WHY MEN REBEL

WRITTEN UNDER THE AUSPICES OF
THE CENTER OF INTERNATIONAL STUDIES
PRINCETON UNIVERSITY
A list of other Center publications appears at the back of the book

WHY MEN REBEL

BY TED ROBERT GURR

PRINCETON UNIVERSITY PRESS
PRINCETON, NEW JERSEY

LC Card: 74-84865
ISBN 0-691-02167-8 (paperback edn.)
ISBN 0-691-07528-X (hardcover edn.)

First Princeton Paperback Edition, 1971

Second Printing, 1971

Third Printing, 1972

Fourth Printing, 1974

This book has been composed in Linofilm Caledonia

Printed in the United States of America
by Princeton University Press, Princeton, New Jersey

To my daughters Lisa Anne and Andrea Mariel

Contents

Introduction

DO WE REALLY KNOW so little about the causes of riot and rebellion that we must invoke contemporary exorcisms like "aggressive instincts" or "conspiracy" to explain them? I think not. Men have rebelled against their rulers for millennia, and during those millennia many perceptive observers have offered careful explanations of why they did so, in particular instances and in general. In a way we know too much about our inclination to violence. The accumulation of monographs and reports and data about this revolution and that, this theory and that, tends to obscure our view of some basic mental and social uniformities. This study tries to identify and order some of those uniformities. Are men inherently aggressive, or aggressive only in response to specific social conditions? We will examine psychological evidence that suggests that men have a capacity but not a need for aggression, and other evidence about the patterns of social circumstance in which men exercise that capacity collectively. Do some men learn to use violence? The answer is obviously yes; what is less obvious is why and how some groups adopt while others eschew violence. Certainly the use of public force to counter private violence, and the nature of human organization, make a difference in the shape and extent of violence. Here again we will discern patterns in much of the reporting and rhetoric; certain uses of force and some kinds of association among people have generally foreseeable effects on political violence.

This book is an exercise in simplification of the kind known as theory-building. I will try to point out the more important uniformities in the causes of violence in politics, drawing from the work of all the human sciences. I will attempt to be precise in describing and defining these uniformities, even at the risk of elaborating some truisms, on grounds that a precisely stated principle is a better tool for understanding than a dull analogy. The uniformities are also documented with a sample of the evidence for them: the laboratory work of experimental psychologists, the speculation of grand and lesser theorists, the case studies of rebellions, the comparative evidence of those who count demands and deaths, and a measure of logical deduction. The tentative explanations that emerge from this process are still complex, not simple. Violence, like those who use it, is complex, but it is not indecipherable. At least that is what I hope this book will demonstrate.

A general explanation of political violence can become a guide to action as well as comprehension, even if it is not ideally precise. It can be used to evaluate, for policy purposes, the "revolutionary potential" of specific nations, and to estimate the effects of various actions on that potential. This theory is not devised for these applications, but many of the characteristics that make it suitable for scholarly inquiry similarly suit it to policy purposes. Social theory can be put to unethical as well as ethical ends, and an author has little control over the use of his work short of refusing to publish. But I am persuaded that insofar as this study has policy uses, it should contribute more to the alleviation of human misery than its perpetuation. There is more than conceit in this concern. The study's impact can at most be marginal, but the world is large and "marginal" impacts can affect thousands of lives.

This book is as likely to be read by rebels as by rulers and suggests as many courses of effective action for one as the other. Rebels should read it, for I think it implies means for the attainment of human aspirations that are more effective and less destructive to themselves and others than some of the tactics they now use. The study will surely be read by men seeking means for the preservation of public order. They will find in it a number of implications for strategies to that end, but they will find little justification for reliance on tactics of repressive control. There is a wealth of evidence and principle that repressive policies defeat their purposes, in the long run if not necessarily in the short run. The public order is most effectively maintained—it can *only* be maintained—when means are provided within it for men to work towards the attainment of their aspirations. This is not an ethical judgment, or rather not just an ethical judgment. It approaches the status of a scientific law of social organization. Some kinds of force may be necessary if revolutionaries or ruling elites are to create and maintain social order in time of crisis, so that constructive means can be established. But exclusive reliance on force eventually raises up the forces that destroy it. This study is in any case not designed for policy ends but for explanation, and that at a general level. If it clarifies the reasons for and consequences of men's violent actions, it will have served its purpose.

The uses of illustrative materials in this study may require a note of explanation. Many of the general relationships to be examined operate in the genesis of each occurrence of violent political conflict. No case of political violence is comprehensively described or analyzed, however. Particular aspects of many specific events, and comparative generalizations about sets of them, are cited to support or illustrate specific hypotheses. None of these references are complete descriptions of the events cited or, unless so specified, are they evidence that the aspects cited are more important than others. For example, a phase of the French Revolution may be summarized in one or two sentences without reference to the fact that it is only one of its facets. The study can justly be criticized according to whether such characterizations are true in the narrow sense. If it is criticized on grounds that specific events are misrepresented because only partly analyzed, the object of the study is misunderstood.

I am indebted to a number of scholars for their advice and criticism in the development of this study. My work on the subject began with my doctoral dissertation, "The Genesis of Violence: A Multivariate Theory of Civil Strife," Department of Government and International Relations, New York University, 1965, work in which I was encouraged and guided by Alfred de Grazia and Thomas Adam. My greatest obligation during the intervening years in which this study was written is to Harry Eckstein, who has been a consistent source of moral support and intellectual sustenance, and who provided detailed criticisms of a draft of the manuscript. A number of other scholars at the Center of International Studies and elsewhere also provided thoughtful and useful commentaries, including Leonard Berkowitz, Mohammed Guessous, Chalmers Johnson, John T. McAlister, Jr., Mancur L. Olson, Jr., J. David Singer, Bryant Wedge, and David Williams. William J. McClung of the University Press gave especially helpful and competent editorial guidance. Responsibility for inadequacies of fact, interpretation, judgment, and logic is of course my own, and in a study of this scope they will no doubt be found in some measure. I also wish to thank June Traube and Mary Merrick of the staff of the Center of International Studies, who spent many laborious hours preparing the manuscript, and James Bledsoe and Mary Fosler, who helped prepare the bibliography.

Initial theoretical work was supported by an award from a National Science Foundation institutional grant to New York University. Empirical work, which contributed to some of the revisions in the theoretical framework, was supported by the Center for Research on Social Systems (formerly SORO) of American University. Writing of the final manuscript was made possible by support of the Center of International Studies and by a basic research grant from the Advanced Research Projects Agency of the U.S. Department of Defense. Support from the last source implies neither that agency's acceptance of this study and its conclusions nor my approval of policies of the U.S. government toward political violence.

WHY MEN REBEL

1. Explanations of Political Violence

> Conflict . . . is a theme that has occupied the thinking of man more than any other, save only God and love.
>
> Anatol Rapoport,
> *Fights, Games, and Debates*

THE INSTITUTIONS, persons, and policies of rulers have inspired the violent wrath of their nominal subjects throughout the history of organized political life. A survey of the histories of European states and empires, spanning twenty-four centuries, shows that they averaged only four peaceful years for each year of violent disturbances.[1] Modern nations have no better record: between 1961 and 1968 some form of violent civil conflict reportedly occurred in 114 of the world's 121 larger nations and colonies.[2] Most acts of group violence have negligible effects on political life; but some have been enormously destructive of human life and corrosive of political institutions. Ten of the world's thirteen most deadly conflicts in the past 160 years have been civil wars and rebellions;[3] since 1945, violent attempts to overthrow governments have been more common than national elections. The counterpoise to this grim record is the fact that political violence has sometimes led to the creation of new and more satisfying political communities. The consequences of the American, Turkish, Mexican, and Russian revolutions testify in different ways to the occasional beneficence of violence.

In this study political violence refers to all collective attacks

[1] Pitirim Sorokin, *Social and Cultural Dynamics, Vol.* III: *Fluctuations of Social Relationships, War and Revolutions* (New York: American Book Co., 1937), 409–475. Twelve countries and empires were studied over the period 500 B.C. to 1925 A.D., none of them for the entire span. Only "important" disturbances were recorded, i.e., those mentioned in standard histories.

[2] Based in part on data for 114 polities reported in Ted Robert Gurr, "A Comparative Study of Civil Strife," in Hugh Davis Graham and Ted Robert Gurr, eds., *Violence in America: Historical and Comparative Perspectives* (Washington, D.C.: National Commission on the Causes and Prevention of Violence, 1969).

[3] According to data collected by Lewis F. Richardson, *Statistics of Deadly Quarrels* (Pittsburgh: The Boxwood Press, 1960), 32–43, to which events after 1948 are added here. The conflicts most destructive of life were World Wars I and II. Of the other eleven all but one were primarily internal wars and all caused more than 300,000 deaths each; the Tai-P'ing Rebellion, 1851–64; the American Civil War; the Great War in La Plata, 1865–70; the post-revolutionary Civil War in Russia, 1918–20; the first and second Chinese Civil Wars, 1927–36 and 1945–49; the Spanish Civil War; the communal riots in India and Pakistan, 1946–48; the Vietnam War, 1961–present; the private war between Indonesian Communists and their opponents, 1964–66 (casualty figures are problematic); and the Nigerian Civil War, 1967–.

within a political community against the political regime, its actors—including competing political groups as well as incumbents—or its policies. The concept represents a set of events, a common property of which is the actual or threatened use of violence, but the explanation is not limited to that property. The concept subsumes revolution, ordinarily defined as fundamental sociopolitical change accomplished through violence. It also includes guerrilla wars, coups d'état, rebellions, and riots. Political violence is in turn subsumed under "force," the use or threat of violence by any party or institution to attain ends within or outside the political order. The definition is not based on a prejudgment that political violence is undesirable. Like the uses of violence qua force by the state, specific acts of political violence can be good, bad, or neutral according to the viewpoint of the observer. Participants in political violence may value it as a means of expressing political demands or opposing undesirable policies. Limited violence also can be useful for rulers and for a political system generally, especially as an expression of social malaise when other means for making demands are inadequate. Ethical judgments are held in abeyance in this study to avoid dictating its conclusions. But it does not require an ethical judgment to observe that intense violence is destructive: even if some political violence is valued by both citizens and rulers, the greater its magnitude the less efficiently a political system fulfills its other functions. Violence generally consumes men and goods, it seldom enhances them.[4]

Despite the frequency and social impact of political violence, it is not now a conventional category of social analysis. Yet some common properties of political violence encourage attention to it rather than more general or more specific concepts. Theoretically, all such acts pose a threat to the political system in two senses: they challenge the monopoly of force imputed to the state in political theory; and, in functional terms, they are likely to interfere with and, if severe, to destroy normal political processes. Empirical justification for selecting political violence as a universe for analysis is provided by statistical evidence that political violence comprises events distinct from other measured characteristics of nations, and homogeneous enough to justify analysis of their common characteristics and causes. For example, countries experiencing

[4] It is possible that political violence can increase the sum total of satisfactions of society's members. This can be true if violence and its immediate effects are intrinsically valued more than the material and human resources it consumes, or if violence serves a popularly approved regulatory function, as it did for the American vigilante movements. A hypothetical relationship of this type is shown schematically in fig. A. It is likely that high magnitudes of violence destroy more than they create, at least in the short run. When the time dimension is taken into ac-

extensive political violence of one kind—whether riots, terrorism, coups d'etat, or guerrilla war—are rather likely to experience other kinds of political violence, but are neither more or less likely to be engaged in foreign conflict.[5] The properties and processes that distinguish a riot from a revolution are substantively and theoretically interesting, and are examined at length in this study, but at a general level of analysis they seem to be differences of degree, not kind.[6] The search for general causes and processes of political violence is further encouraged by the convergence of recent case, comparative, and theoretical studies. One striking feature of these studies is the similarity of many of the causal factors and propositions they identify, whether they deal with revolution, urban rioting, or other forms of political violence. This similarity suggests that some of their findings can be synthesized in a more efficient set of testable generalizations.

However good the prospects seem for a general analysis of political violence, research on it has been quite uneven, both in sub-

---

count, however, intense political violence, though it destroys much in the short run, may have the long-run payoffs either of stimulating rulers to increase outputs or of restructuring society in such a way that total satisfactions are substantially increased. This kind of relationship is sketched in fig. B.

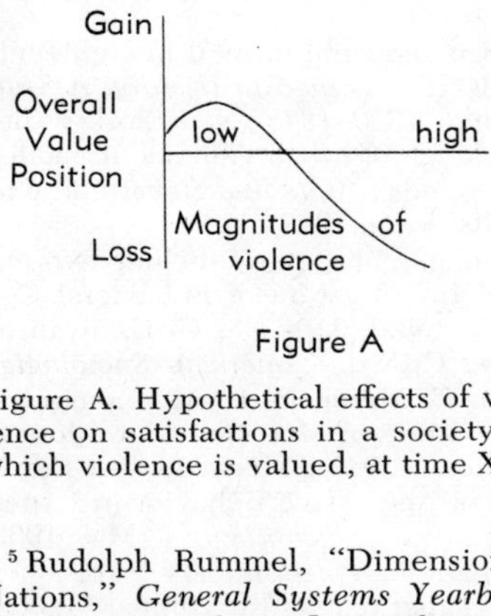

Figure A

Figure A. Hypothetical effects of violence on satisfactions in a society in which violence is valued, at time X.

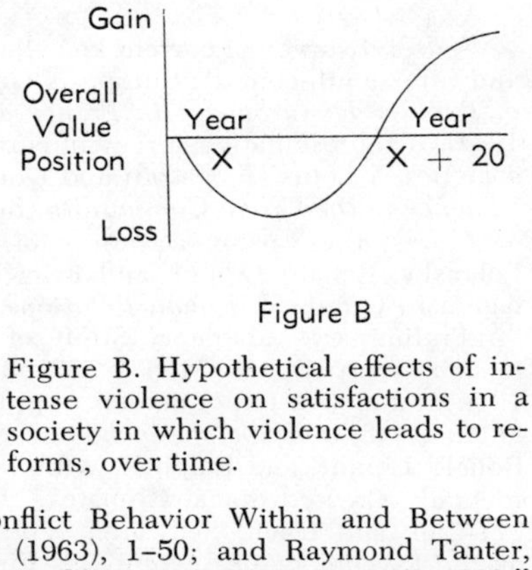

Figure B

Figure B. Hypothetical effects of intense violence on satisfactions in a society in which violence leads to reforms, over time.

[5] Rudolph Rummel, "Dimensions of Conflict Behavior Within and Between Nations," *General Systems Yearbook*, VIII (1963), 1–50; and Raymond Tanter, "Dimensions of Conflict Behavior Within and Between Nations, 1958–1960," *Journal of Conflict Resolution*, X (March 1966), 41–64. There are statistically significant relations among some forms of internal and external conflict, but they are relatively weak. For factor-analytic evidence that types of political violence are independent of most measured characteristics of nations, see Rudolph Rummel, "Dimensionality of Nations Project; Orthogonally Rotated Factor Tables for 236 Variables," Department of Political Science, Yale University (New Haven, July 1964), mimeographed.

[6] Billington points out, for example, that the Russian Revolution comprised an "insurgency" from below—actually extensive rioting and mutinies—followed by a coup d'état and a protracted civil war. James H. Billington, "Six Views of the Russian Revolution," *World Politics*, XVIII (April 1966), 452ff.

stance and in disciplinary approach. There is considerable European historical scholarship on segments of the subject, notably the peasant rebellions of the twelfth through nineteenth centuries and the great revolutions of England, France, and Russia. American and European scholars, most of them also historians, have in recent years contributed a modest case-study literature. American policy scientists have written a small flood of treatises on the causes and prophylaxis of subversive warfare, most of which seem to have had neither academic nor policy impact. The lapses of attention are striking by comparison. Of all the riotous mobs that have clamoured through the streets of history, only the revolutionary crowds of eighteenth- and nineteenth-century Europe and the ghetto rioters of twentieth-century America have attracted much scholarly attention.[7] There are relatively few case studies of political violence in the non-Western world, and fewer systematic comparative studies or attempts at empirical theory. Experimental studies dealing with social-psychological mechanisms of collective violence can be counted on one hand.[8] Among social scientists the historians have been by far the most active; American political scientists have until recently neglected the subject.[9] Of 2,828 articles that appeared in the *American Political Science Review* from its estab-

[7] A useful survey of current knowledge of urban and rural turmoil in eighteenth- and nineteenth-century Europe is George Rudé, *The Crowd in History: A Study of Popular Disturbances in France and England, 1730–1848* (New York: Wiley, 1964). A representative survey of current knowledge of urban violence in modern societies is Louis H. Masotti and Don R. Bowen, eds., *Riots and Rebellion: Civil Violence in the Urban Community* (Beverly Hills: Sage, 1968).

[8] The studies, using a variety of experimental techniques, include Norman Polansky, Ronald Lippitt, and Fritz Redl, "An Investigation of Behavioral Contagion in Groups," *Human Relations,* III (No. 3, 1950), 319–348; G. E. Swanson, "A Preliminary Laboratory Study of the Acting Crowd," *American Sociological Review,* XVIII (October 1953), 522–533; Norman C. Meier, G. H. Mennenga, and H. J. Stoltz, "An Experimental Approach to the Study of Mob Behavior," *Journal of Abnormal and Social Psychology,* XXXVI (October 1941), 506–524; Kurt Lewin, Ronald Lippitt, and Ralph K. White, "Patterns of Aggressive Behavior in Experimentally Created Social Climates," *Journal of Social Psychology,* X (May 1939), 271–299; and David Schwartz, "Political Alienation: A Preliminary Experiment on the Psychology of Revolution's First Stage," paper read at the Annual Meeting of the American Political Science Association, 1967. Many other experimental studies are relevant to collective violence; these deal explicitly with social-psychological factors facilitating violence.

[9] The renaissance of systematic theoretical and empirical work on political violence by political scientists can be dated from the publication of three articles that appeared in 1962 and 1963: James C. Davies, "Toward a Theory of Revolution," *American Sociological Review,* XXVII (February 1962), 5–19; Harry Eckstein, "Internal War: The Problem of Anticipation," in Ithiel de Sola Pool et al., *Social Research and National Security: A Report Prepared by the Research Group in Psychology and the Social Sciences* (Washington, D.C.: Smithsonian Institution, March 5, 1963), published in revised form as "On the Etiology of Internal Wars," *History and Theory,* IV (No. 2, 1965), 133–163; and Rummel, "Dimensions of Conflict Behavior."

lishment in 1906 through 1968, only twenty-nine appear from their titles to be concerned with political disorder or violence. Moreover twelve of the twenty-nine were concerned specifically with revolution, and fifteen appeared after 1961.[10]

Political scientists might be expected to have a greater concern with political violence than others. Authoritative coercion in the service of the state is a crucial concept in political theory and an issue of continuing dispute.[11] Some have identified the distinctive characteristic of the state as its monopoly of physical coercion. Max Weber, for example, wrote that violence is a "means specific" to the state and that "the right of physical violence is assigned to all other associations or individuals only to the extent permitted by the state; it is supposed to be the exclusive source of the 'right' to use violence." [12] Thomas Hobbes, dismayed by the brutish anarchy of men living outside the restraint of commonwealths, conceived the sovereign's control of coercion to be the foundation of the state and the social condition.[13] Schattschneider sees conflict, which subsumes violence, as the central concept of political science.[14] Nieberg emphasizes the positive functions of nonauthoritative violence and its threatened use as an instrument of social change.[15] From any of these perspectives the occurrence of collective, nonauthoritative violence appears to pose two fundamental questions for political science: From what sources and by what processes does it arise, and how does it affect the political and social order?

What Is to Be Explained?

This study proposes some general answers to three basic questions about our occasional disposition to disrupt violently the order we otherwise work so hard to maintain: What are the psy-

[10] By contrast, 111 articles deal specifically with Great Britain, some 140 with the U.S. Congress, and about 250 with constitutions or constitutional issues. These counts were facilitated by the use of the Key-Word-in-Context index of article titles in Kenneth Janda, ed., *Cumulative Index to the American Political Science Review: Volumes 1–57: 1906–1963* (Evanston: Northwestern University Press, 1964).

[11] A useful analysis of alternative conceptions of authoritative violence is E. V. Walter, "Power and Violence," *American Political Science Review,* LVIII (June 1964), 350–360. A survey of the origins, functions, and forms of legitimate and illegitimate violence, within and among states, is Chapter 8, "Civil Conflict and War," Alfred de Grazia, *Politics and Government, Vol. 1: Political Behavior,* rev. edn. (New York: Collier, 1952, 1962), 265–301.

[12] Max Weber, "Politik als Beruf," *Gesammelte Politische Schriften* (Tubingen: J. C. B. Mohr, 1958), 494, translated in E. V. Walter, 359.

[13] Thomas Hobbes, *Leviathan* (Oxford: Basil Blackwell, 1946).

[14] E. E. Schattschneider, "Intensity, Visibility, Direction and Scope," *American Political Science Review,* LI (December 1957), 933–942.

[15] H. L. Nieburg, "The Threat of Violence and Social Change," *American Political Science Review,* LVI (December 1962), 865–873, and *Political Violence: The Behavioral Process* (New York: St. Martin's Press, 1969).

chological and social sources of the potential for collective violence? What determines the extent to which that potential is focused on the political system? And what societal conditions affect the magnitude and form, and hence the consequences, of violence? The study has four primary objects of analysis. Two are intervening variables: the *potential for collective violence* and the *potential for political violence.* Propositionally, *potential for collective violence* is a function of the extent and intensity of shared discontents among members of a society; the *potential for political violence* is a function of the degree to which such discontents are blamed on the political system and its agents. The remaining objects of analysis are dependent variables: the *magnitude of political violence* and the *forms of political violence,* both of which are discussed below.

Theories of revolution are usually concerned with specifying a relationship between some set of preconditions and the occurrence of revolution. Political violence, however, is a pervasive phenomenon, as was suggested above: few contemporary or historical societies have been free of it for long. It may be useful for microanalysis to specify whether political violence is likely in a given society at a particular point in time. For macroanalysis, however, the more interesting questions are the determinants of the extent of violence and of the forms in which it is manifested. If one's interest is the effects of political violence on the political system, the questions of its magnitude and kind are both highly relevant. And if one is concerned in an ethical way with political violence, then almost certainly one wants to assess its human and material costs, and consequently the determinants of its magnitude. Various measures of the relative extent of political violence have been used in recent comparative studies. Sorokin combined measures of the proportion of a nation affected (social area), proportion of population actively involved, duration, intensity, and severity of effects of violence in assessing the magnitude of internal disturbances. Tilly and Rule make use of man-days of participation. Rummel and Tanter have used counts of numbers of events. The Feierabends have developed a scaling procedure that takes account of both number of events and *a priori* judgments about the severity of events of various types.[16] Some researchers have used

[16] Sorokin, *op. cit.;* Charles Tilly and James Rule, *Measuring Political Upheaval* (Princeton: Center of International Studies, Princeton University, Research Monograph No. 19, 1965); Rummel, "Dimensions of Conflict Behavior . . ."; Raymond Tanter, "Dimensions of Conflict Behavior Within Nations, 1955–60: Turmoil and Internal War," *Peace Research Societies Papers,* III (1965), 159–164; and Ivo K. and Rosalind L. Feierabend, "Aggressive Behaviors Within Polities, 1948–1962; A Cross National Study," *Journal of Conflict Resolution,* X (September 1966), 249–271.

the grisly calculus of number of deaths resulting from violence.[17]

The proposed relation between perceived deprivation and the frustration concept in frustration-anger-aggression theory, to be discussed in chapter 2, provides a rationale for a more general definition of magnitude of violence and a more precise specification of what it comprises. The basic frustration-aggression proposition is that the greater the frustration, the greater the quantity of aggression against the source of frustration. This postulate provides the motivational base for an initial proposition about political violence: the greater the intensity of deprivation, the greater the magnitude of violence. (Other perceptual and motivational factors are also relevant to political violence, but many of them can be subsumed by the deprivation concept, as is suggested in chapter 2.) Intense frustration can motivate men either to intense, short-term attacks or to more prolonged, less severe attacks on their frustrators. Which tactic is chosen is probably a function of anticipated gain, opportunity, and fear of retribution, which in political violence are situationally determined. Hence the severity of deprivation affects both the intensity of violence, i.e. in the extent of human and physical damage incurred, and its duration. Moreover there are evidently individual differences—presumably normally distributed—in the intensity of frustration needed to precipitate overt aggression. Extension of this principle to the deprivation-violence relationship suggests that the proportion of a population that participates in violence ought to vary with the average intensity of perceived deprivation. Mild deprivation will motivate few to violence, moderate deprivation will push more across the threshold, very intense deprivation is likely to galvanize large segments of a political community into action.

This argument suggests that magnitude of political violence has three component variables that ought to be taken into account in systematic analysis: the extent of participation within the political unit being studied (*scope*), the destructiveness of action (*intensity*), and the length of time violence persists (*duration*). Sorokin's empirical work takes all three aspects into account; so does mine.[18]

The intensity and scope of relative deprivation and magnitude of

[17] Among them Richardson, especially chap. 2 and 4; Rummel, "Dimensions of Conflict Behavior"; Tanter; and Bruce M. Russett, "Inequality and Instability: The Relation of Land Tenure to Politics," *World Politics,* XVI (April 1964), 442–454.

[18] Ted Gurr with Charles Ruttenberg, *The Conditions of Civil Violence: First Tests of a Causal Model* (Princeton: Center of International Studies, Princeton University, Research Monograph No. 28, 1967); Ted Gurr, "A Causal Model of Civil Strife: A Comparative Analysis Using New Indices," *American Political Science Review,* LXII (December 1968), 1104–1124.

violence are unidimensional variables. Theoretically, and empirically, one can conceive of degrees or quantities of each in any polity. The forms of violence, however, are attributes that do not form a simple dimension. A society may experience riots but not revolution, revolution but not coups d'état, coups d'état but not riots. Hypotheses about forms of violence as dependent variables thus are necessarily different from those about deprivation and magnitude of violence. They are expressed in terms of probabilities (the greater x, the more *likely* y) rather than strict concomitance. The question is how many forms of political violence ought to be accounted for in a general theory. The principle of parsimony, which should apply to dependent as well as independent variables, suggests using a typology with a small number of categories, events in each of which are fairly numerous.

Conventional taxonomies, of which there are many, provide little help. Some, like that of Lasswell and Kaplan, provide simple typologies for revolutions but not for political violence generally.[19] Eckstein proposes a composite typology comprising unorganized, spontaneous violence (riots), intraelite conflicts (coups), two varieties of revolution, and wars of independence.[20] Perhaps the most complex typology is Rummel's list of twenty-five types of domestic conflict, the analysis of which provides an empirical solution to the problem of a parsimonious typology. In Rummel's analysis, and in a number of subsequent studies, data on the incidence and characteristics of various types of political violence were collected and tabulated by country and the "country scores" (number of riots, assassinations, coups, mutinies, guerrilla wars, and so on, in a given time period) were factor analyzed. Whatever the typology employed, the period of reference, or the set of countries, essentially the same results were reported. A strong *turmoil* dimension is characterized by largely spontaneous strife such as riots and demonstrations. It is quite distinct both statistically and substantively from what can be called a *revolutionary* dimension, characterized by more organized and intense strife. This revolutionary dimension has two components that appear in some analyses as separate dimensions: *internal war*, typically including civil war, guerrilla war, and some coups; and *conspiracy*, typically including plots, mutinies, and most coups.[21]

[19] Harold Lasswell and Abraham Kaplan, *Power and Society: A Framework for Political Inquiry* (New Haven: Yale University Press, 1950), 261–268. The types are palace revolution, political revolution, and social revolution.

[20] "On the Etiology of Internal Wars," 135–136.

[21] Rummel's typology appears in "Dimensions of Conflict Behavior," 25–26. Two summary articles on the factor analyses are Rudolph J. Rummel, "A Field

These types are not absolutely distinct. The analyses mentioned on pp. 4–5 indicate that, at a more general level of analysis, political violence is a relatively homogenous universe. Within that universe, however, some kinds of violence tend to occur together, and the occurrence of some types tends to preclude the occurrence of other types. The principal distinction between turmoil and revolution is the degree of organization and focus of violence, a distinction also made by Eckstein in his composite typology. A major difference between the internal war and conspiracy components of the revolutionary dimension is one of scale. General definitions of the three forms of political violence examined in this analysis are as follows:

Turmoil: Relatively spontaneous, unorganized political violence with substantial popular participation, including violent political strikes, riots, political clashes, and localized rebellions.

Conspiracy: Highly organized political violence with limited participation, including organized political assassinations, small-scale terrorism, small-scale guerrilla wars, coups d'état, and mutinies.

Internal war: Highly organized political violence with widespread popular participation, designed to overthrow the regime or dissolve the state and accompanied by extensive violence, including large-scale terrorism and guerrilla wars, civil wars, and revolutions.[22]

In summary, this study is an attempt to analyze, and develop testable general hypotheses about, three aspects of political violence: its sources, magnitude, and forms. The processes by which the potential for violence develops and the kinds of conditions and events that channel its outcome are examined as part of this

Theory of Social Action With Application to Conflict Within Nations," *Yearbook of the Society for General Systems Research,* x (1965), 183–204, and Tanter, "Dimensions of Conflict Behavior."

[22] Eckstein, in "On the Etiology of Internal Wars," reintroduced the term "internal war," but defined it considerably more broadly as "any resort to violence within a political order to change its constitution, rulers, or policies," 133. In ordinary language, however, the phrase connotes a degree of participation and organization of conflict that is not characteristic of the events I have separately categorized under turmoil and conspiracy. The three categories differ from the categories with the same labels in Gurr, "A Comparative Study of Civil Strife," and Gurr, "A Causal Model of Civil Strife," only in their exclusion of nonviolent strife and of violent conflict between apolitical groups.

analysis. Two topics often examined in theories of revolution are examined here only in passing: the immediate precipitants of violence, about which most generalizations appear trivial; and the long-run outcomes of various kinds of political violence, about which there is little empirical evidence or detailed theoretical speculation.

Toward an Integrated Theory of Political Violence

The basic model of the conditions leading to political violence used in this study incorporates both psychological and societal variables. The initial stages of analysis are actor-oriented in the sense that many of the hypotheses about the potential for collective action are related to, and in some instances deduced from, information about the dynamics of human motivation. The approach is not wholly or primarily psychological, however, and it would be a misinterpretation of the arguments and evidence presented here to categorize it so. Most of the relationships and evidence examined in subsequent stages of analysis are those that are proposed or observed to hold between societal conditions and political violence. The psychological materials are used to help provide causal linkages between and among societal variables and the dependent variables specified above: the potential for collective and political violence; the magnitude of political violence; and the likelihood that political violence will take the form of turmoil, conspiracy, or internal war. Use of psychological evidence in this way makes certain kinds of social uniformities more clearly apparent and comprehensible, and contributes to the simplification of theory. At the same time the analysis of societal relationships is crucial for identifying the sources of some common psychological properties of violence-prone men and for generalizing about the many facets of political violence that have no parallels in psychological dynamics. The goal of this analysis, at best only partly realized, was proposed by Inkeles in the context of a discussion of social structure and personality: "What is required . . . is an integration or coordination of two basic sets of data in a larger explanatory scheme—not a reduction of either mode of analysis to the allegedly more fundamental mode of the other."[23]

The outlines of the theory can now be sketched briefly. The primary causal sequence in political violence is first the development of discontent, second the politicization of that discontent, and

[23] Alex Inkeles, "Personality and Social Structure," *Sociology Today* (New York: Basic Books, 1959), 272, quoted in Marvin E. Wolfgang and Franco Ferracuti, *The Subculture of Violence: Towards an Integrated Theory in Criminology* (London: Social Science Paperbacks, 1967), 8.

finally its actualization in violent action against political objects and actors. Discontent arising from the perception of relative deprivation is the basic, instigating condition for participants in collective violence. The linked concepts of discontent and deprivation comprise most of the psychological states implicit or explicit in such theoretical notions about the causes of violence as frustration, alienation, drive and goal conflicts, exigency, and strain (discussed in chapter 2).

Relative deprivation is defined as a perceived discrepancy between men's value expectations and their value capabilities. Value expectations are the goods and conditions of life to which people believe they are rightfully entitled. Value capabilities are the goods and conditions they think they are capable of attaining or maintaining, given the social means available to them. Societal conditions that increase the average level or intensity of expectations without increasing capabilities increase the intensity of discontent. Among the general conditions that have such effects are the value gains of other groups and the promise of new opportunities (chapter 4). Societal conditions that decrease men's average value position without decreasing their value expectations similarly increase deprivation, hence the intensity of discontent. The inflexibility of value stocks in a society, short-term deterioration in a group's conditions of life, and limitations of its structural opportunities have such effects (chapter 5).

Deprivation-induced discontent is a general spur to action. Psychological theory and group conflict theory both suggest that the greater the intensity of discontent, the more likely is violence. The specificity of this impulse to action is determined by men's beliefs about the sources of deprivation, and about the normative and utilitarian justifiability of violent action directed at the agents responsible for it.

Societal variables that affect the focusing of discontent on political objects include the extent of cultural and subcultural sanctions for overt aggression, the extent and degree of success of past political violence, the articulation and dissemination of symbolic appeals justifying violence, the legitimacy of the political system, and the kinds of responses it makes and has made to relative deprivation (chapters 6 and 7). The belief that violence has utility in obtaining scarce values can be an independent source of political violence, but within political communities it is most likely to provide a secondary, rationalizing, rather than primary, motivation. Widespread discontent provides a general impetus to collective violence. However, the great majority of acts of collective violence in recent decades have had at least some political objects, and the more intense those violent acts are, the more likely they are to be focused primarily or exclusively on the political system. Intense discontent is quite likely to be politicized; the primary effect of normative and utilitarian attitudes toward violence is to focus that potential.

The magnitude of political violence in a system, and the forms it takes, are partly determined by the scope and intensity of politicized discontent. Politicized discontent is a necessary condition for the resort to violence in politics. But however intense and focused the impetus to violence is, its actualization is strongly influenced by the patterns of coercive control and institutional support in the political community. Political violence is of greatest magnitude, and most likely to take the form of internal war, if regimes and those who oppose them exercise approximately equal degrees of coercive control, and command similar and relatively high degrees of institutional support in the society. The coercive capacities of a regime and the uses to which they are put are crucial variables, affecting the forms and extent of political violence in both the short and long run. There is much evidence, some of it summarized in chapters 8 and 10, that some patterns of regime coercive control increase rather than decrease the intensity of discontent, and can facilitate the transformation of turmoil into full-scale revolutionary movements. Dissidents, by contrast, use whatever degree of coercive capacities they acquire principally for group defense and for assaults on the regime. The degree of institutional support for dissidents and for regimes is a function of the relative proportions of a nation's population their organizations mobilize, the complexity and cohesiveness of those organizations, their resources, and the extent to which they provide regularized procedures for value attainment, conflict resolution, and channeling hostility (chapter 9). The growth of dissident organization may in the short run facilitate political violence, but it also is likely to provide the discontented with many of the means to alleviate deprivation in the long run, thus minimizing violence.

The preceding three paragraphs are an outline of the framework in which the hypotheses and definitions of this study are developed, and a summary of some of its generalizations. The hypotheses and their interrelationships are summarized more fully and systematically in chapter 10. The Appendix lists all hypotheses developed, categorized according to their dependent variables, and the chapters in which they are proposed.

The three stages in the process of political violence—those in which discontent is generated, politicized, and actualized in political violence—are each dependent on the preceding one, as the outline indicates. It is likely but not necessarily the case that there is a temporal relationship among the three stages, whereby a sharp increase in the intensity of discontent precedes the articulation of doctrines that justify politically violent action, with shifts in the balances of coercive control and institutional adherence occuring subsequently. The conditions can be simultaneously operative, however, as the outbreak of the Vendée counterrevolution in 1793 demonstrates: implementation of procedures for military conscription intensified the discontent of workers and peasants already sharply hostile to the bourgeoisie and the government it ruled. Mass action against the bourgeoisie began in a matter of days; the social context for dissident action was provided in part by preexisting communal and political organization, action that was facilitated by the concurrent weakness of government forces and institutions in the region.[24] The point is that many of the attitudes and societal conditions that facilitate political violence may be present and relatively unchanging in a society over a long period; they become relevant to or operative in the genesis of violence only when relative deprivation increases in scope and intensity. Intense politicized discontent also can be widespread and persistent over a long period without overt manifestation because a regime monopolizes coercive control and institutional support. A weakening of regime control or the development of dissident organization in such situations is highly likely to lead to massive violence, as it did in Hungary in 1956 and China in 1966–68, and as is likely at some future date in South Africa.

The concepts, hypotheses, and models of causes and processes developed in the following chapters are not intended as ends in themselves. Intellectually pleasing filters through which to view and categorize the phenomena of a disorderly world are not knowledge. Systematic knowledge requires us to propose and test and reformulate and retest statements about how and why things happen. We know enough, and know it well enough, only when we can say with some certitude not just why things happened yesterday, but how our actions today will affect what happens tomorrow, something we can always hope to know better, though never perfectly. This analysis may demonstrate that too little is known about the violence men do one another, and that it is known too weakly and imprecisely. It is designed to facilitate the processes by which that knowledge can be increased.

[24] Charles Tilly, *The Vendée* (Cambridge: Harvard University Press, 1964), passim.

The Nature of Social Theory

(In this section I wish to comment on some criteria for social theory and their application to political violence. These criteria are not essential for understanding the substance of the book, but they help explain its approach to analysis and form of presentation. Readers not concerned with these questions may turn directly to chapter 2.)

Many descriptive generalizations and propositions can be made about the origins, processes, and effects of political violence generally, and of its several forms. Variables commonly examined include the kinds of societal and political structures most susceptible to violence, revolutionary ideologies, the developmental sequence of revolutionary movements, the effects of force on the outcome of violence, the nature of revolutionary organization, and much else. Some less common variables for analysis are the nonideological motivations of revolutionaries, the effects of institutional patterns on the forms and objects of violence, the efficacy of different kinds of governmental response, and the long-range consequences of political violence.

Two paradigmatic approaches to "theory" about political violence can be identified. One is to analyze a related phenomenon, like revolutionary organization or ideology, in order to generalize about its origins, characteristics, or effects. An interest in explaining the occurrence or outcome of political violence is often implicit or explicit in such an analysis, but typically the analysis does not pretend to be complete; the relevance of other variables ordinarily is recognized. The second is to choose a particular violent event or class of events as an object of explanation and to specify some more or less exhaustive set of conditions or variables that determines the occurrence, extent, or outcome of the events. Theories of revolution, like those of Edwards, Brinton, Pettee, and Timasheff, are representative of this second approach.[25] A variant of this approach is to select a common, quantifiable property of a variety of events for analysis and explanation (see pp. 8–9).

"Theory" is a term loosely used in the social sciences generally and in the study of political violence specifically. The kind of theory aimed at in this study is an interrelated set of general, falsi-

[25] The three best-known American theories of revolution are Lyford P. Edwards, *The Natural History of Revolutions* (Chicago: University of Chicago Press, 1927); Crane Brinton, *The Anatomy of Revolution* (New York: Norton, 1938); and George Pettee, *The Process of Revolution* (New York: Harper, 1938). A more recent theory of this type is proposed by Nicholas S. Timasheff, *War and Revolution* (New York: Sheed and Ward, 1965).

fiable hypotheses that specify causal or concomitant relationships between independent and dependent variables. The nature of such relationships can be argued inductively from observations about the relevant phenomena at various levels of analysis, or deduced from other statements comprising the theory, or both.[26]

Such "explanatory" theory is distinct from what Eckstein calls pretheoretical exercises, such as the formulation of classificatory schemes and conceptual frameworks, which are sometimes called theory.[27] Nor are descriptive generalizations about relationships among variables theory in the sense intended here, unless the sources and nature of such relationships are stated explicitly and the generalizations themselves interrelated.

Most hypotheses developed in this study are derived from the juxtaposition and generalization of relationships observed in studies of political violence and of the individual behaviors manifest in it. The approach reflects an assumption that social science theory ought to build on what is already known about the subject being theorized about, and that it ought to be consistent with, or at least not directly contradictory to, what is more generally known about the nature and processes of individual and aggregate human behavior. This is not to say that hypotheses must be consistent with what Levy calls "going common sense," but rather that it is nonsensical and inefficient to invest research effort in testing hypotheses that contradict what is precisely known, unless there are compelling logical or empirical grounds for questioning what is assumed to be "precisely known."

The central scientific criterion for theory is that it be subject to empirical assessment. Four attributes of theory that facilitate its assessment are its falsifiability, definitional clarity, identification of relevant variables at various levels of analysis, and applicability to a large universe of events for analysis. The first two are necessary conditions for assessment, the others desirable. A fundamental limitation of most older theories and conceptions

[26] For a critique of what passes for theory in the social sciences and a proposed set of criteria for good theory, see Marion J. Levy, Jr., "'Does It Matter if He's Naked?' Bawled the Child," in Klaus Knorr and James Rosenau, eds., *Contending Approaches to International Politics* (Princeton: Princeton University Press, 1969). For a statement of criteria for theory in a field related to the subject of this book, and a survey of extant "theory," see Wolfgang and Ferracuti, chap. 2.

[27] Harry Eckstein, "Introduction: Toward the Theoretical Study of Internal War," *Internal War: Problems and Approaches* (New York: The Free Press, 1964), 7–29, classifies pretheoretical operations as delimitation (statement of the boundaries of the subject); classification and analysis (meaning by "analysis" the dissection of a subject into its components); and problemation (the formulation of specific problems for theory construction). Most of these "operations" with respect to political violence are attempted in this chapter.

of revolution is the difficulty of deriving falsifiable hypotheses from them.[28] Few if any were formulated with reference to applicable empirical methods. The fact that very few case or comparative studies make use of them is further evidence of their limited usefulness even for taxonomic or conceptual purposes. Two general conventions regarding falsifiability are used in social science. One is to state that an independent (causal) variable is a necessary and/or sufficient condition for the dependent variable one wants to explain. This usually means that both variables are defined in dichotomous terms—"disequilibrium" does or does not occur—even if one or both are continuous variables, and typically leads to propositions that are trivial or falsifiable by a single deviant case. The second is to rely on tests of statistical significance of relationships between variables, which has led to the proliferation of weakly supported but not-quite-falsified hypotheses which have yet to be integrated into a more general and parsimonious theory. A third convention is used in this study: a minimum strength of relationship is postulated for each hypothesis in correlational terms; if the relationship found in an empirical test is weaker than stipulated, and no serious sample or instrument error is likely, the hypothesis is rejected. For example, one basic hypothesis is that the greater the intensity and scope of relative deprivation in a population, the greater the potential for collective violence. The proposed relationship is a strong one: if interval-order measurement of both variables for a substantial number of cases gives a product-moment correlation coefficient less than .45 (less than 20 percent of the variance explained), the hypothesis is rejected.[29]

[28] For example, Edwards, Brinton, and Pettee. A sampling of the older theoretical speculation about revolution and political violence, which seldom finds its way even into the footnotes of current writings, would include the work of Gustave Le Bon, especially *The Psychology of Revolution,* trans. Bernard Miall (London: Unwin, 1913); Brooks Adam, *The Theory of Social Revolutions* (New York: Macmillan, 1913); Everett Dean Martin, *The Behavior of Crowds: A Psychological Study* (New York: Harper, 1920), chap. 7, "The Psychology of Revolutionary Crowds"; Charles A. Ellwood, *The Psychology of Human Society: An Introduction to Sociological Theory* (New York: Appleton, 1925), chap. 8, "Changes Within the Group: Abnormal"; Robert Hunter, *Revolution: Why, How, When?* (New York: Harper, 1940); and Mark A. May, *A Social Psychology of War and Peace* (New Haven: Yale University Press, 1943), chap. 7, "Aggressive Social Movements." The flavor of the literature to 1925 can be sampled in Dale Yoder, "Current Definitions of Revolution," *American Journal of Sociology,* XXXII (November 1926), 433–441. Some writings of this period are curious indeed, for example, Sidney A. Reeve, *The Natural Laws of Social Convulsions* (New York: Dutton, 1933).

[29] The same strength of relationship is required of multiple regression coefficients (R) for studies in which multiple measures of a particular independent variable are used. I have reported evidence to the effect that the .45 threshold is by no means too stringent for the hypotheses mentioned in Gurr, "A Causal Model of Civil Strife." Three composite measures of deprivation related to magnitude of civil strife for 114 polities give an R of .60, despite the presence of considerable measurement error.

Other hypotheses specify relationships of moderate strength, requiring a minimum *r* of .30 if they are not to be discarded. Hypotheses about independent variables that do not meet these criteria are not necessarily false in the conventional sense, but they denote relationships that are too weak to contribute to parsimonious theory.[30]

Independent and dependent variables must be defined with sufficient precision so that a researcher can determine what particular conditions or set of events constitute "X" for purposes of empirical assessment. The definitional inadequacy of many theories, new and old, contributes to the difficulty of assessing them. For example, a great many conditions have been said to "cause" or to constitute a basic potential for collective violence, among them general properties of sociopolitical systems labeled "cramp," "disequilibrium," and "strain"; motivational characteristics of violent men such as "frustration" and "discontent"; and particular institutional patterns such as repressive government and inadequate circulation of, or divisions within, an elite.[31] A difficulty of explanations citing such general properties is that the conditions as defined, if indeed they are defined, can usually be found in most societies and among most men, whether or not revolutionary; and usually they are not formulated precisely enough to permit one to assess the effects of their various elements and degrees. The empirical referents of some concepts are more easily isolated than those of others. The concept "participation in clandestine organization" is more readily made operational than "revolutionary mobilization," and revolutionary mobilization is a more malleable concept than "power deflation." This is not to argue that more general concepts be avoided, but that the more general they are the more necessary it is to define them fully and to catalog their manifestations so that they can be evaluated empirically.

It is desirable that theoretical statements be testable at various levels of generalization. Feldman, for example, attributes revolutionary potential to the increasing salience of goal conflicts between the increasingly numerous subsystems that are said to result from

[30] These two criteria imply an absolute maximum of five strong variables or eleven moderately strong variables for any theoretical system. Hypotheses that are not supported at the .30 level but that nonetheless meet statistical tests of significance should lead to postulation of more general hypotheses that might account for a set of such weak relationships.

[31] See Pettee, passim; Chalmers Johnson, *Revolutionary Change* (Boston: Little, Brown, 1966), especially chap. 4; Neil J. Smelser, *Theory of Collective Behavior* (New York: The Free Press, 1963), passim; Davies, passim; and Ronald G. Ridker, "Discontent and Economic Growth," *Economic Development and Cultural Change*, XI (October 1962), 1–15. A categorization of specific and general causal factors cited in the literature is given in Eckstein, "On the Etiology of Internal Wars," 143–144.

structural differentiation in a society.[32] Ideally it should be possible to observe manifestations of such a process at both the macrolevel of an entire social system, for example eighteenth-century France, and at the level of the community and among small, face-to-face groups.[33] Small-group phenomena are not likely to resemble simply a scaled-down model of macrophenomena, but it should be possible to identify the small-group interactions and individual behaviors that are comprised by macroevents. If this translatability cannot be achieved directly, then at least the macrophenomena postulated in theory should be compatible with what is known about microphenomena. This is not a reductionist argument that analysis of social systems or collective behavior can or should be reduced to analysis of component individual behaviors. The point is that analysis on one level can and should inform the other, and that hypotheses whose relationships are manifested at, and subject to examination at, different levels of analysis are usually more interesting and fruitful than those which refer to one level of analysis only.[34]

The fourth attribute of theory that facilitates its assessment concerns the types and numbers of cases or settings in which the proposed relationships can be examined. The preference is for theory that can be subject to test both in case studies and in large-sample comparative studies using statistical methods. Case studies are useful for elucidating the fine structure of revolutionary events and for providing a sense of understanding of how general variables act and interact. They also can be used to test theoretical statements expressed in dichotomous terms: one can define "accelerators of dysfunction" and "revolution" independently and in sufficiently rigorous fashion that a single case study may be sufficent to falsify the proposition that accelerators of dysfunction are a necessary precondition of revolution.[35] But many variables of interest to social theory can be dichotomized only at great loss of information, and scholars undertaking case studies often find it difficult to distinguish between general relationships and the

[32] Arnold Feldman, "Violence and Volatility: The Likelihood of Revolution," in *Internal War,* 111–129.

[33] Sidney Verba, *Small Groups and Political Behavior: A Study of Leadership* (Princeton: Princeton University Press, 1961), demonstrates the usefulness of relating concepts and findings at one level of analysis to those at another. Tilly's case study of an internal war, *The Vendée,* shows how analysis can proceed from macrolevel concepts such as urbanization and social change to the individual level, and back again.

[34] On the relative merits of using different levels of analysis in social inquiry see David Singer, "The Level of Analysis Problem in International Relations," *World Politics,* XIV (October 1961), 77–92.

[35] This proposition is adapted from Johnson, *op. cit.*

unique historical and cultural circumstances of each case. Hypotheses that specify systematic relations among continuous variables, or between a continuous and a dichotomous variable, are subject to scientific assessment only if substantial numbers of cases are examined. This provides further justification for the choice of political violence rather than revolution as the subject of this study: the former is far more common than the latter.

In this study hypothetical relationships are formally stated and given alphanumeric descriptors. The first term in each hypothesis is its dependent variable. Definitions ordinarily are proposed in the paragraphs immediately following the first appearance of a theoretical term in a hypothesis. Underlining of a term in this context indicates that the sentence in which it appears is a formal definition. Synonyms are used for several of the frequently cited theoretical concepts to avoid the mind-deadening effects of repetition. "Relative deprivation," defined as a perceived discrepancy between men's value expectations and value capabilities, is represented by its initials, RD, and the synonyms deprivation, discrepancy, and, loosely, frustration. "Discontent," the psychological state said to be caused by RD, has as its synonyms anger, rage, and dissatisfaction. Synonyms for "value expectations" are wants, aspirations, and expectations. "Values" are the goods and conditions of life which men seek; the phrase "goods and conditions of life" is used synonymously with values. "Value opportunities," the courses of action people have available to them for attaining or maintaining their desired values, are more simply referred to as "means." These synonyms are used only when there is no ambiguity about their referent; the precisely defined terms are used in the development of the basic theoretical arguments.

2. Relative Deprivation and the Impetus to Violence

> Our desires and pleasures spring from society; we measure them, therefore, by society and not by the objects which serve for their satisfaction. Because they are of a social nature, they are of a relative nature.
>
> Karl Marx and Frieurich Engels, *Wage Labor and Capital*

BENEATH the complexity of human motivation neurophysiologists have identified two great "appetitive systems" that provide the motivating feelings against which everything that happens to us is measured and judged. Stimulation of one of these systems provides our feelings of elation, satisfaction, and love. Stimulation of the other leads to sensations of anxiety, terror, depression, and rage. These feelings color our perceptions of the world and energize our actions. Learning is based on these appetitive systems, first directly, then indirectly: we learn to do and to seek out those things that bring satisfaction, and to avoid those that have noxious effects.[1]

Men's circumstances change, however, and what they have learned does not always prove suitable for deriving satisfactions from changed circumstances. "We become frustrated," Cantril writes, "when we sense a conflict between the significances we bring to a situation and which have worked in the past but seem to have no correspondence . . . to the emerging situation we face. . . ."[2] This conflict or tension is fundamentally unpleasant: to be avoided or overcome if possible; to be released in expressive, "nonrealistic" ways if not. It is the fundamental source of both innovation and destruction in human affairs. Why innovative behavior should occur in response to tension is clear enough: the socialization process teaches men to learn to avoid unpleasant stimuli, and only severe new conflicts are likely to paralyze the adaptive capacities men acquire in that process. Destructive behavior may be explained by reference to another fundamental property of the human organism: if men are exposed to noxious

[1] A brief introduction to the neurophysiological literature, and an interpretation of its implications for motivation generally, are provided by Hadley Cantril, "*Sentio, ergo sum:* 'Motivation' Reconsidered," *Journal of Psychology,* LXV (January 1967), 91–107. The appetitive systems were located by neurophysiologists in the mid-1950s and have been identified and studied in both man and other mammals.

[2] Cantril, p. 99.

stimuli that they cannot avoid or overcome, they have an innate disposition to strike out at their sources. Striking out may or may not reduce the frustration, but it seems to be an inherently satisfying response to the tension built up through frustration.[3] The desire to release tension is not the only source of aggression, however. Innovative responses to tensions may themselves include the resort to violence. Most important, the choice of tactical or "realistic" violence as an innovative response to tension is reinforced by the innate disposition to aggression created by the tension. Distinctions between "realistic" and "nonrealistic" conflict or aggression thus may be analytically useful, but the physiological and psychological evidence suggests that elements of the latter are almost always present.[4] It is likely to be absent only among those who are coerced into participation in collective conflict.

These principles operate in a wide range of individual behavior, including the actions of those in rebellion against their political community. We need concepts and hypotheses better suited to analyzing the social and psychological transactions that provide the impetus to political violence among members of a collectivity. "Relative deprivation" (RD) is the term used in the preceding chapter to denote the tension that develops from a discrepancy between the "ought" and the "is" of collective value satisfaction, and that disposes men to violence. The term's definition is distinct from its conventional sociological usage, but not so different as to warrant using a neologism like "cramp" or "exigency." This chapter examines the RD concept and its subordinate concepts: values, value classes, value expectations, value capabilities, and value opportunities. The frustration-aggression relationship provides the psychological dynamic for the proposed relationship between intensity of deprivation and the potential for collective violence; consequently it is examined in some detail. Other conceptual interpretations of the impetus to political violence are

[3] The drive properties of frustration-induced aggression are examined and documented by Norman R. F. Maier, *Frustration: The Study of Behavior Without a Goal* (New York: McGraw-Hill, 1949), passim, and Leonard Berkowitz, "The Concept of Aggressive Drive: Some Additional Considerations," in Berkowitz, ed., *Advances in Experimental Psychology*, Vol. II (New York: Academic Press, 1965), 307–322, among others. Like the appetitive systems, it appears to be characteristic of man and of higher-order animals generally.

[4] Considerable significance has been attached to the distinction between realistic and nonrealistic conflict by Lewis Coser, *The Functions of Social Conflict* (New York: The Free Press, 1956), 48–55 and passim. The distinction is commonly made in conflict theory, as pointed out by Raymond W. Mack and Richard C. Snyder, "The Analysis of Social Conflict: Toward an Overview and Synthesis," *Journal of Conflict Resolution*, I (June 1957), 221–248.

related to the relative deprivation model, including notions of dissonance, anomie, and social conflict. Finally three patterns of disequilibrium between value expectations and value capabilities are proposed to facilitate dynamic analysis.

Relative Deprivation Defined

Hypothesis V.1: The potential for collective violence varies strongly with the intensity and scope of relative deprivation among members of a collectivity.

Relative deprivation (RD) is defined as actors' perception of discrepancy between their value expectations and their value capabilities. Value expectations are the goods and conditions of life to which people believe they are rightfully entitled. Value capabilities are the goods and conditions they think they are capable of getting and keeping. (These concepts are more precisely defined below.) The emphasis of the hypothesis is on the perception of deprivation; people may be subjectively deprived with reference to their expectations even though an objective observer might not judge them to be in want. Similarly, the existence of what the observer judges to be abject poverty or "absolute deprivation" is not necessarily thought to be unjust or irremediable by those who experience it. As Runciman puts it, "if people have no reason to expect or hope for more than they can achieve, they will be less discontented with what they have, or even grateful simply to be able to hold on to it." [5] The concept of RD was first used systematically in the 1940s by the authors of *The American Soldier* to denote the feelings of an individual who lacks some status or conditions that he thinks he should have, his standards of what he should have generally being determined by reference to what some other person or groups has.[6] The concept is widely used in sociological research, where it is usually assumed for operational purposes that value standards are set by reference to some group or status with which an individual does or is thought to identify.[7] It is more gen-

[5] W. G. Runciman, *Relative Deprivation and Social Justice* (Berkeley: University of California Press, 1966), 9.

[6] See note 27, chap. 1.

[7] See for instance Runciman, 11 ff; David F. Aberle, "A Note on Relative Deprivation Theory," in Sylvia L. Thrupp, ed., *Millennial Dreams in Action: Essays in Comparative Study* (The Hague: Mouton, 1962), 209–214; Gordon Rose, "Anomie and Deviation: A Conceptual Framework for Empirical Studies," *British Journal of Sociology,* XVII (March 1966), 29–45; Peter Townsend, "The Meanings of Poverty," *British Journal of Sociology,* XIII (September 1962), 210–227; and the status-inconsistency literature beginning with Gerhard Lenski, "Status Crystallization: A Non-Vertical Dimension of Social Status," *American Sociological Review,* XIX (August 1954), 405–413.

erally recognized, however, that value standards can have other sources. An individual's point of reference may be his own past condition, an abstract ideal, or the standards articulated by a leader as well as a "reference group." The definition used here makes no assumptions about the sources of value expectations; it is similar to Aberle's definition of RD as "a negative discrepancy between legitimate expectations and actuality."[8]

Values are the desired events, objects, and conditions for which men strive.[9] The values most relevant to a theory of political violence are the general categories of conditions valued by many men, not those idiosyncratically sought by particular individuals. In psychological terms, values are the goal objects of human motivation, presumably attributable to or derived from basic "needs" or "instincts." There have been innumerable attempts to identify and categorize "needs," "goals," or "values" for purposes of psychological, sociological, and political analysis. Freud postulated a single basic need, Eros; Henry Murray listed 12 "viscerogenic" and 28 "psychogenic" needs.[10] Three influential and reasonably parsimonious lists are summarized in table 1 and related to one another. A three-fold categorization that includes *welfare values, power values,* and *interpersonal values* is used here. There is no need for originality in such a scheme; it is a composite typology, representing values common to other schemes and relevant to the genesis of collective RD.

Welfare values are those that contribute directly to physical well-being and self-realization. They include the physical goods of life—food, shelter, health services, and physical comforts—and the development and use of physical and mental abilities. These two classes of welfare values are referred to below as *economic* and *self-actualization* values. Self-actualization values may be instrumental to the attainment of other welfare values and vice versa. Aside from this, however, Maslow and Davies have argued persuasively that "self-actualization" is an end in itself for many men: we take intrinsic satisfaction in exercising our intellects and our hands.[11] *Power values* are those that determine the extent to which men can influence the actions of others and avoid unwanted interference by others in their own actions. Power values especially salient for political violence include the desire

[8] Aberle, 209.

[9] Following the usage of Harold Lasswell and Abraham Kaplan, *Power and Society: A Framework for Political Inquiry* (New Haven: Yale University Press, 1950), 55–56.

[10] Summarily listed and discussed in James C. Davies, *Human Nature in Politics* (New York: Wiley, 1963).

[11] Maslow, passim; Davies, 53–60.

TABLE 1

Four Lists of Value Categories

Maslow's Need Hierarchy[a]	*Lasswell and Kaplan's Values*[b]	*Runciman's Dimensions of Social Inequality*[c]	*Composite Typology*
	WELFARE VALUES		
Physical	Well-being, wealth	Economic class	Welfare values
Self-actualization	Skill, enlightenment	–	
	DEFERENCE VALUES		
Safety, order	Power	Power	Power values
Love, belongingness	Affection	–	Interpersonal values
Self-esteem	Respect	Status	
	Rectitude	–	

[a] A. H. Maslow, "A Theory of Human Motivation," *Psychological Review*, L (1943), 370–396, summarized and discussed in James C. Davies, *Human Nature in Politics: The Dynamics of Political Behavior* (New York: Wiley, 1963), 8–63. Maslow postulates a hierarchy among needs: safety and order needs will not emerge until physical needs are satisfied, love needs emerge only after safety needs are satisfied, etc. The needs are listed here in Maslow's proposed order with the exception of self-actualization, which he suggests emerges after love needs are satisfied.

[b] *Power and Society*, 55–56.

[c] *Relative Deprivation*, chap. 3. Runciman does not treat these explicitly as values or needs but as conditions that groups have in varying degrees, and with respect to which people judge their relative satisfaction or deprivation.

to participate in collective decision-making—to vote, to take part in political competition, to become a member of the political elite—and the related desires for self-determination and security, for example freedom from oppressive political regulation or from disorder. These two classes of power values are referred to below as *participation* and *security* values. *Interpersonal values* are the psychological satisfactions we seek in nonauthoritative interaction with other individuals and groups. These values include the desire for status, i.e., occupancy of a generally recognized role by virtue of which we are granted some measure of prestige by those with whom we interact; the related need to participate in stable, supportive groups—family, community, associations—that provide companionship and affection; and the sense of certainty that derives from shared adherence to beliefs about the nature of society and one's place in it, and to norms governing social interaction. These three classes of interpersonal values are labeled *status, communality,* and *ideational coherence.*

The *value expectations* of a collectivity are the average value positions to which its members believe they are justifiably entitled. *Value position* is the amount or level of a value actually attained. Value expectations refer to both present and future conditions. Men ordinarily expect to keep what they have; they also generally have a set of expectations and demands about what they should have in the future, which is usually as much or more than what they have at present. It is important to note that value expectations are defined with reference to *justifiable* value positions, meaning what men believe they are entitled to get or maintain, not merely what they faintly hope to attain. Hoselitz and Willner make a precisely comparable distinction between expectation and aspiration:

> Expectations are a manifestation of the prevailing norms set by the immediate social and cultural environment. Whether expressed in economic or social terms, the basis upon which the individual forms his expectations is the sense of what is rightfully owed to him. The source of that sense of rightness may be what his ancestors have enjoyed, what he has had in the past, what tradition ascribes to him, and his position in relation to that of others in the society. Aspirations, on the other hand, represent that which he would like to have but has not necessarily had or considered his due. . . .[12]

The value capabilities of a collectivity are the average value positions its members perceive themselves capable of attaining or maintaining. Value capabilities also have both present and future connotations. In the present, value capabilities are represented by what men have actually been able to attain or have been provided by their environment: their *value position.* In the future, value capabilities are what men believe their skills, their fellows, and their rulers will, in the course of time, permit them to keep or attain: their *value potential.* It is possible to distinguish between perceived and actual value potential: men's capacities for attaining their value expectations may be substantially greater or less than they believe them to be. However, it is perceived value potential that determines present behavior. It is also likely that perceived value potential is considerably more important than present value position in determining how people assess their capabilities. The attained value positions of a group may

[12] Bert Hoselitz and Ann Willner, "Economic Development, Political Strategies, and American Aid," in Morton A. Kaplan, ed., *The Revolution in World Politics* (New York: Wiley, 1962), 363.

be quite low with respect to value expectations, but perceived deprivation and manifestations of discontent will tend to be low to the extent that potential is perceived to be high. The obverse relationship characterizes some prerevolutionary societies: attained value positions appear relatively high with respect to value expectations, but the potential for increasing or even maintaining value positions is perceived to be declining. These assertions are documented in the following chapters.

The courses of action people have available to them for attaining or maintaining their desired value positions are their *value opportunities,* three types of which can be distinguished: personal, societal, and political. *Personal opportunities* are individuals' inherited and acquired capacities for value-enhancing action. Inherited capacities are normally distributed in most collectivities and thus have little relevance to a theory of collective violence. The technical skills and general knowledge acquired through education, however, can greatly increase men's sense of personal competence, particularly in improving their material value positions. *Societal opportunities* are the normal courses of action available to members of a collectivity for direct value-enhancing action. Societal opportunities for economic value attainment include the range and number of remunerative occupations, the ease of access to those occupations, and the economic resources available to compensate those engaged. Participation values can be attained through routinized channels for political participation and recruitment to the political elite; the attainment of security values is largely a function of the capacity of the political system for simultaneously minimizing detailed regulation of human activity and maintaining internal order. Interpersonal values are enhanced to the extent that familial and communal life is free from external disruption, and to the extent that there are generally accepted norms on the basis of which status and respect are accorded in interpersonal relations. *Political opportunities* are the normal courses of action available to members of a collectivity for inducing others to provide them with value satisfactions. Political opportunities refer to political actions as means rather than ends; opportunities for political participation as an end in itself are comprised under societal value opportunities. The same procedures and institutions that provide the latter usually also provide the means by which collectivities can demand welfare and power benefits from a government. There are other kinds of opportunities that are "political" in the sense intended here, including collective bargaining procedures by which workers can demand greater welfare benefits from their employers, and associational activity by subcultural groups designed to increase their members' status in dealing with members of other groups.

The *scope* of RD is its prevalence with respect to each class of values among the members of a collectivity. Some deprivations are characteristic of some members of all groups. Deprivation is relevant to the disposition to collective violence to the extent that many people feel discontented about the same things. Unexpected personal deprivations such as failure to obtain an expected promotion or the infidelity of a spouse ordinarily affect few people at any given time and are therefore narrow in scope. Events and patterns of conditions like the suppression of a political party, a drastic inflation, or the decline of a group's status relative to its reference group are likely to precipitate feelings of RD among whole groups or categories of people and are wide in scope. Aberle dichotomizes what is here called scope into two general classes of deprivations, those that are personal and those that are group experiences.[13] Scope is better regarded as a continuum: it should be possible to identify, for example by survey techniques, the proportion of people in any collectivity that feels deprived with respect to any specified class of values.

The *intensity* of RD is the extent of negative affect that is associated with its perception, or in other words the sharpness of discontent or anger to which it gives rise. Runciman similarly speaks of the "degree" of deprivation, defined as "the intensity with which it is felt."[14] Intensity, like scope, is subject to direct empirical assessment: one can infer the intensity of men's feelings about RD using interview, projective, and content analytic techniques, among others.[15] Moreover it is possible to specify a number of properties of value expectations and value capabilities that increase or decrease the scope and intensity of deprivation, and that can be examined without necessarily relying on survey techniques. Some determinants of the scope and intensity of RD are examined in the following chapter.

Potential for collective violence, the dependent variable of the hypothesis stated at the outset of this section, is defined as the scope and intensity of the disposition among members of a collectivity to take violent action against others. For many research purposes this potential may be treated as a hypothetical construct, a disposition to act inferred to exist in the minds of many members

[13] Aberle, 210.
[14] Runciman, 10.
[15] One appropriate interviewing technique, the self-anchoring scale, is used in Hadley Cantril, *The Pattern of Human Concerns* (New Brunswick: Rutgers University Press, 1965).

of a collectivity but measured only in terms of its antecedents, the intensity and scope of RD, or in terms of its consequences, the magnitude of collective violence. If it could not conceivably be assessed more directly there would be no point in stating hypotheses about it; the only testable hypothesis would be that the greater the intensity and scope of relative deprivation, the greater the magnitude of collective violence. In principle, however, the potential for collective violence *can* be independently assessed. One means is the use of interview techniques that specifically ask people whether they are prepared to participate in a riot, or that allow them to project violent sentiments in response to ambivalent stimuli. These techniques can be used in structured or laboratory situations. They also can be and have been employed in natural populations. Louis Harris, for example, has polled black Americans about their willingness to riot.[16] It also is possible to construct simulation studies of prerevolutionary situations and assess the responses of players, an approach being developed by Schwartz.[17] This diversity of approaches seems to justify treating potential for collective violence as a crucial intervening variable between deprivation-induced discontent and political violence, rather than as a merely hypothetical and superfluous construct.

The Sources of Aggression [18]

Psychological theories about the origins of human aggression provide an explicit motivational explanation for the proposed causal link between relative deprivation and collective violence. There is a variety of theoretical writings on this question, some of it speculative, some of it based on empirical research. Some psychological "theories" about the sources of aggressive behavior can be disregarded at the outset. There is little support for pseudo-psychological assertions that most or all revolutionaries or conspirators are deviants, fools, or the maladjusted.[19] Psychodynamic explanations of the "revolutionary personality" may be useful for

[16] William Brink and Louis Harris, *Black and White: A Study of U.S. Racial Attitudes Today* (New York: Simon and Schuster, 1967), 266.

[17] David Schwartz, "Political Alienation: A Preliminary Experiment on the Psychology of Revolution's First Stage," paper read at the Annual Meeting of the American Political Science Association (1967).

[18] Portions of this section first appeared in Ted Gurr, "Psychological Factors in Civil Violence," *World Politics*, XX (January 1968), 247–251.

[19] See for example Kurt Riezler, "On the Psychology of the Modern Revolution," *Social Research*, X (September 1943), 320–336; portions of Eric Hoffer's generally useful *The True Believer: Thoughts on the Nature of Mass Movements* (New York: Harper, 1951); and Donald J. Goodspeed, *The Conspirators: A Study of the Coup d'Etat* (New York: The Viking Press, 1962).

microanalysis of particular events, but contribute relatively little to general theories of collective action.[20] Aggression-prone victims of maladaptive socialization processes are found in every society, and among the actors in most outbreaks of political violence, but they are much more likely to be mobilized by strife than to constitute it in its entirety. Nor can a general theory of political strife be based solely on culturally specific theories of modal personality traits, though it should take account of their effects (discussed in chapter 6). The most generally relevant psychological theories are those that deal with the sources and characteristics of aggression in all men, regardless of culture. Such psychological theory provides a motivational base for theory about political violence and provides a means for identifying and specifying the operation of some explanatory variables.

There are three distinguishable psychological assumptions about the generic sources of human aggression: that aggression is solely instinctive, that it is solely learned, or that it is an innate response activitated by frustration.[21] One or another of these is implicit in most theoretical approaches to civil strife that have no explicit motivational base. The instinct theories of aggression, represented among others by Freud's qualified attribution of the impulse to destructiveness to a death instinct and by Lorenz's view of aggression as a survival-enhancing instinct, assume that most or all men have within them an autonomous source of aggressive impulses, a drive to aggress that, in Lorenz's words, exhibits "irresistible outbreaks which recur with rhythmical regularity."[22] Although there is no definitive support for this assumption, its advocates, including Freud and Lorenz, have often applied it to the explanation of collective as well as individual aggression.[23] The assump-

[20] A recent study of this type is E. Victor Wolfenstein, *The Revolutionary Personality: Lenin, Trotsky, Gandhi* (Princeton: Princeton University Press, 1967).

[21] A threat-aggression sequence is discussed below.

[22] Konard Lorenz, *On Aggression* (New York: Harcourt, Brace, and World, 1966), chap. 4, quotation from xii. The aggressive instinct in animals and man is said ordinarily to be triggered by the presence or approach of another creature. In the absence of such an activator, however, aggression will occur spontaneously. Such assertions are supported by somewhat idiosyncratic observational reports on animal behavior.

[23] See for example Sigmund Freud, *Civilization and Its Discontents*, trans. Joan Riviere (London: The Hogarth Press, 1930); Lorenz, chaps. 13, 14; and Franz Alexander, "The Psychiatric Aspects of War and Peace," *American Journal of Sociology*, LXVI (1941), 504–520. Freud's instinctual interpretation of aggression is advanced in his later works; his early view was that aggression is a response to frustration of pleasure-seeking behavior. For reviews and critiques of other instinct theories of aggression see Leonard Berkowitz, *Aggression: A Social Psychological Analysis* (New York: McGraw-Hill, 1962), chap. 1, and Ralph L. Holloway, Jr., "Human Aggression: The Need for a Species-Specific Framework," in Morton Fried and others, eds., *War: The Anthropology of Armed Conflict and Aggression* (Garden City, New York: Natural History Press, 1968), 29–48.

tion is evident in Hobbes' characterization of man in the state of nature, and perhaps implicit in Nieburg's recent concern for "the people's capability for outraged, uncontrolled, bitter, and bloody violence,"[24] but plays no significant role in contemporary theories of civil strife.

Just the opposite assumption, that aggressive behavior is solely or primarily learned, characterizes the work of some child and social psychologists, whose evidence indicates that some aggressive behaviors are learned and used strategically in the service of particular goals—aggression by children and adolescents to secure attention, by adults to express dominance strivings, by groups in competition for scarce values, by military personnel in the service of national policy.[25] This assumption, that violence is a learned response, rationalistically chosen and dispassionately employed, is common to a number of recent theoretical approaches to collective conflict. Among theorists of revolution, Johnson repeatedly, though not consistently, speaks of civil violence as "purposive," as "forms of behavior *intended* to disorient the behavior of others, thereby bringing about the demise of a hated social system."[26] Timasheff regards revolution as a "residual" event, an expedient "resorted to when other ways of overcoming tensions have failed."[27] Morrison attributes rural discontent and strife in developing nations to "relative deprivation," defined as it is here, but he explicitly assumes rationality in the behavior of the deprived when he hypothesizes that "all attempts to reduce discontent are selected on the basis of the actor's perception of the probability of the attempt's reducing the discontent."[28] Parsons attempts to fit political violence into the framework of social interaction theory, treating the resort to force as a way of acting chosen by the actor(s) for purposes of deterrence, punishment, or symbolic demonstration of capacity to act.[29] Schelling represents those conflict theorists who explicitly

[24] H. L. Nieburg, "The Threat of Violence and Social Change," *American Political Science Review*, LVI (December 1962), 870.

[25] A characteristic study is Albert Bandura and Richard H. Walters, *Social Learning and Personality Development* (New York: Holt, Rinehart and Winston, 1963).

[26] Chalmers Johnson, *Revolutionary Change* (Boston: Little, Brown, 1966), 12, 13, italics added.

[27] Nicholas S. Timasheff, *War and Revolution* (New York: Sheed and Ward, 1965), 154.

[28] Denton E. Morrison, "Relative Deprivation and Rural Discontent in Developing Countries: A Theoretical Proposal," paper read at the Annual Meeting of the American Association for the Advancement of Science (1966), 6.

[29] Talcott Parsons, "Some Reflections on the Place of Force in Social Process," in Harry Eckstein, ed., *Internal War: Problems and Approaches* (New York: The Free Press, 1964), 34–35.

assume rational behavior and interdependence of adversaries' decisions in all types of conflict.[30]

The third psychological assumption is that much aggression occurs as a response to frustration. "Frustration" is an interference with goal-directed behavior; "aggression" is behavior designed to injure, physically or otherwise, those toward whom it is directed. The disposition to respond aggressively when frustrated is part of man's biological makeup; there is a biologically inherent tendency, in men and animals, to attack the frustrating agent. This is not necessarily incompatible with the preceding two assumptions. Frustration-aggression theory is more systematically developed, however, and has substantially more empirical support than theories that assume either that all men have a free-flowing source of destructive energy or that all aggression is imitative and instrumental.

The most influential formulation of frustration-aggression theory was proposed by Dollard and his colleagues at Yale in 1939. The basic postulate is "that the occurrence of aggressive behavior always presupposes the existence of frustration and, contrariwise, that the existence of frustration always leads to some form of aggression." It is clear from the remainder of the study that the second part of the postulate was not intended to suggest either that aggression was the only possible response to frustration, or that there was no difference between the instigation to aggression, subsequently called "anger," and the actual occurrence of aggression.[31] Miller later offered a clarification: frustration produces instigations to various responses, one of which is aggression. If the non-aggressive responses do not relieve the frustration, "the greater is the probability that the instigation to aggression eventually will become dominant so that some response of aggression will occur."[32] Empirical studies identify fundamental responses to frustration other than aggression. Himmelweit sum-

[30] Thomas C. Schelling, *The Strategy of Conflict* (Cambridge, Mass.: Harvard University Press, 1960), 4.

[31] John Dollard and others, *Frustration and Aggression* (New Haven: Yale University Press, 1939), quotation from p. 1. Major summaries of the experimental and theoretical literature include Hilde T. Himmelweit, "Frustration and Aggression: A Review of Recent Experimental Work," in *Psychological Factors of Peace and War,* ed. T. H. Pear (London: Hutchinson, 1950), 161–91; Elton D. McNeil, "Psychology and Aggression," *Journal of Conflict Resolution,* III (June 1959), 195–294; Arnold H. Buss, *The Psychology of Aggression* (New York: John Wiley, 1961); Aubrey J. Yates, *Frustration and Conflict* (New York: John Wiley, 1962), especially chaps. 2–4; and Berkowitz, *Aggression.*

[32] Neal E. Miller and others, "The Frustration-Aggression Hypothesis," *Psychological Review,* XLVIII (July 1941), quotation from 339.

marizes experimental evidence that frustration in children can lead to regression in the form of lowering intellectual performance, and to evasion.[33] Four response patterns were found in an examination of frustration-induced behaviors in a New Guinea tribe: submission, dependence, avoidance, and aggression. The primary emotional response to frustrations among children is rage or anger, modified by later learning experiences.[34] Prolonged frustration, in the form of continuous unemployment, has been observed to result in apathy.[35]

These findings and observations are qualifications of the basic frustration-aggression thesis, not refutations of it. The basic explanatory element that frustration-aggression theory contributes to the understanding of human conflict, and specifically to the analysis of political violence, is the principle that anger functions as a drive. In the recent reformulation of the theory by Berkowitz, the perception of frustration is said to arouse anger. Aggressive responses tend to occur only when they are evoked by an external cue, that is, when the angered person sees an attackable object or person that he associates with the source of frustration. This argument, and the experimental evidence that supports it, suggests that an angered person is not likely to strike out at any object in his environment, but only at the targets he thinks are responsible. The crucial point is that occurrence of such an attack is an inherently satisfying response to anger; if the attacker has done some harm to his frustrator, his anger is reduced, whether or not he succeeds in reducing the level of frustration per se.[36] If frustration continues, aggression is likely to recur. If it is reduced as a result of the attack, the tendency to attack is reinforced, and the onset of anger in the future is increasingly likely to be accompanied by aggression.

Maier has undertaken many studies which support the thesis that innate frustration-induced behaviors become ends in themselves for the actors, unrelated to further goals, and qualitatively different from goal-directed behavior. He suggests that there are four frustration-induced responses, including regression, fixation, and resignation as well as aggression. Frustration-instigated behavior is distinguished from goal-directed behavior by a number of

[33] Himmelweit, 172.

[34] J. M. V. Whiting, "The Frustration Complex in Kwoma Society," *Man*, XLIV (November–December 1944), 140–144.

[35] Marie Lazarsfeld and Hans Zeisal, "Die Arbeitslosen von Marienthal," *Psychologische Monographen*, V (1933), summarized in Himmelweit, 172.

[36] On the drive properties of anger see Berkowitz, "The Concept of Aggressive Drive," and S. Feshbach, "The Function of Aggression and the Regulation of Aggressive Drive," *Psychological Review*, LXXI (July 1964), 257–272.

characteristics: it tends to be fixed and compulsive; it is not necessarily deterred by punishment, which may instead increase the degree of frustration; it takes the form most readily available, little influenced by anticipated consequences; and it is satisfying in itself.[37] Furthermore the original goal which suffered frustration may become largely irrelevant to behavior. "Aggression then becomes a function of the frustration, the previously existing goal response having been replaced by behavior which is controlled by an entirely different process."[38]

The threat-aggression sequence is another behavioral mechanism that a number of psychologists have argued is as fundamental, if not as common, as the frustration-aggression relationship. Clinical and observational evidence suggests that the greater the perceived threat to life, the greater the violent response. According to Wedge, "When the value directly at stake is life, violent response occurs as reaction to fear rather than expression of anger."[39] Surveys of the effects of bombing on Japanese, German, and English civilian populations during World War II show that heavy bombings—including those of Hiroshima and Nagasaki—first produced acute fear, not anger, but also generally led to increased hostility toward both the enemy and the government that failed to prevent the bombings.[40] Experiments with animals provide substantiating evidence: events that immediately and actively threaten the continued existence of the organism trigger avoidance-survival mechanisms, which can include extraordinarily violent behavior. The threat-aggression sequence can be interpreted as a special case of the frustration-aggression relationship, as Berkowitz does. A threat to life is an anticipated frustration; as the degree of threat increases, fear and anger rise simultaneously, and the extent to which fear predominates may be "a function of the individual's perceived power to control or hurt his frustrater relative to the frustrater's power to control or harm him."[41] It nonetheless seems likely that people have a fundamental disposition to respond ag-

[37] Maier, 92–115, 159–161; also see Yates, 24–30, 36–56.

[38] Norman R. F. Maier, "The Role of Frustration in Social Movements," *Psychological Review,* LXIX (November 1942), 587.

[39] Bryant Wedge, "The Case Study of Student Political Violence: Brazil, 1964, and the Dominican Republic, 1965," *World Politics,* XXI (January 1969), 195–196. Also see Jerome Frank, *Sanity and Survival: Psychological Aspects of War and Peace* (New York: Vintage Books, 1968), 75.

[40] I. L. Janis, *Air War and Emotional Stress; Psychological Studies of Bombing and Civilian Defense* (New York: McGraw-Hill, 1951), 4–152. Comparable reactions have been observed in many disaster studies. See for example George W. Baker and Dwight W. Chapman, eds., *Man and Society in Disaster* (New York: Basic Books, 1962).

[41] Berkowitz, *Aggression,* 42–46, quotation from 45.

gressively to extreme fear itself; if so, the response can reinforce and be reinforced by frustration-induced anger. The relationship appears especially relevant in evaluating the effect of police and military actions in precipitating and prolonging collective violence.

The frustration-aggression and the related threat-aggression mechanisms provide the basic motivational link between RD and the potential for collective violence. They are not inconsistent with the presence of learned and purposive elements in acts of individual and collective violence, however. Men feel deprived with respect to what they have learned to value and to what they have learned to do. The beliefs and symbols that determine the timing, forms, and objects of violence are learned. If their anger is powerful and persistent, men can employ much reason and inventiveness in devising ways to give it violent expression. Some such men may learn to value violence for its own sake. But much of this learning takes place after anger has already been aroused; individuals who are dispassionately violent often are using techniques that proved useful and satisfying in response to past frustrations.

There also is an evident sense of purpose among many of the participants in most outbreaks of collective violence, in the sense that they expect violent action to enhance their value position. Revolutionary leaders put their followers' anger to their purpose of seizing power; rioters take advantage of disorder to loot stores for food and furniture; demonstrators hope to persuade their rulers to take remedial action. The nature and strength of these purposes are major determinants of the form and tactics of collective violence. But in most instances they appear to reinforce or channel the impetus to violence, and are infrequently an autonomous motive for violence. This assertion is made without an attempt to support it, but it is suceptible to empirical test. It is true, and the frustration-aggression relationship is significant for political violence, to the extent that actors in political violence manifest or admit to some degree of anger.[42]

In summary, the primary source of the human capacity for violence appears to be the frustration-aggression mechanism. Frustration does not necessarily lead to violence, and violence for

[42] Anger is quite often accompanied by other affective elements, notably excitement; the test proposed here is whether anger is present in substantial degree. Excitement does not seem to be an independent affective state but a general emotional arousal that precedes and accompanies goal-consummatory activity; the angry man who anticipates a riot is excited for much the same reasons that a starving man is excited at the smell of food cooking.

some men is motivated by expectations of gain. The anger induced by frustration, however, is a motivating force that disposes men to aggression, irrespective of its instrumentalities. If frustrations are sufficiently prolonged or sharply felt, aggression is quite likely, if not certain, to occur. To conclude that the relationship is not relevant to individual or collective violence is akin to the assertion that the law of gravitation is irrelevant to the theory of flight because not everything that goes up falls back to earth in accord with the basic gravitational principle. The frustration-aggression mechanism is in this sense analogous to the law of gravity: men who are frustrated have an innate disposition to do violence to its source in proportion to the intensity of their frustration, just as objects are attracted to one another in direct proportion to their relative masses and inverse proportion to their distance. A number of other variables influence the behavior of men, and of objects, in such circumstances: for men, their beliefs, inhibitions, and social environment; for objects in a gravitational field, their energies, configuration, and the properties of the medium in which they are situated. But it seems even less feasible to account for political violence without reference to the properties of men that dispose them to violence than it is to construct a theory of flight without reference to the law of gravitation. On earth, gravity can be assumed a constant; among men, levels of frustration vary greatly.

Relative Deprivation and Analogous Causes of Political Violence

Relative deprivation, defined as perceived discrepancy between value expectations and value capabilities, is sufficiently general to comprise or be related to most of the general "preconditions of revolution" identified in other theoretical analyses. Some of these conceptual relationships are examined here, not to demonstrate that RD is somehow a "correct" concept and that others are not, but to show that in addition to its relatively clear definition it can synthesize diverse other notions.

For Aristotle the principal cause of revolution is the aspiration for economic or political equality on the part of the common people who lack it, and the aspiration of oligarchs for greater inequality than they have, i.e. a discrepancy in both instances between what people have of political and economic goods relative to what they think is justly theirs.[43] Edwards, writing some twenty-three centuries later, asserts that all revolutions are due to "repression of

[43] *The Politics of Aristotle*, trans. J. E. C. Welldon (New York: Macmillan, 1883, 1905), 338–342.

elemental wishes" and that the violence of any revolution is proportional to the degree of such repression. The sense of repression, or "balked disposition," develops when "people come to feel that their legitimate aspirations and ideas are being repressed or perverted, that their entirely proper desires and ambitions are being hindered and thwarted. . . ."[44] Pettee's concept of "cramp" similarly resembles RD. People feel "cramped" when they find that satisfaction of their basic needs for liberty and security is interfered with, and moreover regard this repression as unnecessary and avoidable, hence unjustified. "A revolution takes place when the great majority of the society feel cramped beyond tolerance."[45]

Analogous concepts are used by contemporary theorists. Lasswell and Kaplan attribute political instability to the discrepancy between expectations and the "degree of . . . realization of value for the mass. . . . It is a low degree of realization—disparity between value position and value demanded and expected—which is most directly effective."[46] Zollschan argues that all activity, including revolutionary activity, begins with "exigency," defined as "a discrepancy (for a person) between a consciously or unconsciously desired or expected state of affairs and an actual situation."[47] Both of these concepts make assumptions about states of mind of revolutionary actors, as do the concepts mentioned in the preceding paragraph. Johnson makes no such assumptions in identifying a "disequilibrated social system" as a necessary precondition for revolution, which is explicitly a macro-analytic concept. Its manifestations at the individual level of analysis may be readily interpreted in terms of RD, however: it constitutes a discrepancy between men's value expectations (collectively, their "value structures") and their means for attaining those values (collectively, the social system's "pattern of adaptation to the environment" and its capacity to "fulfill functional requisites").[48]

Some theorists explicitly use the terms "frustration" or "deprivation" to represent the impetus to collective violence. Davies attributes revolutionary outbreaks to the frustration which results

[44] Lyford P. Edwards, *The Natural History of Revolution* (Chicago: University of Chicago Press, 1927), 3–4, 30–33.

[45] George S. Pettee, *The Process of Revolution* (New York: Harper, 1938), chap. 2, quotation from 33.

[46] Lasswell and Kaplan, 264.

[47] George K. Zollschan and Walter Hirsch, eds., *Explorations in Social Change* (Boston: Houghton Mifflin, 1964), xxv, 89.

[48] Johnson, chap. 5. For a similar analysis see Neil J. Smelser, *Theory of Collective Behavior* (New York: The Free Press, 1963), chaps. 2, 3.

from a short-term decline in achievement following a long-term increase that generated expectations about continuing increase.[49] Lerner similarly describes the gap between what people want and what they get as "frustrating" and suggests revolutionary consequences. "The spread of frustration in areas developing less rapidly than their people wish can be seen as the outcome of a deep imbalance between achievement and aspiration . . . aspiration outruns achievement so far that many people, even if they are making some progress toward their goal, are dissatisfied because they get so much less than they want."[50] Crozier says that the one element common to all rebels is frustration, defined as "the inability to do something one badly wants to do, through circumstances beyond one's control."[51] The Feierabends associate political instability with aggressive behavior, which is said to vary with the extent of "systemic frustration." The extent of systemic frustration is the ratio of social want satisfaction to social want formation, or, in RD terms, the discrepancy between present value position and value expectations.[52]

Relative deprivation is related to frustration by Coser, and applied to the explanation of suicide rates.[53] Hoselitz and Willner, extending their distinction between expectations and aspirations, link deprivation with the potential for revolution.

> Unrealized aspirations produce feelings of disappointment, but unrealized expectations result in feelings of deprivation. Disappointment is generally tolerable; deprivation is often intolerable. The deprived individual feels impelled to remedy, by whatever means are available, the material and psychic frustrations produced in him. Whereas disappointment may breed the seeds of incipient revolution, deprivation serves as a catalyst for revolutionary action.[54]

[49] James C. Davies, "Toward a Theory of Revolution," *American Sociological Review*, XXVII (February 1962), 5–19. The Davies thesis is also used by Raymond Tanter and Manus Midlarsky, "A Theory of Revolution," *Journal of Conflict Resolution*, XI (September 1967), 264–280, who characterize the discrepancy as a "revolutionary gap."

[50] Daniel Lerner, "Toward a Communication Theory of Modernization: A Set of Considerations," in Lucian W. Pye, ed., *Communications and Political Development* (Princeton: Princeton University Press, 1963), 327–350, quotations from 330–335.

[51] Brian Crozier, *The Rebels: A Study of Post-War Insurrections* (London: Chatto and Windus, 1960), 15–16.

[52] Ivo K. and Rosalind L. Feierabend, "Aggressive Behaviors Within Polities, 1948–1962; A Cross-National Study," *Journal of Conflict Resolution*, X (September 1966), 250–251.

[53] Lewis A. Coser, *Continuities in the Study of Social Conflict* (New York: The Free Press, 1967), 56–62.

[54] Hoselitz and Willner, 363.

The anthropological literature on American Indian response to white conquest also makes use of the deprivation concept. Nash, for example, shows how deprivation may occur either through acceptance or rejection by Indians of white values and skills, and proposes that the aggressive components in Indian revivalism are a response to that deprivation.[55] Geschwender attributes the American Negro revolt of the 1960s to "relative deprivation," defined in its conventional sociological sense of status discrepancy vis-à-vis a reference group.[56] Galtung, although he does not use the concept of relative deprivation per se, attributes aggression within and among societies to status discrepancy, or "rank disequilibrium," in what is essentially a generalized rephrasing of the Aristotelian thesis with which this catalog of concepts began. If men or groups are high on one dimension of a stratification system, but low on another, e.g., if they have high power or education but low income, they are said to be disposed to use aggression to attain a high or equilibrated position on all dimensions.[57]

This catalog could be extended at length, but only at the risk of belaboring the obvious. Almost all theories that purport to explain violent collective behavior assign a central place to a variable or concept that generally and often specifically resembles RD as it is defined here. Some salient characteristics of the RD variable are not necessarily incorporated in these other concepts, however. Some of them, particularly those making use of "want/get" formulations, make no reference to the justifiability or intensity of men's value expectations, nor to the theoretical desirability of taking into account both actual and anticipated discrepancies between goals and attainments. Moreover, while many of them specify by illustration the kinds of societal and political conditions that constitute the variable or increase its magnitude, few include specific propositions about its determinants, and only some suggest categories for classifying the variable's manifestations. Finally, many theories do not provide a motivational rationale for the causal connection they propose between the variables and the violent events toward which it is supposed to dispose men.

[55] Philleo Nash, "The Place of Religious Revivalism in the Formation of the Intercultural Community on Klamath Reservation," *Social Anthropology of North American Tribes,* ed. Fred Eggan (Chicago: University of Chicago Press, 1937), 377–442.

[56] James A. Geschwender, "Social Structure and the Negro Revolt: An Examination of Some Hypotheses," *Social Forces,* XLIII (December 1964), 248–256.

[57] Johan Galtung, "A Structural Theory of Aggression," *Journal of Peace Research,* No. 2, 1964, 95–119. Galtung also posits several variables that intervene between rank disequilibrium and aggression, including lack of alternative means and the extent of cultural experience in aggression.

There are three other concepts frequently employed in the analysis of disruptive collective behavior that are not directly analogous to RD but that appear to be alternatives to it: dissonance, anomie, and conflict. Without passing judgment on their analytic usefulness in other contexts, it can be suggested that they relate to conditions either more or less specific than RD.

Dissonance is a concept widely used in individual psychology. In Festinger's formulation of cognitive dissonance theory, the term refers to inconsistency between two cognitive elements or clusters of elements. Cognitive elements, "the things a person knows about himself, about his behavior, and about his surroundings," are dissonant if "the obverse of one element would follow from the other."[58] For example, a citizen who believed that his government would begin a war only if attacked and then learned through news media that it had initiated a war without provocation is said to experience dissonance. The assumption is that people sensing dissonance are motivated to reduce or eliminate it, which they can do by changing their behavior or beliefs, by changing the corresponding situation, or by seeking new information to reduce dissonance while avoiding information that would increase dissonance.[59] Depending on the magnitude of dissonance, i.e. the importance or value of the dissonant elements to him, the citizen may change his views about the government, attempt to change the personnel or policies of the government through political action, or, most likely in this instance, deny the validity of the evidence that the war was begun without provocation and be receptive to any evidence of provocation, however flimsy. Many hypotheses have been proposed and considerable empirical research done on effects of dissonance in decision-making, compliance, receptivity to information, social support for mass phenomena, and the influence process in small groups.[60]

The dissonance and RD concepts neither comprise nor subsume one another but overlap. RD is perceived with reference to individuals' welfare, power, and interpersonal value expectations; dissonance can obtain among any set of cognitive elements, not only those that relate to valued goods and conditions of life. Moreover only some perceptions of deprivation entail dissonance, in its original sense of contradiction among cognitive elements.

[58] Leon Festinger, *A Theory of Cognitive Dissonance* (Stanford: Stanford University Press, 1957), quotations from 4, 13. The perception of contradiction can arise on logical, experiential, cultural, or other grounds, according to Festinger.

[59] Festinger, 18–24.

[60] Festinger, passim; Jack W. Brehm and Arthur R. Cohen, *Explorations in Cognitive Dissonance* (New York: Wiley, 1962).

Most black Americans know very well that their expectations of economic and social equality will be only grudgingly and gradually satisfied, if at all; the failure of the political system to take massive remedial action is "dissonant" only for those Negroes who at one time thought that it would. For the great majority the lack of action merely confirms prior cognitions of the system and intensifies discontent. The dissonance concept and hypotheses seem directly applicable to only one particular aspect of the processes by which the perception of RD develops: when an individual first perceives inadequacies in value opportunities he had thought were appropriate and sufficient for attainment of his value expectations, he can be said to experience dissonance. The onset of RD through increasing value expectations, or the existence of a discrepancy between expectations and capabilities per se, does not itself constitute dissonance, however, nor as Festinger pointed out does dissonance exist whenever an individual encounters resistance or frustration in trying to achieve an objective.[61]

Anomie, in the sense Durkheim used it in *Suicide,* is a situation in which either ends (value expectations) outstrip men's means, or ends remain constant while means are severely restricted, and corresponds quite closely to the RD concept. The more generalized sense that Durkheim gave the term in *The Division of Labor in Society,* one which Merton popularized in his essay on "Social Structure and Anomie," is that anomie is a breakdown of social standards governing social behavior, or normlessness. It is specifically a sociological concept: "the degree of anomie in a social system is indicated by the extent to which there is a lack of consensus on norms judged to be legitimate, with its attendant uncertainty and insecurity in social relations." [62] Manifestations of normlessness within individuals are characterized as anomia. Rose, summarizing the literature, identifies three kinds of anomie: weakness of norms per se, the existence of several strong but conflicting norms, and ignorance of norms. All three situations lead to the pervasive sense of uncertainty to which is attributed much deviant behavior, including criminality, suicide and drug addiction, and gang behavior. Merton originally suggested that anomie could lead to widespread deviant behavior and the establishment of alternative norms, which constitutes "rebellion." "When rebel-

[61] Festinger, 278.

[62] Robert K. Merton, "Social Structure and Anomie: Continuities," *Social Theory and Social Structure,* rev. ed. (New York: The Free Press, 1957), quotation from 266–267. This discussion of the anomie concept makes substantial use of Gordon Rose, "Anomie and Deviation," 29–45. A more comprehensive summation of work making use of the concept is Marshall B. Clinard, ed., *Anomie and Deviant Behavior: A Discussion and Critique* (New York: The Free Press, 1964).

lion becomes endemic in a substantial part of the society, it provides a potential for revolution, which reshapes both the normative and the social structure." There seem to have been no substantial later attempts to relate anomie to the occurrence of collective violence other than gang behavior, however.[63]

Anomie can be related to the RD concept, as defined here, in two ways. If group norms are weak or in conflict about how members can satisfy value expectations, value opportunities are thereby limited. This is particularly the case with respect to personal and societal opportunities; the less certain people are about what ways of acting are appropriate for attaining their goals, i.e. the greater their anomia, the lower their value capabilities are likely to be and hence the greater is RD. It should be noted that men can experience normlessness or norm conflict in any social role and outside social roles, for example as subordinates in an authority relationship or as passengers on a jet flight. Thus anomie constitutes or increases RD only when it relates to norms of value-maintaining or value-enhancing activities.

It also can be argued, partly on the basis of cognitive dissonance theory, that sets of internally consistent norms are intrinsically valued and that the breakdown of systems of norms therefore constitutes RD with respect to "coherence" values. The argument is not that everyone who suffers from anomia is therefore deprived; it is that RD is experienced by those persons who at one time accepted an internally consistent set of norms as valid guides to action but have subsequently felt those norms to be seriously challenged, without being replaced by another internally consistent set of norms. Deprivation in this instance results from value loss, i.e. a declining value position with respect to the ideational coherence category of interpersonal values. In an anomic society, however, there are likely to be many people who have never held one unquestioned, consistent set of norms. Never having had a consistent set of norms, they are less likely to be discontented over its lack than those who experience a threat to or loss of strongly held norms.

The most potent effect of anomie on RD probably is its impact on value opportunities. Whether normative systems are intrinsically valued in the sense that economic goods, security, and

[63] Merton, 191. One application to political violence is Elwin H. Powell, "Reform, Revolution, and Reaction as Adaptations to Anomie," *Review of Mexican Sociology*, XXV (1963), 331–355. David C. Schwartz has developed a process model of revolutionary behavior which uses the related concept of alienation and specifies the circumstances in which political alienation occurs, in "A Theory of Revolutionary Behavior," in James C. Davies, ed., *When Men Revolt and Why* (New York: The Free Press, 1970).

status are valued is an empirical question most directly answered by ascertaining the extent to which threats to norm systems anger people. Generally, the anomie and anomia concepts are related to RD in a way comparable to dissonance: they overlap RD, but they cannot be subsumed by it nor do they incorporate all or most aspects of it.

"Conflict" in its collective sense is sometimes defined as a condition, sometimes as a process, and sometimes as an event. Galtung defines it as a condition: "An action-system is said to be in conflict if the system has two or more incompatible goal-states."[64] Coser initially defines it as a process, "a struggle over values and claims to scarce status, power and resources in which the aims of the opponents are to neutralize, injure or eliminate their rivals."[65] In conventional usage conflict is an event, a violent or nonviolent clash between two groups. By either of the first two definitions conflict resembles the RD concept more closely than either dissonance or anomie.[66] One difference is that RD refers both to individual states of mind and their collective distribution, whereas social conflict is generally treated as a property of collectivities without reference to its manifestations in the minds of the individuals involved. Galtung identifies a more consequential difference:

> Conflict should . . . be distinguished from *frustration*, which is the more general case where goals are not achieved (needs are not satisfied, gratification not obtained, values not fulfilled, etc.) for *some* reason. A very simple case is that of scarcity. . . . Another simple case is when something is *blocking* the access to the source of gratification. . . . But the most important special case . . . is the case of *conflict* where efforts by oneself or others to obtain some value can be seen as the source of frustration.[67]

Conflict defined as a condition is essentially a special case of RD in which the source of the discrepancy between value expectations and capabilities is another group competing for the same values. Conflict defined as a process refers to the interaction between groups in their respective attempts to alleviate RD.

[64] Johan Galtung, "Institutionalized Conflict Resolution: A Theoretical Paradigm," *Journal of Peace Research*, No. 4, 1965, 348.

[65] Coser, *The Functions of Social Conflict*, 8.

[66] Conflict also has a psychological usage not examined here, namely the presence in an individual of two (or more) competing and incompatible motives. For a review of this concept and the literature see Yates, esp. chap. 5.

[67] Galtung, "Institutionalized Conflict Resolution," 349.

The conflict concept is less appropriate than RD for the analysis of political violence for several reasons. One is simply that in its connotations of process or class of events it includes by definition some of the variables that this analysis proposes to explain. I hope to account for the forms and extent of violent political conflict by proposing some of their general determinants, not to "explain" them by defining them as conflict. Moreover, conflict defined as a condition in which group X has what group Y wants refers to a particular kind of RD, but by no means exhausts the RD concept. RD refers to any collectively felt discrepancy between a sought and an attainable value position, whether or not some other group has the value sought and whether or not group Y tries to seize it from group X. There are psychological grounds, suggested in the preceding section, for expecting collective violence to result from any RD that is of wide scope and intensity. It also seems evident that many acts of political violence, revolutionary movements in particular, do not involve a struggle for values so much as a demand that systems be reshaped so that they can create new values. In this connection, one difficulty that arises if political violence is treated as a category of conflict is that political violence is thereby assumed to entail a struggle for scarce values, an assumption that forecloses examination of other causal factors.

One last limitation of conflict theory for our purposes is the distinction commonly made by conflict theorists between what is called "realistic" and "nonrealistic" conflict (Coser), or "rational" and "nonrational" conflict (Schelling), or "destructive behavior" and "conflict behavior" (Galtung). The essence of the distinction is between actions instrumental in securing the values sought and actions destructive for their own sake. The analytic usefulness of the distinction is not in question; what *is* questionable is attempting to account for political violence using theoretical approaches that assume that only the instrumental manifestations of violence are relevant or subject to analysis. Coser and Galtung, among other conflict theorists, recognize that both elements are present in most conflict. Coser criticizes others for failure to realize that "conflict may be motivated by two distinct yet intermingled factors—a realistic conflict situation and the affective investment in it. . . ." Galtung similarly makes the theoretical point that underlies this entire discussion: "conflict behavior tends to become destructive behavior (because of the frustration-aggression cycle) and destructive behavior tends to be self-reinforcing."[68]

Despite this recognition, most of the concepts and hypotheses

[68] Coser, 59; Galtung, 349. Also see Mack and Snyder, 219, 222–223.

of conflict theory are concerned with the instrumentalities of strife. This analysis gives equal weight to its nonrational origins and manifestations.

Patterns of Relative Deprivation

In static terms, RD is a discrepancy between value expectations and value capabilities, its intensity and scope determinable in any accessible population by the use of survey and other techniques. Dynamic analysis requires conceptual tools that take into account patterns of changes in value expectations and value capabilities over time. One can begin with the assumption that, because RD is a psychically uncomfortable condition, men tend over the long run to adjust their value expectations to their value capabilities. Societal conditions in which sought and attainable value positions are in approximate equilibrium consequently can be regarded as "normal," however uncommon they may be in the contemporary world, and provide a base-line from which to evaluate patterns of change. Three distinct patterns of disequilibrium can be specified: *decremental deprivation,* in which a group's value expectations remain relatively constant but value capabilities are perceived to decline; *aspirational deprivation,* in which capabilities remain relatively static while expectations increase or intensify;[69] and *progressive deprivation,* in which there is substantial and simultaneous increase in expectations and decrease in capabilities. All three patterns have been cited as causal or predisposing factors for political violence.

DECREMENTAL DEPRIVATION

The model shown graphically in figure 1 represents settings in which group consensus about justifiable value positions has varied little over time, but in which the average attainable value position or potential is perceived to decline substantially. Men in these circumstances are angered over the loss of what they once had or thought they could have; they experience RD by reference to their own past condition. The value position of an entire society may fall because of declining production of material goods, declining capacities of the political elite to provide order or resolve crises, imposition of foreign rule, or loss of faith in the society's integrating structure of beliefs and attendant norms of action. Value capabilities also may fall among one or more segments of society because its members lose out in absolute terms in conflict with other groups over scarce values. Examples in-

[69] These patterns are labeled and described briefly by Morrison, 5.

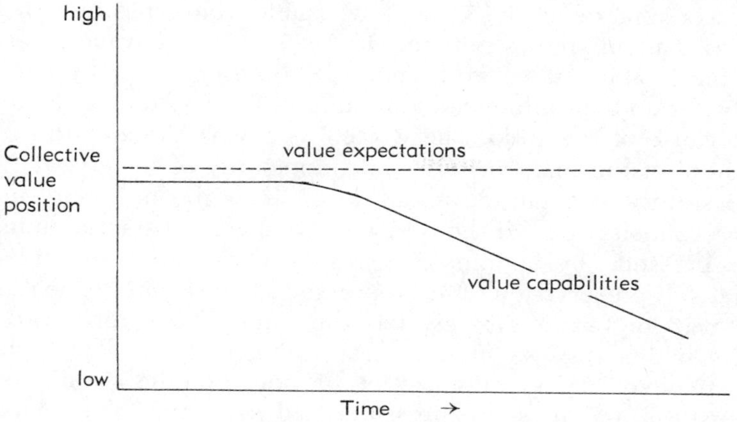

Figure 1. Decremental deprivation.

clude the effects of progressive taxation on the wealthy and of regressive taxation on the poor; the loss of political influence by elites and oppositional groups newly barred from political activity; and the decline in status and influence felt by middle-class groups as the status of working-class groups increases. The value position or potential of a particular group also may seem to decline not because of any diminution or redistribution of total values available in a society but because of the declining number or appropriateness of opportunities, for example the shrinking number of employment opportunities for unskilled labor in highly industrialized societies and the lack of stable communal relationships open to migrants newly arrived in the city from rural villages. The systemic sources of declining value capabilities are examined in more detail in chapter 5.

A number of theorists have attributed political violence wholly or in part to decremental deprivation. The revolutions that Aristotle held to be characteristic of democracies and oligarchies were said to result partly from deprivations of this type. "The main cause of revolutions in Democracies is the intemperate conduct of the demagogues who force the propertied class to combine partly by instituting malicious prosecutions against individuals . . . and partly by inciting the masses against them as a body," whereas in oligarchies one of the two general causes of revolution is seen as the oppression of the masses by the oligarchs.[70] In democracies the relatively high, stable value position of the oligarchs is threat-

[70] Aristotle, *The Politics*, Book v, chaps. v and vi. Quotation from J. E. C. Welldon, trans., *The Politics of Aristotle* (New York: Macmillan, 1883, 1905), 355.

ened, in oligarchies it is the low, stable value position of the masses that suffers interference. In 1925 Sorokin advanced a general thesis about the significance of "repression" in the genesis of revolution that influenced a number of later writers. The immediate cause of revolution, he wrote, "is always the growth of 'repression' of the main instincts of the majority of society, and the impossibility of obtaining for those instincts the necessary minimum of satisfaction." If the desire for food of a substantial number is "repressed" by famine, riots result. If the "reflexes of individual self-preservation" are "repressed" by arbitrary executions, total war, or terror, the result is the same. Other repressed instincts which dispose men toward violence are said to include collective self-preservation, want of housing, the "instincts of ownership" and of self-expression, and so forth.[71] The Marxian view in its original dispensation is similar. Marx and Engels argued the inevitable growth of profound dissatisfactions in the proletariat as a consequence of absolute deprivations or oppressions: the destruction of the worker's pride through his subjection to the machine and the market; economic deprivation because of minimal wages and job insecurity, the latter a consequence of crises in the economic system; and repressive measures of the bourgeois state.

Decremental deprivation is probably most common in "traditional" societies and in traditional segments of transitional societies. Natural disasters in traditional societies often gave rise to collective violence, as Norman Cohn observes in his study of violent millenarianism in medieval Europe:

> Again and again one finds that a particular outbreak of revolutionary chiliasm took place against a background of disaster: the plagues that preluded the First Crusade and the flagellant movements of 1260, 1348–1349, 1391, and 1400. . . . The greatest wave of chiliastic excitement, one which swept through the whole of society, was precipitated by the most universal natural disaster of the Middle Ages, the Black Death. . . .[72]

Hobsbawm says that social banditry was most pervasive in the precapitalist peasant societies of Southern Europe "when their traditional equilibrium [was] upset; during and after periods of abnormal hardship, such as famines and wars, or at the moments

[71] Pitirim A. Sorokin, *The Sociology of Revolution* (Philadelphia: J. B. Lippincott, 1925), 367–369.

[72] Norman R. C. Cohn, *The Pursuit of the Millenium*, 2nd edn. rev. (New York: Harper, 1957, 1961), 315. Also see Smelser, chap. 6.

when the jaws of the dynamic modern world seized these static communities in order to destroy and transform them."[73] Such irresistible events inflicted decremental deprivations on and led to banditry by peasants who had no effective methods of social agitation, i.e., no political value opportunities. The imposition of alien authority on non-Western peoples had similar effects. Colonialism to varying degrees disrupted interpersonal relationships and undermined tribal and other traditional authority. Interpersonal and power deprivations were inflicted on many newly conquered people at the same time that traditional value opportunities, especially political ones, were disrupted. These conditions often generated violent traditionalist resistance that subsequently was transformed into nationalist rebellion.[74]

Decremental deprivation may be less common than other forms of RD in societies undergoing socioeconomic transformation, but it is not uncommon and it can have virulent effects. The great human and material sacrifices of the Russian people during the first World War provided the basic potential for the first Russian Revolution; the refusal of the Kerensky regime to terminate Russia's involvement in the war led directly to the Bolshevik seizure of power and indirectly to the civil war that followed. Almost all analyses of the post-war fascist movements emphasize the absolute deprivations that motivated most of their adherents. In a comparative study of fascist movements in nine countries Carsten concludes that

> certain social groups responded much more strongly to the Fascist appeal than others. This is particularly true of those who were uprooted and threatened by social and economic change, whose position in society was being undermined, who had lost their traditional place, and were frightened of the future. These were above all [segments of] the lower middle classes. . . . Perhaps even more important in the early stages were the former officers and non-commissioned officers of the first world war for whom no jobs were waiting, who had got accustomed to the use of violence, and felt themselves deprived of their "legitimate" rewards.[75]

[73] E. J. Hobsbawm, *Social Bandits and Primitive Rebels: Studies in Archaic Forms of Social Movement in the 19th and 20th Centuries* (Glencoe: The Free Press, 1959), 23–24.

[74] See, for example, William Kornhauser, "Rebellion and Political Development," in Harry Eckstein, ed., *Internal War: Problems and Approaches* (New York: The Free Press, 1964), 145.

[75] F. L. Carsten, *The Rise of Fascism* (Berkeley: University of California Press, 1967), 232.

Cantril's social psychological analysis of the roots of Nazism is similar. Nazism was capable of succeeding as a movement because "old norms, old cultural standards, were no longer able to provide the framework necessary for a satisfying adjustment of the individuals who composed the culture." Decremental deprivation was intense for a variety of groups on many values; there was economic distress, many people had suffered status reductions, and most felt a profound sense of personal insecurity because of the disintegration of both social structures and normative systems.[76]

Any absolute decline in the value position or value potential of a social group constitutes decremental deprivation, and many additional cases of political violence attributable to this pattern of RD could be cited. Some others are examined in chapter 5. Despite the considerable emphasis given in contemporary social analysis to "revolutions of rising expectations," examined below, over the long run of human history decremental RD has probably been a more common source of collective violence than any other pattern of RD. And one can speculate that decremental RD of a given degree probably instigates men to greater intensities of violence than an equivalent level of aspirational RD. Men are likely to be more intensely angered when they lose what they have than when they lose hope of attaining what they do not yet have.

ASPIRATIONAL DEPRIVATION

The aspirational RD model, sketched in figure 2, is characterized by an increase in men's value expectations without a concomitant change in value position or potential. Those who experience aspirational RD do not anticipate or experience significant loss of what they have; they are angered because they feel they have no means for attaining new or intensified expectations. An "increase" in value expectations may reflect demands for a greater amount of a value already held in some degree, for example for more material goods and a greater degree of political order and justice. It may be a demand for new values never previously held, such as political participation for colonial peoples and personal equality for members of lower class and caste groups. Third, it

[76] Hadley Cantril, *The Psychology of Social Movements* (New York: Wiley, 1941), 228–269, quotation from 266. Also see Frederick L. Schuman, *The Nazi Dictatorship: A Study in Social Pathology and the Politics of Fascism* (New York: Knopf, 1935). Individual documentation of the nature and severity of these frustrations is provided by the autobiographical essays of Nazi Party members which are analyzed by Theodore Abel, *The Nazi Movement: Why Hitler Came to Power* (New York: Atherton Press, 1938, 1966).

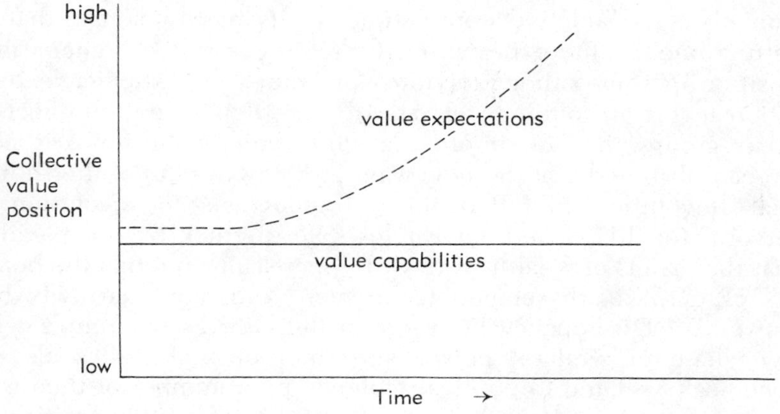

Figure 2. Aspirational deprivation.

may represent intensification of the commitment to (salience of) a value position that earlier was weakly sought, for example intensifying demands for welfare goods among those who experience breakdown of communal life during the early stages of modernization, and intensified demands for access to political elite positions among the upwardly mobile bourgeoisie of seventeenth- and eighteenth-century Europe. Degrees and saliences of value expectations quite often increase simultaneously, but no necessary relation holds between the two. For example, the contemporary demands of black Americans for social equality compared with demands made in the 1940s appear to reflect an increase in the salience of status values among Negroes, a shift from faintly held aspirations for equality to an intensely held belief that equality is deserved now, rather than an increase in the degree of equality sought.

Many sources of increasing value expectations are identified in studies of RD and of political instability. For some traditional peoples mere exposure to, or knowledge of, a better material way of life is assumed to raise expectations. In medieval and early Renaissance Europe the growth of industrial and commercial centers demonstrated new possibilities beyond any that life had to offer the peasant. The new ways attracted the surplus population in particular, but also those who were in some way dissatisfied with manor life. "As social and economic horizons expanded, hardship and poverty and dependence ceased to appear the ineluctable fate of common folk." [77] A special case of the demonstra-

[77] Cohn, 27–28. Also see Neil J. Smelser, *Social Change in the Industrial Revolution* (Chicago: University of Chicago Press, 1959).

tion effect is "relative deprivation" in its narrow sense, that is, setting one's value expectations by reference to the higher value position of some other individual or group. In particular, expectation levels are often accelerated by the demonstration effect of other groups that are improving while one's own group is not. Brogan observed that the new ways and new wealth of the Industrial Revolution impelled many intellectuals to revolutionary fervor. Men like Friedrich Engles "were struck by the paradox that the means of wealth were vastly increasing and that the benefits of that wealth seemed to be more and more narrowly bestowed."[78] Discrepancy between an individual's or group's relative share of welfare, power and interpersonal values also is specifically related to political violence by a number of theorists, among them Aristotle, who wrote that the source of disposition to revolution

> is the aspiration after equality which provokes the commons to sedition when they suppose that they have a small share . . . although they are the equals of the privileged Few, and it is the aspiration after inequality or in other words after superiority which provokes the Oligarchs to sedition, when they imagine that despite their inequality their share is not greater than that of others but is equal or even smaller.[79]

These and other conditions that increase expectation levels beyond the capacities of men to satisfy them, and hence dispose men to collective violence, are examined more closely in chapter 5. Some comparable effects of new beliefs and ideologies are considered there and in chapter 7.

PROGRESSIVE DEPRIVATION

The third pattern of RD, sketched in figure 3, is a generalized version of a model proposed by Davies, who refers to it as the "J-curve" hypothesis: "revolutions are most likely to occur when a prolonged period of objective economic and social development is followed by a short period of sharp reversal."[80] It can be regarded as a special case of aspirational RD, one in which long-run, more-or-less-steady improvement in peoples' value position generates expectations about continued improvement. If value capabilities stabilize or decline after such a period of improve-

[78] Denis W. Brogan, *The Price of Revolution* (London: Hamish Hamilton, 1951), 30.

[79] *The Politics,* Welldon trans., 343–344. For a restatement of the Aristotelian position see Fred Kort, "The Quantification of Aristotle's Theory of Revolution," *American Political Science Review,* LXVI (June 1952), 487.

[80] Davies, "Toward a Theory of Revolution," 6.

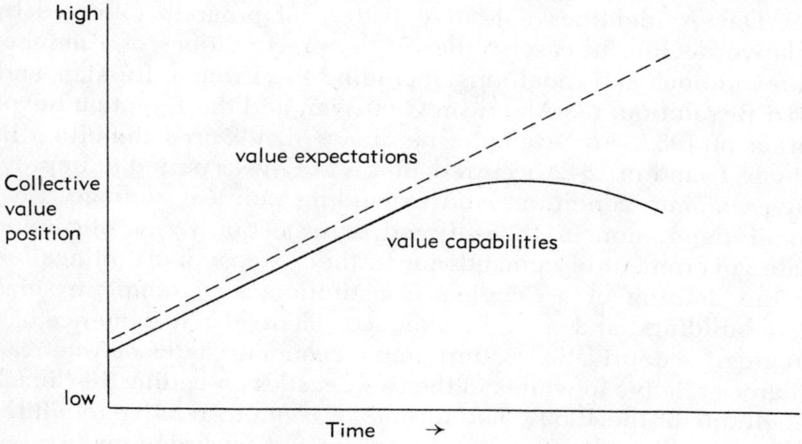

Figure 3. Progressive deprivation.

ment, progressive RD is the result. Such a pattern is most common in societies undergoing simultaneous ideological and systemic change. Economic depression in a growing economy can have this effect. So can the articulation of an ideology of modernization in a society that has structural inflexibilities that prevent expansion of value output beyond a certain point. The model also can be used to subsume some "social change" theories of revolution, which in their general form postulate that political violence is a consequence of decreasing responsiveness of social structures, beliefs, norms, or all three to objective change.

Davies emphasizes that the revolutionary state of mind requires "the continued, even habitual but dynamic expectation of greater opportunity to satisfy basic needs," by which he includes all types of values, physical, social, and political. In addition, what is needed

> is a persistent, unrelenting threat to the satisfaction of these needs: not a threat which actually returns people to a state of sheer survival but which puts them in the mental state where they believe they will not be able to satisfy one or more basic needs. . . . The crucial factor is the vague or specific fear that ground gained over a long period of time will be quickly lost.

The political system is perceptually related to these fears; they are generated "when the existing government suppresses or is blamed for suppressing such opportunity." [81] In support of the the-

[81] *Ibid.*, 8.

sis, Davies identifies a J-curve pattern of progress followed by relative decline in case studies of the preconditions of a number of revolutions and rebellions, including the French, Russian, and Nazi Revolution, the American Civil War, and the Egyptian Revolution of 1952. For example, he shows that Dorr's Rebellion in Rhode Island in 1842 occurred after a forty-year period of improving economic conditions and expanding political suffrage. Economic depression in 1835–40 and the rejection by an oligarchic state government of demands for further extension of suffrage led to the drafting of a People's Constitution, an attempt to seize state buildings, and sporadic violence. There also is evidence of a progressive deprivation pattern in the economic status of American Negroes relative to whites in the two decades preceding the "black rebellion" of the 1960s. The income of Negroes relative to whites of comparable education increased rapidly towards equality between 1940 and the early 1950s but then began to decline, so that by 1960 half the relative gains of the earlier period were lost.[82] In this study's terminology, both cases were characterized by rising value expectations, set in motion by prolonged experience of improving value positions. Diminishing capabilities, evident in politicians' reluctance to extend political rights and in irremediable economic decline, provided the background conditions necessary for the outbreak of violence.

Le Vine's explanation of mob violence by African colonial peoples against their rulers resembles the J-curve argument. Such turmoil is said to be a consequence of psychological conflict generated when colonial officials encouraged expectations of self-rule by their stated policies and practices, but then accompanied or followed those policies with others which, Africans thought, interfered with the attainment of those expectations. Le Vine describes seven cases that appear to support the hypothesis.[83] The J-curve hypothesis is also implicit in Deutsch's interpretation of the relationship between governmental capability and political stability in societies in the early and middle stages of modernization. Increasing capabilities, as an object of government policy, require increasing mobilization of citizens for participation in the market economy and political life. "Such mobilization,

[82] Case studies of the Russian and Egyptian Revolutions and Dorr's Rebellion appear *ibid.* The other studies are included in James C. Davies, "The J-Curve of Rising and Declining Satisfactions as a Cause of some Great Revolutions and a Contained Rebellion," in Hugh Davis Graham and Ted Robert Gurr, eds., *Violence in America: Historical and Comparative Perspectives* (Washington, D.C.: National Commission on the Causes and Prevention of Violence, 1969), 547–576.

[83] Robert A. Le Vine, "Anti-European Violence in Africa: A Comparative Analysis," *Journal of Conflict Resolution*, III (December 1959), 420–429.

however, is usually accompanied by rising needs and expectations, which must not be frustrated if stability is to be preserved." To preserve stability—that is, to minimize progressive RD and the consequent impetus to violence—outputs must continue to increase. Deutsch cites only two types of value outputs, increasing per capita income and expanding governmental activity, but his argument is readily extended to other value classes.[84]

Progressive RD is a common theme in many old and some new theories that attribute revolutionary potential to general social change. Simple versions of these theories emphasize structural inflexibility, i.e. the inability of social and political institutions to adapt their value outputs rapidly enough to changing conditions. Yoder proposes, for example, that change in social life is continual, and that the organized group must and ordinarily does constantly readjust to changing situations, resulting from inventions, discoveries, culture contact, and so forth. In some cases, however, groups within the society desire to preserve the old order—"the traditional institutions, the time-tried folkways, mores, conventions, and customs"—even though irrelevant to present situations. The end of adaptation is the beginning of revolution.[85] Johnson's "social-dysfunction" theory of the origins of political violence is of the same genre, though its vocabulary has a more contemporary ring. One necessary condition of revolution is said to be a disequilibrated social system, i.e. a discrepancy between the belief structure of a society and its division of labor, which may result from any combination of internal or external changes in values or technology. The second necessary cause is elite refusal ("intransigence") to take action designed to relieve the disequilibrium. The consequence is a loss of authority by the elite and its reliance upon force to maintain its position. The sufficient cause of revolution in such a situation is an "accelerator of dysfunction," any condition that decreases the ability of the elite to control its armed forces.[86]

These and other social change theories refer to systems that were able to adapt value outputs to changing environmental require-

[84] Karl Deutsch, "Toward an Inventory of Basic Trends and Patterns in Comparative and International Politics," *American Political Science Review*, XIV (March 1960), 39.

[85] Dale Yoder, "Current Definitions of Revolution," *American Journal of Sociology*, XXXII (November 1926), 440–442. Comparable explanations are proposed by Charles A. Ellwood, *The Psychology of Human Society: An Introduction to Sociological Theory* (New York: Appleton, 1925), chap. 8; Rex Hopper, "The Revolutionary Process: A Frame of Reference for the Study of Revolutionary Movements," *Social Forces*, XXVIII (March 1950), 270–271; and Pettee, passim.

[86] Johnson, *Revolutionary Change*, passim. An earlier and briefer statement of the theory is his *Revolution and the Social System* (Stanford: The Hoover Institution on War, Revolution and Peace, Stanford University, 1964).

ments and to men's changing value expectations up to some point in time, but gradually or abruptly lost their adaptive capacities. In societies that have experienced positive social change, the conditions described in these theories fit the J-curve or progressive deprivation model; in static societies, they more closely resemble the absolute deprivation model. The point is that the RD models correspond generally to many of the abstract theories of the preconditions of political violence.

The RD Models: Some Qualifications and Uses

No one of the RD models is necessarily characteristic of a particular type of society, although absolute RD seems more likely to be found in static societies, while aspirational and progressive RD appear most often in societies undergoing substantial socioeconomic change. In any given society at any given time, however, some groups are likely to experience RD of each type. Moreover, some groups can experience different patterns of RD with respect to different classes of values. For example, large segments of the working classes of the defeated European countries after World War I simultaneously experienced decremental deprivation with respect to security and participation values, and progressive deprivation on welfare values. A complete profile of RD in a society requires specification of the extent and patterns of RD with respect to each class of values for every consequential socioeconomic group.

One operational use of the RD models is that they facilitate systematic inferences about the effects of changes in various indices of economic and political performance. Indicators of economic performance and of governmental fiscal activity provide examples. Rather than resorting to inferences about economic discontent based on such measures as per capita income in country X compared with country Y, or their relative rates of growth, one can infer it more accurately from such patterns as short-term declines in productivity following a period of stable production (decremental RD) and short-term changes in inflation rates, commodity prices, or total productivity relative to rates in the more distant past (decremental or progressive RD). Time-series wage and salary data for various occupational groups are available for many modern and some modernizing societies, from which welfare and in some instances status RD can be inferred. One also can search systematically for evidence of conditions associated with rising expectations, such as rates of increase in schooling and literacy, announcement of programs of reform, articulation by political leaders of ideologies of modernization, and mobilization of previously nonparticipant citizens for purposes of political and associational activity. To assess the effects of governmental action one can examine the changing balance over time between value-depriving and value-satisfying decisions, giving special attention to *relative* increases in the former. Interpersonal RD of various patterns also can be inferred from changes over time in measures of conditions as diverse as internal migration, religious affiliation, changing size and composition of occupational groups, and social origins of elite groups. Procedures for making systematic, comparative inferences of these kinds are not examined here; examples of some of them are reported in other published studies.[87]

The three models of RD proposed do not exhaust all the logically possible relationships between value expectations and value capabilities.[88] Declining expectations might be found in some groups, for example among members of a well-disciplined colonial elite who expect gradually to lose their political authority to indigenous rulers, or among members of a millenarian religious group who expect the social order to deteriorate and collapse as a prelude to the coming of a new order. Somewhat more common may be a "boom and bust" set of expectations about value satisfactions, for example among some traditional societies, under some totalitarian regimes, and perhaps among some groups and isolated individuals in modernized societies. Resigned anticipation of a "time of troubles" following the death of a king was as common in feudal kingdoms of tropical Africa as it was in medieval Europe. Those whose livelihood depends on the land tend to develop a similar tolerance for the vagaries of weather: two years of plenty and one of scarcity is the way of the seasons. The Bemba of South Central Africa, like many other people living near the margin of subsistence, build their way of life around a cycle of nine months of abundance followed by a hunger season of three months.[89] But in all such cycles there is an element of predictability, and if this predictability vanishes RD is the likely result. If, for example, conditions in such a

[87] See Ted Gurr, *New Error-Compensated Measures for Comparing Nations: Some Correlates of Civil Strife*, Center of International Studies (Princeton: Princeton University, Research Monograph No. 25, 1966); Ted Gurr with Charles Ruttenberg, *The Conditions of Civil Violence: First Tests of a Causal Model*, Center of International Studies (Princeton: Princeton University, Research Monograph No. 28, 1967); and Ted Gurr, "A Causal Model of Civil Strife: A Comparative Analysis Using New Indices," *American Political Science Review*, LXI (December 1968), 1104–1124.

[88] A more comprehensive set of models of social change, including variations on the three basic models proposed here, appears in Ivo K. Feierabend, Rosalind L. Feierabend, and Betty A. Nesvold, "Social Change and Political Violence: Cross-National Patterns," in Graham and Gurr, eds., 497–542.

[89] See Audrey I. Richards, *Land, Labour, and Diet in Northern Rhodesia* (London: Oxford University Press, 1939), especially chaps. 1–3.

cycle deteriorate and remains bad, the result is decremental RD; and if value positions stabilize at a high level substantially beyond the expected onset of the next cyclical decline, any subsequent decline would be likely to generate the potential for violent protest.

At the outset of the discussion of the models it was suggested that over the long run men's value expectations tend to adapt to their value capabilities; the discrepancies caused by rising expectations or declining capabilities are temporary. Eventually men collectively either succeed in raising their value capabilities to meet their expectations or, if their circumstances prove impervious to change, lower their expectations. For intensely felt expectations, however, "eventually" may be measured in years, decades, or even generations, which are likely to be characterized by both constructive and destructive struggle. Some of the variables that affect the persistence of RD and typical modes of response to it are examined in subsequent chapters. If any single sentence can summarize the arguments advanced in this chapter, it is that men are quick to aspire beyond their social means and quick to anger when those means prove inadequate, but slow to accept their limitations.

3. The Intensity and Scope of Relative Deprivation

> People foreign to our land and race made up the government; the middle class was ruined through the scarcity of food and the depreciation of money; scoundrels and parasites cheated and robbed us, and in an incredibly brief time ruined undertakings it had taken a whole people centuries to build. People lacked the very essentials of living. . . . Having felt the results of the economic collapse on my own pulse, I was only too happy to take my place in the van of the movement.
>
> A Nazi Party member, 1933 [1]

THE INTENSITY of our anger at its onset is a function of four psychocultural variables. The greater the discrepancy we see between our expectations and capabilities, the greater is our discontent. The greater the importance we attach to the values affected, and the fewer the other satisfactions we have to fall back on, the greater is our discontent. If we have many alternative ways of trying to satisfy our expectations, we are likely to defer discontent over our failures; if we have few alternatives we are likely to feel the anger of desperation. A fifth determinant is time: if our anger is denied expression in the short run it intensifies before it subsides. The greater its intensity, the longer it persists; many men carry the burden of profound grievances throughout their lives and pass them on to their children. The first four variables resemble but are not merely collective manifestations of the three variables that Dollard said determine the strength of instigation to aggression (anger) in the frustration-aggression sequence: the strength of instigation to the frustrated response (salience), the degree of interference with the frustrated response (degree), and the number of frustrated response-sequences (alternative values and opportunities).[2] Runciman specifies two comparable variables as sources of variance in RD. "The magnitude of a relative deprivation is the extent of the difference between the desired situation and that of the person desiring it (as he sees it). . . . The degree of a relative

[1] From an autobiographical essay written in 1933, cited in Theodore Abel, *The Nazi Movement: Why Hitler Came to Power* (New York: Atherton Press, 1938, 1966), 125–126.

[2] John Dollard and others, *Frustration and Aggression* (New Haven: Yale University Press, 1939), 33.

deprivation is the intensity with which it is felt."[3] Hypotheses and corollaries about the effects of these variables and some of their interactions are specified below.

The determinants of discontent apply to each individual and to men collectively. The analysis of discontent must include specification of societal conditions and patterns of events that cause discontent, and identification of its scope in the collectivity. The final section of this chapter identifies a number of types of depriving conditions and events, and suggests research strategies for inferring the scope of discontent from structural properties of the societies in which it occurs.

Determinants of Intensity: The Degree of Relative Deprivation

Hypothesis ID.1: The intensity of relative deprivation varies strongly with the average degree of perceived discrepancy between value expectations and value capabilities.

Corollary ID.1.1: Any increase in the average level of value expectations in a collectivity without an accompanying increase in value capabilities increases the intensity of relative deprivation.

Corollary ID.1.2: Any decrease in the average level of value capabilities in a collectivity without an accompanying decrease in value expectations increases the intensity of relative deprivation.

In the case of aspirational and progressive RD, the *degree* of discrepancy is the distance perceived between the value position sought and value potential. In the case of decremental RD, the degree of discrepancy is the perceived distance between the value position previously held and the residual value position. Operational definitions are suggested below.

The two corollaries follow deductively from hypotheses V.1 (chapter 2) and ID.1, and the definitions given of their terms. Corollary ID.1.1 underlies the "revolution of rising expectations" and the violent consequences postulated for it by Lerner and others. The decremental RD model is characterized by the pattern of decreasing value capabilities specified in corollary ID.1.2.

Psychological evidence demonstrates unequivocally that the intensity of anger varies with the degree to which the response is frustrated. For example, McClelland and Apicella exposed college students working on a card-sorting task to varying levels of frustration (as measured by the proportion of times they were made to fail) and found that the frequency of aggressive comments at the

[3] W. G. Runciman, *Relative Deprivation and Social Justice* (Berkeley: University of California Press, 1966), 10.

experimenter increased as the extent of failure increased.[4] Several studies have examined the effects of frustration of group tasks on intragroup hostility, varying the extent to which group members were dependent on one another in carrying out the tasks. The more members were required to work together, i.e. the greater the interference they caused one another in pursuing their tasks, the greater the overt aggression expressed within the group. If group members could work relatively independently of one another, however, levels of hostility were low.[5] The most precise evidence has been obtained in experiments by Hamblin and others which strongly suggest that instigation to aggression follows general psychophysical laws. In the most definitive experiment, three hypotheses were tested: the classic one that instigation to aggression varies directly with the degree of interference, and the psychophysical hypotheses that aggression is a logarithmic or power function of interference. Small groups of subjects were put to a problem-solving task with a money incentive, with leaders who deliberately caused the groups to fail in each of successive stages of the tasks. After various stages the subjects gave their evaluation of the leaders by several methods which permitted measurement of the intensity of hostility towards the leaders. The results show that aggression is a power function of degree of interference: if magnitude of aggression is plotted against degree of interference, the result is a sharply rising "J-curve."[6]

These aspects of the frustration-aggression relationship correspond to the general psychophysical law of human behavior that "the magnitude of the subjective response does increase as a power function of the magnitude of the physical stimulus."[7] This is further evidence that the frustration-aggression sequence is a fundamental behavioral mechanism, not a deviant one. Hamblin also found that the power exponents by which magnitude of aggression increased varied rather widely among individuals. Although the cases were too few for distribution curves to be drawn, it is likely from what is known of other human traits that, in a large

[4] D. C. McClelland and F. S. Apicella, "A Functional Classification of Verbal Reactions to Experimentally Induced Failure," *Journal of Abnormal and Social Psychology*, XL (July 1945), 376–390, cited in Leonard Berkowitz, *Aggression: A Social Psychological Analysis* (New York: McGraw-Hill, 1962), 60.

[5] J. R. P. French, Jr., "Organized and Unorganized Groups Under Fear and Frustration," in Kurt Lewin *et al.*, *Authority and Frustration* (University of Iowa Studies in Child Welfare, Iowa City: University of Iowa Press, 1944), and Edwin J. Thomas, "Effects of Facilitating Role Interdependence on Group Functioning," *Human Relation*, X (No. 4, 1957), 347–366, summarized in Berkowitz, 61–62.

[6] Robert L. Hamblin and others, "The Interference-Aggression Law?" *Sociometry*, XXVI (June 1963), 190–216.

[7] Hamblin and others, 193.

population, a normal distribution curve of magnitude of aggressive response would be found. One implication of this is that the likelihood and level of aggressive response are more accurately regarded in distributional or probabilistic terms than in terms of "thresholds." Finally, it is plausible that the J-curve relationship between degree of frustration and magnitude of aggression should characterize the relationship between degree of RD and magnitude of collective violence. Compatible with this inference, though not bearing directly on it, is the logarithmic distribution curve that characterizes cross-national measures of the intensity of collective violence.[8]

Almost all the literature on collective violence assumes a causal connection between the existence of RD or some equivalent concept and the occurrence of violence. A direct relationship between the degree of discrepancy and the intensity of violence is usually implicit, sometimes explicit as it is in the formulations by Ridker, Lasswell and Kaplan, and the Feierabends.[9] Edwards also was explicit on this point. He identified four classes of human motives and proposed that "All revolutions may . . . be conceived as due to the repression of one or more of these elemental wishes, and the violence of any revolution is, it is assumed, proportional to the amount of such repression." [10] Quantitative evidence also indicates that degrees of deprivation or discontent are associated with degrees of disorder. Some of these studies are based on within-nation comparison of aggregate measures. Rostow has shown graphically that poor economic conditions—in the form of high wheat prices and high unemployment—corresponded with the severity of overt mass protest in England between 1790 and 1850.[11] Variations in bread prices and the extent of mob violence were associated in revolutionary France.[12] There is correlational evidence that the

[8] Bruce M. Russett et al., *World Handbook of Political and Social Indicators* (New Haven: Yale University Press, 1963), 97–100; Ted Gurr with Charles Ruttenberg, *The Conditions of Civil Violence: First Tests of a Causal Model* (Princeton: Center of International Studies, Princeton University, Research Monograph No. 28, 1967), 38–41.

[9] Ronald G. Ridker, "Discontent and Economic Growth," *Economic Development and Cultural Change*, XI (October 1962), 1–15; Harold Lasswell and Abraham Kaplan, *Power and Society* (New Haven: Yale University Press, 1950), 261–268; Ivo K. and Rosalind L. Feierabend, "Aggressive Behaviors Within Polities, 1948–1962; A Cross-National Study," *Journal of Conflict Resolution*, X (September 1966), 250–251.

[10] Lyford P. Edwards, *The Natural History of Revolution* (Chicago: University of Chicago Press, 1927), 3–4.

[11] Walt W. Rostow, *British Economy of the Nineteenth Century* (Oxford: Clarendon Press, 1948), chap. 5.

[12] George Rudé, "Prices, Wages, and Popular Movements in Paris During the French Revolution," *Economic History Review*, VI (April 1954), 246–267; and *The Crowd in History, 1730–1848* (New York: Wiley, 1964), chap. 7.

frequency of lynchings in the American South between 1882 and 1930 varied inversely with indices of economic well-being, although the relationship is a relatively weak one, with reported correlation coefficients of the order of .6 and .3.[13]

Cross-national studies using aggregate data also support the hypothesis. It has been suggested that voting support for extremist political parties is a nonviolent manifestation of discontent. Kornhauser, for example, reports a correlation of −.93 between per capita income and the Communist share of the vote in national elections in sixteen Western democracies in the late 1940s, and another of +.85 between the percentage of the labor force unemployed and the percentage of extremist voting in nine nations in 1928–32.[14] Among Latin American countries, Bwy found that economic growth rates in the 1950s (presumably an indicator of economic capabilities) correlated −.63 with levels of organized group violence and −.33 with anomic violence in the 1960s.[15] The Feierabends inferred the extent of "systemic frustration" in 84 nations from the ratio between measures of "want formation" such as literacy and urbanization, and measures of "want satisfaction" such as income and caloric intake per capita. The correlation between their frustration index and a composite measure of political stability is .499.[16] I constructed three composite measures of the degree and scope of RD, including short-term economic and political deprivation and persisting deprivation, and related them to a measure of magnitude of civil strife for 114 polities; the multiple correlation coefficient obtained is .60.[17]

One limitation of these studies is that their measures of RD or discontent are relatively indirect; states of mind are inferred from aggregate measures. More direct data also are available. Ringer and Sills found that economically discontented Iranians in the late 1940s were more likely than others to take politically extreme positions on the left or right;[18] Zeitlin found that the Cuban workers most

[13] Carl Hovland and Robert Sears, "Minor Studies in Aggression, VI: Correlation of Lynchings with Economic Indices," *Journal of Psychology,* IX (April 1940), 301–310, report the stronger correlation. The weaker is reported in a reinterpretation of the data by Alexander Mintz, "A Re-examination of Correlations Between Lynchings and Economic Indices," *Journal of Abnormal and Social Psychology,* XLI (April 1946), 154–160.

[14] William Kornhauser, *The Politics of Mass Society* (New York: The Free Press, 1959), 160.

[15] Douglas Bwy, "Political Instability in Latin America: The Cross-Cultural Test of a Causal Model," *Latin American Research Review,* III (Spring 1968), 46–48.

[16] Feierabend and Feierabend, 258–262.

[17] Ted Gurr, "A Causal Model of Civil Strife: A Comparative Analysis Using New Indices," *American Political Science Review,* LXII (December 1968), 1122.

[18] Benjamin B. Ringer and David L. Sills, "Political Extremists in Iran: A Secondary Analysis of Communications Data," *Public Opinion Quarterly,* (Winter 1952–53), 258–262.

likely to have supported the Castro movement before 1959 were those who had experienced the greatest unemployment.[19] Wedge has made a comparative interview study of student participation in revolutionary violence in the Dominican Republic in 1965 and Brazil in 1964, and concludes that violence was much more intense in the Dominican Republic partly because Dominican student rebels had experienced considerably greater deprivation than had their Brazilian counterparts.[20] The most persuasive evidence is provided by a secondary analysis of Cantril's fourteen-nation study of the "pattern of human concerns." Respondents in the Cantril study were asked, among other questions, how they compared their past, present, and likely future value positions with their ideals of the good life, on an eleven-point scale. The nationally averaged discrepancies between their actual status at the time of the interviews (between 1957 and 1963) and their personal ideals are shown in table 2, compared against a rank-order measure of the magnitude of turmoil for 1961–65. The rank-order correlation between the two measures is a substantial .59: the greater the degree of RD, operationally measured here as the gap between aspirations and present value position, the greater is turmoil.[21]

Most of the evidence cited above is based on measures of RD with respect to welfare values. Complete assessment of the degree of RD in a collectivity could make use of general value-position rating scales, such as Cantril's, or of scales for measuring degrees of RD with respect to each of the several categories of values defined in chapter 2. Although this study is not primarily concerned with developing operational means for assessing the theoretical variables, two operationally useful definitions of degree of RD may be suggested. One is the ratio of the discrepancy between expected and attainable value position to the expected position, or $\frac{ve - vc}{ve}$, where *ve* is the expected value position and *vc* is the value position perceived to be attainable. Definition in these terms assumes that some order of quantitative measurement is possible. For example, Italian industrial workers were asked in 1955 what their monthly salaries were and what they thought they should be; they received an average of \$80 but expected \$176. By comparison, French workers received an average of \$114 but thought

[19] Maurice Zeitlin, *Revolutionary Politics and the Cuban Working Class* (Princeton: Princeton University Press, 1967), chap. 3.

[20] Bryant Wedge, "The Case Study of Student Political Violence: Brazil, 1964, and Dominican Republic, 1965," *World Politics*, XXI (January 1969), 183–206.

[21] Data are from Hadley Cantril, *The Pattern of Human Concerns* (New Brunswick: Rutgers University Press, 1965), 187. See notes to table 2.

TABLE 2
Aspirational RD in Thirteen National Populations, ca. 1960, and Magnitudes of Turmoil 1961–65

Country	*Year of Survey* [a]	*Average Units of Deprivation* [b]	*Rank Order of RD*	*Rank Order of Magnitude of Turmoil, 1961–65* [c]
Dominican Republic	1962	8.4	1	1
India	1962	6.3	2	4
Poland	1962	5.6	3	11
Brazil	1961	5.4	4	5
Nigeria	1963	5.2	5.5	2
Panama	1962	5.2	5.5	3
Philippines	1959	5.1	7	9
Yugoslavia	1962	5.0	8	12.5
Japan	1962	4.8	9	6
Israel	1962	4.7	10.5	7
West Germany	1957	4.7	10.5	8
Egypt	1960	4.5	12	12.5
Cuba	1960	3.6	13	10

Rank-order correlation coefficient: .59 [d]

[a] Representative cross-national samples reported in Hadley Cantril, *The Pattern of Human Concerns* (New Brunswick: Rutgers University Press, 1965). Data for the United States are excluded from this comparison on grounds that its high levels of turmoil in the 1960s were attributable to the segmental RD of black Americans, which are inaccurately represented in any summary national measure of RD. The overall U.S. score for average deprivation units is 3.4.

[b] The average number of units, on an eleven-point scale, between respondents' value position at the time of the survey and their aspirational value position, from Cantril, 184. The upper and lower ends of the scale were "anchored" by asking each respondent to describe his best possible and worst possible future; he then was asked to indicate his rank at the time of the interview.

[c] Based on a revision of data from Gurr, "A Causal Model of Civil Strife." The magnitude of turmoil measure takes into account the proportion of population participating in turmoil such as demonstrations and riots, the duration of the events, and their proportional intensity. The relatively high level of deprivation in Poland and Yugoslavia relative to their magnitudes of turmoil may be a function of the coercive policies of their regimes.

[d] Spearman's r_s. The correlation is significant, for $n = 13$, at the .05 level.

they should have $170.[22] If we equate *vc* with present wages and *ve* with desired wages, the degree of RD for the Italian workers is .55, for the French workers .33. An individual worker who was laid off and had no prospects of other income or future employment would experience the maximum possible degree of RD, 1.00. Ratio calculations also can be used for value positions defined in dichotomous terms. For example, one could define a threshold on

[22] Hadley Cantril, *The Politics of Despair* (New York: Collier Books, 1958, 1962), 67.

the status-value continuum and assign scores of 1 to individuals and groups with more than the threshold value, 0 to those with less. The only possible RD degree scores for separately-scored groups are 0 and 1.0, but such scores can be averaged for any set of individuals or groups.

An alternative operational definition of degree of deprivation is that it is the *difference* between expected and attainable value positions. For example, an ordinal scale could be devised for the political participation value dimension, including as categories "no participation" (0), "periodic voting with effective choices" (3), "leadership of local political organization" (5), and "national political leadership" (8). An individual or set of individuals who expected to attain the fifth-ranked condition but were able to attain only the third would have a rank-difference degree of RD of two, a rank difference that could be compared and averaged with that of others.

Determinants of Intensity: Value Salience

Hypothesis ID.2: The intensity of relative deprivation varies strongly with the average salience of the value class with respect to which discrepancy is experienced.

Hypothesis ID.3: The intensity of relative deprivation varies moderately with the proportion of value classes with respect to which discrepancy is experienced.

The *salience* of a class of values for an individual is the strength of his motivation to attain or maintain the desired value position. The salience of a class of values for a collectivity is the average strength of commitment to the desired value position. Salience may be assessed in absolute terms or relative to motivation to other values. The value hierarchy in a country whose population is on the subsistence margin might be, in decreasing order of salience, economic, security, communality, coherence, status, participation, and self-realization values. In a modernizing, postcolonial society, the power values of participation and security might be more salient than either welfare or interpersonal values. Generally, economic values are likely to be most salient for most people. Specific class and functional groups, including politically active groups, may have value hierarchies quite different from the larger group, however. Thus, any empirical assessment of value saliences should take into account the value hierarchies of a variety of subpopulations, as well as the specific content and levels of their value expectations.

The sense of hypothesis ID.2 is that the more strongly people are motivated toward a goal, or committed to the maintenance of an attained level of values, the more sharply they resent interference and the greater is the consequent instigation to violence. However, their response to RD affecting one class of values is partly determined by their capabilities for attaining substitute satisfactions.[23] For example, the intensity of RD caused by interference with a moderately salient value, such as political participation, is likely to be reduced if more salient welfare and security values are increased as a result. Similarly, taxation is justified to citizens on grounds that it is necessary for the maintenance of security and communal values. If the net effect of any such policy is to enhance a group's total value capabilities, the intensity of RD is reduced; if other value capabilities are reduced as well, RD intensifies.

Hypothesis ID.3 refers to the "last straw" relationship, and is derived from the preceding argument. Men are likely to tolerate the loss of moderately important values if they can still attain other classes of values. But if they experience RD with reference to most or all other value classes as well, deprivation affecting a previously satisfied value expectation will strongly increase the intensity of RD. The psychological evidence for the "salience" and "last straw" hypotheses is considerably better than the evidence from studies of political violence. For example, Hamblin and others found that subjects working with a money incentive responded much more aggressively to frustration than those who had no such incentive.[24] McNeil mentions five studies in which subjects kept records of incidents that provoked their anger, the motives interfered with, and the nature of the frustration sensed. "Although diaries and lists of things that annoy people are not the most reliable form of evidence, it seems clear that the stronger the drive being frustrated, the greater will be the instigation to an intense or aggressive response."[25] Graham and others found that physical attacks directed against subjects were more likely to produce strong aggressive reactions than were less direct, verbal attacks.[26]

Theories of political violence generally assume that revolution

[23] For a review of the limited psychological evidence on the substitutability of human goals, or values, see Aubrey J. Yates, *Frustration and Conflict* (New York: Wiley, 1962), 76–77, 83–84.

[24] Hamblin and others.

[25] Elton D. McNeil, "Psychology and Aggression," *Journal of Conflict Resolution*, III (June 1959), 204–205.

[26] F. K. Graham and others, "Aggression as a Function of the Attack and the Attacker," *Journal of Abnormal and Social Psychology*, XLVI (October 1951), 512–520. For a more complete review of the evidence see Berkowitz, 52–58.

occurs when men's most salient or fundamental values are threatened, but analyses that identify value hierarchies or demonstrate that the salience of particular values increases in prerevolutionary situations are not common. Some of the influence of ideologies on political violence can be attributed to the salience variable. The articulation of nationalistic ideologies in colonial territories of Asia and Africa in the first half of the twentieth century evidently strengthened preexisting desires for political independence among among the colonial bourgeoisie, at the same time that it inspired quite a new set of political expectations among other groups.[27] Similarly, it has been argued that the desire of the nineteenth-century European factory worker for a better economic lot was intensified as well as rationalized by Marxist teachings. It also is likely that the civil rights movement in the United States in the late 1950s and early 1960s had as much or more effect on the salience of black expectations of equality as it did on their relative level.

THE RELATIVE SALIENCE OF VALUE CLASSES

Some revolutionary theorists suggest that a single class of values is salient for political violence, or at least for its revolutionary facet. For Marx, of course, the underlying value is economic, while Arendt attributes revolution to the repression of aspirations for freedom.[28] Monocausality is less common than pancausality, however. Edwards, Pettee, and Sorokin all suggest that repression of any and all types of human values can lead to political violence.[29] The same approach is assumed in Lasswell and Kaplan's proposition that political stability is a function of disparities in value distribution, though their discussion focuses on economic and power values.[30] Ridker is concerned exclusively with economic values, Aristotle with economic and power values.[31] This analysis contends that RD with reference to any class of

[27] For example, see Rupert Emerson, *From Empire to Nation* (Cambridge: Harvard University Press, 1960), especially chaps. 10 to 14; Thomas Hodgkin, *Nationalism in Colonial Africa* (New York: New York University Press, 1956, 1957); and S. N. Eisenstadt, "Sociological Aspects of Political Development in Underdeveloped Countries," *Economic Development and Cultural Change*, v (July 1957), 289–307.

[28] Hannah Arendt, *On Revolution* (New York: The Viking Press, 1963), 2 and passim.

[29] George S. Pettee, *The Process of Revolution* (New York: Harper, 1938), 11; Lyford P. Edwards, *The Natural History of Revolution* (Chicago: University of Chicago Press, 1927), 3–4; Pitirim A. Sorokin, *The Sociology of Revolution* (Philadelphia: Lippincott, 1925).

[30] Lasswell and Kaplan, 261–262.

[31] Ridker, passim; Aristotle, *The Politics*, Book V, chaps. v and vi.

commonly held welfare, power, or interpersonal values can lead to collective violence.

The basic factual question raised by these and many other interpretations is: Which classes of human values are most salient in what populations? Evidence for a universal answer is provided by results of Cantril's cross-national survey of human concerns. People in twelve of the nations surveyed were asked four questions:

– All of us want certain things out of life. When you think about what really matters in your own life, what are your wishes and hopes for the future?
– Now, taking the other side of the picture, what are your fears and worries about the future?
– Now, what are your wishes and hopes for the future of our country?
– And what about your fears and worries for the future of our country?

The concerns or values expressed were classified, percentages of each type of response were tabulated for each country, and the percentages for each class were weighted according to the population of each country. The results are rank orderings of the personal and the national concerns of some 863 million people; 129 classes of specific concerns were sufficiently common to be held by at least four million people.[32] A sevenfold typology derived from the classificatory scheme for values proposed in chapter 2 is used to consolidate this data, with the results shown in table 3.

Material values are clearly of greatest concern to the people of the world; nearly half of all values mentioned are of this category, for example hopes and fears about standards of living, health, technological advances, economic stability, and owning a house or land. There is no substantial difference among nations in the importance of material values: at least 60 percent of the respondents in every country voiced personal economic hopes or fears. Personal economic hopes were the most commonly expressed hopes in every nation, economic fears the most common fears in all except three Western nations in which people were slightly more concerned over their health.[33] By far the most common power value is security: fear of war was of concern to more than twice as many people as any other issue affecting their nations.

[32] Cantril, questions 23, summary data by categories, 276–279.
[33] *Ibid.*, chaps. 4–8.

TABLE 3

Value Concerns Among 863 Million People in 12 Nations ca. 1960 [a]

Class of Values	*Proportion of all Personal Concerns*	*Proportion of all National Concerns*	*Proportion of Total Concerns*
WELFARE VALUES			
Economic	55%	35%	46%
Self-actualization	7	4	5
POWER VALUES			
Participation	<1	12	5
Security	5	37	20
INTERPERSONAL VALUES			
Status	4	3	4
Communality	27	2	16
Ideational coherence	2	7	4
Totals	100%	100%	100%

[a] From Cantril, 276–279, based on my classification of 129 categories of personal and national concerns. The percentages refer to proportions of all concerns mentioned by respondents, weighted by the population of country to permit summary comparison. The respondents represent twelve nations in which surveys were conducted between 1957 and 1963: India, United States, Brazil, West Germany, Nigeria, Philippines, Egypt, Yugoslavia, Cuba, Dominican Republic, Israel, and Panama.

Concerns here classified as expressions of participation values included fears of dishonest or unrepresentative government and hopes for continued or strengthened national independence. About half of all interpersonal concerns relate to the family, notably to children's welfare and to family health and happiness. Other communality values include desires to be useful to others, fears of being alone, and hopes for better public health and social security. Many status aspirations are probably represented in expressions classified as economic hopes or fears; specifically identifiable status concerns include hopes for acceptance by others, hopes and fears about discrimination and inequality, and fears of social injustice. Concerns classified as expressions of valuation of coherent normative and belief systems include hopes for resolution of religious or ethical problems; hopes for improved sense of social and political responsibility in the community; and fears over the lack of moral or ethical standards in the community.

People may hold unarticulated values whose importance to them becomes evident only when they are threatened. It is also likely that value hierarchies vary substantially among subgroups of national populations; participation values, for example, are probably greater among political activists than among an entire national population. Nonetheless, it is plausible that the concerns people express in response to unstructured questions of the kinds asked in the Cantril survey indicate the relative salience of different classes of values within most large, heterogeneous (i.e. national) populations. On the basis of this data a corollary of hypothesis ID.2 is suggested:

Corollary ID.2.1: In any heterogeneous population, the intensity of relative deprivation is greatest with respect to discrepancy affecting economic values, less with respect to security and communality values, least with respect to participation, self-realization, status, or ideational coherence values.

PROXIMITY OF A GOAL AND VALUE SALIENCE

Another relevant psychological relationship is the "goal-gradient" principle: the closer an organism is to a goal, the stronger the tendency to approach the goal. An experimental study by Haner and Brown suggests its applicability to the questions of value salience and aggression. Children played a game that was interrupted by a buzzer, to which they were obliged to respond by striking a plunger that ended the game. The closer they were to ending when the buzzer sounded, the harder they hit the plunger. Berkowitz's interpretation of this and several other studies is that "frustration-induced emotional reactions apparently increase in strength the closer the person is to the goal of his activities, presumbably because the strength of the thwarted tendency also increases with nearness to this goal."[34] This finding has counterparts in observations about political violence. Hoffer is representative of theorists who point out that "discontent is likely to be highest when misery is bearable; when conditions have so improved that an ideal state seems almost within reach. . . . The intensity of discontent seems to be in inverse proportion to the distance from the object fervently desired."[35]

The amount of effort invested in attaining or maintaining a value position seems as relevant as the closeness of the desired position itself, however. That is, if men have a relatively low value position but have worked hard toward a high value position, and believe that it is close at hand, the average intensity of drive, or salience, is high—almost certainly greater than if little effort had been expended. A hypothetical native clerk who has studied and im-

[34] C. F. Haner and P. A. Brown, "Clarification of the Instigation to Action Concept in the Frustration-Aggression Hypothesis," *Journal of Abnormal and Social Psychology,* LI (September 1955), 204–206, discussed in Berkowitz, 53–54.

[35] Eric Hoffer, *The True Believer* (New York: Harper, 1951), 27–28.

proved his skills for ten years in an effort to pass a civil service examination for a major promotion is likely to suffer a greater sense of deprivation when he fails than does the Melanesian adherent of "Marching Rule" or a Cargo Cult who performs certain rituals and then waits passively for the gods or the white men to provide him the material blessings of life.[36]

The increasing salience of a goal as men approach it varies with its *perceived* not its actual closeness. The event that inflicts the sense of RD may be simply the realization that a goal thought to be near at hand is still remote. The intense anger of underemployed university graduates in developing nations is partly a consequence of their pre- or postgraduate loss of innocence, the discovery that they cannot attain the good positions and high status they expected education to make possible.[37] The progression of African colonies to independence was marred by violence when that progression was reversed by official recalcitrance. In the Congo the frustration of unrealistic expectations about the utopia of independence fueled the rebellions of the "second independence" in 1963.[38] Vietnam provides two contemporary examples. The French reoccupation in 1946 was a massive assault on the power position the Viet Minh had attained at great cost during the Japanese occupation, and led to intense revolutionary resistance.[39] Members of the National Liberation Front in South Vietnam experienced comparable frustration when United States escalation began in 1963, at a time when the NLF had all but succeeded in seizing control of the country. The increased revolutionary activity in both situations is partly attributable to decisions by the revolutionary elites to maintain their position, but the goal-gradient and the frustration-aggression principles suggest that such patterns of events also generated sharply intensified drives toward

[36] On the Cargo Cults as a customarily nonviolent response to relative deprivation see C. S. Belshaw, "The Significance of Modern Cults in Melanesian Development," *Australian Outlook,* IV (1950), 116–125, and Peter N. Worsley, *The Trumpet Shall Sound: A Study of "Cargo" Cults in Melanesia* (London: MacGibbon and Kee, 1957).

[37] For African interview evidence on this phenomenon see Hugh H. Smythe and Mabel M. Smythe, *The New Nigerian Elite* (Stanford: Stanford University Press, 1960), chap. 10. For Latin American evidence see Robert C. Williamson, "University Students in a World of Change: A Colombian Sample," *Sociology and Social Research,* XLVIII (July 1964), 397–413.

[38] On preindependence violence see Robert A. Le Vine, "Anti-European Violence in Africa: A Comparative Analysis," *Journal of Conflict Resolution,* III (December 1959), 420–429. On the Congo see, among others, Crawford Young, *Politics in the Congo: Decolonization and Independence* (Princeton: Princeton University Press, 1965).

[39] One of the best of the many studies of this period is John T. McAlister, *Vietnam: The Origins of Revolution* (New York: Knopf, 1969).

"nonrealistic" aggression among the cadres and rank-and-file members who had been so long in the struggle. This discussion supports two additional corollaries about the determinants of the saliency of value expectations:

Corollary ID.2.2: The salience of a value tends to vary with the average effort invested in attaining or maintaining the desired position on that value.

Corollary ID.2.3: In instances of aspirational deprivation, the salience of a value tends to vary with the perceived closeness of the desired value position at the time discrepancy is first experienced.

Determinants of Intensity: Number of Opportunities

The degree of RD is a function of the discrepancy between value expectations and capabilities; salience is a characteristic of value expectations per se. The third determinant of intensity of RD is a characteristic of value capabilities: the number and range of alternative courses of action men have for attaining their conception of the good life.

Hypothesis ID.4: The intensity of relative deprivation varies strongly with the proportion of value opportunities with which interference is experienced or anticipated.

Much evidence and observation supports the general notion, stated more precisely in hypothesis ID.4, that increasing men's opportunities decreases the potential for civil disorder. The relevant proposition in the frustration-aggression model is that the greater the number of frustrations, the greater the instigation to aggression. Berkowitz found that subjects receiving two successive hostile notes were more aggressive toward their partners than subjects getting only one or no hostile communications.[40] Palmer noted that convicted murderers had been subjected to significantly more physiological and psychological frustrations during childhood than a comparable group of nonmurderers, and also had been taught fewer socially acceptable forms of aggression release.[41] Miller proposed a more general interpretation of the "number of frustrations" hypothesis, to the effect that though anger is aroused by any frustration, other, nonaggressive responses may be dominant (and are likely to be, in any well-socialized

[40] Leonard Berkowitz, "Repeated Frustrations and Expectations in Hostility Arousal," *Journal of Abnormal and Social Psychology,* LX (May 1960), 426.

[41] S. Palmer, "Frustration, Aggression, and Murder," *Journal of Abnormal and Social Psychology,* LX (May 1960), 430–432.

adult). If these nonaggressive responses remove the frustration, hostile behaviors probably will not occur. But if the alternative responses available to the individual do not reduce frustration, they are likely to be abandoned and aggression is increasingly likely to occur.[42] When adults were frustrated in an experimental situation devised by Marquart, they proved slow to learn new responses. They were given an insoluble problem and punished in varying degrees for failing to learn; the rules were then changed, unknown to them, so that further trial and error made it possible to solve the problem. Members of the most severely punished group took nearly twice as long as others to learn the correct solution, which Maier interprets as evidence of the existence of a frustration threshold.[43] Members of the group presumably crossed the threshold, became fixated on their last nonaggressive response alternative, and probably did not become aggressive because of lack of available cues or targets for aggression.

Considerable societal evidence suggests that narrow ranges of opportunities increase the impetus to collective violence. Olson attributes the political instability of modernizing societies to the relative dearth of societal value opportunities:

> . . . societies in the early stages of industrialization rarely have suitable institutions for mitigating the adversities that the losers in the process suffer. While traditional social institutions . . . often have appropriate ways of helping those among them who suffer adversities, and while mature industrial societies have developed welfare institutions, the society in an early stage of rapid industrialization will probably not have adequate institutions to care for those who suffer from the economic advance.[44]

Ridker makes a comparable point in more general terms. "A person who sees no possibility of satisfying his aspirations in productive ways is more likely to express dissatisfaction in destructive ways than is the person who believes there are socially acceptable alternatives to his present position." He identifies three value alternatives: the number of suitable jobs open to the individual

[42] Neal E. Miller, "The Frustration-Aggression Hypothesis," *Psychological Review*, XLVIII (July 1941), 337–342, summarized in Berkowitz, *Aggression*, 62–63.

[43] Dorothy Marquart, "The Pattern of Punishment and its Relation to Abnormal Fixation in Adult Human Subjects," *Journal of General Psychology*, XXXIX (July 1948), 107–144, discussed in Norman R. F. Maier, *Frustration: The Study of Behavior Without a Goal* (New York: McGraw-Hill, 1949), 74–76.

[44] Mancur Olson, Jr., "Growth as a Destabilizing Force," *Journal of Economic History*, XXIII (December 1963), 550–551.

(societal value opportunities), the individual's perception of possibilities for creating suitable jobs for himself (personal value opportunities), and the possibilities of migrating to places where economic opportunities are available.[45] Theoretical arguments about stability-enhancing effects of pluralism assume the efficacy of multiple political value opportunities. Tannenbaum, for example, argues that political stability and freedom require the existence of a multiplicity of small societies, each with its own sphere of political action.[46] The existence of many small political units signifies a large number of alternative structures, or structural positions, for the satisfaction of power value expectations.

Case study and comparative evidence also documents the thesis. Brogan remarks that by the mid-nineteenth century English workers had abandoned revolutionary methods, in sharp contrast to the French working class, and cites as reasons the English laborers' resort to "self-help, self-education, organization and permeation of the existing order. . . . There were the new co-operatives; there were the friendly societies, there were the trade unions. . . . There were building societies doing something to redeem the horrors of overcrowding. . . ."[47] Kling attributes the chronic coups d'etat of a number of Latin American nations to the lack of adequate opportunities for elite aspirants who have economic ambitions; political office, seized illicitly if necessary, is said to provide opportunity for satisfying those ambitions.[48] Migration as an alternative response to discontent is cited by a number of writers. Sorokin, citing data on Russia, Ireland, and many other cases shows that migration is a response to natural disasters and war as well as to prerevolutionary situations.[49] Greer has demonstrated that the most turbulent cities and departments of revolutionary France had the highest emigration rates—including not only departments which favored the Revolution but coun-

[45] Ridker, 6.

[46] Frank Tannenbaum, "On Political Stability," *Political Science Quarterly*, LXXV (June 1960), 160–180.

[47] Denis W. Brogan, *The Price of Revolution* (London: Hamish Hamilton, 1951), 34. For comparative studies of violent French and English labor protest in the eighteenth and nineteenth centuries see Rudé, *The Crowd in History*, chaps. 4 and 8; and Charles Tilly, "Collective Violence in European Perspective" and Ben C. Roberts, "On the Origins and Resolution of English Working-Class Protest," in Hugh Davis Graham and Ted Robert Gurr, eds., *Violence in America: Historical and Comparative Perspectives* (Washington, D.C.: National Commission on the Causes and Prevention of Violence, 1969), 197–220.

[48] Merle Kling, "Toward a Theory of Power and Political Instability in Latin America," *Western Political Quarterly*, IX (March 1956), 21–35.

[49] Pitirim A. Sorokin, *Man and Society in Calamity* (New York: Dutton, 1942), 107–111. Also see Edwards, 33; and Hoffer, 19–20.

terrevolutionary areas as well.[50] The inference is that the dissatisfactions and deprivations that produced the Revolution and the reaction to it had previously stimulated some men to migrate. Data compiled by Tilly on the Vendée similarly show a significant emigration of priests and nobles from centers of patriotic strength during the years before the counterrevolution.[51]

Three general types of value opportunities are identified in the preceding chapter: personal, societal, and political, referring respectively to personal skills for value attainment, normative means for value attainment in the society, and the capacity to influence others to provide value satisfactions. The range of opportunities of each type varies substantially within and among nations. For example, the illiterate peasant in a modernizing society has rather limited personal means for economic value attainment: he knows how to raise a few crops within a narrow range of environmental conditions, and how to build and maintain a farmstead, but if traditional methods fail him or if he aspires to monetary income he has only his farming skills and his strength to offer on the labor market. The economic value opportunities in his immediate social setting also are likely to be limited: the village may have stockpiled food against the possibility of famine, but agricultural loans and extension services are not likely to be available, and the opportunities for wage labor are few unless he migrates to a city. His political opportunities are even more limited. If he has tenant farmers or is influential in the village political hierarchy, he may be able to demand an increase in customary tribute. A regional or national political organization may provide for local input activity, but one man's voice or vote is unlikely to have significant effects.

The literate clerk in the same society has considerably greater economic value opportunities. Personally he has acquired skills that are less diverse than those of the peasant farmer, but they open up for him a wider range of societal opportunities for employment. The restrictions on employment are determined in part by economic diversification, the demand for his skills, and discriminatory barriers to his employment or promotion. If he sees no chance of satisfying his value expectations he has recourse to potent political means, including action as a union member to compel employers to increase wages, and participation in political

[50] Donald Greer, *The Incidence of the Emigration During the French Revolution* (Cambridge: Harvard University Press, 1951).

[51] Charles Tilly, *The Vendée* (Cambridge: Harvard University Press, 1964), 192–195.

movements aiming to break down traditional barriers to economic growth and mobility.

To say that the clerk has more diverse value opportunities does not necessarily mean that his value capabilities are greater than those of the peasant. The clerk's value expectations are almost certainly higher than the peasant's, and his value opportunities in all their diversity may prove less effective for satisfying his expectations than the peasant's skills at subsistence agriculture are for meeting his material needs. Hypothesis ID.4 stipulates that when the peasant and the clerk experience RD, their anger will increase as a function of the *proportion* of opportunities that remain open to them; the peasant's anger is likely to increase more rapidly as opportunities fail him because he has fewer of them. Corollary ID.2.2 suggests an important qualification of the process: the clerk, by investing greater energy in testing out his opportunities, becomes increasingly committed to the value he is pursuing, so that if and when he does exhaust all opportunities the intensity of his anger is likely to be greater and the magnitude of violent response greater. This relationship is shown graphically in figure 4 and its implications for intensity of RD stated in generalized form in corollary ID.4.1. A on the graph represents the increase in intensity of RD (anger) for a person or group as it exhausts a limited set of value opportunities, B the increase in RD for a person or group with a large number of opportunities. The outbreak of violence by A, at x_a, is likely to occur more quickly but with less magnitude than the outbreak by B at x_b.

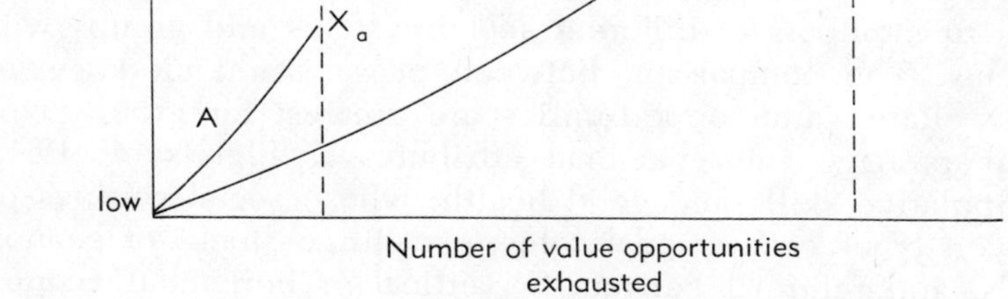

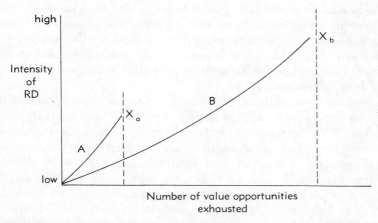

Figure 4. Intensity of RD preceding the outbreak of violence given varying numbers of value opportunities.

Corollary ID.4.1: The intensity of relative deprivation varies moderately with the number of actively pursued value opportunities with which interference is experienced or anticipated.

This relationship holds only for actively pursued value opportunities because increases in value salience, and hence potential RD, are a function of effort invested in value attainment; the elimination of value opportunities that are considered but not pursued because of anticipated failure does not increase value salience.

If this relationship is generally applicable, it has substantial implications for the outcome of various strategies of governmental response to demands for value increases. A common response to such demands is to establish new programs designed to increase societal value opportunities. Latin American demands for land reform have been met in some nations by widely publicized programs of resettlement and redistribution (for example in Mexico, Chile, Bolivia, Venezuela, and Colombia). American Negro demands for greater economic opportunity led to creation of the Job Corps and a number of other public and private programs to increase job skills and opportunities. But such programs typically promise more than can be delivered. To the extent that land-hungry peasants and unemployed ghetto residents perceive new programs as an increase in their value opportunities, the edge is taken off their discontent. To the extent that they try to use these opportunities and find that they don't pay off, the edge of discontent is sharpened. Moreover, their bitterness is likely to be focused on the agency of their final disappointment, the government which offered what proved to be a false hope, rather than on the sources of their previous frustrations. In short, the announcement of a reform program to deal with popular grievances tends to reduce the immediate potential for violence, but, to the extent that it fails, it tends to increase the long-range potential and to focus it on the would-be reformers.

There are systematic differences in ranges of value opportunities open to members of different social systems and groups within systems. The comparison between peasant and clerk suggests that welfare value opportunities are greatest for groups whose members have such personal attributes as high symbolic and manipulative skills and good health; whose social settings offer a diversity of occupational roles, expanding stocks of economic goods, and minimal barriers to vertical or horizontal economic mobility; and whose political structures promote pluralistic associations, encourage high levels of input activity, and have and exercise substantial capacity for generating and redistributing welfare values. This could be taken as a description of an ideal-typical modern social democracy; such conditions also may hold, in varying degrees, for such subnational collectivities as the upper middle classes and traditional oligarchies in societies that differ radically from that ideal type. Opportunities for satisfying interpersonal value expectations—status, communality, and coherence values—are likely to be greatest in rather different cultural settings. Such personal characteristics as noncompetitiveness, accommodation, and rectitude seem most instrumental for attaining interpersonal values. Appropriate societal characteristics are stability of kinship and communal patterns, stability and homogeneity of belief systems, and access to political means for reinforcing belief systems and protecting stable social relationships from internal and external threat. In other words, a social system or subsystem with substantial *Gemeinshaft* characteristics appears to offer greater opportunities to its members for attaining high levels of interpersonal values than does a predominantly *Gesellshaft* system. A qualification to this is that even in highly industrialized societies there are many relatively homogeneous, stable communities and neighborhoods that offer such value opportunities, and persistent efforts to establish new patterns of association that can satisfy interpersonal needs.

Some Effects of Anticipation and Persistence of RD

Hypothesis ID.5: The intensity of relative deprivation varies curvilinearly over time following the onset of discrepancy.

Corollary ID.5.1: The greater the salience of the value affected by discrepancy, the longer RD persists.

This hypothesis and corollary attempt to synthesize and generalize some of the diverse evidence on the effects of the time variable on the intensity and outcome of RD. Considerable evidence suggests that if people anticipate repeated interference with particular goal-seeking activities, in the long run they are likely to readjust their value expectations. In an anthropological application of the frustration-aggression hypothesis, Bateson pointed out that Balinese mothers repeatedly tempt their children and then refuse to gratify them, thereby giving the children a high toleration for frustration and a disposition to seek other courses of action or other goals when they anticipated frustration.[52] In an

[52] Gregory Bateson, "The Frustration-Aggression Hypothesis and Culture," *Psychological Review*, LXVIII (July 1941), 354–355.

experimental study, Cohen and others similarly found that once their subjects became accustomed to frustration of their desires for social reinforcement, they were less likely to seek it.[53] Berkowitz, using paired subjects who received hostile and friendly notes from one another in various combinations, found the greatest level of unfriendliness (aggression) among subjects who received two successive hostile notes, but that the increase of hostility on receipt of the second note was less than the level of hostility caused by the first note, probably because the subjects anticipated the second hostile note.[54] Another study indicates that even a very brief delay in the expression of an aggressive response after the onset of frustration increases the intensity of aggression when it does occur.[55]

The relationships proposed above seem consistent with all these findings. The onset or anticipation of frustration increases the intensity of RD in proportion to the degree and salience of the value affected (hypotheses ID.1 and ID.2, above). To the extent that value salience is low and substitute value satisfactions can be sought (hypothesis ID.4), the intensity of anger will be low and readily inhibited or diverted. If the degree of deprivation and value salience are high, however, and if the victim of RD has no effective alternatives or means of avoiding it, he will react with increasingly intense anger. Moreover, if he is disposed to strike out at the source of his discomfort but cannot—for fear of retribution, for want of means, for lack of definition of the responsible agency—his anger will continue to increase over the short run. In the long run, however, levels of value expectation, or the salience of values, or both are likely to decline; the victim is likely to become resigned to his condition.

An analogous pattern is observable in collective behavior. Apathy and resignation are a common response to continuous unemployment in ghetto areas, depressed rural regions, and in communities affected by economic depression. Himmelweit, commenting on one systematic study of apathetic response to unemployment, suggests that "the reason for this reaction lies probably in the prolonged character of the frustrating experience and may well

[53] Arthur R. Cohen and others, "Commitment to Social Deprivation and Verbal Conditioning," *Journal of Abnormal and Social Psychology*, LXVII (November 1963), 410–421.

[54] Berkowitz, "Repeated Frustrations and Expectations in Hostility Arousal."

[55] J. W. Thibaut and J. Coules, "The Role of Communication in the Reduction of Interpersonal Hostility," *Journal of Abnormal and Social Psychology*, XLVII (October 1952), 770–777. For further evidence see Leonard Berkowitz, "Aggressive Cues in Aggressive Behavior and Hostility Catharsis," *Psychological Review*, LXXI (March 1964), 104–122.

have succeeded reactions of protest."[56] This is the sequence of responses of American Indians to their subjection by the U.S. Army and white settlers during the last half of the nineteenth century. Active warfare against whites was repressed with increasing effectiveness in the 1870s, and the Plains Indians turned in increasing numbers to new religions. Among the most widespread in the 1880s was the militant Ghost Dance, which emphasized the fantasied destruction of whites but occasionally resulted in outbreaks of violence, such as the Sioux Disturbance of 1890–91. Suppression of these sporadic outbursts and of the Ghost Dance movement was followed by the appearance of the Peyote Religion, nativistic but not militant. Smelser, from whom this example is drawn, concludes that under continuous repression such movements evolve "progressively toward the most passive and least politically threatening form of organization. . . ."[57] When troops were withdrawn early in the twentieth century, however, there was no outbreak of violence; the levels of value expectation and salience apparently had declined to what was attainable within the confines of reservation life under white control.

Another case in point is the pattern of response of nonwhite South Africans to *apartheid* policies. These policies, which impose substantial and diverse value-deprivations on nonwhites in the urban areas in particular, were put into effect principally in the 1950s. The parliamentary discussion and subsequent implementation of the policies of the early 1950s inspired substantial violence. The imposition of more restrictive race laws and regulations, and enforcement of identity pass requirements for Africans living outside tribal reserves, resulted in a wave of strikes and riots that began with the Sharpeville massacre in March 1960 and continued for several months. By the late 1960s, however, when the level of restrictions was greater than in any previous era, antiwhite violence was minimal. This was in part the result of the massive and unhesitatingly used coercive capacity of the regime, but that capacity was not sufficient to deter earlier outbreaks of violence. It is likely that there has been some decline in the salience of the participatory and status values affected, if not in levels of justifiable expectations per se.[58]

[56] Hilde Himmelweit, "Frustration and Aggression: A Review of Recent Experimental Work," *Psychological Factors of Peace and War*, ed. T. H. Pear (London: Hutchinson, 1950), 172, summarizing Marie Lazarsfeld and Hans Zeisal, "Die Arbeitslosen von Marienthal," *Psychologische Monographen*, v (1933).

[57] Neil J. Smelser, *Theory of Collective Behavior* (New York: The Free Press of Glencoe, 1963), 366.

[58] On the initial period of apartheid see Gwendolen M. Carter, *The Politics of Inequality: South Africa Since 1948* (New York: Praeger, 1958).

The existence of external restraint, in the form of coercive police or military control of disaffected populations, is the most common source of displacement of RD over time. Even if repression is continuous over a long period it does not necessarily lead to declining expectations. The students and middle classes of Hungary rebelled in 1956 after more than fifteen years of first Nazi and then Communist repression. Convulsive popular reaction to military dictatorship in the Dominican Republic broke out in 1965, thirty-four years after the establishment of the Trujillo dictatorship. The people of the Belgian Congo had been under colonial control for more than seventy years before the outbreak of bitter antiwhite hostilities that accompanied independence in 1960. None of these are clear-cut cases. In each there are sources of rising expectations, and of recent deprivations imposed by weakening regimes, that may partly account for the impetus to violence. It is nonetheless likely that many of these people shared an intense sense of persistent grievance, based on legends or recollections of a past era of personal freedom and communal security.

Another source of RD displacement over time is the exhaustion of economic resources or changes in the structure of an economy, which reduce the means of livelihood of regional or occupational groups like the soft-coal miners of Appalachia and of Wales who were dispossessed by changing technologies and depletion of resources, and the cottage weavers of early nineteenth-century England who lost out to the newly mechanized cotton industry. The miners responded at first with strikes and sporadic violence, the cotton weavers with the Luddite riots whose aim was to destroy the new mechanical looms.[59] These events occurred in dynamic industrial societies in which many workers were able to find alternative economic opportunities. Those who could not lapsed into apparent apathy. When loss of livelihood occurs in more static societies, however, violent protest often becomes chronic and endemic. Peasant anarchism in Andalusia developed in the sixth decade of the nineteenth century, apparently as a response to the massive disruption of economic and communal relationships imposed by the introduction of capitalist legal and social relationships into the countryside; millenarian rural uprisings occured in the region down through the 1930s, well beyond the lifespan of the generation affected by the initial breakdown.[60]

[59] On the Luddite riots see Rudé, *The Crowd in History*, chap. 5.

[60] E. J. Hobsbawm, *Social Bandits and Primitive Rebels: Studies in Archaic Forms of Social Movement in the 19th and 20th Centuries* (New York: The Free Press, 1959), chap. 5.

Even more strikingly protracted has been the response of Peruvian Indians of the *sierra* to the alienation of their lands by Creole landowners, a process that began in the sixteenth century and continued into the nineteenth. Indian resistance was largely sporadic and unorganized but it never ceased, and any faint hope or sign was enough to precipitate reassertion of old claims. When President Belaúnde was inaugurated on July 28, 1963, having promised a program of land reform during his campaign, a wave of land invasions by Indians took place throughout the country.[61]

These examples demonstrate that the sense of RD can endure for a community almost indefinitely after its onset. This seems an especially likely consequence of decremental RD that affects a number of value classes of groups living in relatively static societies, i.e. societies in which there are few alternative values and value opportunities. In such circumstances, one generation is likely to pass legends on to the next about the good life that was lost, and teach the new generation that they should demand the restoration of what was taken from their fathers or grandfathers.

Determinants of the Scope of Relative Deprivation

The intensity of RD is a psychocultural variable; the basic unit of analysis is the individual, and the intensity of consequent anger in a collectivity is the aggregate (or average) anger felt by its members. The scope of RD is a societal variable; the unit of analysis is the collectivity and the operational question is the proportion of its members who share specified levels of discontent, a question that can be answered either by survey techniques or inferred from properties of the social system. It is essential that the question be answered. For example, a pattern of prolonged economic growth followed by an abrupt decline can be observed in various underdeveloped societies which have not experienced the revolution that Davies postulates as an outcome of such a pattern. This is partly because the J-curve or progressive-deprivation pattern is not a sufficient but only a predisposing condition for political violence. More important, the proportion of people affected by progressive economic RD varies greatly among types of societies. A sharp decline in the gross national product of Tanzania or Thailand is likely to affect at most only that ten or fifteen percent of the workers who are dependent on the monetary economy; a com-

[61] David Chaplin, "Peru's Postponed Revolution," *World Politics*, XX (April 1968), 399–400, 415.

parable decline in the United States or Argentina would have—and in the case of Argentina did have—revolutionary consequences, because virtually their entire working populations are affected by economic depression. Similarly, assessment of potential for collective violence in the United States and South Africa must take account of both the relative intensity of nonwhite anger about discrimination and its relative scope; in South Africa discriminatory patterns affect 81 percent of the population, in the United States 12 percent.

There is some discontent among almost all members of all societies, so that in a global analysis that makes no distinctions among social groups or types or intensities of RD, the scope of RD approaches 1.0. But in any given group there is likely to be a range of discontent, shown in general from in figure 5. The crucial empirical question is what proportion of the population, or what specific segments of it, are likely to be discontented with an intensity beyond some threshold X. The threshold chosen depends on one's specific empirical purposes and procedures. Using survey techniques, one possible threshold is respondent agreement with such a statement as, "I think people should take any kind of action, legal or illegal, to remedy the present state of affairs." Using societal data one can estimate the approximate proportion of a population that, in structural terms, is likely to be affected adversely by a particular kind of event or condition. Since the latter approach is most applicable to historical and cross-national comparative studies of collective violence, it may be

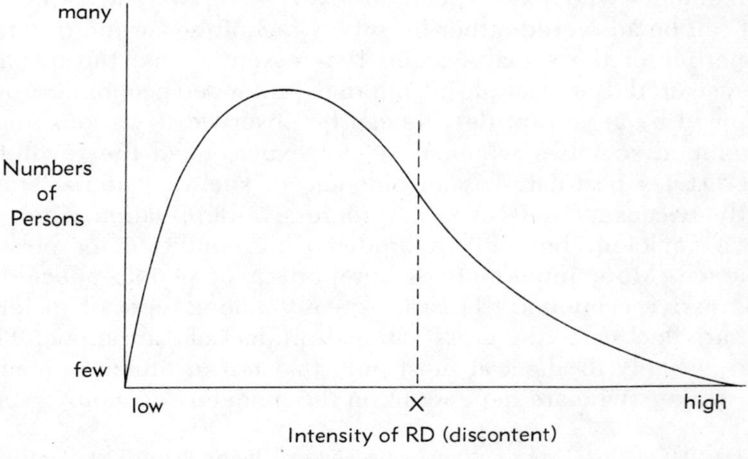

Figure 5. Hypothetical distribution of intensities of RD in a collectivity.

useful to suggest alternative research strategies for inferring the scope of RD and to propose some guidelines for determining the scope of RD caused by various types of value-depriving conditions. The discussion will also illustrate further the kinds of events and conditions that can be inferred to cause RD.

A SOCIAL STRATIFICATION APPROACH

In this approach, the scope of groups potentially affected by RD is assessed first, and intensities of RD then evaluated with reference to these predetermined groups. The first step is to identify a set of socioeconomic, political, or regional strata comprising all the population of the society being studied. For case study purposes the set of strata might be complex and idiosyncratic to the country; for comparative purposes a small set of generally identifiable strata would be more appropriate. Census data or estimates of relative class size can then be used to estimate the relative size of each strata. Two alternative sets of strata are suggested below for societies in the middle stages of economic development, with hypothetical proportions specified:

Class and Demographic Strata	
Lower classes:	
rural	.55
urban	.20
Lower middle classes:	
rural	.10
urban	.10
Upper middle classes:	
rural	.01
urban	.02
Upper classes:	
rural	.01
urban	.01

Economic Strata	
Subsistence farmers	.30
Cash-crop farmers	.30
Unskilled laborers	.20
Skilled workers	.10
Bourgeoisie and professional employees	.06
Entrepreneurs and large landowners	.01
Political elite and governmental employees	.03

The next step in this research strategy is to examine each group in turn, or groups of special interest, using more or less precise guidelines to evaluate the intensity of each group's RD with respect to each class of values. The simplest procedure, too imprecise for any except the most general comparative studies, is

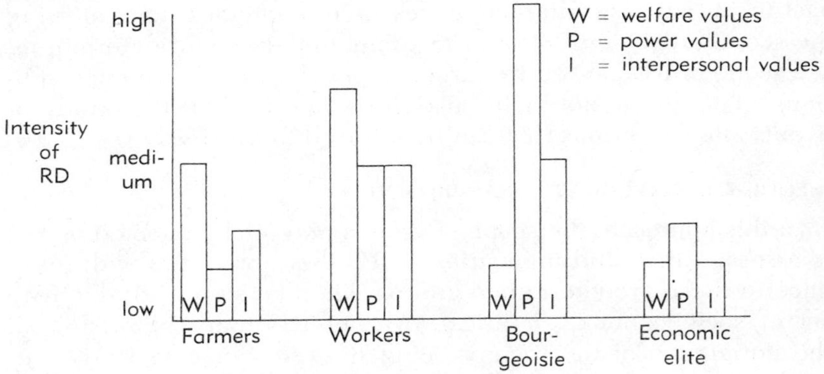

Figure 6. Hypothetical distribution of intensity of RD in a collectivity, by social strata and by class of values.

to make an impressionistic judgment on the basis of general information about the extent to which each group is mildly, moderately, or strongly deprived with respect to each salient value. The prerequisite for such judgments is knowledge of the value hierarchies of each group and their past and immediate social conditions. The more detailed the information available, the more precisely such judgments can be made. Alternatively, one can use specific indicators of RD for each class of values examined, for example relative income levels as indicators of economic RD, migration rates as indicators of communal breakdown, repressive governmental policies as indicators of power RD, and so forth. Whatever procedures are followed, the results can be graphically summarized in a profile of RD by social strata and class of value, as they are hypothetically in figure 6. The proportions determined for each strata are measures of the scope of each class of RD. If numerical scores are assigned to points along the RD intensity continuum, it is possible to calculate comparable scores for each class of RD for each strata and for all strata, weighted for scope, and a total RD score for all strata. The example applies to strata of a national population; the procedures can be used to develop comparable profiles of sets of stratifiable collectivities of any scale, including nations, regions, cities, small groups, and also any one such collectivity at different points in time.

A PATTERN OF DEPRIVATION APPROACH

This approach makes use of predetermined definitions of events and conditions that induce discontent; the scope of RD is inferred from the structural characteristics of the collectivities in which such events are observed. The initial step in this research strategy is operational specification of conditions that are assumed to be depriving in the collectivity or collectivities being examined; the severity of the conditions should be assessed as well as their occurrence. Some kinds of RD may be inferred from aggregate statistics, such as absolute levels of inflation; relative declines in economic productivity; and measures of inequality of land or income distribution.[62] Others can be inferred from conditions such as systematic discrimination against ethnic, linguistic, or religious communities; discrepancies between norms of distributive justice and actual distribution patterns; and events such as restrictions on political participation.[63] Examples of several types of such patterns and conditions are suggested below, without general definition because they are used here for illustrative purposes, and guidelines are proposed for estimating the scope of their effects.

Examples of *general economic adversity* include depression, inflation, and declining commodity prices in export-oriented monocultural economies. The population "at risk" for such conditions comprises people who are dependent on money incomes, most of whom are likely to be adversely affected by economic malfunction in some fashion, and hence likely to be discontented in some degree. Operationally, the intensity of discontent can be assumed to vary with the severity of depression or inflation. Its scope can be operationally defined as the number of all wage and salary workers as a proportion of all economically active men; such data are available for most countries for the 1950s and 1960s, and for many countries for earlier periods.[64] Proportions of the working population in the monetary economy vary with the level of economic development; in undeveloped countries the proportion seldom exceeds .10, whereas in countries in the early stages of development the proportion is usually between .20 and .40; in middle stages of development between .50 and .80; and in the most highly developed countries .90 or more.[65]

[62] For a survey of measures of inequality see Hayward R. Alker, Jr., *Mathematics and Politics* (New York: Macmillan, 1965), chap. 3. Bruce M. Russett has analyzed the relationship between measures of inequality of land distribution and measures of collective violence for a substantial number of nations in "Inequality and Instability: The Relation of Land Tenure to Politics," *World Politics*, XVI (April 1964), 442–454.

[63] For examples of specific indices of this sort see Gurr, "A Causal Model of Civil Strife."

[64] See *International Labour Yearbook*, various years (Geneva: International Labour Organisation, annual).

[65] *Ibid.*

Economic adversity usually has differential effects on different groups, and it often is possible to isolate and determine the scope of such groups. Conditions likely to generate *economic RD with primary impact on blue-collar workers* include restrictive wage regulations, worsening conditions of employment, intensive demands for improved wages, and governmental policies that diminish the socioeconomic or political standing of workers relative to that of the middle and upper classes. The population "at risk" for many such conditions can be assumed to include wage-earning blue-collar employees in the nonagricultural sectors or some segment of them. Other types of economic RD have *primary impact on agricultural sectors,* for example declining crop prices, worsening conditions of agricultural employment, restriction of tenure conditions for small-holders, and drought. For most contemporary societies there are estimates of proportions of persons engaged in agricultural and related occupations, which provide the basis for a "scope" estimate for consequent discontent.

Some kinds of economic RD, and power and interpersonal RD as well, are most likely to affect particular class or demographic groups. To use an economic example, the population at risk in *fiscal adversity,* for example capital flight and confiscatory policies against entrepreneurs, consists of capitalists, business owners and shareholders, and self-employed persons in the commercial classes. In least-developed societies these groups seldom comprise more than .01 of the population; in countries in the middle stages of development about .02; and in the most highly developed societies seldom more than .05.[66] Other *conditions with primary impact on upper and middle classes* include progressive tax policies, governmental actions that diminish the relative socioeconomic or political advantages of the middle classes, and restrictive regulation of the commercial sector. Labor census data also can be used to infer the scope of discontent caused by such conditions. The population at risk might be operationally specified as professional, administrative, clerical, sales, and related white-collar workers; such groups comprise approximately .05 of the economically active population of undeveloped countries, .10 in countries in early stages of development, .20 in middle stages, and .30 at the highest level of development. As examples of the scope of depriving conditions with *impact on demographic groups,* imposition of universal military conscription presumably affects men of the specified draft age; curtailment of university enrollments affects current secondary school graduates; imposition of martial law in a province

[66] *Ibid.*

affects the population of the province as a proportion of total population.

Most of the above examples are of depriving conditions which affect welfare values. Similar procedures for comparative specification of the scope of various kinds of power discontent can be developed. For example, one common type of participatory RD results from *restrictions and crises affecting all political activities,* such as dissolution of national representative bodies, banning of all political party activity, and widespread dereliction of duty by public officials. Since many citizens even of politically developed societies are uninterested in their political circumstances, it is questionable to assume that all of them are sensitive to such actions. A better estimate of scope might be the portion who voluntarily participate in political activity. In multiparty democracies this portion could be operationally defined as the proportion of voting-age population that voted in recent national elections. Participatory deprivation also can be inferred from *restrictions or crises affecting a political faction,* for example the banning or restriction of a specific party, legislation designed to maintain one party in power to the detriment of other parties, or proposals to implement a new form of government or political procedure opposed by some political factions. Supporters of the affected political factions or viewpoint are those at risk for RD in such cases. A good estimate of scope is the proportion of voters who supported the affected faction in the most recent contested election, weighted by the proportion of the population participating politically (above). An example will clarify the suggested procedure. Assume that 45 percent of the voting-age population participated in the Peruvian presidential election of 1962, which was won by the *Aprista* candidate with 33 percent of the total vote. The military subsequently seized power to prevent the *Aprista* candidate from assuming office and called for another election, which was won by Belaunde of Popular Action. The scope of population most clearly and directly aggrieved in this case was the active *Aprista* electorate, which constituted $.45 \times .33 = .15$ of the adult population.[67]

RD affecting security and interpersonal values can be inferred from *general repression of or widespread demands for freedom and order,* for example national states of siege or emergency, infringement of generally valued constitutional guarantees, widespread and indiscriminate use of terror by a regime or its opponents, and the general breakdown of public order. No one procedure can be

[67] See Richard W. Patch, "The Peruvian Elections of 1963," *American Universities Field Staff Report* (July 1963). The .45 estimate of voter participation is hypothetical.

used to determine the scope of discontent induced by such conditions. The breakdown of order and the spread of terror most sharply affects those in the cities and regions in which it occurs, and those who have some measure of goods and security to lose. Temporary or permanent suspensions of civil liberties are likely to be of greatest concern to the better-educated groups; scope measures might be based on estimates of literacy or of proportions of population with secondary education.

Segmental restrictions affecting mobility and distributive equality provide a final set of examples of RD conditions whose scope can be inferred from structural data on societies. Segmental restrictions exist when groups defined on the basis of their ascribed characteristics are systematically denied economic, participatory, or status values. The existence of caste, class, ethnic, linguistic, regional, or religious barriers to value attainment does not necessarily lead to discontent, although demands for sociopolitical equality and distributive justice in the contemporary world are so pervasive that discontent could be inferred to exist from their presence alone. But any imposition of segmental restrictions where none existed before, or widespread demands for elimination of existing restrictions, is strong evidence of the existence of decremental RD in the first instance and aspirational RD in the second. Discontent over lack of participatory values is frequently expressed in demands for greater political participation and agitation for regional autonomy. Segmental economic and status discontent may be manifest in demands for removal of restrictions or for remedial programs and compensatory values, or in ideologies justifying rebellion by under classes against upper classes. It also can be inferred from legislative, bureaucratic, or military infringements on traditional privileges or practices of a segmental or regional group. The maximum estimate of the scope of the segmental RD is the proportional size of the segmental group, but often only some of its members are discontented.[68] Intense demands for autonomy in Brittany and the Swiss Jura seem shared by only a few inhabitants of those regions, inasmuch as the demands have not received widespread political support. The demand of Walloons in Belgium and of French-Canadians for greater autonomy, however, are expressed in almost unanimous support for regional political parties and ideologies; the scope of

[68] Discriminated and separatist groups in some 100 polities as of 1960 are identified and their proportions specified in Ted Gurr, *New Error-Compensated Measures for Comparing Nations: Some Correlates of Civil Violence* (Princeton: Center of International Studies, Princeton University, Research Monograph No. 25, 1966), 67–90.

discontent in these groups seems virtually the same as their proportional size in the national population.

Hypotheses about the determinants of the scope of RD are not formally proposed here—those I considered seemed either too narrow or trivial—but instead detailed approaches are proposed for empirical determination of the scope of societal conditions that can be inferred, from the "intensity" hypothesis, to cause widespread discontent. The specific procedures may require more precision than is possible for comparative studies of some historical eras. But the general approaches should be applicable even if the specific suggestions are not. Any careful attempt to understand which social groups have been discontented about what, even if their relative sizes and the intensities of their grievances can be specified only roughly, should advance and make more precise the social history of turmoil and revolution.

4. Social Origins of Deprivation: Sources of Rising Expectations

> Talking once with a miner I asked him when the housing shortage first became acute in his district; he answered, "When we were told about it," meaning that till recently people's standards were so low that they took almost any degree of overcrowding for granted.
>
> George Orwell,
> *The Road to Wigan Pier*[1]

THE HYPOTHESES of the preceding chapter specify a set of variables that determines the potential for collective violence in any group at any time. The potential would be greatest in a nation most of whose citizens felt sharply deprived with respect to their most deeply valued goals, had individually and collectively exhausted the constructive means open to them to attain those goals, and lacked any nonviolent opportunity to act on their anger. One can identify groups and whole nations that, from an external perspective, might be so described: Parisian workers in 1848, Mexican peasants in 1910, the German *Kleinburgertüm* in the early 1920s, Hungarians in 1956, black South Africans in the 1960s. The statements and actions of the people involved provide evidence of intense deprivation in these circumstances, which may suffice for retrospective explanation. Contemporary analysis and accurate forecasting are facilitated by generalizations about the social and political processes that are likely to generate widespread and intense discontent. This and the next chapter identify some of these processes by developing hypotheses supported by assertions and empirical findings about the sources of rising expectations and of perceptions of declining value capabilities.

The bases of the hypotheses developed here are stated in corollaries ID.1.1 and ID.1.2. Any increase in the level or salience of men's value expectations without a comparable increase in their value capabilities increases their RD; any decrease in their value capabilities has a comparable effect. Consequently, one can infer a likely increase in RD as a result of social processes and patterns systematically associated either with rising expectations or declining capabilities. Three distinguishable sources of rising expectations are examined below: the demonstration effect, in its various manifestations; the articulation of new beliefs that justify height-

[1] *The Road to Wigan Pier* (London: Victor Gollancz, 1937), 64.

ened expectations; and the effects of increasing value position. Among the societal characteristics associated with static or declining value capabilities, discussed in chapter 5, are the presence of fixed-sum perspectives on values and structural inflexibilities that reduce value outputs or limit value opportunities. Together these hypotheses do not account for the processes determining value expectations and capabilities as comprehensively and parsimoniously as the set of social psychological hypotheses that identify the determinants of intensity of RD. The reasons are not far to seek: our knowledge of the workings of men's minds is at present greater and more precise than our understanding of the workings of society that influence collective perceptions, and there are far fewer studies of the dynamics of social processes than static analyses on which generalization can be based.

Men who aspire to a better way of life than they have, or than their fathers had, are not necessarily discontented. They may be fortunate enough to be members of a society that provides the means by which they can satisfy those expectations. Thus, analysis of the scope of increasing and intensifying expectations is not of itself sufficient for inferring increasing RD; capabilities should be given a parallel examination. However, men's expectations appear more susceptible to escalation than are the resources and institutions that determine their capabilities. The inference is that conditions which generate rising expectations may not be as potent sources of RD as disequilibrium between expectations and capabilities per se, but they nevertheless are likely to be closely associated with RD. It was pointed out in chapter 2 that "rising expectations" can be manifest in demands for greater amounts of values already held, demands for new values, or increasing salience of unsatisfied value demands. A variety of conditions having such effects in transitional and industrialized societies can be specified.

Demonstration Effects: Exposure to New Modes of Life

One of the more facile generalizations of research on modernization is that exposure of non-Western peoples to the material culture of the West promptly led them to aspire to new goods and ways of life. Blanksten defines the process as one in which "people on a lower standard of living become acquainted with the benefits of a higher standard, and in consequence of this 'demonstration effect' come to desire or demand the goods of the higher level."[2] Lerner characterizes the consequences of such exposure as the "revolution

[2] George Blanksten, "Transference of Social and Political Loyalties," in Bert Hoselitz and Wilbert Moore, eds., *Industrialization and Urbanization* (Paris: UNESCO, 1963), 184.

of rising frustrations" and states that its source is increasing aspiration unmatched by achievement. Among the sources of increased aspiration he identifies "new leaders . . . who encouraged their people to believe in the immanence of progress and the fulfillment of their new, often millennial, hopes," and, more pervasively, the demonstration effect of the content of new communications media.[3] Representative evidence is Holton's conclusion, on the basis of a survey of goods and services demanded in developing economies, that imitative consumption is practiced most by the industrial labor force, often for prestige, and that imitative consumption is self-reinforcing and increases at an accelerating rate.[4] Olson cites empirical studies that suggest that "the demonstration or evidence of higher consumption patterns in one's neighbors will increase one's desire for additional consumption, in the sense that it leads to saving a smaller proportion of income."[5]

Various mechanisms of exposure to the new are cited. Cole suggests that a principal source of rising expectations in the early stages of non-Western peoples' exposure to the West was missionary activity.[6] Turnbull poignantly depicts the dysfunctional effects of mission education on African lives in his biographical sketches of several Congolese.[7] The development of urban centers is said to set new standards for those who live on their periphery and to attract workers who by exposure to the wealth of urban bourgeoisie acquire new tastes, which are frequently unsatisfiable. Cohn says of the marginal men who were drawn to medieval European cities that they

> merely acquired new wants without being able to satisfy them; and in them the spectacle of a wealth undreamt-of in earlier centuries provoked a bitter sense of frustration. In all the over-populated, highly urbanized and industrialized areas there were multitudes of people living on the margin of society, in a state of chronic insecurity. There industry even at the best of times could

[3] Daniel Lerner, *The Passing of Traditional Society* (New York: The Free Press, 1958), 330–331, 335ff. A systematic analysis is Elizabeth E. Hoyt, "Want Development in Underdeveloped Areas," *Journal of Political Economy*, LIX (June 1951), 194–202.

[4] Richard H. Holton, "Changing Demand and Consumption," in Wilbert E. Moore and Arnold S. Feldman, eds., *Labor Commitment and Social Change in Development Areas* (New York: Social Science Research Council, 1950), 210–216.

[5] Mancur Olson, Jr., "Rapid Growth as a Destabilizing Force," *Journal of Economic History*, XXIII (December 1963), 538.

[6] A. H. Cole, "The Relation of Missionary Activity to Economic Development," *Economic Development and Cultural Change*, IX (January 1961), 120–127.

[7] Colin Turnbull, *The Lonely African* (New York: Doubleday, 1962, 1963).

> never absorb anything like the whole of the surplus population. Beggars crowded in every market place and roamed in gangs. . . . Many became mercenaries. . . . And even among artisans in employment many found themselves more defenceless than peasants on the manor.[8]

The Youngs, on the basis of Mexican questionnaire data, argue that the cities have a strong attractive influence on people in the surrounding villages that is mediated through kinsmen who already have an urban outlook. "Not only will a young man hear about the urban-industrial world but he may be exposed to the 'demonstration effect' of observing or learning from a relative working in a factory job."[9]

Literacy and Western education are often asserted to be major sources of rising expectations. The child of traditional society who invests his time and energy in formal education is assumed to be set in motion toward new goals, perhaps nebulous at first but increasingly distinct as education progresses. His levels of expectations are likely to increase along with the salience of the values he seeks. The notion that completion of elementary, or secondary, or higher education puts him close to his goals—of money, of status, of political participation—is also common. If he then finds jobs scarce, pay low, his kin hostile or parasitic, and his political capabilities low, disillusionment and anger are likely consequences.[10] Fallers describes the structural pattern that leads to such consequences in many developing countries:

> In some areas, the expansion of educational facilities in response to popular demand has run ahead of the growth and differentiation of the occupational system, with the result that large numbers of persons enter the labor market with expectations of employment that the occupational system cannot fulfill. The sense of grievance felt by the under-employed secondary-school or university graduate results . . . from the fact that governments in the new states are held directly responsible for the welfare and progress of their people in a way that was less true in the West during comparable phases of modernization. In facing these re-

[8] Norman R. C. Cohn, *The Pursuit of the Millennium,* 2nd edn. rev. (New York: Harper, 1957, 1961), 28. The depriving effects of urban migration on interpersonal value attainment are examined in a subsequent section of this chapter.

[9] Frank W. and Ruth C. Young, "Individual Commitment to Industrialization in Rural Mexico," *American Journal of Sociology,* LXXI (January 1966), 373–383, quotation 374.

[10] On the nature of literate vis-à-vis nonliterate societies see J. Goody and I. Watt, "The Consequences of Literacy," *Comparative Studies in Society and History,* V (April 1963), 304–345.

> sponsibilities, governments find it easier to expand educational facilities than employment opportunities, and this results in a constant decline in the market value of education. In consequence, the educated under-employed or unemployed are in many of the new states a more serious source of alienation and political disaffection than are industrial workers.[11]

Various country and regional studies support this argument. A questionnaire study of some 600 Colombian university students shows them to be convinced that education is their principal means for upward social and economic mobility, but dissatisfied both with their immediate environment and with prospects for achievement in the socioeconomic world toward which their expectations and training propel them.[12] In a psychological study of Guatemalan villagers, *Ladinos*—those of Spanish ancestry, oriented toward an urban, relatively modern world—were found to respond aggressively to Rorschach and other projective tests about five times as frequently as their Indian neighbors. The proposed explanation is that Indian culture tends to be "homogeneous, integrated, relatively self-sufficient," while *Ladino* culture is less integrated and creates "wants and desires which cannot be fully satisfied by the cultural resources" of the village community.[13] Field studies by Doob of three African peoples—the Luo and Ganda of East Africa and the Zulu of South Africa—using projective and interview techniques indicate that the higher the level of education, considered as a measure of extent of conversion to Western culture, the greater the degree of discontent expressed.[14] The Ainsworths, in a similar study, found that more acculturated Ugandan secondary students were more aggressive than less acculturated Kenyan students. The Ugandans "were more frequently frustrated by authority, by the aggression of others, and by their own failure or inability, and less frequently . . . feared aggression or viewed it and rebellion against authority to be wrong." [15]

[11] Lloyd Fallers, "Equality, Modernity, and Democracy in the New States," in Clifford Geertz, ed., *Old Societies and New States: The Quest for Modernity in Asia and Africa* (New York: The Free Press, 1963), 192–193. An African study of some of the consequences is Archibald Callaway, "Unemployment Among School Leavers," *Journal of Modern African Studies*, I (September 1963), 351–371.

[12] Robert C. Williamson: "University Students in a World of Change: A Colombian Sample," *Sociology and Social Research*, XLVIII (July 1964), 397–413.

[13] Otto Billig, John Gillin, and William Davidson, "Aspects of Personality and Culture in a Guatemalan Community: Ethnological and Rorschach Approaches, Part II," *Journal of Personality*, XVI (March 1948), 326–368, quotation 365.

[14] Leonard W. Doob, *Becoming More Civilized: A Psychological Exploration* (New Haven: Yale University Press, 1960), 282–283.

[15] Mary D. and Leonard H. Ainsworth, "Acculturation in East Africa, II. Frus-

These assertions and findings suggest that exposure to modernization raises expectations for welfare and interpersonal values—economic goods, personal development, status, the pleasures of urban social life. The demonstration effect also operates with respect to power values. Such a political demonstration effect seems partly responsible for the succession of rebellions by the Creole elites of Latin America that freed them from incompetent Spanish autocracy between 1810 and 1830.[16] The February 1848 revolution of Parisian workers and liberal bourgeoisie that overthrew Louis Philippe clearly was the inspiration for subsequent risings by Germans, Italians, Czechs, and Magyars later in the year.[17] Ghana's attainment of independence in 1957 intensified expectations of political independence among African leaders throughout the continent and thus indirectly contributed to political violence in regions like the Belgian Congo and Angola where progress toward effective African political participation was dilatory or nonexistent. The rebellions of Somalis in the Horn of Africa in the early 1960s provide another, less familiar example. The Somalis until 1960 were divided among Italian-mandated Somalia, British and French Somaliland, northern Kenya, and Ethiopia's Haud and Ogaden. In that year the Somali Republic was formed by union of the first two territories, and the Somali Republic began stridently to advocate the union of Ethiopian, Kenya, and French Somalis in a Greater Somalia. Although Kenyan Somalis had almost no Western-educated leaders and the one million Ethiopian Somalis none at all, the fact of Somali Republic independence and its advocacy of union apparently sufficed to instigate separatist political violence throughout the Horn from 1961 through 1967. The inference is that independence for Somalia and its advocacy of union served to raise political expectations markedly among other Somalis; the uncompromising response of Kenya and Ethiopia to the demands increased RD to the point that sustained violence developed.[18] These political demonstration effects are also closely associated with

---

tration and Aggression," *Journal of Social Psychology,* LVII (August 1962), 401–407, quotation 407.

[16] See Robert A. Humphrey and John Lynch, eds., *The Origins of the Latin American Revolutions, 1808–1826* (New York: Knopf, 1965).

[17] See especially Priscilla Robertson, *Revolutions of 1848: A Social History* (Princeton: Princeton University Press, 1952), passim, and also Robert B. Merriman, *Six Contemporaneous Revolutions* (Oxford: Clarendon Press, 1938), 209–210.

[18] Saadia Touval, *Somali Nationalism: International Politics and the Drive for Unity in the Horn of Africa* (Cambridge: Harvard University Press, 1963), 73–76, 132–153; and Ted Gurr, "Tensions in the Horn of Africa," in Feliks Gross, *World Politics and Tension Areas* (New York: New York University Press, 1965), 316–334.

variables examined in subsequent chapters. One successful revolution may provide angry men with a suitable model for action where one was previously lacking (chapter 7), and suggest that theirs may also be successful, i.e. may reduce the apparent coercive capacity of the regime they oppose (chapter 8).

There are findings that challenge the ethnocentric argument that Western ways of life are so compellingly attractive that mere exposure to them or education about them is enough to make non-Westerners discontented with what they have. Oberschall, in a recent survey, found no consequential differences in dissatisfaction among urban and rural Ugandans that could be attributable to urban or rural residence, or to the extent of their exposure to the mass media. Moreover, although the great majority of respondents were concerned about economic difficulties, the younger the respondent and the greater his educational level, the better he thought life had gotten in his village in the preceding five years. On the basis of these and other findings, Oberschall argues that "While there are demands, sometimes even very strong ones, even in remote rural areas, for material improvements, for consumer goods, and for jobs, these demands occur within a still viable traditional context in which provision of a minimum of economic, social, and psychological security dampens whatever frustrations unfulfilled demands generate."[19] Surveys of six Middle Eastern nations in 1950–51 showed that "transitional" people, those caught up in the "revolution of rising expectations," were generally more happy than traditional people. Even in Egypt and Syria, countries then experiencing little social or economic progress, the "transitionals" were no more discontented than the "traditionals."[20] Evidence from a 119-nation study of relations between measures of educational levels and the extent of civil strife similarly challenges simple assumptions about the dysfunctional consequences of excessive education. By and large, the greater the relative increase in skilled men in a country's nonagricultural labor force in the 1950s, the less likely was turmoil and the lower were levels of strife in the early 1960s. The relationship was strongest in nations in the early stages of development. Measures of relative levels of education provide similar results: the greater the proportion of a population that has formal schooling, controlling for levels of economic development, the less likely and less extensive is strife. The implication of these

[19] Anthony Oberschall, "Rising Expectations, National Unity and Political Turmoil" (paper read at the annual meeting of the African Studies Association, November 1967), no page nos.

[20] Daniel Lerner, *The Passing of Traditional Society* (Glencoe: The Free Press, 1958), 100–103.

and related findings is that education tends to be functional in both developing and developed societies; it seems to serve less to raise expectations to an unsatisfiably high level than to provide ambitious men with the sense that they have better means for attaining their expectations.[21]

The argument that migration to urban centers is associated with the raising of men's expectations to an unsatisfiably high level and hence leads to violence also is open to question. Fals Borda suggests that in Latin America the flight to the city is in some respects a conservative movement, a value-enhancing alternative for discontented rural people that in the short run reduces rather than increases the potential for revolution.[22] Tilly has made a series of studies of the incidence of and participants in urban violence in eighteenth- and nineteenth-century France, with comparable results: there was no direct relationship between rates of urban growth and mass violence, while participants in urban strife were predominantly established urban workers acting in the context of organized political movements, not new migrants acting anomically.[23] Studies of the 1967 ghetto riots in Newark and Detroit show that substantially greater proportions of the participants than nonparticipants were raised in the ghettos rather than in the rural South, and that levels of anger and sympathy for the riots were even more disproportionately characteristic of the black of Northern heritage. In Detroit, for example, 75 percent of rioters were raised in the North compared with 36 percent of the noninvolved; comparable figures for Newark are 74 percent and 52 percent.[24] The 119-nation cross-national study cited above provides further evidence for the 1950s and 1960s: there was no substantively

[21] Ted Gurr with Charles Ruttenberg, *The Conditions of Civil Violence: First Tests of a Causal Model* (Princeton: Center of International Studies, Princeton University, Research Monograph No. 28, 1967), 58–60, 71–75.

[22] Orlando Fals Borda, "Unfinished Revolutions in Latin America," (paper read at a conference on "The United States in a Revolutionary World," Princeton University, April 1968), 4–5.

[23] See Charles Tilly, "A Travers le chaos des vivantes cités," paper read at the Sixth World Congress of Sociology, Evian-les-Bains, September 1966, and Charles Tilly, "Collective Violence in European Perspective," in Hugh Davis Graham and Ted Robert Gurr, eds., *Violence in America: Historical and Comparative Perspectives* (Washington, D.C.: National Commission on the Causes and Prevention of Violence, 1969), 5–34.

[24] See *Report of the National Advisory Commission on Civil Disorder,* Otto Kerner, Governor of Illinois, Chairman (New York: Bantam Books, 1968), 173, and Governor's Select Commission on Civil Disorder, State of New Jersey, *Report for Action* (Trenton: State of New Jersey, February 1968), 129–131; and Robert M. Fogelson and Robert D. Hill, "Who Riots," *Supplemental Studies for the National Advisory Commission on Civil Disorders* (Washington, D.C.: U.S. Government Printing Office, 1968), 217–248.

or statistically significant relationship for all nations or any group of nations between rates of urban immigration in the 1950s and the likelihood or levels of strife in the early 1960s.[25]

These somewhat-contradictory sets of assertions and findings about the operation of the demonstration effect require a more general explanation. None of the findings indicates that the demonstration effect of other people's material and political culture does not operate. The implication is rather that it raises expectations only in certain circumstances, and that when it does so it does not necessarily lead to increased discontent and to political violence.

Under what circumstances is the demonstration effect operative? Doob suggests that alone it is seldom sufficient to stir new strivings. His fieldwork suggests that it is ordinarily some form of discontent with traditional life that motivates men toward new goals. The "man in motion"—the phrase is Daniel Lerner's—may be set in motion because "he may be generally discontented with his society either because too many of its institutions fail to satisfy his needs or because one specific frustration, being severe, colors his entire outlook. This latter kind of discontent may be facilitated by catching a glimpse of the new, since radical rejection of the old is more likely to occur after the individual has been convinced that life as a whole conceivably can be sweeter."[26] McClelland's studies of the need for achievement, which can be generally though not precisely equated with intensifying expectations, similarly indicate, in a variety of cultural settings, that partial exposure to an alien culture through education is ineffective by itself in raising need for achievement. Exposure increases the need for achievement only when it involves "'ideological conversion' of the total group in which the experience occurs. There is even some evidence that . . . partial exposure to other 'foreign' value systems may be disruptive and even lower *n* [need for] Achievement."[27] Whatever the motivation to attempt the new, learning its ways can disrupt older norms and beliefs, and the complexity of the new may of itself be frustrating. Doob suggests that in such circumstances men may become uncertain about their roles, but that the most fundamental bitterness and despair are likely to occur

[25] Gurr and Ruttenberg, 57–60. Among "personalist"—predominantly Latin American—countries there was a significant inverse relationship of the type suggested by Fals Borda: the greater the rates of urban migration the lower the levels of strife.

[26] Doob, 72–73.

[27] David C. McClelland, *The Achieving Society* (Princeton: Van Nostrand, 1961), 411–417, quotation 416.

> when the individual, fired to change himself, discovers that for reasons he cannot control the way to change is obstructed. He cannot obtain the money needed to carry on his education. He is the victim of prejudice and hence certain jobs are automatically barred to him. He would mingle socially with people already civilized, and he finds that he is either discouraged or prevented from doing so.[28]

The first general relationship suggested in these comments can be summarized in the following hypothesis.

Hypothesis VE.1: The susceptibility of a group to conversion to rising value expectations through symbolic exposure to a new mode of life varies strongly with the intensity and scope of preexisting relative deprivation in the group.

Conversion is the abandonment of some or all the norms and beliefs that establish existing expectation levels and provide the means for their attainment, and their replacement by new beliefs that justify increased or different expectations. In other words, some degree of RD is a precondition for the operation of the demonstration effect. The greater the intensity of RD the more prone people are to seek out and be receptive to norms and beliefs that justify new expectations and that promise means of attaining them. The greater the scope of RD in a collectivity, the more likely converts are to find communal support for their conversion.

The argument that conversion to new value expectations is most likely to occur among those already sharply discontented may seem to beg the central question of this chapter, which is what patterns of change over time cause changes in value expectations and capabilities. But other hypotheses developed above, and in subsequent sections, suggest what some of those changes are. The general pattern that is most likely to lead to intensifying discontent in static, traditional societies is decremental RD, i.e., a temporary deterioration in value performance compared with the more-or-less static secular trend. Similarly, a decline following a prolonged period of improvement in value position is likely to cause increasing deprivation (hypothesis VE.5 below). It is in situations such as these that men are most likely to be converted to new perspectives on life that justify new and intensified expectations. One such relationship, a modification of the decremental RD model developed in chapter 2, is sketched in figure 7. The

[28] Doob, 73.

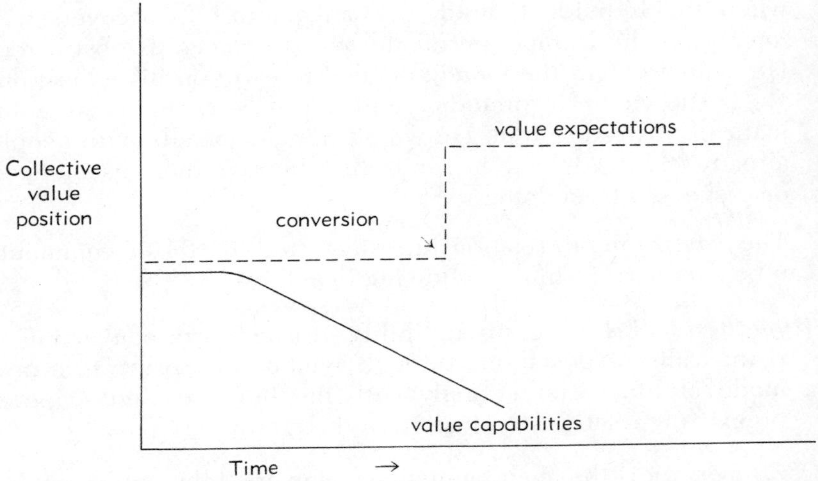

Figure 7. Potential effects of intensifying RD on conversion to new value expectations.

dotted line symbolizes the conversion effect of exposure to new modes of life following an experience of intensifying RD.

A second relationship also is implied in these and some of the preceding comments.

Hypothesis VE.2: The susceptibility of groups to conversion to rising value expectations varies moderately with the perceived availability of value opportunities for attaining those expectations.

That is, exposure to the material and power benefits of a "better way of life" is unlikely to bring about conversion even for intensely discontented people unless they see that they have some chance of attaining those goods themselves. The peasant may aspire to a better life, but as long as he sees no courses of action open to him to attain them he is unlikely to abandon the unsatisfying but familiar way of life he knows.

In any society there are likely to be "deviant" or "maladjusted" or adventurous individuals who will be sufficiently dissatisfied with their lot in life to be converted by encounters with representatives of a new mode of life. In "peasant" societies the number of such discontents may be greater than is commonly believed. In sharp contrast to the idyllic picture of harmony, compassion, and mutual supportiveness that is sometimes assumed to characterize peasant life, Bequiraj argues that "the peasant [meaning most members of most peasant communities throughout human history] is confronted with a gap between expectations and attainments which causes his achievements in all spheres of activity to fall short of his hopes." The following quotation summarizes his argument:

> the strong loyalty and benevolence within peasant primary groups are not generated by satisfaction and contentment but function as necessary counterweights to disruption and dissent; . . . the social benevolence evident in these primary groups enables the member to endure the heavy weight of centralized authority and repressed internal dissent. In other words, the world of the individual peasant is one of suffering and repressed dissent, reflecting the response of the average individual to coercive authority, the inefficient guidance and unchallenged power of elders, the prescriptive nature of peasant virtues, the severe character of rigid mores, and the confinement of standards based upon identification by kin affiliation.[29]

If this interpretation is essentially or even only partly accurate, it accounts for the readiness of many peasant communities to undergo rather prompt conversion to Westernization and modernization. It is compatible with Lerner's finding, mentioned above, that peasants in the Middle East are more dissatisfied than their modernizing countrymen. It also provides a tentative explanation for the differential responsiveness of non-Western peoples to Western influence, for example the alacrity with which the Yoruba, living in an overpopulated and agriculturally marginal part of West Africa, accepted Christian education and Western mores, compared with the persistent resistance of the Ganda, members of a centralized and well-endowed state, to acceptance of most of the trappings and beliefs of Christianity. Finally it suggests an explanation for the relatively low levels of participation in collective violence by recent migrants into cities noted in several studies above: the appalling poverty and decay of *favelas, bidonvilles,* workers' suburbs, and black ghettos may represent a marked improvement in personal freedom and economic opportunity, if not economic attainment, for men and women fleeing the constraints and hopelessness of rural settlements.

Demonstration Effects: New Ideologies

Hypothesis VE.1 also provides an interpretation for the expectation-intensifying effects sometimes attributed to the articulation

[29] Mehmet Bequiraj, *Peasantry in Revolution* (Ithaca: Center for International Studies, Cornell University, 1967), quotations from 1, 8.

of new ideologies. A token of faith among many Communist writers, accepted by many vehement anticommunists as well, has been that the vision of earthly paradise held out to the impoverished worker and peasant in popularized Marxist teachings should be sufficient to mobilize him into revolutionary activity. The necessary catalyst, however, seems to be that he must be subjectively aware of his impoverishment before he becomes susceptible to revolutionary ideologies. Ideologies of progress and revolution are most effectively articulated not in static societies but among men who have experienced profound upheaval. Trotsky made the point in his well-known statement that

> the mere existence of privations is not enough to cause an insurrection: if it were, the masses would be always in revolt. It is necessary that the bankruptcy of the social regime, being conclusively revealed, should make these privations intolerable, and that new conditions and new ideas should open the prospect of a revolutionary way out.[30]

The revolutionary, chiliastic movements of the later Middle Ages occurred at times of natural and social disaster, when material well-being and communal patterns were deteriorating.[31] Hobsbawm points out that the formative period of socialism, the first half of the nineteenth century, was characterized by "depression, falling money-wages, heavy technological unemployment, and doubts about the future expansive prospects of the economy." The new socialist writers were inspired by these conditions, and their doctrines of progress toward a new society were persuasive among workers and intellectuals, not because economic conditions were bad but because they were getting worse in relative and for some groups in absolute terms.[32] In China, Communist nationalism became an effective ideology for sustaining peasant mobilization for revolutionary activity in the early 1940s, not because of rural economic distress per se, as Johnson demonstrates, but in substantial part because of the repressive policies of the Japanese invaders, which deprived the Chinese peasantry of the modicum of security they had.[33] When men have experienced disruption they

[30] Leon Trotsky, *The History of the Russian Revolution* (Ann Arbor: University of Michigan Press, 1957).

[31] See Johan Huizinga, *The Waning of the Middle Ages* (London: Arnold, 1924), passim, and Cohn, passim.

[32] E. J. Hobsbawm, *The Age of Revolution 1789–1848* (New York: Mentor, 1962, 1964), chap. 13, quotation 286–287.

[33] Chalmers, A. Johnson, *Peasant Nationalism and Communist Power: The Emergence of Revolutionary China 1937–1945* (Stanford: Stanford University Press, 1962, 1966), chaps. 1 and 2.

are susceptible to conversion to ideologies justifying new and intensified expectations. When their circumstances of life are relatively static and coherent they are unlikely to be attracted by new ideologies even if, in the observer's perspective, they are in a condition of objective deprivation. Some effects of new ideologies and beliefs in focusing discontents are examined in chapter 7.

Demonstration Effects: Value Gains of Reference Groups

Another, more consequential, source of rising expectations is the demonstration effect of one social group's upward mobility in raising the expectations of other groups. The argument is an extension of the conventional sociological view of RD, of which Runciman's development is particularly useful. RD is said to arise when individuals compare their own situation with that of a reference group which has what they want and think they should have. The greater the individuals' negative discrepancy, the greater their RD. People may set their standards by a variety of reference groups, of course, and as Runciman points out the individual may either take his aspirations from a comparative reference group, or choose it as a reference group because he was already dissatisfied with his value position. For societies containing pervasive poverty, and for subordinate classes in a larger but relatively static social system, comparative reference groups tend to be limited.

> The situation of a number of comparable people who are very much better off is not readily brought home. . . . In the absence of an external stimulus, the limited reference groups by which relative deprivation is kept low . . . tend to be self-perpetuating. . . . Once the vicious circle has been broken, this may set off a rising spiral of expectations and comparisons which will continue until a new equilibrium is reached. But some external influence is needed.[34]

Among the external influences Runciman mentions are war and its consequent expectations of reward and social dislocation, the introduction of new standards from outside the group, and economic change. He suggests that "prosperity can break the vicious circle between poverty and conservatism by making people aware of the possibility of a higher standard than it would previously have occurred to them to hope for. Conversely, a decline in prosperity, if not too violent, can restrict the sense of relative deprivation by inhibiting comparisons with more fortunate groups."[35]

[34] W. G. Runciman, *Relative Deprivation and Social Justice* (Berkeley: University of California Press, 1966), 23–24.
[35] *Ibid.*, 25.

This relationship may underlie the impression that revolutions are apt to occur at times of rising prosperity: as mobility increases for some groups but not for others the less mobile groups tend to set their expectations by reference to the most mobile. Lipset, in his discussion of economic development and the democratic order, concludes from various evidence that people whose experiences and significant communications are primarily with persons at their own socioeconomic level tend to be "more conservative than people who may be better off but who have been exposed to the possibilities of securing a better way of life. The dynamic in the situation would seem to be exposure to the possibility of a better way of life rather than poverty as such."[36] An interview study of 283 black clerks working in South African cities shows a distinct tendency for their job-related frustrations to increase in proportion to increasing contact with European society.[37] In a summary of thirteen studies of members of the radical National Farmers' Organization and of the more conservative Farm Bureau, Morrison and Steeves show that NFO members generally are more prosperous but have considerably higher aspirations, express higher dissatisfaction, and are more disposed to drastic means of change. Their economic aspirations are attributed not to membership in the NFO per se but to their higher levels of education and greater contacts than more conservative farmers with "economically advantaged nonfarm groups and the styles and standards of such groups. This carries the strong suggestion of an increased likelihood that NFO members have, as a result of these contacts, acquired higher income aspirations through more affluent reference groups."[38]

Related studies suggest a qualification: *similar* groups tend to be chosen as reference groups. Runciman cites evidence, from studies by Hyman of American workers and by Stern and Keller of Frenchmen, that the aspirations of the less fortunate are modified by their position. Those near the bottom of the class ladder "are likely, even in a society with an egalitarian ideology, to choose reference groups nearer the bottom than self-conscious egalitarianism would imply."[39] A more recent study by Hamilton of at-

[36] Seymour M. Lipset, *Political Man: The Social Bases of Politics* (Garden City: Doubleday, 1960), 63.

[37] Rae Sherwood, "The Bantu Civil Servant," unpublished ms. (Johannesburg: National Council for Social Research, National Institute for Personnel Research, 1959), summaried in Doob, 75.

[38] Denton E. Morrison and Allan D. Steeves, "Deprivation, Discontent, and Social Movement Participation: Evidence on a Contemporary Farmers' Movement, the NFO," *Rural Sociology*, XXXII (December 1967), 414–434, quotation 424.

[39] Herbert H. Hyman, "The Value Systems of Different Classes," in Reinhard Bendix and Seymour M. Lipset, eds., *Class, Status and Power* (Glencoe: The

titudes of U.S. white-collar workers found that those moving from what they perceived as a working-class background into white-collar occupations tend to continue to identify with their class of origin.[40] Most people probably choose their reference groups from among those groups they perceive to be socioeconomically similar to themselves, but, among such groups, they are most likely to set their expectations by those experiencing the most rapid increase in well-being. Thus New York City policemen justify their demands for higher salaries not by reference to the income of municipal white-collar employees, but to the salaries of city firemen. Landless Mexican peasants in the decades after the Revolution of 1910 did not demand the perquisites of urban workers, but their own land, which other peasants had seized or received in land distribution programs. The following hypothesis summarizes the relationship and qualification:

Hypothesis VE.3: The rate at which group value expectations rise varies strongly with the rate of value gain of the most rapidly gaining group of similar socioeconomic status.

The hypothesis is applicable particularly to value gains that are readily perceived and symbolized, as economic, participatory, and status values typically are, and as self-realization and interpersonal values other than status are not.[41]

Studies of structural inequalities within and among nations also support hypothesis VE.3. Pareto's statements about the political implications of variances in income distribution led Davis to infer that economies with either highly dispersed or highly concentrated incomes would have political disturbances, while only those with a "normal" distribution are politically stable. Specifically, whenever a critically high concentration of income prevails, revolution is likely; and whenever the concentration ratio is below a critical minimum (i.e. widely dispersed), civil war is likely. Davis reports evidence that the French and Russian Revolutions, and the Spanish Revolution of 1931, occurred in societies with critically high concentrations; and that the Spanish Civil War of 1936–39 and the

---

Free Press, 1953), 426–442, and Eric Stern and Suzanne Keller, "Spontaneous Group References in France," *Public Opinion Quarterly*, XVII (No. 2, 1953), 208–217, summarized in Runciman, 26–27.

[40] Richard F. Hamilton, "The Marginal Middle Class: A Reconsideration," *American Sociological Review*, XXXI (April 1966), 192–199.

[41] Methods for estimating relative economic deprivation from disparities in rates of economic improvement among social sectors are demonstrated by Alfred Sauvy and Françoise Leridon, "Du calcul des Révenus dans une population à la frustration sociale," *Population*, XVI (October-December 1961), 605–624.

American Civil War occurred when the ratio was below the minimum.[42] Russett proposes that extreme inequality of land distribution is most likely to lead to instability "in those poor, predominantly agricultural societies where limitation to a small plot of land almost unavoidably condemns one to poverty." Measures of poverty and inequality in land tenure together account for substantial variance ($R^2 = .50$) in levels of collective violence in forty-seven nations, most of them at the middle or higher levels of economic development.[43] If hypothesis VE.3 is correct, one would expect the proposed Davis-Pareto relationship between high concentration and revolution, and the Russett hypothesis regarding land inequality and strife, to be strongest in countries undergoing rapid socioeconomic change, weakest in more static societies.

Finally, there is some evidence that regional differences in economic development, among or within nations, lead to political violence by people in the less-privileged regions. AlRoy suggests this as a partial explanation for the discontents underlying the Cuban revolution. "There was no lack of development in Cuba so much as a development of consumption patterned after the extremely productive society nearby, but without the corresponding ethos of production. . . . The resulting stagnation was not complete but neither sufficiently splendiferous for all."[44] The interpenetration of the Cuban and American economies, and the visible affluence of American tourists in Cuba, intensified such a demonstration effect. Midlarsky and Tanter found general relationships of this sort between the United States and Latin American countries. The greater the degree of American involvement in the economy of a Latin American country in the mid-1950s, taking into account concentration of trade and per capita investment, the greater the number of conspiracies and anti-U.S. demonstrations in the late 1950s.[45] A study of the patterns of regional rebellion in recent Indonesian history suggests that interregional hostility has not been systematically associated with ethnic, linguistic, or other cleavages conventionally associated with separatist movements, but with relative levels of social and economic develop-

[42] Harold T. Davis, *Political Statistics* (Evanston: Northwestern University Press, 1948), 185–202, summarized in Fred Kort, "The Quantification of Aristotle's Theory of Revolution," *American Political Science Review*, XLVI (June 1952), 490–491.

[43] Bruce M. Russett, Jr., "Inequality and Instability: The Relation of Land Tenure to Politics," *World Politics*, XVI (April 1964), 442–454.

[44] Gil AlRoy, "Revolutionary Conditions in Latin America," *Review of Politics*, XIX (July 1967), 419.

[45] Manus Midlarsky and Raymond Tanter, "Toward a Theory of Political Instability in Latin America," *Journal of Peace Research*, No. 3, 1967, 209–227.

ment; the poorest regions have been the most rebellious.[46] The protracted rebellion of the black, predominantly pagan southern Sudanese against the nation's northern, predominantly Muslim leaders that began in 1961 was in part the consequence of ethnic and religious hostility, but an equally important grievance was deliberate and increasing economic disparity between the southern Sudan and the north.[47] The same general explanation has been suggested for the American Civil War: many Southerners were fundamentally dissatisfied with the relative economic stagnation of the South vis-a-vis the industrializing North, and regarded the trend toward abolition as a further step toward the economic and political subjugation of the South.[48] A supplemental explanation to the proposed regional demonstration effect is that in most of these cases the wealthier country or region was, or appeared to be, drawing off resources of the poorer for its own benefit. An exploitative relationship, individually or collectively, is likely to intensify the sense of injustice associated with RD.

Demonstration Effects: Value Disequilibria

A discrepancy between a group's relative share of welfare values vis-à-vis its share of participatory or status values also is said to have a kind of demonstration effect on value expectations. The argument, briefly, is that if a group has attained a high rank relative to other groups in the distribution of one value, its members will demand an equal rank on other values. Aristotle discusses this disquilibrium with reference to economic and participatory values (chapter 2). Kort's restatement of Aristotle's view is that "inequality in the sense of an incongruity of the respective political and economic status within social classes is a factor which promotes political disorders." [49] Galtung proposes that all kinds of

[46] Mohammed Ansori Nawawi, "Regionalism and Regional Conflicts in Indonesia," (Ph.D. dissertation, Department of Politics, Princeton University, June 1968), chap. 10.

[47] The south's relative economic deprivation is emphasized in Joseph Oduho and William Deng, *The Problem of the Southern Sudan* (London: Oxford University Press, 1963), chap. 12, and "Six-Year Revolt in Sudan Leaves Untold Casualties," *New York Times*, April 15, 1968, 1, 16. For another interpretation see Mohamed Omer Beshir, *The Southern Sudan: Background to Conflict* (New York: Praeger, 1968).

[48] On the origins of the Civil War, and the general issue of assessing causation, see Lee Benson and Cushing Strout, "Causation and the American Civil War: Two Appraisals," *History and Theory*, I (No. 2, 1961), 163–185. For a progressive deprivation interpretation see James C. Davies, "The J-Curve of Rising and Declining Satisfactions as a Cause of some Great Revolutions and a Contained Rebellion," in Graham and Gurr, eds.

[49] Fred Kort, "The Quantification of Aristotle's Theory of Revolution," *American Political Science Review*, LXVI (June 1952), 487.

human aggression, including crime, rebellion, and war, are caused by "rank disequilibria": a lack of consistency in the rankings of individuals, groups, or nations on whatever value hierarchies are relevant to them.[50] Geschwinder applies the proposition to groups: "A group which possesses a number of status attributes which are differently ranked on the various status hierarchies will be dissatisfied and prone to rebellion."[51]

A narrower version of the hypothesis attributes a disposition to revolution to those who experience economic or status value gains without a comparable increase in their ability to participate in politics. Heberle cites this as one of several necessary conditions for revolution:

> First, there has to be a social class or several social classes dissatisfied with the existing distribution of political power; this usually happens because the classes feel the discrepancy between their actual importance in society and their legal and political position. . . . The actively revolutionary groups are usually those classes or subclasses that, just because they are no longer poor, feel unduly restrained in their economic activities or in their participation in political decisions.[52]

Smelser suggests a comparable motive for group participation in "value-oriented" (revolutionary) movements: "improvement on absolute grounds [may involve] deprivation on relative grounds; for the same groups, with their new gains in one sphere (e.g. economic, cultural) often are held back in another (e.g. political)."[53] The observational basis for the assertion is considerable. The closed merchant oligarchies that ruled many of the early Renaissance cities were repeatedly challenged by economically advancing and rebellious craft guilds seeking a voice in governing councils. Middle-class participants in the English, American, and French revolutions demanded for themselves a role in governing the state commensurate with their role in its economic life. The Chartist Rebellion in England, 1838–42, took the form of explicitly political demands for manhood suffrage, the secret ballot, and annual parliaments, principally by members of the more advanced,

[50] Johan Galtung, "A Structural Theory of Aggression," *Journal of Peace Research*, No. 2, 1964, 95–119.

[51] James A. Geschwender, "Social Structure and the Negro Revolt: An Examination of Some Hypotheses," *Social Forces*, XLIII (December 1964), 249.

[52] Rudolf Heberle, *Social Movements: An Introduction to Political Sociology* (New York: Appleton-Century-Crofts, 1951), 368.

[53] Neil J. Smelser, *Theory of Collective Behavior* (New York: The Free Press, 1963), 340.

organized working class. A recent study of the South African black bourgeoisie identifies tensions arising from the contrast of the high occupational status they hold as professionals with their low social and civil status.[54]

The causal question is why this kind of relationship should hold. Aristotle's answer was that men's conception of social justice determines their response to what is here called value disequilibria. "Whenever one part or the other fails to enjoy such a political influence as is consistent with its own conception of *justice*, it becomes the author of sedition." [55] In other words, men whose economic lot is improving will aspire to greater political participation if they hold beliefs that justify such participation. But this answer begs the question, which is whether there is some universal human trait whereby experience of an advance toward economic equality, or superiority, makes men believe they should have comparable status on other values. Galtung suggests that there is. If a person experiences disequilibrium, he

> will be constantly reminded of his objective state of disequilibrium by the differential treatment he is exposed to. This will force a correspondence between his objective situation and his subjective perception of it . . . and the idea of rectification may occur. However, we do not have to presuppose . . . that an ideology of rectification has to be fully developed, or even perceived at all—only that the objective existence of disequilibrium will cause an instability in the life-style of the person or the nation, and cause what is often referred to as an "unstable self-image." [56]

Geschwinder suggests a more restricted relationship. If other groups achieve value gains because they have such characteristics as education or wealth, and if the perceivers, individual or group, have these same characteristics but do not experience improvement, they will feel entitled to the same gains and be discontented over their lack.[57]

But Geschwender's proposal does not seem to account for many of the cases of status or political expectations associated with value discrepancies. The French bourgeoisie were not resentful of any

[54] Leo Kuper, *An African Bourgeoisie* (New Haven: Yale University Press, 1965).

[55] Aristotle, *The Politics*, Book V, Quotation from J. E. C. Welldon, trans., *The Politics of Aristotle* (New York: Macmillan, 1883, 1905), 357, translator's emphasis.

[56] Galtung, "A Structural Theory of Aggression," 99.

[57] Geschwender, 256.

upward mobility among the nobility, whose economic position seems to have been static or declining in relative terms; they wanted some measure of that nobility's present status and former political influence. The Chartists in nineteenth-century England may have been emulating the growing political power of the urban middle classes; they also were seeking political means to protect themselves against the pervasive and recurrent economic disasters that affected the working class.[58] This is in fact a common theme in descriptions of cases of value-disequilibrium RD: men rebel in order to adjust their power or status position to their rising economic position because the lack of power or status appears to threaten the gains they have struggled for. For example, only when the newly gained wealth of the English middle classes was directly threatened by actions of the crown did the Puritan Revolution occur. As Edwards observes, "the English middle class . . . were thus driven to revolution by the two most compelling of economic incentives—the prospect of great gain and the fear of great loss."[59] Prior to the French revolution, erratic government economic policies, for example the tariff reduction treaty with England in 1786, posed a serious threat to segments of the bourgeoisie—who had, after all, held considerable economic and some political power for several generations without supporting a revolution.[60] The following hypothesis summarizes the proposed causal relationship between upward mobility on one class of values and rising expectations for other values.

Hypothesis VE.4: The rate at which group value expectations for a discrepantly low value rises varies moderately with the extent to which the discrepant value is a primary base value for other values.

Base value is used in the sense given it by Lasswell and Kaplan, as a value which people use to justify and obtain improved positions on other values.[61] In other words, if lack of power, as a base value, is perceived as a threat to maintaining and increasing a group's economic well-being or relative status, power will be demanded. The relationship is probably most common among groups

[58] See George Rudé, *The Crowd in History, 1730–1848* (New York: Wiley, 1964), chap. 13, and Ben C. Roberts, "On the Origins and Resolution of English Working-Class Protest," in Graham and Gurr, eds.

[59] Lyford P. Edwards, *The Natural History of Revolution* (Chicago: University of Chicago Press, 1927), 81.

[60] See Crane Brinton, *The Anatomy of Revolution* (New York: Norton, 1938), 45–46.

[61] Harold Lasswell and Abraham Kaplan, *Power and Society: A Framework for Political Inquiry* (New Haven: Yale University Press, 1950), 83–96.

that experience upward economic mobility without compensatory increases in political participation, which they may find necessary to increase their security from economic restrictions. It also is possible that groups experiencing upward political mobility will feel their chances for maintaining power are reduced by the lack of material goods or lack of recognition, and therefore demand commensurate economic or status mobility.

Some Effects of Value Mobility

The Davies theory of revolution, summarized in chapter 2, is that "revolutions are most likely to occur when a prolonged period of objective economic and social development is followed by a short period of sharp reversal."[62] The hypothesis can be generalized to other forms of political violence as well. The underlying causal mechanism is that the period of improvement generates expectations about continued improvement. If those expectations are frustrated by declining value output or repressive governmental action, violent protest is a likely consequence. The expectation-intensifying effects of value mobility can be summarized hypothetically:

Hypothesis VE.5: The rate at which group value expectations rise varies strongly with the rate and duration of the group's past value gains, except for groups with maximum value positions.

Groups have maximum value positions if they have the maximum conceivable amount of a value. One can distinguish between "ceiling" values such as power and status, which have maximums—only one group can have the highest status or all power in a society—and "nonceiling" values such as welfare and communality, which can be sought in limitless quantity. Expectations about the former presumably stabilize when the ceiling is reached; expectations about the latter may continue to rise even after a group surpasses all others in the society. Ordinarily, group value gains occur in societies in which overall value performance is increasing. But even in a static society, or in one in which total values are shrinking, some groups may experience relative increases in economic, power, or other values at the expense of other groups. It should be noted that whereas hypothesis VE.4 refers to effects of gains on one value vis-a-vis expectations about other values, hypothesis VE.5 asserts that mobility with reference to a single value generates expectations about continued gains on that value.

[62] James C. Davies, "Toward a Theory of Revolution," *American Sociological Review*, XXVII (February 1962), 6.

A few theoretical views and cases support the hypothesis. Soule is representative of many theorists who associate change rather than oppression with revolution:

> When the people are in their most desperate and miserable condition, they are often least inclined to revolt, for then they are hopeless. . . . Only after their position is somewhat improved and they have sensed the possibility of change, do they revolt effectively against oppression and injustice. What touches off insurrection is hope, not lack of it, rising confidence, not bleak suffering.[63]

The obverse relationship, that lack of change contributes to political stability, is postulated by Wilson in a discussion of the Thai farmer:

> the peasantry's inarticulate acquiescence to government and indifference to national politics are fundamental to the political system. A tolerable economic situation which provides a stable subsistence without encouraging any great hope for quick improvement is no doubt the background of this political inaction. In the foreground is a real freedom from political and social pressures. Relatively secure in his property rights and usually safe from bandits and plunderers, the Thai farmer may go about his vital activities in security. . . .[64]

The general explanations of the Puritan, American, and French revolutions offered by scholars like Brinton and Soule are consistent with the Davies hypothesis. Brinton, writing of these three and the Russian Revolution, attributes primary importance to "the existence among a group, or groups, of a feeling that prevailing conditions limit or hinder their economic activity." It was specifically the economically improving groups, the "chief enterprising groups," that found their opportunities for continued improvement unduly limited.[65] Soule's analysis of the same four revolutions leads him to similar conclusions. The Puritan Revolution, for example, was characterized by a struggle of the rising middle classes, notably "the landed gentry who were made richer and more aggressive by the enclosures, the eviction of peasants and the seizure of church lands." They sought to acquire more

[63] George Soule, *The Coming American Revolution* (New York: Macmillan, 1935), 20.

[64] David A. Wilson, "Thailand," in George McT. Kahin, ed., *Governments and Politics of Southeast Asia* (2nd edn., Ithaca: Cornell University Press, 1959, 1964), 33.

[65] Brinton, 54.

lands, "to free themselves from the tithes, fees, laws, and jurisdiction of the clergy so that they could accumulate capital, trade freely and exploit the chances for profit in the newly born capitalist world. . . ." [66]

All these views imply the presence of rising economic expectations generated by economic improvement, whose continued attainment was thwarted first by economic adversity and second by the inability or unwillingness of the political system to take remedial action. Several studies of other forms of violence suggest the same interpretation. An analysis of violent rural protest in France in 1961, which began among Breton farmers and included protest meetings, riots, and sabotage, suggests that it resulted not from economic "repression" but from farmers' dissatisfaction at lack of continued improvement in prices, public investment, and government services.[67] The conditions leading up to the ten days of rioting which devastated Bogota, Colombia, in April 1948, leaving 3,000 dead, followed a more complex pattern of essentially the same kind. Following the end of the depression of the 1930s there was a long, gradual improvement in the economic position of the urban workers, but their position inevitably deteriorated because of the restrictive effects of World War II on the export economy. Late in the war exports increased rapidly and an economic boom began, but a drastic inflationary spiral soon channeled most of the benefits of the boom into the hands of entrepreneurs and speculators. The income of workers and the lower middle class wage earners lagged further and further behind the cost-of-living curve at a time when they had every expectation of sharing in the new prosperity. The "social vomiting," as Kalman Silvert called the subsequent rioting, was precipitated by the assassination of a Liberal politician.[68]

Political violence also has been attributed in part to the failure of an elite to tolerate continued expansion of political rights or privileges. A major grievance in Dorr's Rebellion, for example, was the failure of the Rhode Island legislature to continue its expansion of suffrage.[69] On a much larger scale, Merriman argues that a factor in the Puritan Revolution of 1640–60 was the desire of townsmen, yeomen, country squires, and others of the middle classes for continued expansion of their political role, which was

[66] Soule, 22–30, quotations 26, 27.

[67] Henri Mendras and Yves Tavernier, "Les Manifestations de Juin 1961," *Révue Française de Sciences Politiques* XII (September 1962), 647–671.

[68] See Vernon Lee Fluharty, *Dance of the Millions: Military Rule and the Social Revolution in Colombia 1930–1956* (Pittsburgh: University of Pittsburgh Press, 1957), chap. 6.

[69] Davies, 8–10.

threatened by the fumbling and unpopular attempts of the Stuart kings, James I and Charles I, to restore some of the prerogatives of royal absolutism.[70] Attempts by George III to reestablish some measure of political control over the American colonies after a century of increasing political autonomy was clearly a major instigation to rebellion.[71] Among twentieth-century colonial peoples, political violence has often followed the imposition of restrictions after a period of expansion of political rights. The Mau Mau movement offers a case in point. During the 1920s and 1930s the Kenyan government had been increasingly responsive to African and especially Kikuyu political demands. A protest movement in 1921 against African wage reductions, for example, received favorable government action. During the 1930s and especially after 1945 the government gave considerable latitude to African political activity, whose leadership was predominantly provided by Western-educated Kikuyu. After 1945, however, the British government increased its encouragement of white settlement and was acquiescent to increasingly intransigent settler demands for greater political participation. The Mau Mau movement was an organized response of the most alienated young Kikuyu to these policies; it was relatively limited and largely intratribal until the declaration of the Emergency in October 1952 and the arrest of a number of nationalist leaders. In form, Mau Mau was largely a traditional response to oppression, but the frustrations which brought it about were those affecting Westernized Kenyans with intense, modernizing political demands, and it occurred only after a generation of gradual improvement in the political status of the Kenyans most committed to modern politics and its forms.[72]

Postcolonial restrictions on expanding political rights also has

[70] See Merriman, 27–50. For a review of other interpretations see Philip A. M. Taylor, ed., *The Origins of the English Civil War: Conspiracy, Crusade, or Class Conflict?* (Boston: D. C. Heath, 1960).

[71] On the origins of the American Revolution, see, for example, the selections in Edmund S. Morgan, ed., *The American Revolution: Two Centuries of Interpretation* (Englewood Cliffs, N.J.: Prentice-Hall, 1967), and John C. Miller, *Origins of the American Revolution* (Stanford: Stanford University Press, 1943, 1959).

[72] For comparable interpretations see Robert A. Le Vine, "Anti-European Violence in Africa: A Comparative Analysis," *Journal of Conflict Resolution,* III (December 1959), 423–424, and Carl G. Rosberg, Jr., and John Nottingham, *The Myth of "Mau Mau": Nationalism in Kenya* (New York: Praeger, 1966). The "traditionalist" nature of Mau Mau is a matter of some dispute; it has been suggested that many of its rites were borrowed from accounts of medieval European witchcraft, not from Kikuyu tradition. A more "nativistic" or decremental RD interpretation of the rebellion is Annette Rosenstiel, "An Anthropological Approach to the Mau Mau Problem," *Political Science Quarterly,* LXVIII (September 1953), 419–432. For the colonialist interpretation see F. D. Corfield, *Historical Survey of the Origin and Growth of Mau Mau* (London: H. M. Stationery Office, 1960).

been responsible for political violence in some countries. The post-1945 history of Ghana was one of fairly rapidly expanding political rights. At independence in 1957, the urban bourgeoisie had the longest tradition of political participation and influence (dating from the late-nineteenth century), but were gradually restricted in its exercise by the Nkrumah government, culminating in an almost complete exclusion from elective or appointive positions or party activity. The sporadic small-scale terrorism of the early 1960s and the popularly backed Army coup of February 1966 were apparent consequences. The identity of most of the terrorists has not been revealed; it is significant that many of the Army officers active in the coup were of urban bourgeois background.[73]

All the above examples associate political violence with the interruption of medium-to-long-range trends of economic and participatory mobility. Other statements and examples suggest that in some circumstances a marginal increase in value position, or simply a promise of reform, is sufficient to precipitate violence. This is particularly the case with political or governmental reforms in situations in which the masses have few or no means of political participation. De Tocqueville makes the general case:

> Only a great genius can save a prince who undertakes to relieve his subjects after a long oppression. The evil, which was suffered patiently as inevitable, seems unendurable as soon as the idea of escaping from it is conceived. All the abuses then removed seem to throw into greater relief those which remain, so that their feeling is more painful. The evil, it is true, has become less, but sensibility to it has become more acute. Feudalism at the height of its power had not inspired Frenchmen with so much hatred as it did on the event of its disappearing.[74]

The great revolutions again provide examples. In prerevolutionary France the calling of the Estates-General, for the first time in over 170 years, generated at first cautious and then exponentially increasing expectations among the bourgeoisie, the workers, and ultimately among the peasants that grievances of recent decades could be remedied.[75] In Russia before 1918, Pettee notes, "the utmost repression and occasional barbarism was accompanied by

[73] See Henry Bretton, *The Rise and Fall of Kwame Nkrumah: A Study of Personal Rule in Africa* (New York: Praeger, 1966).

[74] Alexis de Tocqueville, *L'Ancien Régime*, trans. M. W. Patterson (Oxford: Basil Blackwell, 1947), 186.

[75] Relevant interpretations include Hobsbawm, 80–84, and Georges Lefebvre, *The Coming of the French Revolution 1789*, trans. R. R. Palmer (Princeton: Princeton University Press, 1947), chaps. 5, 6.

spasmodic reforms in industry and politics."[76] Such efforts posed a threat to relatively privileged groups on the one hand; more importantly they raised great hopes among workers and disaffected members of the middle class. Even greater unsatisfied expectations can be attributed to the February 1917 revolution, some of whose leaders promised peace but whose government prosecuted war and, when attacked in October, found few willing to support it. Brinton says that one of the "most evident uniformities" among the revolutions he examined was that efforts were being made to reform the machinery of government.

> Nothing can be more erroneous than the picture of the old regime as an unregenerate tyranny, sweeping to its end in a climax of despotic indifference to the clamor of its abused subjects. Charles I was working to "modernize" his government. . . . George III and his ministers were trying very hard to pull together the scattered organs of British colonial government. . . . In both France and Russia, there is a series of attempted reforms. . . . It is true that these reforms were incomplete, that they were repealed or nullified by sabotage on the part of the privileged. But they are . . . an essential part of the process that issued in revolution in these countries.[77]

In most of these cases, however, the reforms that were promised, or hoped for, affected people who already had substantial and long-standing grievances. With the exception of the American colonies, where the effect of reforms was to restrict the privileges of the middle and upper classes, the attempts at partial reform seem to have generated widespread expectations that all grievances would be remedied. This interpretation suggests a corollary to hypothesis VE.5:

Corollary VE.5.1: Marginal increases in value capabilities among deprived groups tend to increase the salience of the groups' value expectations.

That is, a promise of improvement for deprived men intensifies their hopes that all the deprivations they have suffered in the past will be alleviated. If these hopes are soured, the consequences are virulent.

A number of contemporary cases can be cited in support of the generalization. Crozier suggests such an interpretation of events preceding four anti-Communist rebellions in the 1950s, including

[76] George S. Pettee, *The Process of Revolution* (New York: Harper, 1938), 94.
[77] Brinton, 51–52.

a revolt of North Vietnamese peasants in 1956 and the uprisings in Hungary, East Berlin, and perhaps Tibet. "The people revolted in a period of slight relaxation and disappointed hopes. It is scarcely surprising that disappointed hope should prove a stronger stimulus to rebellion than no hope at all."[78] The pattern is especially distinct in Hungary. The first period of liberalization in postwar Hungary began in 1953, after twelve years of severe political oppression and seven years of Communist rule, and led to some peasant unrest. In 1955, however, the Party elite closed ranks and instituted new repressive measures. The second relaxation of control began early in 1956 when the "thaw" that originated in the Soviet Union brought dissension in the elite into the open, led to the replacement of the Stalinist premier Rákosi, and increasing agitation for political reform that escalated into the student demonstrations in Budapest with which the revolution began. The two successive periods of relaxation unquestionably raised hopes among the Hungarian people, especially the intellectuals, professional people, and urban workers who were most subject to governmental repression, that major reforms were possible; there is little question from their statements that they thought them desirable. The expectation-intensifying effects of the first relaxation probably were greatest; the second seems to have demonstrated that the regime was too weak to resist satisfaction of those expectations. Kecskemeti writes,

> Hungarian revolutionary behavior was not a sudden desperate reaction to intolerable pressure and deprivation. It was, rather, a delayed reaction to all the negative experiences of the past, a reaction released when elements of weakness appeared in the image of the regime, and elements of strength bulked larger in one's own self-image.[79]

Two African examples suggest that the effect is not restricted to repressive monarchical or Communist regimes. Colonial and postcolonial violence repeatedly has been associated with promises and improvements in political and economic performance that aroused substantial but subsequently unfulfilled expectations. The insurrection in Madagascar in 1947–48, one of the least-known of the postwar colonial rebellions, was rooted at least in

[78] Brian Crozier, *The Rebels: A Study of Post-War Insurrections* (London: Chatto and Windus, 1960), 92–104, quotation 104. For supporting evidence see Stefan Brant, *The East German Rising* (New York: Praeger, 1957), and Paul Kecskemeti, *The Unexpected Revolution: Social Forces in the Hungarian Uprising* (Stanford: Stanford University Press, 1961).

[79] Kecskemeti, chaps, 2–8, quotation 117.

part in frustrated political expectations. Madagascar had a long tradition of precolonial political autonomy, and the dominion of its traditional land-holding elite had never been entirely destroyed by the French administration. The immediate events of the postwar years, in particular the activities of the nascent political party movement and the provisions of the constitution of the Fourth Republic regarding the conferral of self-government on colonial territories, raised political expectations among many groups, including the dominant Merina class, that went unsatisfied. The colonial administration at the same time became increasingly unresponsive to local problems. The insurrection which began in March 1947 had the avowed purpose of overthrowing the French administration and reestablishing independence, and was repressed at the cost of at least 11,000 lives.[80]

The experience of the Congo-Kinshasa after independence illustrates the same general pattern. The people of the Congo were more intensively exposed to European culture and education, and more of them mobilized into wage employment, than the people of almost any other tropical African country. Fox points out that as one consequence "the expectations, disappointments and frustrations of Congolese living in villages, centers, and cities are so similar as to be almost identical . . . a complex amalgam of 'traditional' and 'modern' elements. . . ."[81] The very rapid progress of the Congo toward independence in 1959 and 1960 raised expectations that all the oppressions and injustices of "Boula Matari" would be alleviated and that long-sought material riches would be obtained. The goal of *"le bien-être materiel"* subsequently was written into the preamble of the Congolese Constitution. The settling of accounts that accompanied independence in 1960 was a manifestation of the repressed hostilities against

[80] Crozier gives a brief summary, 199–201. A more comprehensive account appears in Virginia Thompson and Richard Adloff, *The Malagasy Republic: Madagascar Today* (Stanford: Stanford University Press, 1965), chaps. 3 and 4. A much different, essentially psychoanalytic, interpretation is suggested by O. Mannoni, *Prospero and Caliban: The Psychology of Colonization,* trans. Pamela Powesland (New York: Praeger, 1956, 1964), to the effect that the Malagasy felt a profound dependence on and inferiority to the colonial Europeans and this psychologically satisfying dependence was threatened by the abortive movement toward greater self-determination.

[81] Renée C. Fox, "The Case of Congo-Kinshasa" (paper read at the annual meeting of the African Studies Association, November 1967), 3–4. As evidence of the relative modernization of the Congolese, the Congo in the late 1950s ranked as follows among the thirty larger tropical African polities (excluding South Africa and Southern Rhodesia): first in literacy, fourth in proportion of school-age children in school, fourth in proportion of population in wage-and-salary employment, fourth in the proportion of adherents to Christianity, and seventh in urbanization.

colonial rule, but was largely over by 1961. A far more violent reaction to the disappointments of independence began with the Kwilu rebellion at the end of 1963, spreading rapidly in 1964 and 1965 throughout two-thirds of the nation. The new Congolese leaders had assumed all the privileges of the former rulers and inflicted greater oppression and injustice; their incompetence and the limitations of the economy sharply disillusioned the Congolese of their millennial expectations about the benefits of independence. The violence of their reaction can be judged from the fact that at least 50,000 Congolese died in the rebellions the Congolese called the "Second Independence" that followed.[82]

These cases demonstrate that collective violence is likely when discontented people are offered unfulfilled hopes that their discontents will be remedied. Neither the cases nor the corollary imply that anticipation of improvement necessarily leads to violence. The potential for violence can be minimized during years when widespread and intense RD is being remedied by a steady increase in capabilities. This in turn requires such policies as the continuous expansion of both value outputs and opportunities (chapter 5), the maintenance of patterns of control (chapter 8), and the strengthening of institutional loyalties (chapter 9).

* * *

To summarize some of the foregoing arguments, men are not likely to be mobilized by new, revolutionary hopes unless they feel sharply deprived by the circumstances in which they live (hypothesis VE.1). Exposure to a new way of life or to ideologies depicting a golden millennium seldom themselves generate either dissatisfaction or new expectations. But to the extent that men are already discontented and see opportunities open to them to attain those goals (hypothesis VE.2), they are strongly susceptible to ideological conversion. An especially violent, often revolutionary response is likely when men who have been persistently deprived of valued goods and conditions of life are led to believe that their government is about to remedy that deprivation, but then find the hopes false (corollary VE.5.1). Once socioeconomic change is underway within any segment of a society, other processes become operative. If a number of groups experience value gains, the most rapidly gaining groups are most likely to be chosen as the reference groups by which other men set their expectations (hy-

[82] This summary is based on Fox; Crawford Young, *Politics in the Congo* (Princeton: Princeton University Press, 1965), chap. 13; Renée C. Fox and others, "'The Second Independence': A Case Study of the Kwilu Rebellion in the Congo," *Comparative Studies in Society and History*, VIII (October 1965), 78–109; and my data.

pothesis VE.3). Moreover, those groups that do experience consistent increases in well-being develop expectations about continued improvement (hypothesis VE.5). The experience of growing well-being in one sector of life may generate expectations about greater well-being in others, but usually only to the extent that continued well-being in one sector proves dependent on well-being in the others (hypothesis VE.4).

Whether men are in fact able to satisfy their new expectations depends on the capacities of their societies for generating and distributing values. The following chapter examines some of the conditions that determine how these capacities are perceived.

5. Social Origins of Deprivation: Determinants of Value Capabilities

> Man and all the political, social, economic, religious, intellectual, aesthetic and psychological systems by which he has so far organized his life, are persistently being rendered incoherent. . . . This breaking of connections, and therefore the destruction of the capacity to deal with the most basic issues of social life, is the persistent and permanent challenge of the modern age.
>
> Manfred Halpern,
> "A Redefinition of the Revolutionary Situation" [1]

MEN'S VALUE CAPABILITIES are defined in chapter 2 as the value positions they perceive themselves capable of attaining and maintaining. They are, in other words, a function both of what men have and of what they believe they can attain. The most fundamental structural constraint on men's value capabilities is the stock of values available for distribution in a society. If a society has extensive resources and a demonstrated capacity to convert them into more satisfying conditions of life, and if people have varied and reasonably effective opportunities for sharing the benefits, perceived value capabilities are likely to be high. But if resources are limited and past value performance poor, or if opportunities are few and narrow, people are likely to have poor hopes for their future.

General Determinants of Value Capabilities

Four general patterns of experience and belief that limit men's value capabilities are identified in the following hypotheses. Subsequently, we will examine some characteristics of economic, belief, and political systems that demonstrate the relevance of the hypotheses to the genesis of particular kinds of political violence.

PERSPECTIVES ON VALUE STOCKS

Both intrinsic and perceived limitations on the availability of values in a society vary among societies and among groups within societies. A basic distinction is made in the theory of games between fixed- or zero-sum and variable-sum situations. In fixed-

[1] *Journal of International Affairs*, XXIII (No. 1, 1969), 57–58.

sum situations there is a fixed amount of a desired good or condition; any increase in one actor's position on that value necessarily entails a decrease in other actors' value positions. In variable-sum situations there may be either undistributed values (such as unused land, unoccupied elite positions) or the potential for increases in value stocks. Groups in a society whose members are in, or perceive themselves to be in, a fixed-sum situation are not necessarily in conflict with other groups. They may be satisfied with their value positions, or they may be willing to give up a less salient value for a more salient one, although their possibilities for doing so depend on the existence of other groups with expendable excess values. In some feudal societies, for example, freeholders and barons were willing to give up some of their participatory and economic values to a centralizing monarchy in exchange for an increase in security. The allocation process by which such exchanges are made or resisted can lead to a more or less equitable distribution both of values and of deprivations; but in any society with a fixed stock of values it is unlikely that there will be enough goods to satisfy all expectations. Even the equilibrium situation is inherently unstable because any intensification of the expectations of any group, or of any individual with great power, is likely to lead to demands and actions which disrupt the equilibrium—if indeed one ever existed.[2]

The dichotomous distinction between fixed-sum and variable-sum values may be applicable to gaming situations. For collectivities, value stocks are more usefully thought of in continuous terms: any value is more or less expandable, and values generally are perceived to be more or less expandable. The relevance of the distinction to the concept of value capabilities is nonetheless clear. In societies with relatively fixed or inflexible value stocks, value capabilities of most groups are likely to be static. Any value gain by one group is likely to reduce other groups' value positions, and to be perceived as declining value capabilities. In societies with relatively flexible value stocks, these consequences are less likely. It cannot be assumed, of course, that the actual availability of value stocks coincides with perceptions of their availability. There may be societies in which most or all values are perceived in zero-sum terms, even if it is technologically or politically feasible to increase value stocks. There also may be societies in which long-term socioeconomic progress has generated a pervasive optimism that values are infinitely expandable,

[2] The application of game-theory concepts to value analysis is developed by Karl W. Deutsch, "Some Quantitative Constraints on Value Allocation in Society and Politics," *Behavioral Science*, XI (July 1966), 245–252.

without reference to natural limitations imposed, for example, by diminishing resources. The Sprouts have shown that Britain in the 1950s and 1960s faced the dilemma of inadequate resources for continued growth, only partly resolved by governmental policies of shifting resource allocations and controls on consumption.[3] These are only qualifications to the basic relationships summarized in these two general hypotheses:

Hypothesis VC.1: Perceived value capabilities vary strongly with the extent to which value stocks in a society are perceived to be flexible.

Hypothesis VC.2: To the extent that the stock of any value in a society is perceived to be inflexible, perceived group capabilities for that value vary strongly and inversely with upward mobility of other groups on that value.

As an example, a zero-sum perspective on value stocks seems to be characteristic of many Latin American societies. "Subnational thinking" is Silvert's label for this mode of thought in Argentina. "Argentina's class-bound politics assume that no public measure can be good for almost everybody, that the benefit of one group is the automatic loss of all others. Life is an inelastic pie. . . ." The revolutionary reforms introduced under the Perón regime led to a counterrevolutionary response after his overthrow in 1955, which demonstrates the attitude in practice: "Argentines take it as axiomatic that increased freedom of action for lower groups between 1945 and 1955 implied a necessarily restricted freedom for others, and that with the fall of Perón nothing could have been more natural than a return to restriction of freedom for those below and a regrowth of freedom for those above." These shifts affected not only political freedom and participation but income as well; real wages for workers increased 35 percent between 1945 and 1951 but by 1958 had returned to 1945 levels, partly because of economic decline but also because of redistribution policies.[4] The same attitudes seem reflected in other Latin American practices: the obdurate resistance of landholders to land redistribution or to increasing productivity; the reluctance of many democratic leadres to permit effective participation by underclasses,

[3] Harold and Margaret Sprout, "The Dilemma of Insufficient Resources," *World Politics,* XX (July 1968), 660–693.

[4] Kalman H. Silvert, "The Costs of Anti-Nationalism: Argentina," in Silvert, ed., *Expectant Peoples: Nationalism and Development* (New York: Random House, 1963), 350–351. A similar zero-sum perspective on economic values is attributed to Cubans by Wyatt MacGaffey and Clifford Barnett, *Cuba: Its People, Its Society, Its Culture* (New Haven: Human Relations Area Files Press, 1962), 58.

and their unwillingness to give up power once obtained; the preference of many businessmen for lowering productivity and increasing prices in response to competition; and the resistance of the upper middle classes to upward status mobility by others.

Such generalizations are far from universally applicable; they may apply less to Mexico and Brazil than most other Latin countries. Zero-sum thinking nonetheless seems widely prevalent in the Latin cultures and appears to underlie much of the political turmoil of the continent. If any group's value gain tends to be regarded as another group's value loss (hypothesis VC.2), groups with rising expectations are likely to have low value capabilities and to believe that their expectations can be satisfied only by seizing what they want from those who have it. Similarly, increasing demands by any group are likely to threaten the value capabilities of other groups. Thus, Peruvian workers expect to use demonstrative violence to gain their political and economic demands, and employers and civilian regimes respond to those demands in proportion to the degree of threat.[5] Coups have been chronic, especially in the less-developed Latin countries, because political power was the only effective path to wealth thought to be open to ambitious men of nonelite background.[6] Radicals demand revolution rather than reform because they do not believe that the elites are willing to share or expand economic and power values, and the elites confirm the radicals' interpretation by responding to every demand for change as a threat of irreparable deprivation. Whether or not these attitudes are pervasive in Latin culture—and the evidence for their existence is indirect—they appear by no means idiosyncratic to Latin Americans, as examples in subsequent analysis suggest.

INFLEXIBILITIES IN VALUE PERFORMANCE AND OPPORTUNITIES

The expandability of value stocks at the societal level strongly influences, but is neither a necessary nor a sufficient condition of, high value capabilities for particular groups. The past experience of a group and its social circumstances are more immediate determinants of whether its members believe they can maintain

[5] See James Payne, "Peru: The Politics of Structured Violence," *Journal of Politics*, XXVII (May 1965), 362–374.

[6] On the correspondence between relative poverty and coups, 1907–1966, see Egil Fossum, "Factors Influencing the Occurrence of Military Coups d'État in Latin America," *Journal of Peace Research*, No. 3, 1967, 229–232. On the inferred motives of *golpistas* see Merle Kling, "Toward a Theory of Power and Political Instability in Latin America," *Western Political Quarterly*, IX (March 1956), 21–35.

or improve their condition. Hypothesis VE.4 (chapter 4) stipulates that collective experience of value gains generates expectations about continued value gains, a special case of the more general argument that people's previous experiences dominate their anticipations of the future. The analogous relationship is that groups which have had prolonged experience of stable or declining value positions are likely to expect those trends to continue, barring societal transformation or the group's conversion to doctrines of millennial change. If a group's economic or status position remains unchanged for generations, as it ordinarily did in traditional peasant societies, its members are likely to regard their capabilities as static. If people's share of economic, participatory, or other values begins to decline, as it did for Amerindians displaced by white settlement, they may at first anticipate a reversal of the trend, but the longer the decline continues the more hopeless they are likely to judge their prospects. In the long run, their value expectations tend to decline to coincide with their declining capabilities, as hypothesis ID.5 specifies (chapter 3), but the short-run effect is an increase in RD and hence in the potential for collective violence.

Hypothesis VC.3: Perceived value capabilities vary strongly and inversely with the rate of a group's past experience of value loss.

The sense of incapacity caused by zero-sum perspectives on values, and static or declining group value position, can be intensified or minimized by a group's immediate societal circumstances. Hypothesis ID.4, developed in chapter 3, specifies that the intensity of RD varies with the proportion of individuals' value opportunities blocked. It was suggested that RD could be decreased at least temporarily by increasing the number and variety of value opportunities. Hypothesis VC.4, below, generalizes this relationship as it applies to collective value capabilities: any increase in the courses of value-enhancing action open to members of a group increases their value capabilities, any decrease reduces them. These relationships hold irrespective of value stocks available for distribution in a society. Even if material goods are limited, for example, young men usually can increase their personal opportunities for economic well-being by acquiring technical skills. Similarly, participatory values are inherently inflexible, but expansion of channels for political participation and broadening of the base of recruitment for elite positions increases the societal opportunities of newly eligible groups. Such expansions of franchise and elite eligibility also increase the affected groups' political opportunities: participation, in addition to being intrinsically valued, is a base value that can be used to enhance welfare, security, and interpersonal values.

Hypothesis VC.4: Perceived value capabilities vary strongly with the number and range of value opportunities open to a group's members.

The inverse relationship is that any decrease in a group's value opportunities tends to reduce its value capabilities, even if value stocks are large and increasing. A special case of this relationship is the situation of groups in developing societies whose members are denied the use of value opportunities open to some other groups. Hypothesis VE.3 (chapter 4) implies that group value expectations for welfare and participatory values, for example, are likely to increase during processes of economic expansion and political democratization. This is likely even for groups that do not share in the benefits of expansion, because of their identification with more mobile reference groups. Hypothesis VE.5 implies that members of a group which experiences some gains will expect more. If opportunities are differentially low for these groups, their perceived capabilities are likely to be especially low and their sense of grievance intense. The following corollary is suggested:

Corollary VC.4.1: The greater the rate of expansion of value stocks in a society, the greater the intensity of relative deprivation among groups with differentially low value opportunities.

A group's value opportunities are *differentially low* if its members are barred on ascriptive grounds from using value-enhancing techniques open to other groups. Workers who are barred from some types of employment because of their ethnic or social status, and union members whose right to collective bargaining is restricted by governmental action, are likely to be more intensely discontented in a growing economy than in a static one. In an analysis of the correlates of civil violence in Western and Eastern European nations in the early 1960s we found evidence of a similar relationship: violence was greatest in those countries experiencing rapid economic expansion and simultaneous static or declining educational opportunities.[7] Other examples are the

[7] Ted Gurr with Charles Ruttenberg, *The Conditions of Civil Violence: First Tests of a Causal Model* (Princeton: Center of International Studies, Princeton University, Research Monograph No. 28, 1967), 99.

discriminatory barriers which have restricted the educational mobility of French-Canadians vis-à-vis English-speaking Canadians, and which have kept professionally trained black Americans from getting jobs with pay and status equal to those of whites with comparable training. RD is not necessarily inherent in racial, ethnic, or class discrimination; discrimination is a source of RD only if the affected groups aspire to more than their "betters" are prepared to let them have. But the greater the rate of growth or "progress" in a society, the greater the likelihood that differential lack of opportunity to share in its benefits will be intensely resented.

* * *

A general question raised by the foregoing hypotheses is: What properties of social systems contribute to the zero-sum perspectives on values and to the restrictions on value output and distribution which give so many groups, sometimes whole societies, dim prospects for realizing their members' expectations? A necessarily partial answer to this question is provided by an analysis of some of the inherent and socially created limitations on the performance of social and political systems. Some sources of low output of welfare, interpersonal, and power values are separately examined in the following three sections, with special reference to those theoretically and empirically associated with political violence. It is beyond the scope of this analysis to summarize all such properties of social systems, or to develop formal hypotheses that relate them causally to political violence through the set of intervening variables examined thus far, namely value capabilities and scope and intensity of RD. The causal connections will nonetheless be apparent in the discussion.

Welfare Value Capabilities and Political Violence

Most welfare values are inherently flexible, though in different degrees among types of societies and according to the perspectives of groups within them. Deutsch points out that economic values are variable-sum to the extent that "unused factors of production can be brought quickly into play, in adequately balanced combinations, as required by current production functions." He proposes a similar interpretation for the flexibility of the other Lasswellian values I have summarily labeled welfare values (see chapter 2, table 1):

> Well-being, skill and enlightenment can also be procured in some considerable measure by almost every mature individual for himself and by his own efforts. To the extent that well-being,

> skill, and enlightenment can thus be produced autonomously by individuals for themselves—or by small groups for their members—the allocation of these values . . . becomes a variable-sum game.

But these are less subject to impersonal exchange among individuals than economic goods per se.[8]

Economic goods can be expanded to the extent that a society has unused natural resources; technology and skills to make use of them; labor to apply those skills to resources; capital to provide labor with the tools to work; societal structures capable of organizing these factors of production and of distributing new outputs; and systems of beliefs and norms that make cooperation possible in carrying out production and distribution. The first four factors are to some extent substitutable, but in the absence of all of them there can be no expansion of economic goods. In such a situation no group can attain more or aspire to attain more without restricting others' value capabilities (hypothesis VC.2). If the economic expectations of some groups do increase, the consequent instigation to political violence is greater than that caused by a similar increase in a society with rising economic performance. In the latter, aspirational RD for one group does not necessarily imply decremental RD for another; in the former it does. A special aspect of this argument concerns the effects of government policies of economic value redistribution. A regime can induce the perception of rising economic capabilities in a large portion of a population, even in an economically static society, by taking symbolic actions such as expropriating the wealth of a minority. The rising expectations of the larger groups are thus temporarily satisfied at the expense of a numerically small group, i.e. such policies are symbolic evidence for the poor and landless that the political system is capable of improving their condition. But if redistributions or economic development plans do not increase economic value stocks, the long-range effect is to increase the instigation to political violence: expectations that are intensified by marginal increases in value capabilities lead to virulent grievances if the expectations prove unattainable (corollary VC.5.1).

Another general point is that economic values are more salient for most people than other values, partly because some minimal level of economic goods is necessary for continued physical existence. Men also tend to be more sensitive to small changes in economic value position than to changes on other values because the degree to which they are attained in monetary societies, and

[8] Deutsch, 248–249, quotation 249.

many nonmonetary ones as well, is easily expressed in quantitative terms. Individuals tend to think of their economic well-being in terms of monthly incomes of *X* dollars or cruzeros, or possession of *Y* number of cattle, or cultivation of *Z* hectares of rice paddy. Such a calculus is seldom available for their social status, their security, or their political participation. There is nonetheless a natural threshold below which economic impoverishment will not lead to revolt, whatever men's expectations, namely the "starvation threshold." If economic deprivation is so great that men are reduced to or below the level of physical subsistence, they are literally incapable of rebellion. The point is very nearly a cliché in the literature, for example Hobsbawm: "When people are really hungry they are too busy seeking food to do much else; or else they die"; [9] and Hoffer: "To be engaged in a desperate struggle for food and shelter is to be wholly free from a sense of futility." [10] Men often have rioted for more food, for example in the price-reducing "bread riots" of eighteenth-century England and France, but it is evident that their participants were far from starvation. They were responding to rising prices that threatened starvation, not to its actual presence. The impetus to violence increases as men's economic value position drops towards the subsistence margin, but decreases sharply when the margin is reached.

When economic values are inflexible and men live close to the subsistence margin, almost any marginal economic decline can precipitate violence. Natural disasters like drought and plague have frequently led to turmoil, especially in peasant societies. Increases in taxes or food prices have repeatedly had the same effects. In the classic jacquerie, *les effrois* of northern France in 1358 broke out when the ineffectual French nobility required the peasantry to pay taxes to ransom nobility captured by the English at Poitiers.[11] Resentment against new demands for taxation was a fundamental cause of the elite and mass Catalonian rebellion against the Castilian crown in 1640–52, and of the revolt of the Neapolitan people against Spanish rule in 1647, as it was a factor in four other mid-seventeenth century antimonarchical revolutions.[12] Of some 275 riots in rural England between 1735 and

[9] E. J. Hobsbawm, *Social Bandits and Primitive Rebels* (New York: The Free Press, 1959), 79.

[10] Eric Hoffer, *The True Believer: Thoughts on the Nature of Mass Movements* (New York: Harper, 1951), 26.

[11] Maurice Dommanget, *La Jacquerie: 600 anniversaire des "Effrois"* (Creil, l'Oise: Syndicate des instituteurs de l'Oise, 1958), summarized in Chalmers Johnson, *Revolution and the Social System* (Stanford: Hoover Institution of War, Revolution and Peace, Stanford University, 1964), 31–32.

[12] Roger Merriman, *Six Contemporaneous Revolutions* (Oxford: Clarendon Press, 1938), passim.

1800, Rudé finds that two-thirds were occasioned by a shortage or sudden rise in the price of food.[13] Western Pennsylvanian farmers rose in rebellion in 1794 against the new government because of the imposition of taxes on the whiskey they distilled.[14]

Dislocations of production are frequently cited causes of declines in economic performance that lead to collective violence in economically transforming societies. Changes in economic structure often push some groups of workers into chronic unemployment and violent protest. Unemployment in the textile industry of the Vendée, beginning in the 1780s, generated beggary, banditry, political agitation, many localized acts of collective violence, and ultimately provided many of the most active participants in the Vendée counterrevolution of 1793.[15] A century earlier London silk-weavers had repeatedly rioted and demonstrated against the impact on their trade of French workers, French imports, and the introduction of the engine-loom.[16] In the twentieth century the closing of unproductive coal mines in Appalachia, Wales, Belgium, and the Ruhr has led to worker violence. Inflation similarly is associated with collective violence, especially when it occurs in economically static societies, where its typical effect is income redistribution that imposes decremental RD on workers with low economic bargaining power.[17] War also is a common source of economic dislocation leading to violence. After World War I, Italy suffered the effects of demobilization, unemployment, and a rising cost of living, as well as continual political crises and ineffective government. At the end of 1920 there were about 100,000 unemployed, increasing to 600,000 at the beginning of 1922, a measure both of worsening economic conditions and of potential recruits for the Fascisti, many of whom followed Mussolini in his march on Rome in the fall of 1922.[18] Similar dislocations had comparable effects throughout postwar Europe.

The relationship between economic decline and collective

[13] George Rudé, *The Crowd in History, 1730–1848* (New York: Wiley, 1964), 47–65.

[14] See Leland D. Baldwin, *Whiskey Rebels: The Story of a Frontier Uprising* (Pittsburgh: University of Pittsburgh Press, 1939).

[15] Charles Tilly, *The Vendée* (Cambridge: Harvard University Press, 1964), 308–314.

[16] Max Beloff, *Public Order and Popular Disturbances 1660–1714* (London: Frank Cass, 1938, 1963), 82–87.

[17] Long-term inflation was an underlying cause of extensive rioting in Chile in 1957. See Kalman H. Silvert, *The Conflict Society: Reaction and Revolution in Latin America* (New Orleans: Hauser Press, 1961), 194–196.

[18] F. L. Carsten, *The Rise of Fascism* (Berkeley: University of California Press, 1967), chap. 2.

violence is so widely recognized that studies designed to assess the relative importance of the relationship in various types of societies and among different forms of violence are more needed than further case-study documentation. As preliminary evidence on this question, a cross-national study shows that for 114 nations in the early 1960s a composite measure of short-term economic deprivation correlates .44 with magnitude of civil strife. In other words about 20 percent of the variation among contemporary nations in levels of strife is attributable to relative economic decline.[19]

Some examples of welfare values that are *not* flexible can also be mentioned. A notable one is life itself, which when threatened or restricted by military conscription, for example, has often led to political violence. The most severe, violent manifestations of French-Canadian separatism before 1968 occurred during the two world wars, in response to governmental attempts to impose conscription.[20] The announcement of conscription was the deprivation that precipitated the Vendée counterrevolution in postrevolutionary France.[21] The bloodiest riot in American history occurred in New York City in July 1863 in protest of a new draft quota; the riot lasted four days during which an estimated 500 people were killed.[22] Opposition to the draft was a primary motive in the antiwar protest movement in the United States during the 1960s; between 1965 and fall of 1968 an estimated 700,000 people participated in some 170 antiwar demonstrations, about twenty-five of which involved significant violence.[23] Land is an inflexible value in most peasant societies, and threats to land itself, its uses, or the conditions of its tenure have often been sources of violent protest. For example, in Tanganyika's mountainous Morogoro District the imposition of a terracing scheme for land conservation in the early 1950s not only failed to improve productivity but appeared to threaten traditional tenure practices. Traditional political leaders capitalized on the consequent deprivation; the subsequent rioting during the last half of 1955 resulted in temporary loss of government control of the area and

[19] Ted Gurr, "A Causal Model of Civil Strife: A Comparative Analysis Using New Indices," *American Political Science Review*, LXII (December 1968), 1117.

[20] Frank L. Wilson, "French-Canadian Separatism," *Western Political Quarterly*, XX (March 1967), 116–131.

[21] Tilly, 308–314.

[22] Willard A. Heaps, *Riots U.S.A. 1765–1965* (New York: Seabury Press, 1966), chap. 6. A fuller account is David Garson, "The Politics of Collective Violence in America: 1863–1963" (Ph.D. dissertation, Department of Government, Harvard University, 1969), chap. 2.

[23] My summary of data reported by Irving Louis Horowitz, "The Struggle is the Message" (Paper prepared for the Task Force on Group Protest and Violence, National Commission on the Causes and Prevention of Violence, September 1968).

abandonment of the scheme.[24] The Hukbalahap rebellion that began in the Philippines in 1945 was motivated largely by grievances over the oppressive nature of share-cropping tenancy practiced on the haciendas of Central Luzon, where a feudal subjugation of tenant to master was reinforced by a system of credit at high interest that kept the peasant perpetually in debt. Peasants do not always or necessarily rebel over the lack of or threats to land, but land is very often a common denominator among the diverse deprivations that motivate peasant rebellions.[25]

Short-term economic declines are all but inevitable in modernizing societies, and the consequent declines in perceived economic capabilities are likely to increase potentials for collective violence. But most of these conditions are subject, in theory and in the eyes of many of the world's people, to manipulation and control by the governing institutions of society. Moreover, economic value stocks are flexible in almost every society. Most societies have either some unused factors of production or at least the means to obtain them through cooperation with other nations. The principal obstacles to mobilization of these factors, and to minimization of disruptive economic conflict, are the lack of effective ideologies of cooperation and development, and the lack of appropriate political arrangements. High economic value performance requires high interpersonal and power value capabilities, some of whose aspects are examined below.

Interpersonal Value Capabilities and Political Violence

IDEATIONAL COHERENCE

Some of the most general explanations of the origins of revolution and other forms of collective violence attribute it to the loss of ideational coherence: men's loss of faith in, or lack of consensus about, the beliefs and norms that govern social interaction. Ideational coherence is both ends and means, and consequently

[24] Roland Young and Henry A. Fosbrooke, *Smoke in the Hills: Political Tension in the Morogoro District of Tanganyika* (Evanston: Northwestern University Press, 1960), 141–167.

[25] On the Hukbalahaps see Alvin H. Scaff, *The Philippine Answer to Communism* (Stanford: Stanford University Press, 1955); Frances Lucille Starner, *Magsaysay and the Philippine Peasantry: The Agrarian Impact on Philippine Politics, 1953–1956* (Berkeley: University of California Press, 1961); and Edward J. Mitchell, "Some Econometrics of the Huk Rebellion," *American Political Science Review*, LXIII (December 1969). For a critical examination of evidence about the motives for peasant participation in political violence see Gil Carl AlRoy, *The Involvement of Peasants in Internal Wars* (Princeton: Center of International Studies, Princeton University, Research Monograph No. 24, 1966).

the loss of coherence is both a decline in value position and a decline in value opportunities. The argument for regarding ideational coherence as an end, i.e. an intrinsically valued condition, is that people have a need for beliefs which provide an interpretation of the world, and norms which relate that interpretation to their daily behavior. If members of a group hold a set of beliefs and norms they believe to be correct, they have a high ideational value position. To the extent that they experience conflict among competing ideational systems, find some norms irrelevant to concrete situations, or lose faith in general social myths, their value positions are low. Ideational coherence also affects men's value opportunities. If they hold norms of goal-seeking behavior which facilitate attainment of their value expectations, then their value opportunities are by definition adequate (chapter 2), though not necessarily numerous or diverse. But if the norms people have accepted in the past become less appropriate to their goals, then their value capabilities are likely to decline.[26]

One implication of this interpretation is that ideational systems seldom lose their coherence in a social vacuum. Ideational disintegration usually is a consequence of other conditions: culture contact with divergent practices or beliefs or, more commonly, long-term loss of other values because of structural malfunction or ecological change. Several writers make this point. Pettee, for example, remarks that "frustrated men will question the symbols which lead them into frustration, and according to their capability for participation they will invent or find new ones."[27] Johnson similarly suggests that "only occasionally is an innovation produced or accepted in . . . the value structure." Most disequilibrating changes, he suggests, arise not in the ideational system but as a consequence of environmental changes or technological innovations which demonstrate the inapplicability of beliefs and norms.[28] A case in point is Schuman's interpretation of the success of the Nazi movement. The fundamental cause was economic RD, whose lack of resolution was popularly associated with "the degradation of . . . symbols of patriotism" and the absence of a strong state authority embodying principles and symbols that could be respected and obeyed. The Nazi theory of the state, based on the *Führerprinzip,* the role of personal leader-

[26] This is a recapitulation of the effects attributed to anomie in chap. 2, 42–44.

[27] George S. Pettee, *The Process of Revolution* (New York: Harper, 1938), 45.

[28] Johnson, *Revolutionary Change,* 65–67, quotation 67. Also see Neil J. Smelser, *Theory of Collective Behavior* (New York: The Free Press, 1963), 59–64, 287–292, 338–347.

ship, symbolized "the emotional satisfaction of having found at last in Hitler a symbol of absolute authority. . . ."[29] The argument that the sense of ideational incoherence is largely a function of declining capabilities for the attainment of other valued goods and conditions, can be stated as a corollary to hypothesis ID.3, which specifies a causal relationship between the proportion of values affected by RD and the intensity of RD:

Corollary ID.3.1: The greater the intensity of relative deprivation with respect to welfare, power, status, and communal values, the greater the likely decline in ideational coherence.

Two somewhat different causal connections are proposed in the literature between the loss of ideational coherence and the occurrence of political violence. One is that loss of coherence leads to a breakdown in the social order, which, for reasons not always specified, leads to violence. Sebastian de Grazia, for example, attributes revolutionary violence to "acute anomie," a state of profound anxiety which is said to arise from the deterioration and disintegration of belief systems. He distinguishes such deterioration from simple anomie, confusion among members of a group due to conflict among belief systems, which does not have revolutionary consequences.[30] Heberle accounts for the rise of all social movements, including revolution, in terms of the loss of the "sense of community":

> Dissatisfaction with a social order arises when individuals no longer consider the values and norms on which the order is based to be the best or only possible values and norms. The agreement on social values and norms is the essence of social solidarity. . . . The sense of community is the foundation of any social order.[31]

A variation of this argument attributes revolution to elite or mass loss of faith in specifically political myths. "We may regard it as an established historical law," wrote Michels, "that races, legal systems, institutions, and social classes, are inevitably doomed to destruction from the moment they or those who represent them

[29] Frederick L. Schuman, *The Nazi Dictatorship: A Study in Social Pathology and the Politics of Fascism* (New York: Knopf, 1935), 107–108, 123.

[30] Sebastian de Grazia, *The Political Community: A Study of Anomie* (Chicago: University of Chicago Press, 1948), especially 72–74.

[31] Rudolph Heberle, *Social Movements: An Introduction to Political Sociology* (New York: Appleton-Century-Crofts, 1951), 454–455.

have lost faith in their future."[32] Lasswell and Kaplan's version of the proposition is that political stability depends upon the intensity of conviction among both elite and mass in the political doctrines that sustain the elite.[33] Janos provides a final example: the first step in the process of revolution "is a decline in social consensus. Doubts arise concerning the policies and aspirations of the ruling classes, and the doubts are followed by popular withdrawal and alienation."[34]

The second kind of causal argument is that the loss of ideational coherence is accompanied, either as cause or effect, by the appearance of competing belief systems. Conflict between adherents of the several belief systems then leads to violence. Deutsch suggests that belief systems usually are regarded in zero-sum terms, when several belief systems are operative in a system. His argument is worth quoting at length. If a set of beliefs

> prescribes a corresponding code of conduct, if the believer has internalized this code, and if he now perceives himself as living up to it, he is also likely to experience a gain in his own feelings of righteousness. . . .
>
> At any moment, its experience is to a large extent internal to the individual. . . . In fact, however, righteousness contains a large and often crucial interpersonal component. It is from other persons, particularly from their own families, and ultimately from society, that individuals learn the codes of conduct which they then make their own and from which they then draw some of their self-respect. . . .
>
> To the extent that the value of righteousness depends upon interpersonal relations, it is subject to processes of social and political allocation, and to the distinction between zero-sum and variable-sum games. Governments can lend support and legitimacy to the learning and acting out of certain moral codes, while penalizing and frustrating the observance of others, or associating them with intolerable conflicts with the pursuit of other values.

[32] Robert Michels, *Political Parties: A Sociological Study of the Oligarchical Tendencies of Modern Democracy*, trans. Eden and Cedar Paul (Glencoe: The Free Press, 1915, 1949), 243.

[33] Harold Lasswell and Abraham Kaplan, *Power and Society: A Framework for Political Inquiry* (New Haven: Yale University Press, 1950), 270.

[34] Andrew Janos *The Seizure of Power: A Study of Force and Popular Consent* (Princeton: Center of International Studies, Princeton University, Research Monograph No. 16, 1964), 4.

> To the extent that society and government can only support, tolerate, or facilitate the observance of a rigidly limited set of codes, politics and ethics become once more a zero-sum game. *Any gain for one code, religion, philosophy, or view of morality can occur only to the detriment of others.*[35]

Deutsch points out that societies, and governments, can enhance men's capacities to tolerate a wide range of codes of conduct. But many coherent communities, including entire traditional societies and many smaller groups in modern societies, have a very limited tolerance for competing systems of beliefs and norms. By its very existence a competing code of beliefs and behavior may raise questions about the validity of one's own views, and hence inflict deprivation.

General theories of revolutionary causation often emphasize ideological incoherence and conflict. Pettee's concept of "ideological cramp" is an example. "In an integrated society all men's wills are governed by a commonly accepted system of symbols, which constitute common standards of reference." Mediation of this sytem, or myth, to the mass is the "whole social function of the leadership. . . . Without it there would be no cultural continuity." Social solidarity and political power are weakest where mediation is least coherent. In general, "any society in which opposed myths are present is to a degree subject to disintegration and faction. This . . . contributes to cramp through the confusion and disorder of cross purposes."[36] Three contemporary sociological explanations speculate more precisely about the kinds of ideational incoherence which have revolutionary consequences. In summary comparison, revolutionary potential is attributed by Stinchcombe to lack of consensus on the means or norms of interorganizational competition; by Feldman to lack of interorganizational consensus on goal hierarchies; and by Johnson to competition between adherents of alternative ideational systems.

Stinchcombe says that revolutionary potential in modernizing societies is a function of instability in the stratification system of society caused by a shift from an emphasis on ranking of individuals or families to a ranking of organizations. This shift is accompanied by a lack of consensus on the relative ranks of organizations, and lack of commitment by their leaders to norms governing

[35] Deutsch, 249–250. "Righteousness" as Deutsch uses it corresponds rather closely with my concept of ideational coherence. A psychological discussion of the zero-sum nature of conflicts between belief systems appears in Jerome Frank, *Sanity and Survival: Psychological Aspects of War and Peace* (New York: Vintage Books, 1967, 1968), 131–132.

[36] Pettee, 42–45.

the interorganizational distribution of values. This ideational incoherence, in my terms, is manifested in a lack of restraint in competition among organizations, leading to either the growth of uncontrolled coercion by governments, or the growth of unrestrained opposition to governments, or both.[37] Feldman similarly focuses on the process of social differentiation in societies undergoing modernization. Differentiation involves the creation of new systems, which constitute norms that are "more *internally consistent* and *externally discontinuous*" than those of older systems. The goals of these systems are likely to come increasingly in conflict, not because of goal changes but because different goal hierarchies develop among subsystems. "When such goal changes are either relatively rapid or relatively unpredictable . . . revolutionary potential should be quite high."[38] Johnson is concerned with the sources and consequences of disintegration of society wide sets of norms and beliefs. One of the two necessary conditions of revolution is said to be disequilibrium between environment and "value systems," the shared cognitions which provide people with definitions of situations and standards of behavior. Value systems provide justification for the division of labor and legitimation for authority; they also typically comprise norms through which conflicts can be resolved. Patterns of value-environmental synchronization may deteriorate because of exogenous sources of value change, e.g. various kinds of external demonstration effects, or by endogenous sources of change, specifically articulation of new value systems or symbols by innovative individuals or groups. The consequence of these changes, if sudden or intense, may be to destroy procedures for self-maintenance, and to make men receptive to new ideologies which facilitate resynchronization of a system. "Given sufficient time . . . an ideology will cause the disequilibrated society to divide into one group of allies seeking to change the structure of the system and another seeking to maintain it."[39]

An example of rebellion instigated by conflict between competing belief systems is the antigovernment uprising of members of

[37] Arthur L. Stinchcombe, "Social Structure and Organization," in James G. March, ed., *Handbook of Organization* (Chicago: Rand McNally, 1965), 169–180. Stinchcombe cites several variables that minimize the revolutionary consequences of unrestrained competition: normative limitations on military and police coercion; the availability of other means of competition; and elite socialization into cooperative activity.

[38] Arnold Feldman, "Violence and Volatility," in Harry Eckstein, ed., *Internal War: Problems and Approaches* (New York: The Free Press, 1964), quotations from 122, 123.

[39] Johnson, *Revolutionary Change*, 15–39, 64–87. Environmental changes are said to have the same effect. For a parallel interpretation see Smelser, 247.

the Lumpa religious sect of Northern Rhodesia during July and August, 1964. Such separatist African churches are said to offer "purification and hope, intense group identification, a sense of individual worth and self-accommodation" for those caught up in the tensions of culture change. Among the Lumpas, however, these beliefs were under steady pressure from the United National Independence Party (UNIP), as well as from orthodox religious bodies, beginning in the late 1950s. The Lumpas formally withdrew from political activity in 1963 on the ideological grounds "that politics was a kind of terrestrial witchcraft." The UNIP, however, continued to demand that Lumpas join the Party, and had set July 20, 1964, as the date for the Lumpas to leave the stockaded villages they had built in a collective response to these pressures. Fernandez interprets the uprising as "a reaction to the movement's situation of increasing insecurity in the face of growing political and orthodox mission hostility."[40] In the terms of this analysis, the demands of the UNIP were a major threat to the coherence of the beliefs which had helped the tribesmen accommodate themselves to the deprivations inflicted by erratic socioeconomic change.

An equally important characteristic of competing belief systems that affects the genesis of collective violence is that they establish general lines of social cleavage and targets for violence resulting from other factors. The effect of exposure to adherents of contrary beliefs and different codes of behavior may itself be only mildly threatening, far below the threshold of violence. But if adherents of one belief have been disliked in previous circumstances by another group, they can become targets for violence arising from subsequent deprivations, whatever the source of those deprivations. The psychological basis for this focusing or "scapegoating" effect of intergroup hostility is discussed in the following chapter.

The history of relations between groups of different social beliefs affords many examples of genocide, civil war, communal rioting, repression, discrimination, and defensive withdrawal. It also affords enough examples of assimilation, coexistence, and cooperative interaction to demonstrate that one group's ideational coherence is not necessarily a threat to a different group's beliefs. Groups holding different social myths have sometimes been able to live in close association without doing violence to one

[40] James W. Fernandez, "The Lumpa Uprising: Why?" *Africa Report*, IX (November 1964), 30–32. For background on the Lumpa Church see Robert Rotberg, "The Lenshina Movement of Northern Rhodesia," *Rhodes-Livingstone Institute Journal*, XXIX (June 1961), 63–78.

another because in some cases they reinterpreted their myths so that they appeared mutually compatible; in others because of norms of tolerance for diverse beliefs held by one or both groups; and in still others, including heterogenous Western societies, because many people have become accustomed through repeated exposure to a diversity of beliefs and practices among their neighbors.[41]

STATUS

Unsatisfied group status aspirations and the resistance of higher status groups to those aspirations are often cited as sources of collective violence. Deutsch, in his analysis of value flexibility, says of prestige (status) that its allocation is a variable-sum game "so long as additional capacities for mutual attention, communication, and responsiveness can be brought into play rapidly. . . ."[42] The perquisites of status may be flexible in absolute terms, but in relative terms only one group can occupy the top of a status hierarchy. If *relative* status is valued more than such specific status perquisites as mutual attention and responsiveness, status is a zero-sum value and the games played for it have potentially violent consequences which are well-documented in contemporary and historical analyses.

Fascist movements in Western Europe were rooted in the relative loss of status by marginal middle-class groups. Lipset asserts that the principal support for Austrian, Italian, and German Fascism of the 1920s and 1930s, and for Poujadism and McCarthyism in the 1950s, came from the "small independents" of rural areas and provincial cities, "the declining 'liberal' classes living in declining areas. The petty bourgeoisie of these sections not only suffer deprivation because of the relative decline of their class, they are also citizens of communities whose status and influence within the larger society is rapidly declining." Declining value positions lead to low value capabilities and growing discontent for these groups, and discontent in turn "leads them to

[41] Some cases of relatively peaceful coexistence among culturally diverse groups are described by F. B. Tolles, "Non-violent Contact: The Quakers and the Indians," *Proceedings of the American Philosophical Society*, CVII (April 15, 1963), 93–101; Morton Klass, *East Indians in Trinidad: A Study of Cultural Persistence* (New York: Columbia University Press, 1961); and R. E. Crow, "Religious Sectarianism in the Lebanese Political System," *Journal of Politics*, XXIV (August 1962), 489–520. Tensions and violence are more common, of course. R. I. Burns describes extended Christian rioting against Moslems of the conquered Moorish kingdom of Valencia, despite evolution of a philosophy of tolerance toward the Moslems by clerics and lawyers, in "Social Riots on the Christian-Moslem Frontier (Thirteenth-Century Valencia)," *American Historical Review*, LXVI (January 1961), 378–400.

[42] Deutsch, 248.

accept diverse irrational protest ideologies."[43] The frustration of lower-class aspirations for status mobility also leads to political protest. Lipset attributes leftist protest voting to unsatisfied needs for income security, satisfying work, and "social recognition of one's value and freedom from degrading discrimination in social relations."[44] When workers demand status that is not accorded by higher classes because it threatens their own status and prestige, one has the ingredients of a classic zero-sum game that Alfred de Grazia calls the "class war" of modern European nations:

> Ranked against one another are the working classes who appeal to the universal principle of equality, and the middle classes who feel their social rank slipping. While many industrial workers are organizing, gaining higher pay and better working conditions, and claiming that the future belongs to them, many members of the middle class are finding clerical skills less rare and less valued than in the past. They are losing their financial advantage over manual workers and are finding promotion to positions of ownership or high income more difficult to achieve. The upper ranks of society also are directly threatened; the deference, the honor, the bows, the respectful address given their status for centuries hang at issue in the class struggle. . . . The use of violence by one class against another, then, is more easily understood when one appreciates the threat that an aggressive working class poses to the classes above it.[45]

The perceived incapacity of upwardly mobile Africans and Asians to satisfy their status expectations was and is a source of instigation to violence in colonial and postcolonial societies. The peasants who migrated to colonial cities often gained welfare values that compensated for the sometimes severe interpersonal deprivations they suffered; their children, educated in Western ways, frequently developed status expectations whose satisfaction was firmly resisted by white societies. An example of this is provided by the leaders of the Nyasaland "rising" of 1915, the first modernizing rather than traditionalist rebellion in tropical Africa. The leaders were "educated natives" or "proto-intellectuals," marginal men who had sought education for its personal and social advantages. A number owned stores or small estates, and John

[43] Seymour M. Lipset, *Political Man: The Social Bases of Politics* (Garden City: Doubleday, 1960), 70.

[44] *Ibid.*, chap. 7, especially 232, 238.

[45] Alfred de Grazia, *Politics and Government*, Vol. 1, *Political Behavior*, rev. edn. (New York: Collier, 1952, 1962), 273.

Chilembwe, the rebellion's leader, was the founder and director of a prosperous mission station. Yet these men, ambitious for acceptance by Europeans as well as for economic goods, were repeatedly exposed to European prejudices and hostilities. These often were petty, sometimes severe: whites expected that if Nyasa Africans had the temerity to wear a hat and "ape the European" they should raise it when meeting a white; shopkeepers refused to serve Africans in European dress; Chilembwe and his wife were excluded from local white society; three churches of his mission were burned on grounds that they were potential centers of agitation against the management of an adjacent European plantation. It is clear that many members of this nascent bourgeoisie

> felt a strong sense of frustration, part of which may have been the result of a sense of their own failure to adopt European methods and manners as effectively as they wished, and part from the economic, political and social circumstances of the Protectorate which did not operate in favour of the rapid advancement of aspiring Africans.[46]

Power Values and Political Violence

The distribution and uses of power values in a political system have two rather different effects on the value capabilities of its members. If the circulation of elite individuals is high and opportunities for political participation wide, citizens' power value capabilities are likely to be high. Desires for participation and leadership seem to motivate some men in every society; if power values are not widely shared, their participatory RD is likely to be intense. The second and more general effect of power on value capabilities is a function of its potential and actual uses to remedy deprivations. Power can be used, and in most contemporary societies is expected to be used, to remedy the sources of discontent. It can be used to increase the societal and political value opportunities of discontented groups; to increase the output of and reallocation of economic goods, and sometimes participatory and status values; to create and maintain security; and to reinforce ideational coherence. To the extent that leaders use their power to fulfill these functions, citizens' value capabilities are likely to be high.

[46] George Shepperson and Thomas T. Price, *Independent African: John Chilembwe and the Origins, Setting, and Significance of the Nyasaland Native Uprising of 1915* (Edinburgh: Edinburgh University Press, 1958), 226–227, 240–247, quotation from 247.

Power is not always widely distributed, nor is it always effectively used for adjustive purposes. When it is not, value capabilities may decline to the point at which collective violence is likely. Theory and evidence examined below identify some of the sources and consequences of the dysfunctional uses of power.

THE DESIRE FOR POWER

The capacity of a political system to satisfy the participatory value expectations of those who desire high levels of power, the elite aspirants, is a function of the ratio between the number of elite aspirants and the number of elite positions, weighted by the frequency of change in incumbents. If the ratio is high—many roles and rapid turnover in their incumbents, but relatively few aspirants—participatory value capabilities are high. The same argument applies to a system's capacity to satisfy demands for lesser degrees of influence: if there are many opportunities for participation in decision-making compared with the number of activists, participatory value capabilities are high. The inverse relationships also hold for both cases. Participatory power values are not highly flexible, however, as Deutsch points out:

> Power over men depends on their capacity to obey in ways that are still meaningful and rewarding to the powerholders, and on the latter's capacity to perceive such acts of obedience as having these functions for themselves. Up to the point at which these capacities can be expanded quickly, some actors can increase their social or political power without diminishing the power of others. Beyond it, claims to power become inflationary, and the allocation of actual power becomes a fixed-sum game.[47]

Limitations on the availability of participatory values for distribution are considerable, especially for high power positions. In most societies the proportion of political elite positions is very small and incumbents are reluctant to be replaced. Such proportions are smallest in authoritarian and centrally controlled democratic systems. The greatest proportions of relatively high power positions characterize decentralized democratic systems, with their panoply of legislative and executive bodies at several levels below the national level.

If the participatory value position of ordinary citizens is low, their value capabilities can readily be expanded in almost any type of political system by the development of political party organizations, interest associations, expansion of the franchise, and in-

[47] Deutsch, 249.

creased frequency of elections. Such expansion is typically opposed by elites in centralized political systems, and in the more modern democratic systems the increasing complexity of decision processes and of government functions substantially reduces the perceived effectiveness of conventional methods of participation, and consequentially reduces the participatory value positions of the nonelite. The increasing use of techniques such as demonstrations, general strikes, and riots to influence government policies in democracies can be attributed in part to this phenomenon. Many groups, especially students, regard the institutionalized procedures for participation and for expressing grievances as ineffective. Their initial grievances or deprivations are consequently intensified by a perceived decline in their participatory value capabilities, leading to increasingly aggressive protest.[48]

Several general views attribute revolution to innate desires for freedom, or participation, or power. Repression of man's inalienable political rights has been the classic justification for revolution in the modern world, cited with equal facility by the leaders of the French and American revolutions, the people of colonial territories, and political philosophers. Arendt writes that the aim of revolution "was, and always has been, freedom." She assumes a fundamental desire of all men to govern their own affairs, which is given tangible expression in the pervasive development of political leadership and councils "outside all revolutionary parties and groups" at the local level during the American, French, and Russian revolutions. The essence of the revolutionary spirit is this quest for such "spaces" of political freedom, though it is customarily subverted by the reconcentration of power in oligopolistic political institutions.[49] Arendt's argument parallels that made in the preceding paragraph: any centralized political order tends to limit effective non-elite participation in decision-making. The same view is inherent in Tannenbaum's interpretation of the sources of political stability:

> If anything definitive can be said about political revolutions, it is that they do not and cannot take place in countries where political strength is dispersed in a thousand places, and where myriads of men feel personally involved in the continuing prob-

[48] Two useful studies of student protest in Asia are George R. Packard, III, *Protest in Tokyo: The Security Treaty Crisis of 1960* (Princeton: Princeton University Press, 1966), and Ann Ruth Willner, "Some Forms and Functions of Public Protest in Indonesia," paper read at the annual meeting of the Asian Studies Association, Philadelphia, 1968.

[49] Hannah Arendt, *On Revolution* (New York: The Viking Press, 1963), especially 259–278, quotations from 2, 266.

lems of a self-governing parish or township and participate in making the rules for the larger unit, county, state or nation.[50]

Other interpretations argue that elite aspirants have a strong desire for political power, and that if they are denied access to its locus, central political authority, they will be angered to the point of revolt. The source of RD in such situations is restricted to what Keller calls "circulation of elite individuals."[51] For example, Pareto's explanation for the collapse of any political elite takes restrictions on elite circulation into account as well as declining ideational coherence. He attributes the French Revolution and the final collapse of the Roman Empire to a differentiation of basic attitudes between elite and mass, and, coincidentally, demands for power among members of the intrinsic elite—those who had elite qualities but were excluded from political power.[52] Brinton suggests that

> one clue to this problem of the circulation of the elite may lie in a stoppage of that circulation in a particular and very delicate spot, such as the professions, and especially the 'intellectual' professions; that is, among people especially liable to the feeling of frustration, of being excluded from good things.[53]

A variant of this thesis is Pettee's suggestion that lack of elite circulation prevents many members of the intrinsic elite from using their talents or obtaining appropriate rewards from them. "If members of the intrinsic elite can find no other outlet for their talents they will always revolt."[54] The "new nations" are often said to be particularly susceptible to revolutionary violence resulting from lack of elite circulation. Crozier suggests such an explanation for some of the major participants in the Indonesian revolution. It was "the frustration of the sound technician prevented from doing his job" that impelled two high-ranking officials, Dr. Sumitro and Dr. Sjafruddin, "into the discomfort and uncertainty of rebellion."[55]

[50] Frank Tannenbaum, "On Political Stability," *Political Science Quarterly*, LXXV (June 1960), 161–180, quotation from 169.

[51] Suzanne Keller, *Beyond the Ruling Class: Strategic Elites in Modern Society* (New York: Random House, 1963), chap. 10.

[52] Vilfredo Pareto, *Mind and Society* (New York: Harcourt Brace, 1935), paragraphs 2182–2193, especially 2191, 2199, 2250.

[53] Crane Brinton, *The Anatomy of Revolution* (New York: Norton, 1938), 78.

[54] Pettee, 11.

[55] Brian Crozier, *The Rebels: A Study of Post-War Insurrections* (London: Chatto and Windus, 1960), 80. A full account of the Indonesian revolution is George McT. Kahin, *Nationalism and Revolution in Indonesia* (Ithaca: Cornell University Press, 1952). On its aftermath see Herbert Feith, *The Decline of Constitutional Democracy in Indonesia* (Ithaca: Cornell University Press, 1962).

The lack of relative loss of power by men who sought it has been associated with innumerable outbreaks of collective violence. The revolt of Portugal against the Spanish crown in 1640, instigated and largely carried out by the Portuguese nobility, was a successful attempt by a thwarted political elite to regain lost powers and privileges.[56] Members of the nobility and the higher clergy displaced by the French Revolution played leading roles in the Vendée counterrevolution. Mosca suggests that the 1773–74 rebellion of Russian peasants and Cossacks, led by Pugachev, was a reaction to the loss of freedom at the hands of the expanding, centralized bureaucracy and its German agents.[57] Attempts by the British crown to reassert its political control over the colonial legislatures and administration in the late 1760s and early 1770s was almost certainly the major grievance of the leaders of the American Revolution.[58] The Irish rebellions of 1916–23 and the Hungarian revolution of 1956, among many others, were fueled by a variety of economic and social grievances and a sense of political repression by hated regimes that were unwilling to tolerate an expansion of political opportunities commensurate with popular demands.[59]

Other examples can also be cited. Underlying the ethnic riots between the Sinhalese and Tamil communities of Ceylon in 1958 was the belief among educated Sinhalese that Tamils were receiving preference for governmental positions, i.e. a situation in which one group's improvement was felt as a decline in the value capabilities of another.[60] The same kind of underlying grievances among regional and tribal groups appears responsible for the decimation of Ibo communities in Northern Nigeria in spring 1966 following a January coup d'état by predominantly Southern (Ibo and Yoruba) officers, and for the subsequent countercoup by Northern officers and the civil war fought by the Yoruba of Biafra. Each community's members saw political power in Nigeria in terms of a zero-sum game, with disastrous consequences.[61] The Zanzibar revolution of 1963 originated in a combination of historical political repression along lines of Arab-African cleavage, followed

[56] Merriman, 1–10.

[57] Gaetano Mosca, *The Ruling Class*, trans. Hannah D. Kahn (New York: McGraw Hill, 1896, 1939), 212.

[58] See footnote 71, chap. 4.

[59] On the Irish uprising see Edgar Holt, *Protest in Arms: The Irish Troubles, 1916–1923* (New York: Coward-McCann, 1961).

[60] Tarzie Vittachi, *Emergency '58: The Story of the Ceylon Race Riots* (London: Andre Deutsch, 1959).

[61] See Edward Feit, "Military Coups and Political Development: Some Lessons from Ghana and Nigeria," *World Politics*, XX (January 1968), especially 187–192, and "Six Views of the Nigerian War," *Africa Report*, XIII (February 1968), 8–49.

by efforts of one group to increase its power at the expense of the other. The Arab minority had controlled the political and economic life of Zanzibar for centuries and maintained political control at the time of independence, despite being outvoted at the polls and despite the growing resentment of the African majority. The Arab government then passed a series of laws that further threatened the power position of the African majority by assuming arbitrary censoring power, endorsing pro-Arab hiring practices within the bureaucracy, and replacing the predominantly African police with pro-Arab personnel. The enunciation of these policies decreased further the participatory capabilities of members of the nationalistic, egalitarian Afro-Shirazi Party, already caught up in their own "revolution of rising political expectations," and precipitated a convulsive political revolution.[62]

Such a list could be extended almost indefinitely. Political motives—the demand for power values, and more specifically for participation and self-determination—has been voiced by leaders of most internal wars of the past century and of many similar events in preceding centuries. What is not at all certain is whether specifically political deprivations were primary in the minds of their followers. It is demonstrated in chapter 3 that the vast majority of people in the contemporary world are more concerned about welfare, interpersonal, and security values than they are about political participation. Frustration of power motives is likely to be a dominant characteristic of those who lead conspiracies and revolutions, but for many, perhaps most, of their followers, demands for political values are probably secondary. The political demands of leaders provide hope and justification for others to act on their economic and communal grievances. This argument and some evidence in support of it is developed in the following chapter.

THE USES OF POWER

The ultimate responsibility for remedying economic deprivation, for resolving conflicts arising from competing goals and ideational systems, and for maintaining and reinforcing the dominant ideational system of a society and its supportive political myths rests with the political regime. This assertion is not an empirically demonstrable one; it *is* demonstrable that most citizens of most countries in the twentieth century share this perspective on government. A number of theorists ascribe revolution in the most

[62] See Michael F. Lofchie, *Zanzibar: Background to Revolution* (Princeton: Princeton University Press, 1965), especially 257–281.

general sense to the state's failure to adjust itself to changes in society. Half a century ago Adam attributed social revolutions to inadequate administrative adjustment to changing economic conditions and demands.[63] Ellwood wrote that "the real cause or stimulus which provokes a social revolution must be sought in the system of social control," meaning primarily the political system. "When that system is immobile, inflexible, and especially when it represses free expression . . . it is bound sooner or later to bring about the revolt of large masses of the group." [64] According to Pettee, "no revolution can actually occur unless the state has become a barrier to change, and the state cannot become a barrier to change unless its own form is in some way out of adjustment to the society it is supposed to serve." [65] Johnson's second necessary cause of revolution is summarily labeled "elite intransigence," the traditional explanation in modern guise. "In its grossest form, elite intransigence is the frank, willful pursuit of reactionary policies by an elite—that is, policies which exacerbate rather than rectify a dissynchronized social structure, or policies that violate the formal, envalued norms of the system. . . ." [66]

The more consequential question is: What attributes of the political system contribute to its adjustive capacities, and in particular to its ability to maintain perceived capabilities at a level sufficiently high to minimize violence? A comprehensive review of the literature suggests that one answer is, "Almost everything"—ranging from constitutional structure to high levels of economic development to elite ideologies of mobilization.[67] Adjustive capacity is said to be high if political elite incumbents have skills relevant to stresses on the system; or if they have resources with which to work; or if they share fundamental attitudes about the desirability of resolving problems cooperatively; and if their roles enable them to exercise authority in ways familiar both to them and to those over whom they exercise it. To the extent that such conditions are lacking, adjustive capacity is likely to be low, and value capabilities low as a result.

The inappropriateness or inefficiency of extrinsic elites is a

[63] Brooks Adam, *The Theory of Social Revolutions* (New York: Macmillan, 1914).

[64] Charles Ellwood, *The Psychology of Human Society: An Introduction to Sociological Theory* (New York: Appleton, 1925) 255.

[65] Pettee, 7, 8.

[66] Johnson, *Revolutionary Change,* chap. 5, quotation from 94.

[67] In an unpublished study, Harry Eckstein and his students at Princeton University have identified and systematically summarized some 180 propositions in the literature on comparative government identifying conditions said to have some causal or interactive relationships with the stability of democratic regimes.

causal variable often cited in the literature on revolution. Elites may be relatively open but fail to attract rising talents, or may occupy roles or have skills irrelevant to changing needs, or may for other reasons perform elite functions inadequately. "Social estrangement from the world of reality"—the phrase is Keller's—develops in an elite that is incapable of meeting changing value expectations. A feudal aristocracy is unlikely to comprehend or resolve the problems of economic growth, though it may make the attempt. Of equal consequence, those affected by new stresses are likely to perceive that a feudal elite is unable to resolve them, whatever its actual capacity to do so. Mosca's classic statement applies:

> Ruling classes decline inevitably when they cease to find scope for the capacities through which they rose to power, when they can no longer render the social services which they once rendered, or when their talents and the services they render lose in importance in the social environment in which they live.[68]

He attributes the periodic upheavals of dynastic China to decline in governmental efficiency, corruption of public officials, and the loss of will to rule. Under such conditions an adventurer or minor official, abetted by general discontent, would dispossess the old dynasty and found a new one, which would in turn eventually weaken.[69]

However talented and dedicated an elite may be, high adjustive capacities also require organizational efficiency and substantial resources. Brinton says that inefficiency in government was one of the four conditions common to the prerevolutionary governments of the four great Western revolutions:

> The governmental machinery is clearly inefficient, partly through neglect, through a failure to make changes in old institutions, partly because new conditions—in the societies we have studied, pretty specifically conditions attendant on economic expansion and the growth of new monied classes, new ways of transportation, new business methods—these new conditions laid an intolerable strain on governmental machinery adapted to simpler, more primitive conditions.[70]

Inefficiency led to attempts at reform, but such policies are more easily proposed than implemented, especially when resources are

[68] Mosca, 65–66. For a critical analysis of Mosca's work see James H. Meisel, *The Myth of the Ruling Class: Gaetano Mosca and the Elite* (Ann Arbor: University of Michigan Press, 1958).

[69] Mosca, 207ff.

[70] Brinton, 48–63, quotation from 287–288.

limited. Ill-conceived attempts at modernization can generate the forces that overthrow the reformers, as Zolberg suggests in an explanation of declining political capabilities and increasing political disorder in the new African nations. Their leaders assumed, on independence, the dual objectives of maintaining themselves in power and satisfying their own and their countrymen's expectations of modernization. The limited natural, financial, and human resources of their countries led to a growing gap between these expectations and implementation of the requisite policies. In the elites' attempts to secure and maintain themselves in power, political participation was rapidly expanded, leading to the politicization of communal cleavages and disputes. Almost simultaneously an "inflationary spiral of demands" developed among groups whose support was most crucial for governmental operations, namely government employees, military personnel, and unemployed young school-leavers. Increasing demands by elite aspirants and the nascent middle-classes, exacerbation of primordial conflicts among these same groups, and demonstration of the limitations of the resources of the systems undermined the legitimacy of many elites and made it necessary for most of them to shift from reliance on authority per se to force to maintain themselves in office. The process that Parsons calls "power deflation" set in, conflict between the incumbents and elite aspirants increased, and with growing frequency the military has taken the side of the opponents to the civilian elites and has seized power.[71] These military and other revolutionary leaders throughout the developing world demand power not only as an intrinsic value but, usually more consequentially, because they believe the value capabilities of the society can be increased only if they can themselves manage the political system.

A set of political-cultural variables that influences adjustive capacity is popular and elite attitudes about the political system. Certain basic orientations toward communal problems are requisites for political problem-solving. One is a belief by members of the political elite that they have an obligation to resolve societal problems, not merely to maintain and enhance their own positions. This is the crux of the "ideologies of modernization" which have been widely disseminated in the third world. Making such a problem-solving attitude operational requires an equally fundamental recognition by rulers that their circumstances are amenable to manipulation. Many traditional groups still believe their per-

[71] Aristide R. Zolberg, "The Structure of Political Conflict in the New States of Tropical Africa," *American Political Science Review*, LXII (March 1968), 70–87, quotation 76. The power deflation argument is presented in Talcott Parsons, "Some Reflections on the Place of Force in Social Process," in Eckstein, ed., 33–70.

sonal circumstances are not manipulable. The root cause of the Yemeni civil war which began in 1963 is said to have been the discontent of would-be modernizers with the utter incompetence and resistance to change of the Sayyid oligarchy.[72] A third prerequisite for political flexibility is a sense of cooperativeness and mutual interdependence among and within both the elite and citizens. Some degree of cooperativeness is necessary if any society is to persist over time, but such attitudes vary in both intensity and scope. For example, Moreno suggests that the very limited sense of what he calls social responsibility is a fundamental handicap to effective government in Latin America.[73] If cooperative attitudes are limited among elites as well as most of the mass—which they appear to be in many countries, including such European nations as Italy, Spain, and, to a lesser degree, France—the prospects of a political system maintaining and increasing value capabilities are limited except when authoritarian leaders, if they are so disposed, enforce collective solutions.

Such structural-political variables as constitutions that give the executive the power to dissolve the legislature, and the existence of a well-institutionalized party system, are also said to affect the effectiveness and durability of political systems. Eckstein's "congruence theory" attributes high performance not to a particular structural arrangement but to the resemblances among political and social structures. The basic hypothesis is that the greater the resemblance between the exercise of authority in government and the ways authority is exercised in the social institutions most crucial for political socialization and elite recruitment, the better the performance of the political system. The rationale is that if congruence among interacting social units is reasonably high, members of the political elite should be sufficiently familiar with their roles to respond effectively to crises, as well as to meet the recurrent demands of governmental activity. Moreover, their directives are likely to be obeyed because citizens are likely to perceive them as having been made by individuals occupying familiar, legitimate roles and using legitimate means.[74] Congruence theory applies especially but not only to representative systems. Moreno

[72] See for example William R. Brown, "The Yemeni Dilemma," *Middle East Journal,* XVII (Autumn 1963), 349–367.

[73] Frank Jay Moreno, "Latin America: The Fear Within," *The Yale Review,* LV (December 1965), 165–166.

[74] The initial statement of congruence theory is reprinted in Harry Eckstein, *Division and Cohesion in Democracy: A Study of Norway* (Princeton: Princeton University Press, 1966), 225–288. A revised statement is Eckstein, "Authority Relations and Governmental Performance: A Theoretical Framework," *Comparative Political Studies* II (October 1969).

has proposed a similar theory of "authoritism," arguing that a prerequisite for stable and legitimate government in societies with authoritarian political cultures is the establishment of an institutionalized, authoritarian executive. The thoery has special application to Latin America, in which, Moreno argues, only Chile and Mexico have developed and maintained such a system for any length of time.[75]

* * *

Four highly general determinants of group value capabilities have been identified in this chapter, and hypotheses about their effects illustrated with evidence and theoretical assertions about the almost infinite diversity of conditions and events that have reduced men's means below their limits of toleration. If men believe that the stocks of values available in their society are limited and unexpandable, a common perspective in traditional and some modern societies, they are likely to regard their value capabilities as static (hypothesis VC.1). Some values are inherently less expandable than others, in particular political participation—especially at the elite level—and ideational coherence. Elite positions are few in number, their incumbents seldom willing to expand them. And it is a lamentable but apparently pervasive facet of the human condition that men feel their psychological security threatened by exposure to people who live by sets of beliefs and norms other than their own. To the extent that any valued goods or conditions are inflexible, or perceived as such, any group that aspires to improve its position threatens the value positions of other groups (hypothesis VC.2). When people have such zero-sum perspectives on value distribution, violence is more likely both as a tactic of value enhancement and as a response to attempts by others to improve their relative position than it is when men believe there are possibilities of generating new values.

Perceptions of value capabilities are affected not only by the total stocks of values available for distribution but by men's recollections of how well or badly things were for them in the past. If they have been unable to improve their conditions, or worse, if their value position has steadily deterioriated, either absolutely or relative to other groups, they are likely to see their future prospects in static or declining terms. The worse things have been in the past, the lower their value capabilities are likely to be (hypothesis VC.3). The greater their opportunities for attaining their expectations, however—whether or not value stocks are fixed and

[75] Francisco Jose Moreno, *Legitimacy and Stability in Latin America: A Case Study of Chilean Political Culture* (New York: New York University Press, 1969).

whatever their past position—the greater capabilities are likely to be (hypothesis VC.4). One implication of this relationship is that an expansion of value opportunities even without other changes should lead to a short-run decrease in the potential for violence, though to a long-run increase in that potential if the opportunities prove false. A contingent relationship, especially relevant to expanding societies, is that differential restrictions on value opportunities are a potent source of deprivation among groups that are thus excluded from an equitable chance to share well-being (corollary VC.4.1). In plainer language, discrimination breeds violence, but the relationship is both more precise and more general than the truism suggests.

This chapter concludes the analysis of the sources of collective violence. Subsequent chapters examine the psychological orientations and societal conditions which focus the impetus to collective violence on the political system, and the structural conditions that finally determine its magnitude and form.

6. Perspectives on Violence and Politics: Socialization, Tradition, and Legitimacy

> Aggression breeds aggression. One comes to *expect* aggression to be a way of solving all problems. . . . Thus aggression is pretty much of a habit; the more you express it the more you have of it.
>
> Gordon Allport,
> "The Role of Expectancy" [1]

PRECEDING CHAPTERS ATTRIBUTE the basic disposition towards collective violence to a complex interplay among men's biosocially determined psychological properties, their social environment, and their perceptions of changes in that environment. This discontent is only an unstructured *potential* for collective violence. Discontent leads men to political violence when their attitudes and beliefs focus it on political objects, and when institutional frameworks are weak enough, or opposition organizations strong enough, to give the discontented a sense of potency. This chapter examines some sources of men's underlying attitudes towards violence in politics, and suggests how these attitudes influence the likelihood that they will take collective action against their rulers and political competitors. Men also hold specific beliefs about the uses of political violence in response to specific situations, beliefs they acquire through nurture, experience, conversion, or calculation. The next chapter identifies some sources and effects of doctrinal and utilitarian beliefs about political violence, and the role of communication systems in their dissemination. Even if the members of a political community are commonly and intensely motivated to violent action against political objects, however, political violence does not necessarily occur. The patterns of coercive control and institutional support commanded by the regime and political dissidents are the final determinants in the causal sequence linking hostile motivations to the magnitude and forms of political violence, and are examined in chapters 8 and 9.

Two Basic Hypotheses

Men have two related but distinguishable kinds of perspectives on political violence that influence their decisions to resort to it.

[1] In Hadley Cantril, ed., *Tensions That Cause Wars* (Urbana: University of Illinois Press, 1950), 52.

They are likely to hold norms about the extent to which and the conditions under which violence generally, and political violence specifically, is proper. They also are likely to have expectations about the relative utility of violence as a means for value attainment. The greater men's normative justifications for violence, the more likely they are to be willing to participate in political violence. Similarly, the greater the utility people attribute to tactics of violence in getting what they want, the more readily they will resort to political violence. The argument for analyzing normative and utilitarian justifications for political violence separately is, briefly, that they have distinguishable psychological and social origins and that they can vary independently. They are independent in the sense that there is no necessary logical or psychological connection between holding the beliefs that political violence is proper and that it will be successful. Men who believe that it is both proper and useful are more likely to resort to it than men who think it is neither. But if they think that violence is proper but not useful, the may still act violently to express their anger. And if utilitarian motives are sufficiently strong, normative prohibitions against violence can be overcome. The two basic arguments of this and the following chapter are summarized in the following hypotheses:

Hypothesis V.2: The potential for political violence varies strongly with the intensity and scope of normative justifications for political violence among members of a collectivity.

Hypothesis V.3: The potential for political violence varies strongly with the intensity and scope of utilitarian justifications for political violence among members of a collectivity.

If these hypotheses were truistic they would be stated as postulates. The nontrivial theoretical questions they raise are, first, whether the relationships are "strong" in the sense specified in chapter 1, and, second, whether the two relationships are appropriately regarded as independent. The basic problems for empirical analysis of such attitudes follow from these two questions: they are the importance of normative and utilitarian attitudes about political violence relative to other causal variables, and the major determinants of the intensity and scope of people's perspectives on violence in politics. Some of these determinants are identified in the twelve hypotheses derived in this and the following chapter. The two basic hypotheses and most of the twelve qualifying hypotheses can be applied to collective violence generally, but since my concern is to identify the sources of specifically political violence, I have drawn primarily on evidence about its attitudinal determinants and restrict the hypotheses to their political consequences. The psychological and cultural mechanisms by which people acquire aggressive habits are nonetheless basic to an understanding of perspectives on political violence, and consequently are reviewed in the first half of this chapter.

Political violence is defined in chapter 1 as all collective attacks within a political community against the political regime, its actors—including competing political groups as well as incumbents—or its policies. *Normative justifications* for political violence are the attitudes and beliefs men hold about the intrinsic desirability of taking or threatening such action. *Utilitarian justifications* for political violence are the beliefs men hold about the extent to which the threat or use of violence in politics will enhance their overall value position (defined in chapter 2) and that of the community with which they identify. Perspectives on both threatened and actual violence are included in the analysis because of the apparent correspondence of their political consequences. Men who normatively accept the threat of violence as a means of collective behavior frequently cross the threshold from verbal aggression to overt violence. Those who threaten political violence from utilitarian considerations often decide that it is necessary to resort to actual violence to maintain the credibility of their threats. References to "justifications for political violence" in this and the following chapter should be taken to mean both actual and threatened violence, unless otherwise specified. "Perspectives" is used as a generic term for all men's normative and utilitarian attitudes toward and beliefs about political violence.

The *intensity* of justifications for political violence is a function first of the *range of circumstances* to which actual or threatened violence is thought to be an appropriate response, and second of the *relative desirability* of violence, in normative or utilitarian terms, vis-à-vis other responses. The *scope* of justifications refers to the prevalence of supporting attitudes and beliefs among members of a collectivity. An impressionistic comparison between justifications for political violence among Scandinavian and southern European university students illustrates these distinctions. The intensity of justifications for violence appears to be less among Scandinavian students with respect to *range of circumstances:* violence against the political system is an appropriate response only to threats to a very narrow range of highly salient values, including their own lives, the existence of the political community, and the lives of those groups with whom they closely identify. Among southern European students, however, violence is an appropriate response to circumstances as diverse as undesirable governmental policies affecting university life; political opposition by student and nonstudent groups; and ideologically distasteful foreign policies of government. Differences in the *relative desirability* attributed to political violence among response alternatives may be less. For Scandinavian students, violence appears to be a last resort, justified only when other methods of influence and protest fail. Southern European students may hold similar norms but have fewer alternatives open to them. Differences in the *scope* of perspectives justifying violence similarly are problematic. If differential participation rates in politically motivated student strife are an indication, however, the scope of such justifications is less among Scandinavian than southern European students. If representatives of the two populations were asked whether political violence was justifiable as a last resort, it is likely that fewer northerners than southerners would answer "yes." Such a question has been asked of black Americans in Watts. Those who were militant, defined in terms of sympathy for black radical organizations, were three times as likely as nonmilitants to endorse the use of violence as a legitimate last resort. Moreover they were twice as likely as nonmilitants to claim participation in the 1965 Los Angeles riots.[2]

These examples suggest that the opinion survey is one reasonably direct technique for assessing the intensity and scope of justifications for political violence among collectivities. Justificatory attitudes and beliefs also can be inferred from what rebels do and say, of course. The approach to the development of the hypotheses below is to specify general and more readily observable properties of cultures and communication from which intensities and scope of justifications for violence can be inferred.

Several other theoretical points about hypotheses V.2 and V.3 need to be made before examining some evidence. Their dependent variable, *potential for political violence,* is a subset of the dependent variable of hypothesis V.1 (chapter 2), potential for collective violence. It is necessary for both empirical and theoretical purposes to specify formally the relationship that holds between the two dependent variables, and what relationships are likely to hold among the independent variables specified, namely intensity and scope of RD (hypothesis V.1), and intensity and scope of normative (hypothesis V.2) and utilitarian (hypothesis V.3) justifications for political violence. RD is a necessary precondition for col-

[2] T. M. Tomlinson, "The Development of a Riot Ideology Among Urban Negroes," *American Behavioral Scientist,* XI (March-April 1968), 28.

lective violence, including political violence, but the relationship is not exact. Depending on people's perspectives on violence and politics, RD-induced discontent may be either focused on or deflected from the political system. If, for example, government is held responsible by acts of commission or omission for discontent and is thought to be in appropriate, most or all discontent is likely to be focused on political targets. To the extent that other agents are held responsible and the political system invested with an aura of legitimacy, discontent is likely to lead to action against other objects. Nonetheless, the potential for political violence ought to vary quite strongly with the potential for collective violence. If both variables could be directly assessed, a correlation in the range of .7 to .9 could be expected. In hypothetical form,

Hypothesis V.4: The potential for specifically political violence varies strongly with the potential for collective violence generally.

Assuming the validity of this relationship, a corollary can be derived regarding the relationship between the independent variables determining discontent, those determining the potential for political violence, and the magnitude of political violence itself. If discontent has a dominant causal relationship with potential for political violence, then justifications for political violence should have a contingent rather than independent relation to magnitude of political violence. If justifications are strong but discontent low, less political violence is likely than if justifications are weak and discontent strong. The highest magnitudes of political violence are likely if both are strong. The following corollary should therefore hold:

Corollary V.4.1: The greater the intensity and scope of relative deprivation, the stronger the relationship between the intensity and scope of normative and utilitarian justifications for political violence and the magnitude of political violence.

Finally, interaction effects are also likely between characteristics of normative and utilitarian justifications. There is no compelling reason for assuming that if members of a collectivity normatively accept some kinds of violence they will therefore regard it as useful, but it is quite possible that if they normatively accept violence, they are more likely to make utilitarian calculations about its consequences and to be susceptible to new beliefs about its usefulness than if they had strong normative inhibitions against violence. It also is plausible that if people anticipate substantial gains through violence but hold normative prohibitions against it, they are susceptible to conversion to new norms that justify violent action. The following corollary to hypothesis V.3 is suggested:

Corollary V.3.1: The intensity and scope of normative justifications for political violence vary strongly with the intensity and scope of utilitarian justifications for political violence in a collectivity.

The plan of this chapter is to examine first some psychocultural sources of normative justifications for violence, then some characteristics of perspectives on politics that affect both normative and utilitarian justifications.

Psychocultural Justifications for Violence

Several kinds of normative justifications for violence can be distinguished analytically. Some of men's perspectives on violence are psychocultural in origin, the result of socialization patterns that encourage or discourage outward displays of aggression, and of cultural traditions which sanction violent collective responses to various kinds of deprivation. These perspectives are underlying attitudes about, or normative predispositions toward, violence. There is considerable variation in such attitudes within most cultures; evidence also suggests that modal dispositions toward violence vary significantly from one nation to another and from one subculture to another within nations. These underlying attitudes are separable from the doctrines that men accept in the course of their lives which provide them with specific justifications for violence in response to their immediate political circumstances. Such doctrines conventionally are categorized as "ideologies," which in their most elaborate form can serve to stimulate mutual awareness among the discontented, provide them with elaborate explanations about the causes of their discontent, give normative sanction to violent action against political objects, and identify utopian objectives to be attained by so acting. Comprehensive ideologies are more commonly held by leaders of political violence than by those who follow them, however, and are as often articulated after the revolutionary fact as before it (see chapter 7). The ideas which immediately justify violence for most participants in most acts of political violence have the character of slogans, rumors, prejudices, or simplified fragments of ideologies, not of integrated belief systems.

Some psychocultural factors are examined in this chapter, ideological ones in the next. There are two kinds of psychocultural approaches to explaining aggression and consequent violence that emphasize general social influences. Klineberg characterizes them as the "individual aggressiveness" and "cultural" approaches. The first refers to explanations of aggression in terms of "the actual experiences of individuals, usually in early life, which create a need for, or at least a tendency toward, aggressive behavior." The cultural approach stresses "the extent to which aggression is accepted or rejected through the mores or folkways of a community."[3] A comparable distinction is made below between the sources and effects of individual aggressiveness as it affects general normative perspectives on violence, and the development and consequences of cultural traditions of collective political violence. Much of the evidence summarized in the discussion of individual and cultural aggressiveness is subsequently shown to be relevant to the questions of ideological and utilitarian justification as well.

INDIVIDUAL AGGRESSIVENESS

The basic assumption of "individual aggressiveness" explanations is that individuals acquire differential dispositions to, or needs for, aggression during the socialization process. Some kinds of child-raising practices and interpersonal relationships in the family impose greater frustrations than others. There also is great variation in the kinds of psychological defense mechanisms and response hierarchies for dealing with frustrations which people acquire in socialization. There is an enormous body of theory and evidence about the specific patterns of socialization that lead to high aggressiveness. In anthropology, culture-stress theory posits that cultures differ substantially in the degree of stress they place on their members. The demands and prohibitions of socialization, securing a livelihood, and interacting with others are more or less painful to the individual. The more painful or stressful they are, the more common are manifestations of personal dysfunction likely to be, including neuroses, psychosomatic illnesses, suicide, homicide, alcoholism, use of narcotics, and so forth. Naroll, from whom this brief summary is drawn, shows that cultures with high levels of one kind of such dysfunction tend to have high levels of others.[4] Many studies relate specific kinds of socialization experience to personal disorder. Bandura and Walters found, for example, that both parents of aggressive adolescent boys encouraged their sons' aggression outside the home but that fathers would not tolerate dis-

[3] Otto Klineberg, *Tensions Affecting International Understanding: A Survey of Research* (New York: Social Science Research Council, 1950), 188.

[4] Raoul Naroll, *Data Quality Control: A New Research Technique; Prolegomena to a Cross-Cultural Study of Culture Stress* (New York: The Free Press, 1962), chaps. 2 and 3. Also see John W. M. Whiting and Irvin L. Child, *Child Training and Personality* (New Haven: Yale University Press, 1953).

plays of aggression toward themselves and showed little affection toward the boys. The aggressive boys thus learned to express aggression outside the home in a relatively direct and uninhibited way, and because they resented their fathers tended to displace aggression onto external authority figures.[5] Studies of murderers suggest that they are exposed to relatively severe childhood as well as adult frustrations and tend to have comparatively weak inhibitions against aggression.[6]

Other studies emphasize the relationship between personality characteristics acquired during socialization and aggressiveness. Eysenck has found substantial empirical evidence of an association among tough-mindedness, undersocialization, extraversion, and aggressiveness.[7] Stagner reports that individuals who are aggressive in one sphere of life tend to be aggressive in others, and to be aggressive in both overt and verbal behavior.[8] The central characteristic of the "authoritarian personality," studied in a variety of cultures, is repression of strong hostility originally directed at parents and other authority figures, which is manifest in such personality traits as high valuation of conventional morality, exaggeration of differences between one's own group and others, strong emphasis on the importance of force in human affairs, and prejudice toward and displacement of aggression onto outgroups.[9] Epstein, in a representative experimental study, found that highly authoritarian subjects were significantly more likely than low authoritarians to imitate aggressiveness against a Negro "victim."[10] Himmelweit summarizes ten studies of individual differences in tolerance to frustration, which "demonstrate conclusively that an unstable person has a lower frustration tolerance than a stable person."[11] Many other

[5] Albert Bandura and Richard H. Walters, *Adolescent Aggression* (New York: Ronald Press, 1959), especially chaps. 3 and 7. Similar findings are reported by L. D. Eron et al., "Social Class, Parental Punishment for Aggression, and Child Aggression," *Child Development,* XXXIV (December 1963), 849–867.

[6] A summary of such studies is given by Leonard Berkowitz, *Aggression: A Social Psychological Analysis* (New York: McGraw-Hill, 1962), 318–322.

[7] H. J. Eysenck, *The Psychology of Politics* (London: Routledge and Kegan Paul, 1954), chap. 7.

[8] Ross Stagner, "Studies of Aggressive Social Attitudes," *Journal of Social Psychology,* XX (August 1944), 109–140.

[9] The initial study is Theodor W. Adorno et al., *The Authoritarian Personality* (New York: Harper, 1950). Subsequent studies using its concepts and techniques number in the hundreds.

[10] Ralph Epstein, "Aggression toward Outgroups as a Function of Authoritarianism and Imitation of Aggressive Models," *Journal of Personality and Social Psychology,* III (No. 5, 1966), 574–579.

[11] Hilde T. Himmelweit, "Frustration and Aggression: A Review of Recent Experimental Work," in T. H. Pear, ed., *Psychological Factors of Peace and War,* (London: Hutchinson, 1950), 178–180.

studies could be cited; these suffice to illustrate the generalization that different socialization and personality patterns lead to individual differences in potential for aggression.

Two somewhat distinct approaches are used to link individual attitudes about aggression to political violence. One focuses on the sources of aggressive dispositions of revolutionary leaders. Lasswell argues on the basis of psychoanalytic theory and case studies that political agitators are strongly narcissistic men, whose yearning for emotional response—acquired in the maturation process—is displaced upon generalized objects and manifest in a desire to arouse emotional responses from the community at large.[12] In the same vein is Wolfenstein's comparative study of Lenin, Trotsky, and Gandhi as examples of the "revolutionary personality." His results support the hypothesis that

> the revolutionist is one who escapes from the burdens of Oedipal guilt with ambivalence by carrying his conflict with authority into the political realm. For this to happen two conditions must exist: the conflict with paternal authority must be alive and unresolvable in the family context as adolescence draws to a close, and there must exist a political context in terms of which the conflict can be expressed.[13]

This approach is essentially a psychopathological one, suited to microanalysis of political violence. Examination of the psychological characteristics that dispose particular individuals, leaders in particular, to revolutionary activity can provide a fuller understanding of the origins, nature, and direction of specific revolutionary movements. But analysis of this sort can contribute only marginally to the explanation of cross-cultural variation in levels of political violence.

The second approach linking personality characteristics to collective violence generalizes directly from the presence of aggressive personalities in a society to the occurrence of revolution and war. Lasswell makes this kind of analytic leap in his argument that "Political movements derive their vitality from the displacement of private affects upon public objects." During a political crisis, he writes, "the unconscious triumphantly interprets [the fall of a leader] as a release from all constraint, and the individuals in the community who possess the least solidified personality structures

[12] Harold Lasswell, *Psychopathology and Politics* (Chicago: University of Chicago Press, 1930), especially 125.

[13] E. Victor Wolfenstein, *The Revolutionary Personality: Lenin, Trotsky, Gandhi* (Princeton: Princeton University Press, 1967), quotation 307.

are compulsively driven to acts of theft and violence."[14] Durbin and Bowlby provide a comparable explanation for war. Primary aggression arising from possessive urges and their frustration, they say, is common to all men. Identification of the self with the state, and subordination to its authority, both of which are pervasive twentieth-century phenomena, transform aggression. When citizens become "so educated, so frustrated, and so unhappy" that internal aggression becomes intolerable, "they have reached a point at which war has become a psychological necessity."[15] Other examples are provided by Hoffer, who attributes revolutionary movements in part to widespread psychological disturbance,[16] and by Riezler, who argues that the core of revolutionary movements is comprised of fools, deviants, and the maladjusted.[17]

Some "revolutionary personalities" presumably are present in all societies, and some societies probably produce them in larger numbers than others. However, for a general, cross-cultural theory of political violence the most relevant factors are those which lead to substantial and culture-wide differences in normative dispositions toward aggressiveness. In other words our primary concern should be with pervasive cultural or subcultural socialization practices, not with uncommon deviances, however significant the latter may be for the interpretation of participation and leadership in particular outbreaks of political violence. Moreover,

[14] Lasswell, 173, 180.

[15] E.F.M. Durbin and John Bowlby, *Personal Aggressiveness and War* (London: Kegan Paul, Trench, Trubner, 1939), 7–50, quotations 27, 28. There are many comparable views of the origins of war in innate or frustration-induced aggression, for example J. F. Brown, "The Theory of the Aggressive Urges and Wartime Behavior," *Journal of Social Psychology,* XV (1942), 355–380, and Franz Alexander, "The Psychiatric Aspects of War and Peace," *American Journal of Sociology,* XLVI (1941), 504–520. Empirical studies of the origins of war provide little support for them. Quincy Wright, in his monumental *A Study of War* (Chicago: University of Chicago Press, 1942), concludes that war among modern states "seldom springs from the behavior patterns of the masses but from the calculations of the leaders" (144). Abel examined the decision to go to war in twenty-five cases and concluded that in none of them did emotions or sentiments appear dominant among decision-makers; war seemed to be chosen deliberately, as an instrumental means toward specific goals. Theodore F. Abel, "The Element of Decision in the Pattern of War," *American Sociological Review,* VI (December 1941), 853–859.

[16] Hoffer, passim.

[17] Kurt Riezler, "On the Psychology of the Modern Revolution," *Social Research,* X (September 1943), 320–336. Riezler's generalization is derived largely from an examination of Fascist movements. A useful and more balanced discussion of revolutionary leadership is Carl Leiden and Karl M. Schmitt, *The Politics of Violence: Revolution in the Modern World* (Englewood Cliffs, N.J.: Prentice-Hall, 1968), chap. 5. A detailed set of studies of the social backgrounds and career patterns of Nazi, Fascist, and Soviet and Chinese Communist leaders, dealing principally with those who were active after the attainment of power, is Harold D. Lasswell and Daniel Lerner, eds., *World Revolutionary Elites: Studies in Coercive Ideological Movements* (Cambridge: M.I.T. Press, 1965).

the degree of stress or frustration imposed in socialization appears less consequential than the ways people are taught to deal with their aggressive impulses. Frustrations are imposed in all socialization processes, and whereas there are apparent differences in their degree, those differences appear relatively small and seem empirically associated with variations in types and levels of individual deviance rather than collective behavior. More striking cross-cultural variation is evident in the extent people learn to act out or to internalize their anger, and there is evidence that links these differences to specific kinds of individual *and* collective aggression.

One basic dimension along which socialized attitudes toward aggression vary is the degree to which members of a culture internalize aggression. In some societies, and among some subcultures and status groups, the emphasis is *intrapunitive,* i.e. people acquire a normative disposition to blame their frustrations on themselves and to inhibit or turn inward their aggressive feelings. In others there is an *extrapunitive* disposition, i.e. people tend to attribute blame to others and to regard as justifiable the acting out of aggression against others.[18] It is likely that the greater the emphasis on extrapunitiveness in the socialization process, the more commonly will people feel that collective as well as individual violence is justified. The relationship is probably sufficiently strong and pervasive to affect attitudes toward collective political violence, and hence to be stated in hypothetical form.

Hypothesis JV.1: The intensity of normative justifications for political violence varies moderately with the degree of emphasis placed on extrapunitiveness in socialization.

Indirect evidence for the hypothesis is provided by studies that account for varying incidences of suicide and murder in terms of differences among cultural and status groups in intrapunitive and extrapunitive attitudes. Henry and Short argue that internalization of harsh parental demands, accompanied by punishment for outward displays of aggression, leads to a higher "psychological probability" of suicide than of homicide, i.e. to high frustration and intrapunitive attitudes. On the other hand if parents are harsh but do not threaten to withdraw affection from children who act aggressively, aggression is likely to be expressed outwardly. The

[18] The classification is developed by Saul Rosenzweig, "Types of Reaction to Frustration: A Heuristic Classification," *Journal of Abnormal and Social Psychology,* XXIX (October-December 1934), 298–300, and has been widely used in the literature. He also suggests a third category, "impunitive," to denote substitute responses.

"psychological probability" interacts with "sociological probability": if there are strong external restraints in adult life, extrapunitive responses (homicide) are likely responses to frustration, because the sources of external restraint provide targets for aggression; if external restraints are weak, the individual is more likely to turn his aggression against himself. Together these patterns are said to account for the empirical finding that frequency of homicides varies inversely with social status, suicides directly. People of low status tend to be subject to strong and visible sources of restraint and also to be "under-socialized" vis-à-vis high-status individuals.[19]

In another comparative study Hendin attributes Denmark's high suicide rate to dependency built up in childhood by solicitous mothers who suppress aggression while manipulating guilt feelings as a disciplinary device, i.e. an intrapunitive pattern. High Swedish suicide rates are said to be a result of the trauma of early separation from parents, channeling of consequent anger into highly competitive performance, and self-hatred if failure occurs. In Norway, by contrast, aggression is not so rigorously suppressed, nor are mother-child relationships overprotective or traumatic, and consequently suicide rates are relatively low.[20] This is not to say that Norwegian culture inculcates extrapunitive attitudes, but rather that childhood frustrations are less and attitudes less intrapunitive than in Sweden and Denmark. Hackney, an historian, challenges interpretations such as those of Henry and Short, and of Hendin, which he examines in an attempt to account for the high murder and low suicide rates of white and black American southerners compared with white and black northerners. His proposed explanation is that there is a southern world view which justifies extrapunitive rather than intrapunitive behavior, by locating "threats to the region outside the region and threats to the person outside the self."[21]

These and many other explanations are consistent in general if not specific terms. They can be interpreted as manifestations of cultural or subcultural dispositions to extrapunitive or intrapunitive responses, and their differences attributable to different sources

[19] Andrew F. Henry and James F. Short, Jr., *Suicide and Homicide: Some Economic, Sociological, and Psychological Aspects of Aggression* (New York: The Free Press, 1954, 1964), chaps. 5 to 7. For cross-cultural evidence see Arthur L. Wood, "A Socio-Structural Analysis of Murder, Suicide, and Economic Crime in Ceylon," *American Sociological Review*, XXVI (October 1961), 744–753.

[20] Herbert Hendin, *Suicide and Scandinavia* (New York: Grune and Stratton, 1964).

[21] Sheldon Hackney, "Southern Violence," *American Historical Review*, LXXIV (February 1969), 906–925, quotation 925.

of extrapunitive norms. Henry and Short emphasize the interaction of child-raising and social structural factors as determinants of the direction of aggression. Hendin emphasizes primarily the child-raising factors, Hackney an historical tradition that presumably is implanted in the socialization process and that may be manifest in distinctive child-raising practices. All three kinds of causal factors probably interact in the development of extrapunitive attitudes, some of them being more consequential for some groups than others.

More speculative evidence links socialization characteristics through extrapunitiveness to collective violence. Among the Balinese, for example, Bateson has identified a pattern of conditioning whereby children are taught not to expect culmination in their acts but to take pleasure in preliminary steps with no defined goal, "to live in the immediate present not in some distant goal."[22] Another Balinese characteristic is a strong normative inhibition against overt aggression, presumably inculcated as part of the same process. These two traits may help account for the high apparent toleration of Balinese for frustration, which, if exceeded, leads to extraordinarily intense outbursts of suicidal individual violence analogous to the Malay *amok* and to collective violence like the massacre of hundreds of thousands of Indonesian Communists in 1965–66 – massacres that were particularly intense in Bali.[23] Pye attributes the high incidence of political murders, and other forms of Burmese violence, at the most fundamental level to Burmese child-rearing practices and more immediately to the tensions created by the politics of modernization and the prevalence of beliefs about the inevitability of violence.[24] Results of interviews with sixty-seven Harlem Negroes after a 1943 riot provide a third, less direct example. Clark identified underlying attitudinal differences between those who accepted the riot and those who rejected it. The two groups appeared equally *concerned* about the status of Negroes; but the rejectors responded in terms of a general attitudinal rejection of violence, the acceptors in terms of a restricted frame of reference in which specific racial injustices were sufficient to justify violence.[25] Differences in socialization patterns of the two groups

[22] Gregory Bateson, "The Frustration-Aggression Hypothesis and Culture," *Psychological Review*, XLVIII (July 1941), 355.

[23] Ann Willner of the Center of International Studies, Princeton University, suggested several of these points, but I assume responsibility for the interpretation placed on them.

[24] Lucien Pye, *Politics, Personality, and Nation Building: Burma's Search for Identity* (New Haven: Yale University Press, 1962), 136–143, 163–167.

[25] Kenneth B. Clark, "Group Violence: A Preliminary Study of the Attitudinal Pattern of its Acceptance and Rejection: A Study of the 1943 Harlem Riot," *Journal of Social Psychology*, XIX (1944), 319–337.

were not examined, but the findings are consistent with the argument that intrapunitive individuals acquire generalized inhibitions against aggression, whereas extrapunitive individuals learn to respond more directly and overtly to specific frustrations.

As one example of comparative evidence, Lipset's analysis of multinational survey data shows a rather consistent relationship between lower-class status and intolerance and authoritarianism. Psychological evidence cited above indicated a relationship between authoritarian attitudes and aggressive dispositions; more generally, aggressive political movements in industrial democracies tend to be based on the working class.[26] Hackney's data on the United States show that relative to suicide rates murder rates are greatest among black Americans, less among white Southerners, and least among white Northerners, the proposed explanation for which is variations in subcultural extrapunitive attitudes. The same hierarchy is apparent in the magnitude of collective violence in which members of the three subcultures participate: in recent decades, strife by blacks has been more common than strife by white Southerners, strife by them more common than by white Northerners.[27]

This evidence is suggestive, not wholly persuasive. In particular it is not clear to what extent the extrapunitive attitudes which appear to facilitate collective violence are acquired by children in the process of childhood socialization, rather than in adulthood by exposure to cultural norms justifying violence or to generally frustrating societal conditions. The evidence that cultural traditions of political violence facilitate violence among later generations is more extensive, as the evidence of the following section demonstrates. The two variables, socialization of extrapunitive attitudes and the existence of violent cultural traditions, presumably interact. How they do so and which is more consequential remain to be determined empirically.

CULTURAL TRADITIONS OF POLITICAL VIOLENCE

There are persistent differences among societies in styles, incidence, and levels of political violence. Within most complex societies some groups, and some regions, manifest types of violence

[26] Seymour M. Lipset, *Political Man: The Social Bases of Politics* (Garden City: Doubleday, 1960), chap. 4. Also see William Kornhauser, *The Politics of Mass Society* (New York: The Free Press, 1959), passim.

[27] The proposed relationship with levels of collective violence is mine, not Hackney's. Nor does he explicitly suggest extrapunitiveness as an explanation for high murder rates among black Americans, although the relationship is implicit in his analysis.

different from, and magnitudes of violence greater than, those of other groups and regions. Such continuities are in part a manifestation of persisting societal and subcultural patterns of deprivation, and of patterns of coercive control and institutional support that facilitate violent protest. Eckstein however emphasizes the feedback relationship between the occurrence of political violence and the development of attitudinal predispositions toward future violence:

> political disorientation may be followed by the formation of a new set of orientations, establishing a predisposition toward violence that is inculcated by the experience of violence itself. In such cases, internal wars result not from specifiable objective conditions, and not even from the loss of legitimacy by a particular regime, but from a general lack of receptivity to legitimacy of any kind. Violence becomes a political style that is self-perpetuating, unless itself "disoriented." [28]

More specifically, evidence examined below suggests that the traditions embodying these attitudes or "orientations" specify the kinds of situations to which collective action is an appropriate response, establish particular modes and targets of violence, and thereby increase normative justifications for violence.

It is analytically useful to distinguish the effects of violent events on the perceived likelihood of future violence from their effects on attitudes of justifiability. The occurrence of one riot, one rebellion, or one coup d'etat in a nation is not likely to create widespread expectations about their repetition. The more frequently they occur, however, and the more closely spaced they are in time, the more common people will expect them to be in the future. The American experience with ghetto riots and political assassinations in the 1960s is illustrative. The Watts riot in 1965 seemingly was regarded by many Americans as a rare, epiphenomenal occurrence, unlikely to recur. By 1968 it was widely believed that riots would be common for an indefinite period. The assassination of President Kennedy in 1963 was thought to be an isolated event, requiring explanation but not anticipation of recurrence. After the killing of his brother in 1968, Americans were telling one another with titillated horror that assassination had become a norm of American politics.

The expectation of violence does not necessarily lead to its normative justification. There is nonetheless something of a self-fulfilling

[28] Harry Eckstein, "On the Etiology of Internal Wars," *History and Theory*, IV (No. 2, 1965), 150–151.

prophecy in such expectancies. They may divert attention from remedying underlying causes to preparation for repetition. Moreover, people with weakly held or conflicting norms are susceptible to accepting others' practices as norms, especially if those practices are intrinsically attractive—which aggression is for those who are discontented. Mosca calls this disposition "mimetism," defining it as "the tendency of an individual's passions, sentiments, and beliefs to develop in accord with the currents that prevail in the environment."[29] In other words if discontent is widespread in a society, anomie (normlessness) common, and political violence frequent, there is a tendency for attitudes of expectancy of violence to be converted into norms justifying violence. The process of violence-expectancy-justification-violence tends to perpetuate itself, contingent on the persistence of some level of RD and on a favorable balance between costs and benefits for its participants. If political violence proves at least partially effective in alleviating the initial deprivation, and not disastrously costly to the participants in other terms, the process is reinforced. If the costs to participants are high, and if the intensity of deprivation is reduced without apparent relationship to the occurrence of violence, the process is likely to be terminated.

The argument is summarized in the following hypothesis and corollaries; the "corollaries" in this instance stipulate the causal arguments from which hypothesis JV.2 is derived.

Hypothesis JV.2: The intensity and scope of normative justifications for political violence vary strongly with the historical magnitude of political violence in a collectivity.

Corollary JV.2.1: The more frequent the occurrence of a particular form of political violence in a collectivity, the greater the expectation that it will recur.

Corollary JV.2.2: If expectancy of violence is great, the intensity and scope of normative justifications for political violence will vary strongly with the intensity and scope of relative deprivation.

The scope of justifications is likely to vary with past levels of political violence (hypothesis JV.2) on grounds that the more common violence has been, the greater the proportion of people who are likely to have had direct or mediated exposure to it. An operational question is the period that should be considered in evaluating the "historical" magnitude of political violence (hypothesis JV.2) and the "frequency" of a particular kind of event (corollary

[29] Gaetano Mosca, *The Ruling Class*, trans. Hannah D. Kahn (New York: McGraw-Hill, 1896, 1939), 184.

JV.2.1). Men's collective memories about revolutions and civil wars appear longer than their memories about turmoil. The chronic riots of rural and urban England of the seventeenth through nineteenth centuries seem to have left little ideological residue in modern Britain; the French revolutionary tradition still provides justifications for student and worker action. A period of at least a century should be examined for evidence of traditions of internal wars, whereas a generation should suffice for evaluating historical magnitudes of turmoil.

Varied evidence and arguments indirectly support the contention that a society's historical experience with political violence affects its prospects for future violence. Much of this evidence applies equally well to the development of utilitarian justifications for violence. Psychological studies cited below suggest how habits of individual aggressiveness are acquired but do not examine directly the attitudes toward aggressiveness which presumably are acquired in the learning process. Other psychological and survey studies document the existence of collective justifications for overt aggression of various kinds without identifying their sources. Comparative evidence demonstrates the existence of distinctive patterns of violence by specific groups over long periods of time, but seldom indicates directly what attitudes and beliefs shaped the patterned response. Such evidence implies the importance of widespread normative and utilitarian justifications for strife as intervening variables in the process of political violence, but is suggestive not definitive.

Experimental studies identify some patterns by which habits of individual aggression develop. In a number of studies children have been shown others being aggressive and have then been put in a similar situation. If the child or adult who provided the aggressive model was rewarded, or at least not punished, the children tended to imitate his aggression and display other kinds of aggression as well. If the aggressive model was punished the children did not imitate him—unless the source of punishment or prohibition was removed, in which case they showed the same level of imitative aggression. Experiments with adolescent subjects using film sequences depicting aggression have comparable results: if the film violence was presented as justifiable, for example by other "subjects'" expressed approval, the real subjects became more overtly aggressive.[30] Other studies show that if an individual is

[30] Richard H. Walters, "Implications of Laboratory Studies of Aggression for the Control and Regulation of Violence," *Annals of the American Academy of Political and Social Science*, CCCLXIV (March 1966), 63–66. Another summary of evidence is Jerome D. Frank, *Sanity and Survival: Psychological Aspects of War and Peace* (New York: Vintage Books, 1968), "How Children Learn Aggression," 68–74.

rewarded for aggression intermittently, he develops habits of aggression which are even stronger than those acquired if aggression is always rewarded. Still other experimental evidence identifies some effects of catharsis—tension-reduction following aggression—on the development of aggressive habits. The naive, Aristotelian version of the catharsis argument is that expression of an emotion purges the individual of it. There is some evidence that aggression against a frustrater does reduce tension, if no guilt or punishment accompanies it. Such tension-reduction is satisfying, however, and hence is more likely to be resorted to when the person becomes angry again in the future; it becomes a satisfying habit. Moreover, "even if his aggressive act does lessen the thwarted person's immediate anger . . . the frustrater may acquire the stimulus properties which, under the appropriate conditions, can cause him to evoke aggressive responses from his victim on some later occasion."[31] In other words, "catharsis" not only tends to make aggression a habit, it tends to make certain targets habitual as well.

The relevance of these findings for the development of collective traditions of violence is evident. Angry people are likely to imitate others' violence, especially if they get the impression that violence is justified; such an impression is conveyed either by the fact that the violent models "get away with it" or by others' intimations that violence is justifiable. If people find rewards in violence, either through attainment of their goals or through the satisfaction of acting out their anger without harmful consequences, they are increasingly likely to be violent in the future. The more common collective violence is in a society, the more likely it is that some individuals will find it rewarding and hence be prepared to engage in it in the future. And the more common such violence is, the more likely it is that nonparticipant observers will choose to emulate the behavioral models it provides.

Some survey evidence suggests the extent of group differentials in collective attitudes toward the normative justifiability of violence. Recent surveys show that collective violence is widely tolerated in Afro-American culture. Between 20 and 23 percent of both southern and northern blacks agreed in 1963, before Watts, and in 1966, that they can win their rights only through an "eye for an eye and a tooth for a tooth" struggle.[32] Between a third and a half of Watts residents interviewed after the 1965 riot approved of those

[31] Walters, 66–67, 70–71; Leonard Berkowitz, "Aggressive Cues in Aggressive Behavior and Hostility Catharsis," *Psychological Review*, LXXI (March 1964), 104–122, quotation 111. Also see Berkowitz, *Aggression*, chap. 8.

[32] William Brink and Louis Harris, *Black and White: A Study of U.S. Racial Attitudes Today* (New York: Simon and Schuster, 1966), 260.

who supported the riots.[33] Another survey found that 29 percent of Watts residents thought violence justified to gain attention or as an only way out, views also held by 13 percent of Oakland blacks and 26 percent of Houston blacks. An additional 47, 44, and 24 percent respectively of the people interviewed in these cities thought that violence was justified in self-defense.[34] In other words, between half and three-quarters of black urban Americans apparently believe that violence is justified in some circumstances. If this attitude is a recent phenomenon it could be attributed to the demonstration effects of the riots of the 1960s or to a new protoideology of violence rather than to the historical experience of black riots (infrequent) and violent white racism (more common). However, one bit of interview evidence suggests that these contemporary attitudes reflect a long tradition. After the Harlem riots of 1943, interviews were conducted with an "approximately representative" sample of some 60 Harlem residents, of whom 30 percent condoned the riots, a proportion not substantially lower than the Watts proportion. Moreover, the justifications for acceptance, both utilitarian and normative, have a remarkably contemporary ring: "It was really grand. If we had more of them things would be better for us." "Only way Negroes get government to pay attention to them." "Broke white people's stores and showed them how we feel." [35]

A handful of other survey results provide a rough standard of comparison. Interviews with forty-one white Americans in Geneva, New York, in 1964 suggest that black Americans are not alone in favoring violence: 39 percent said they would join a movement to forcibly overthrow the government if its laws became "very unjust and harmful"; 51 percent said they would do so if the President with army backing disbanded Congress and made himself ruler for life; and 37 percent were willing to play an active part in the fighting.[36] In contrast, in 1963 a survey was conducted of separatist sentiment among French-Canadians. Although about 40 percent were separatists, wanting either independence or union with the United States, *none* would countenance the use of violence toward that goal.[37] In 1966, samples of peace marchers in Britain and Denmark were interviewed. Norms against violence were sufficiently strong among these highly committed individuals that about half

[33] Tomlinson, 28.

[34] William McCord and John Howard, "Negro Opinions in Three Riot Cities," *American Behavorial Scientist*, XI (March-April 1968), 26.

[35] Clark, 322–323.

[36] Young C. Kim, "Authority: Some Conceptual and Empirical Notes," *Western Political Quarterly*, XIX (June 1966), 223–234.

[37] Frank L. Wilson, "French-Canadian Separatism," *Western Political Quarterly*, XX (March 1967), 126.

in each country said they would not march if they "knew in advance that some windows might be broken."[38]

Another kind of evidence of the existence and duration of cultural traditions of violence is provided by descriptive studies of chronic turmoil in Europe in the eighteenth and nineteenth centuries. The frequency with which Parisian workers and shopkeepers took to the streets in the years and decades following the "days" of 1789 is evidence of one such tradition, established by the great *journées* of 1789 to 1795 and manifested in many later riots and demonstrations, most dramatically in the revolutions of 1830, 1848, and 1871.[39] Pinkney, for example, suggests that the riots of the Revolution of 1830 "were an expression of timeless economic complaints, of loyalties within traditional crafts, of popular resentments against symbols of the old regime, and of eighteenth-century ideas of liberty, equality, and fraternity."[40] The statement could be applied almost word for word to the description of the French riots and general strike of May 1968. Traditions of violent protest were as common, perhaps more so, in rural areas. Food riots were an established feature of the rural English landscape in the eighteenth century. At least 275 occurred between 1735 and 1800, in close correlation with the occurrence of harvest failures and high food prices.[41] Hobsbawm documents the development of traditions of millennarian violence among the southern European peasantry in stereotyped response to persisting deprivation.

> Some millennarians . . . merely retire to await the next revolutionary crisis. This is naturally easiest where the economic and social conditions of revolution are endemic, as in Southern Italy, where every political change in the 19th century, irrespective from what quarter it came, automatically produced its ceremonial marches of peasants with drums and banners to occupy the land, or in Andalusia where . . . millennarian revolutionary waves occurred at roughly ten-year intervals for some sixty or seventy years.[42]

[38] Robin Jenkins, "Who are these Marchers?" *Journal of Peace Research*, No. 1, 1967, 46–60. Their pacifism presumably affected their responses.

[39] See for example George Rudé, *The Crowd in History, 1730–1848* (New York: Wiley, 1964), chap. 6 and 11; Charles Tilly, "Reflections on the Revolutions of Paris: An Essay on Recent Historical Writing," *Social Problems*, XII (Summer 1964), 99–212; and Frank Jellinek, *The Paris Commune of 1871* (New York: Grosset and Dunlap, 1937, 1965).

[40] David H. Pinkney, "The Crowd in the French Revolution of 1830," *American Historical Review*, LXX (October 1964), 17.

[41] Rudé, chap. 2.

[42] E. J. Hobsbawm, *Social Bandits and Primitive Rebels* (New York: The Free Press, 1959), chaps. 4 and 5, quotation 63–64.

The forms and targets as well as the fact of protest become enshrined in tradition. French and English food rioters repeatedly imposed ceilings on the price of wheat, flour, and bread; farmers, millers, or bakers either were forced to sell their products at a price thought "fair" or had it confiscated, sold by the rioters at the "fair" price, and were given the proceeds. Rose has shown examples of such practices in England over the period 1693 to 1847.[43] Machinebreaking as a response of unemployed weavers to mechanization reached a peak in the Luddite riots of 1811–16, but was in an English tradition with cases on record as early as 1710. Arson, particularly the burning of farmers' stacks of hay or corn, was an established technique in English agrarian violence.[44] Edwards suggests the generalization that "a crowd is open to suggestions that are in line with its previous experiences—and to no others," and in support of the generalization observes that

> Ancient Jewish mobs always stoned their victims to death, Alexandrian mobs nearly always threw theirs from the tops of high buildings. . . . Medieval mobs regularly decapitated those they killed. Except in unusual circumstances American mobs use the noose. A Belfast mob could no more be brought to lynch negroes than a Chicago mob could be brought to lynch Catholics.[45]

Non-European examples also are easily found. Von der Mehden has compared relative levels and types of political violence in Burma and Thailand in the twentieth century. Burma has had substantially greater levels of anomic rural violence such as assassinations, agrarian revolts, religiously oriented uprisings, and banditry. Urban riots and demonstrations have similarly been much more common in Burma and have increased in frequency in the past twenty years. Burma also has a tradition of large-scale insurgency and rebellion that is unmatched in Thailand. The differences are attributed primarily to the breakdown of traditional political authority under the impact of colonial rule in Burma, and Thailand's avoidance of foreign rule. But the fact that violence has

[43] R. B. Rose, "Eighteenth-Century Price Riots and Public Policy in England," *International Review of Social History*, VI (No. 2, 1961), 277–92; Rudé, chap. 2.

[44] Rudé, 81, 241. On the conditions which led to the ultimate decline of English agrarian and worker violence see Ben C. Roberts, "On the Origins and Resolution of English Working Class Protest," in Hugh Davis Graham and Ted Robert Gurr, eds., *Violence in America: Historical and Comparative Perspectives* (Washington, D.C.: National Commission on the Causes and Prevention of Violence, 1969), 197–220.

[45] Lyford P. Edwards, *The Natural History of Revolution* (Chicago: University of Chicago Press, 1927), 99.

continued, indeed increased, in Burma since independence suggests that traditions of particular kinds of political violence were established during the colonial period and have persisted. In Thailand there also appears to be a tradition justifying a particular form of political disorder, namely coups and attempted coups, eleven of which occurred during the twenty-six years between 1932 and 1958.[46]

Latin America also provides many examples of societal traditions of particular forms of violence. In Venezuela, Gude points out, the attainment of independence by violence was followed by a comparably violent century of attempts at constitutional rule. "The system became, however, quite regularized. Violence and *caudillo* armies were the predictable means of political succession. This was the *de facto* . . . and accepted style of Venezuelan politics."[47] In a comparison of differential responses of Brazilian and Dominican students to revolutionary situations in 1964 and 1965, Wedge suggests that violence was inhibited in the former country by the Brazilian tradition of resolving political conflict with minimal violence and loss of life. In the Dominican Republic, by contrast, *caudillos* had repeatedly been overthrown in violent civil uprisings; there was little adherence to revolutionary ideology among those who participated in the battles of April and May 1965, but Dominican history provided a wealth of examples.[48] In qualification of this comparison, Busey has demonstrated that the Brazilian tradition of minimal violence in politics is not justified by the historical record.[49] What seems operant in the Brazilian case is not the actual historical magnitude of political violence, but Brazilians' belief that they are a nonviolent people.

Further evidence linking past with future levels of civil strife is provided by the previously cited cross-national study of strife in 114 nations during the early 1960s. As a partial test of the proposition, an imprecise measure of magnitude of strife by country for the 1946–59 period was constructed and correlated with more precise measures of magnitudes of the three basic forms of strife in 1961–65. Past strife correlated .30 with total magnitude of 1961–65 strife, .30 with magnitude of turmoil, and .24 with magnitude of con-

[46] Fred R. von der Mehden, "Political Violence in Burma and Thailand: A Preliminary Comparison" (paper read at the Annual Meeting of the Asian Studies Association, Philadelphia, March 1968).

[47] Edward W. Gude, "Political Violence in Venezuela: 1958–1964" (paper read at the 1967 Annual Meeting of the American Political Science Association, Chicago), quotation 10.

[48] Bryant Wedge, "The Case Study of Student Political Violence: Brazil, 1964, and Dominican Republic, 1965," *World Politics*, XXI (January 1969), 183–206.

[49] James L. Busey, "Brazil's Reputation for Political Stability," *Western Political Quarterly*, XVIII (December 1965), 866–880.

spiracy—all statistically significant relationships. Measures of RD and institutional characteristics also were included. An analysis of the causal sequences implicit in the correlation matrix suggests that past strife is an intervening not immediate cause of current strife, except in the case of turmoil, where it has a direct facilitative effect. The findings directly support the hypothesis that collective violence breeds collective violence. And they are consistent with the argument that chronic strife reflects, and contributes to, attitudes that facilitate future strife, irrespective of levels of persisting deprivation or of variations in institutional structure.[50]

The Politicization of Discontent

One striking characteristic of civil strife in the contemporary world is the extent to which its participants have political motives and direct their demands at political targets. Data on the numbers, types, reported targets, and apparent motives of initiators of civil strife events in 114 nations for 1961–65 suggest how strong and pervasive this relationship is. Of fifty-six internal wars (defined in chapter 1) identified, forty-nine were directed toward overthrowing or drastically modifying political systems; seven were "private wars," protracted and widespread violence among members of hostile ethnic or in several cases political groups. Some 200 violent conspiracy events were noted; all but a handful were political in character. Instances of violent turmoil included 315 isolated outbreaks and 122 series of related events. Of the total, 71 percent were antigovernment riots and localized rebellions, 15 percent were clashes among political opponents. The remainder were nonpolitical clashes and banditry. On the basis of form alone, therefore, about 90 percent of reported outbreaks of collective violence were "political." Nonpolitical violence is likely to be underreported, especially if it is localized and sporadic. It is all but certain, however, that nearly all large-scale outbreaks of collective violence are in some respects political in character, as are the majority of smaller-scale events.

Information on participants' targets and motives supports the generalization. Some 1,100 strife events were identified, including nonviolent events like demonstrations, general strikes, and plots. Table 4 shows the categorization of motives, by general type, attributed to the participants in news reports. "Political" motives

[50] Ted Gurr, "Urban Disorder: Perspectives from the Comparative Study of Civil Strife," *American Behavioral Scientist,* XI (March-April 1968), especially 52–54; and Gurr, "A Causal Model of Civil Strife: A Comparative Analysis Using New Indices," *American Political Science Review,* LXII (December 1968), 1104–1124.

TABLE 4

Apparent Motives for Civil Strife
1007 Events in 114 Polities, 1961–65 [a]

Motives	*Turmoil* ($n = 653$)	*Conspiracy* ($n = 295$)	*Internal War* ($n = 55$)
Political	90%	93%	98%
Economic	18	8	36
Social	43	32	87

[a] From Ted Robert Gurr, "A Comparative Study of Civil Strife," in Graham and Gurr, eds. Percentages add to more than 100 because multiple motives were attributed to participants. Events with missing "motives" data are excluded from the n's and percentages.

include demands on or opposition to the regime, its incumbents, its policies, foreign governments, or competing political groups. "Economic" motives comprise demands for material goods and opposition to economic actors (employers, competitors). "Social" motives include promotion of ideational systems and community maintenance, opposition to representatives of other belief systems and communities (linguistic, ethnic, religious, etc.), and demands for self-realization and interpersonal values. Political motives apparently predominate in all forms of strife. It is possible that news sources selectively report political motives, and highly likely that they accept leaders' or government spokesmen's assertions about motives. However, an analysis of the targets of violence—those persons or symbols who are attacked—shows the same pattern. Political actors were among the objects of threatened or overt violence in 83 percent of recorded turmoil events, 85 percent of conspiracies, and 93 percent of internal wars, while political symbols like government buildings were the targets in many of these events and some others.[51]

Some partial information suggests how common this politicization of violence has been in other eras. Studies of turmoil in Europe from the seventeenth through nineteenth century clearly indicate that turmoil was much more motivated by communal and economic issues and directed at the competing craftsmen, neighboring villagers, bakers, speculators, and industrialists who were immediately responsible.[52] Major rebellions of this and

[51] Ted Robert Gurr, "A Comparative Survey of Civil Strife," in Graham and Gurr, eds., 459–460.

[52] See Charles Tilly, "Collective Violence in European Perspective," in Graham and Gurr, eds.; and also Rudé, chapter 14; Hobsbawm, passim; Max Beloff, *Public Order and Popular Disturbances, 1660–1714* (London: Frank Cass, 1938, 1963), passim; and George Rudé, *The Crowd in the French Revolution* (London: Oxford University Press, 1959), chap. 13.

earlier eras usually had political objectives, as do contemporary internal wars, but economic motives seem to have been more salient than at present.[53] An historical trend toward politicization of collective violence is highly likely; its degree is less certain. The natural question is why it has occurred. One possible answer is that the preponderance of political violence in the twentieth century is a reflection of underlying discontents—that violence is political because more people perceive deprivation with reference to power rather than economic or interpersonal values. But cross-national survey evidence summarized in chapter 3 suggested that people in the 1950s and 1960s have been considerably more concerned about and dissatisfied with their economic lot than political issues. More directly, in the cross-national study of the conditions of civil strife in the early 1960s I found that a composite measure of economic deprivation correlated somewhat more closely with total magnitude of civil strife ($r = .44$) than did a measure of political deprivation ($r = .38$).

The implication is that most discontents in the modern world are not political but politicized. Two characteristics of contemporary societies have contributed to the focussing of diverse discontents on the political system: the ambiguity of origin of many deprivations in increasingly complex societies, and the widening scope of governmental responsibility in fact and in popular expectation for resolving value-distribution conflicts and generating new values.[54] The consequences of ambiguity have been examined in psychological studies of the frustration-aggression relationship. Whether aggression actually occurs after frustration depends upon the presence of stimuli associated with the source of frustration. In other words there must be some cue in the frustrating situation that suggests who or what is responsible for the interference.[55] In experimental situations the source of frustration is ordinarily highly visible. In modern and modernizing societies, however, the origins of many deprivations are obscure. The most knowledgeable citizen may have difficulty in identifying what group or institution is responsible for inflation, unemployment, declining religious morality, or status insecurity. If he is both intensely discontented and

[53] See for example Norman R. C. Cohn, *The Pursuit of the Millennium,* rev. edn. (New York: The Free Press, 1961), passim, and Gil Carl AlRoy, *The Involvement of Peasants in Internal Wars,* Research Monograph No. 24 (Princeton: Center of International Studies, Princeton University, 1966).

[54] The historical role of political and labor organizations in politicizing discontent in nineteenth-century Europe is examined by Tilly, "Collective Violence in European Perspective," in Graham and Gurr, eds.

[55] See Berkowitz, *Aggression,* 32–35, and the discussion in chap. 7, below, of receptiveness to revolutionary ideologies.

unable to find concrete sources of responsibility in his social environment, he is highly susceptible to new doctrines which provide palatable explanations, a characteristic of ideologies that is examined in the following chapter.

The increasing specialization of roles and functions in modern societies, and the corresponding development of complex social and economic interdependencies over ever-larger areas, have contributed to increased ambiguity about the sources of socioeconomic malaise. The political system is the agent most likely to be held responsible in the modern and modernizing nation, not simply by default but because of widespread organizational ideological, or elite-generated expectations that the state has ultimate responsibility not only for a narrow set of security and regulatory functions but for the general welfare of its citizens. Guessous argues that as a consequence of the processes of social and economic change set in motion in modernizing societies, "social life becomes integrated in such a way that no local problem can be solved without concomitant action on the wider national scene, and no limited aim can be achieved without a radical transformation of nearly all the major aspects of social life." The only institution that seems to command the resources and authority necessary for system transformation is the state. The ultimate consequence is that "the political system becomes the chief means as well as the chief end of action."[56] Ahmed describes this process as "the transformation of private problems into public issues." Rural people in developing societies, he suggests, are increasingly affected by and made dependent on developing urban centers, in the process of which the local community loses many of its traditional political and economic functions to new, often political, agencies. One result is that rural people begin to see themselves as part of a larger society and to attribute their private, local problems to a wider system which has failed to improve their life and the lives of comparable groups. Another result is a radicalization of conflict. For people newly aware both of common problems and the potential for resolving them at the national level, politics is perceived not just as a contest for offices but for the power to transform, or not transform, an entire society.[57]

Several studies provide evidence about the settings in which

[56] Mohammed Guessous, "An Approach to the Study of the Algerian Revolution" (Center of International Studies, Princeton University, March 1965, mimeo.), 22, 23.

[57] Eqbal Ahmed, "Unfinished Revolutions in the Third World" (paper read to the National Conference on "The United States in a Revolutionary World," Princeton University, April 1968).

politicization of discontent occurs. Danziger has analyzed "future autobiographies" written by black high school students in South Africa at several different periods. He found that, because of social and political restrictions imposed under apartheid policies, students' interest in individual economic success declined and their aspirations were increasingly expressed in political terms.[58] The process appears analogous to those described by Guessous and Ahmed; in South Africa the political system has severely limited opportunities for students' future value attainment and by doing so has made it more evident to them that their prospects depend on political opportunities. Willner suggests that Indonesian protest demonstrations tend to focus on a single issue that symbolizes a more basic source of dissatisfaction, which she attributes to a cultural preference for minimizing overt conflict. Thus a demonstration against rising rice prices can reflect fundamental discontent over the whole pattern of governmental economic policies, and a demonstration against a particular parliamentary policy may be based on a desire by its leaders to make fundamental alterations in the structure of the regime.[59] This example suggests more generally that varied discontents, arising from economic and interpersonal as well as power deprivations, clear or ambiguous in origin, can be channeled into an act of protest that apparently has a narrow, political focus. A characteristic of the political regime that contributes to the politicization of discontent is the degree to which power and resources are concentrated in particular political institutions. Payne proposes that because of the highly centralized nature of Peruvian government "the President is considered omnicompetent and hence, omniresponsible . . . when anything goes wrong the executive is considered to have committed a sin of commission or omission." As a result, groups affected by deprivations of any conceivable type tend to organize and focus violence on a single point, the executive.[60]

Several of these interpretations and examples imply that discontent is likely to be politicized to the extent that a regime affects, or is thought to have the potential to affect, the lives of most or all its citizens. The greater its demonstrated or promised ability to take remedial action, and the greater the number of groups and

[58] Kurt Danziger, "The Psychological Future of an Oppressed Group," *Social Forces,* LXII (October 1963), 31–40.

[59] Ann Ruth Willner, "Some Forms and Functions of Public Protest in Indonesia" (paper read to the Annual Meeting of the Asian Studies Association, Philadelphia, March 1968), 3–5.

[60] James Payne, "Peru: The Politics of Structured Violence," *Journal of Politics,* XXVII (May 1965), 366–367.

range of problems with which it does deal, the more likely it is to be regarded as capable of remedying other problems and alleviating the discontents of other groups. Effective action against one set of problems thus is likely to generate or reinforce existing normative expectations that others should be dealt with, and utilitarian expectations that they *can* be dealt with. If a regime's past performance has been broad in scope and relatively effective, it is likely to be subject to demands to deal with new problems. If demands articulated through conventional channels lead to responses that the discontented find inadequate, they are increasingly likely to resort to demonstrative, sometimes violent tactics. *In extremis,* when people are intensely discontented and believe that the political system has the capacity and resources to resolve their deprivation but feel that no effective action will be taken by the incumbents, they are likely to resort to revolutionary or conspiratorial tactics in order to seize control of the regime and place it in the service of their interests. The crux of this argument, summarized hypothetically below, is that the more effective a political system has been in resolving past problems the greater are popular expectations that it will do so in the future, and the greater the likelihood that its discontented citizens will feel justified, on both normative and utilitarian grounds, in resorting to political violence to compel attention to unresolved problems.

Hypothesis JV.3: The intensity and scope of normative and utilitarian justifications for political violence vary moderately with the effectiveness and scope of past regime action in alleviating relative deprivation.

Previous regime action was *effective* to the extent that it implemented policies that remedied RD. The *scope* of such action is the proportion of the population that benefited from the distribution of values.

The hypothesis appears paradoxical in its implication that political systems that have effectively resolved past crises are more susceptible to future political violence than those that have not. But note that it applies to the development of attitudes justifying violence, attitudes likely to be operative only when a system that resolved problems in the past fails to take effective action in response to present problems. Recent strife in France and the United States may be manifestations of another aspect of this relationship: both political systems, France since 1958 and the United States since the 1930s, have had a high demonstrated capacity to resolve problems, but both have been selective in the problems to which resources were devoted. In both countries the groups resorting to collective action are those whose discontents have received least attention: workers, students, and farmers in France; blacks and pacifists in the United States. These examples suggest a simultaneous relationship analogous to that in hypothesis JV.3, namely, that if a political system concurrently devotes extensive resources to the resolution of one type of problem—maintenance of international position in these two instances—but few resources to others, those affected by the unresolved problems are rather likely to feel justified in violent response.

Hypothesis JV.4: The intensity of normative and utilitarian justifications for political violence varies moderately with the proportional difference in allocation of regime resources to the alleviation of the relative deprivation of different groups.

For example, if policies are devised that provide compensatory values for half the RD of one group but for only 10 percent of another, the less advantaged group is likely to resort to collective protest to increase its share of values. The relationship is a special case of and supported by parallel arguments for the effect identified in hypothesis VE.3 (chapter 4): members of groups tend to set their value expectations by reference to the value positions of the most rapidly improving groups in a society. That relationship applies to the effects of differential group increases in value position on value expectations whatever the source of value increase for the favored group; hypothesis JV.4 asserts that if several groups are deprived and the political system is the source of differential value increases among them, the less fortunate will feel justified in directing their anger at the responsible political agents. The scope of the effect is not intrinsically affected by differentials in value increments but by the size of the relatively disadvantaged group.

The Legitimacy of Political Systems

A dense thicket of scholarly concepts and distinctions has grown out of attempts to specify the sources, nature, and consequences of men's attitudes towards their rulers and political institutions. These perspectives and the conditions associated with them have variously been described as "legitimacy,"[61] "political commu-

[61] Most influentially by Max Weber, for example in *The Theory of Social and Economic Organization*, trans. A. M. Henderson and Talcott Parsons (New York: Oxford University Press, 1947), 124–132.

nity,"[62] "political myth,"[63] "support,"[64] "authoritativeness,"[65] "political trust,"[66] "system affect,"[67] "political allegiance,"[68] and "loyalty," to cite some representative concepts. Some of these, the first three, are usually used as macroconcepts: they refer to properties of political systems. They assume, either explicitly or implicitly, popular attitudes toward politics described as "feelings of legitimacy," "sense of political community," and "adherence to political myth." The others are microconcepts, identifying such attitudes directly. The macroconcepts are sometimes regarded in dichotomous terms: regimes are said to be either legitimate or not. The microconcepts can be applied dichotomously to individuals—a citizen is either loyal or he is not—but more commonly are regarded as variables: citizens individually and collectively have varying degrees or intensities of feelings toward their rulers and institutions. Some of these variables are described in terms of polarities: Lane, for example, distinguishes among feelings of allegiance (positive), alienation (negative), and divorcement (neutral),[69] while Gamson labels the opposite of political trust "discontent."[70] Goldrich distinguishes three types of what he calls "legitimacy orientations"—supportive, acquiescent, and opposed.[71] Other variables, like system affect and authoritativeness, are or can be used as zero-point variables, varying from none or low to high.

Some writers make distinctions among the *objects* of attitudes toward politics. Almond and Verba speak of "output affect," people's expectations about the treatment they can expect from government officials, and "input affect," their feelings about participatory processes.[72] Easton distinguishes among attitudes of support

[62] For example Sebastian de Grazia, *The Political Community* (Chicago: University of Chicago Press, 1948).

[63] Harold D. Lasswell and Abraham Kaplan, *Power and Society: A Framework for Political Inquiry* (New Haven: Yale University Press, 1950), 116–125.

[64] Richard Rose, "The Problematic Nature of the Legitimacy of Regimes" (Department of Politics, University of Strathclyde, Glasgow, n.d., mimeo.), 9ff; David Easton, *A Systems Analysis of Political Life* (New York: Wiley, 1965), 163 and passim.

[65] Kim, 223.

[66] William A. Gamson, *Power and Discontent* (Homewood, Ill.: Dorsey Press, 1968), chap. 3.

[67] Gabriel A. Almond and Sidney Verba, *The Civic Culture: Political Attitudes and Democracy in Five Nations* (Princeton: Princeton University Press, 1963), chap. 4.

[68] Robert E. Lane, *Political Ideology: Why the American Common Man Believes What He Does* (New York: The Free Press, 1962), chap. 10.

[69] *Loc.cit.*

[70] Gamson, chap. 3.

[71] Daniel Goldrich, *Sons of the Establishment: Elite Youth in Panama and Costa Rica* (Chicago: Rand McNally, 1966).

[72] Almond and Verba, 101.

for the political community, the regime, and its incumbents.[73] Gamson identifies four objects of "political trust": incumbents, political institutions, the public philosophy of a regime, and the political community. "They may be considered hierarchical, each being a generalization of trust attitudes at the previous level."[74] The justification for such distinctions is that citizens can vary in the intensity of their feelings toward political objects: one can talk precisely about intensities of support only by weighting feelings toward different objects.

An underlying theme of this theoretical work is that positive perspectives on politics make men good subjects—willing to support and obey, unwilling to attack the political system. The kinds of perspectives that relate most closely to political violence are those conventionally discussed in connection with legitimacy. The behavioral manifestation of legitimacy is the compliance of citizens with directives of the regime, its attitudinal character a generalized sense of identification with and feelings of obligation toward the regime that motivate citizens to comply. Citizens can have other motives for compliance than a sense of identification and obligation, the most common one being fear of sanctions for noncompliance. Recent discussions of legitimacy usually assume that regimes are not legitimate if compliance is based primarily on coercion, for if it is, compliance is likely to decline whenever coercion is removed. Consequently, most definitions associate legitimacy with supportive attitudes. The following hypothesis summarizes the implied causal relationship between attitudes toward a regime and about political violence.

Hypothesis JV.5: The intensity and scope of normative justifications for political violence vary strongly and inversely with the intensity and scope of regime legitimacy.

For the purposes of this analysis, regimes are said to be *legitimate* to the extent that their citizens regard them as proper and deserving of support. *Regime* is used in a general sense to mean the political unit itself, its governing institutions (regime in the narrow sense), and their incumbents. By these definitions a highly legitimate regime does not necessarily get universal compliance. Specific laws may be widely disobeyed out of principle or narrow self-interest. Advocates of civil disobedience in the United States illustrate the possibility that a regime can be highly legitimate but some of its laws highly illegitimate in the eyes of some of its citi-

[73] Easton, 1963; David Easton, *A Framework for Political Analysis* (Englewood Cliffs, N.J.: Prentice-Hall, 1965), 116.
[74] Gamson, 50–52.

zens. The relationship between legitimacy and compliance is generally a close one, however. If people feel intensely about the propriety of their government, only strong countervailing motives are likely to compel them to act against it. The relationship between legitimacy and political violence is not likely to be as strong as that between legitimacy and compliance generally, however. If a highly legitimate regime imposes a policy that substantially violates popular expectations about what the regime should do, people are motivated to protest the policy not only because of the direct deprivation it imposes but because it is inconsistent with their image of the regime. If the regime resists pressures to change through normal channels, participatory RD may increase to the point at which demonstrative violence occurs, directed against both the policy and the incumbents who imposed it. As a last resort, intensely discontented citizens may feel that a highly legitimate political unit can be preserved only by violent opposition to both incumbents and institutions which are acting in an improper, i.e. illegitimate, way. In general, people who regard their regimes as legitimate will regard political violence as unjustified, but if a highly legitimate regime acts in ways inconsistent with the expectations on which its legitimacy is based, it may run a greater risk of political violence, particularly turmoil, than a regime that has persistently lacked popular support. Such circumstances are uncommon, however.

The *intensity* of regime legitimacy is the extent to which the political unit, its governing institutions, and the incumbents are thought proper and worthy of support. Citizens are likely to regard the legitimacy of the unit as more important than that of institutions, and the legitimacy of institutions more important than that of incumbents, following the hierarchy suggested by Gamson. But there is no necessary relationship among the intensities of support for the three types of political objects. In new nations, for example, the legitimacy or lack of legitimacy of a national leader like Nasser, Ayub Khan, or Nyerere may be far more consequential in peoples' attitudes toward overall regime legitimacy than their feelings about the propriety of the state or its institutions. The *scope* of legitimacy is the proportion of people in the political unit with feelings of legitimacy above some specified threshold.

The relationship in hypothesis JV.5 is specifically restricted to feelings of legitimacy above a zero-point of neutrality or disinterest. Illegitimacy is the polar opposite of legitimacy and can be defined in terms of the extent people regard their regimes as improper and deserving of opposition. But illegitimacy sentiments are a particular type of discontent that arises from RD with respect to power values—i.e., a discrepancy between people's expectations about the kinds of participation and security values their regimes should provide and those they actually provide. If the legitimacy-illegitimacy continuum is related to the magnitude of political violence in its entirety, the relationship is likely to be linear and inverse throughout, but different causal mechanisms are operating on either side of the zero point: positive feelings toward the regime are causally linked with normative inhibitions against political violence (hypothesis JV.5), negative feelings toward the regime are a direct instigation to violence, although they are unlikely to be sufficient unless combined with other discontents.

Various causal and temporal sequences have been said to underlie the development of legitimacy or lack of it. Some explanations focus on the individual and the determinants of his hostile or supportive feelings about government. Lane, for example, derives a portrait of "the impoverished self" from his interviews with fifteen Americans and from theoretical literature. Individuals characterized by low self-acceptance, low self-esteem, and low ego strength are unlikely to be supportive of democratic governing processes. The "democratic personality" has all these qualities in substantial degree.[75] Merelman argues that the development of legitimacy is analogous to the individual learning process. He interprets the origins of legitimacy as "a special case of reinforcement learning, whereby symbolic rewards come to replace material rewards for societies, whereby such rewards and the processes and exertions necessary to gain them are rationalized into a sense of legitimacy." Once this process has taken place, symbols of legitimacy like "our way of life" and "the Constitution" are "learning aids" which can be invoked by political leaders to "hasten the acceptance of and compliance with new policies put forth in the sytem." Although the argument is sometimes stated in organismic terms, as though the society as a whole were a learning mechanism, it is clear that Merelman regards the process as one typically concentrated in one or several generations in a nation's history, whose members acquire legitimacy symbols which they pass on to subsequent generations; the whole process is not ordinarily or necessarily repeated in the political socialization of all future citizens.[76]

Other explanations for the development of legitimacy emphasize

[75] Lane, 409–412.

[76] Richard M. Merelman, "Learning and Legitimacy," *American Political Science Review*, LX (September 1966), quotations 560, 561. For a study of the origins of children's attitudes toward incumbents see Fred I. Greenstein, *Children and Politics* (New Haven: Yale University Press, 1965). For qualifying evidence see Dean Jaros, Herbert Hirsch, and Frederic J. Fleron, Jr., "The Malevolent Leader: Political Socialization in an American Sub-culture," *American Political Science Review*, LXII (June 1968), 564–575.

system characteristics. Almond and Verba, for example, suggest a structural correlate of high input affect in democracies: "an effectively functioning democracy implies that a substantial proportion of its members are involved in the political system through the meshing of the more diffuse structures of the community with the more differentiated ones of the polity." If there is inadequate structural articulation, "the polity may lose touch with the intimate moods and needs of its members. People may withdraw emotionally from the political system or relate themselves to it by passively accepting the displacements, projections, and other irrationalities of extremist movements."[77] Eckstein attributes the extent of feelings of legitimacy in all kinds of regimes to the degree of congruence (similarity) among nonpolitical and political institutions in the structures and processes of decision-making and exercise of authority. The argument is that if the directives of the regime are formulated and implemented in ways which are valued by and familiar to the individual, on the basis of his experience with authority in his primary and immediate associations, he is likely to feel that governmental authority is proper.[78] Gusfield proposes that "inability of political elites to deal with crisis is . . . one strong source of mass alienation from a political institution."[79] Varied evidence and speculation, summarized below, supports the relationship proposed in hypothesis JV.5 between legitimacy, whatever its origins, and justifications for political violence. Psychoanalytic and psychological theory and evidence suggest why feelings of support and identification for political objects inhibit attacks on them. Psychoanalytic theory attributes inhibition of individual aggression first to "instinct-renunciation due to dread of an aggression by external authority. . . . Then follows the erection of an internal authority, and instinctual renunciation due to dread of it—that is, dread of conscience."[80] Frank suggests, without specifying psychodynamic sources, that "obedience to legitimate authority is one of the strongest motivating forces in the life of all normal members of organized societies," an obedience

[77] Almond and Verba, chap. 5, quotation 144.

[78] Harry Eckstein, "A Theory of Stable Democracy," Appendix B in *Division and Cohesion in Democracy: A Study of Norway* (Princeton: Princeton University Press, 1966), 225–287.

[79] Joseph R. Gusfield, "Mass Society and Extremist Politics," *American Sociological Review*, XXVII (February 1962), 25. An all but exhaustive list of variables which contribute to legitimacy appears in Richard Rose, "Dynamic Tendencies in the Authority of Regimes," *World Politics*, XXI (July 1969), 602–628.

[80] Sigmund Freud, *Civilization and its Discontents*, trans. Joan Riviere (London: Hogarth Press, 1930, 1951), 112–113. A brief review of psychoanalytic theory of destructiveness related to internal violence is Alfred de Grazia, *Politics and Government*, Vol. I: *Political Behavior*, rev. edn. (New York: Collier, 1962), 275–277.

that makes men willing to commit virtually unlimited aggression at the dictates of legitimate authorities as well as to obey their injunctions against violence even under severe provocation. "A person submitting to a legitimate authority hands his conscience over, in effect, for since the authority decides what is right and wrong, the subordinate's own conscience is suspended."[81] To link these arguments, men can acquire in the socialization process perceptions of the regime as an ultimate source of authority, internalize prohibitions against aggression toward it, and at the same time respond to it as an external surrogate of conscience whose dictates supersede those of conscience.

Some experimental evidence on the frustration-aggression relationship is relevant. Pastore, for example, found that when subjects thought that a frustration was reasonable or justifiable, they gave fewer aggressive responses to it than when they perceived it as arbitrary.[82] Similarly, Cohen reports that aggression is a more likely experimental response to arbitrary than nonarbitrary frustrations.[83] What is "reasonable" or "nonarbitrary" frustration is of course a function of social learning. Extrapolating to the ways people learn about politics, it is likely that in a country with a legitimate regime, children and youth learn that the deprivations imposed by the regime through its demands for compliance and value sacrifice are "reasonable" because people are or will be compensated for them by symbolic and material rewards. Other experimental evidence suggests that the "reasonableness" of frustration does not diminish the intensity of anger per se but, as hypothesis JV.4 proposes, serves to inhibit the aggressive response. Rothaus and Worchel found that under nonarbitrary frustrations, people become angered but inhibit aggression because of the nature of the situation. The more maladjusted the individual, however, the more likely he is to react aggressively to both arbitrary and nonarbitrary frustrations.[84] In a parallel study Kregarman and Worchel found that the reasonableness of a frustration does not significantly reduce mild forms of aggression and that anticipation of frustration—perhaps analogous to expectations that a regime will demand compliance—does not substantially reduce anger but rather leads

[81] Frank, 81–84, also chap. 12.

[82] Nicholas Pastore, "The Role of Arbitrariness in the Frustration-Aggression Hypothesis," *Journal of Abnormal and Social Psychology*, XLVII (July 1952), 728–731.

[83] Arthur R. Cohen, "Social Norms, Arbitrariness of Frustration, and Status of the Agent of Frustration in the Frustration-Aggression Hypothesis," *Journal of Abnormal and Social Psychology*, LI (1955), 222–226.

[84] Paul Rothaus and Philip Worchel, "The Inhibition of Aggression under Nonarbitrary Frustration," *Journal of Personality*, XXVIII (March 1960), 108–117.

subjects to inhibit external aggressive responses.[85] If these findings can be applied to learning about politics, either through political socialization or through adult experience with government, they all suggest that people tend to refrain from aggressive responses to actions of a regime which they have learned to think of as proper and as acting for their own long-range interests.

Small-group studies by Raven and French show a relationship between legitimacy and compliance. They found that group support for leaders is related to feelings about the legitimacy of the leaders' position, and that the legitimation of leaders through election gives them greater influence over group members than assumption of leadership without election.[86] The implication is not necessarily that election is a requirement for legitimate authority; it is likely to be in democratic societies, not necessarily so in others. More generally, people are more likely to comply with directives from leaders chosen by whatever means are regarded as proper. In his interview study of forty-one American respondents, Kim found a clear negative relationship between what he calls "authoritativeness" and expressed willingness to participate in antigovernment violence. Authoritativeness was defined as the degree to which respondents thought that government output (directives) should be accepted as binding. The more authoritative or legitimate these Americans thought government was, the less willing they were to attack it.[87] Also relevant is an experimental study of Midwestern college students' willingness to join what they thought was a real lynching mob; almost all who were prepared to do so said they thought that the law would be ineffective in dealing with the supposed murderers.[88] In this instance violence was not political, but potential participation in it was facilitated by a lack of trust in the efficacy of the judicial system.

Low levels of legitimacy or allegiance in new nations are widely cited as a source of political instability. The nationalism generated in the movement toward independence may provide a sense of allegiance and purpose, but as Halpern observes, "the nationalization of human souls solves only the problem of who is to be in

[85] John J. Kregarman and Philip Worchel, "Arbitrariness of Frustration and Aggression," *Journal of Abnormal and Social Psychology,* LXIII (July 1961), 183–187.

[86] B. H. Raven and J. R. P. French, Jr., "Group Support, Legitimate Power, and Social Influence," *Journal of Personality,* XXVI (September 1958), 400–409; and "Legitimate Power, Coercive Power, and Observability in Social Influence," *Sociometry,* XXI (June 1958), 83–97.

[87] Kim.

[88] Norman C. Meier, G. H. Mennenga, and H. J. Stoltz, "An Experimental Approach to the Study of Mob Behavior," *Journal of Abnormal and Social Psychology,* XXXVI (1941), 506–524.

charge, not the problems of stability or purpose."[89] Shils emphasizes the lack of positive attitudes toward the political community and its rulers in new states:

> the prepolitical matrix is in a most rudimentary condition. The constituent societies on which the new states rest . . . certainly do not form a single civil society. . . . They lack the affirmative attitude toward rules, persons, and actions that is necessary for consensus. . . . The sense of identity is rudimentary, even where it exists. The sense of membership in a nation-wide society, and the disposition to accept the legitimacy of the government, its personnel, and its laws are not great.[90]

Geertz emphasizes the difficulties of adjusting "primordial ties" to the requirements for new, civil identifications.[91] In his comparative study of political violence in Burma and Thailand, von der Mehden attributes the relatively high levels of political violence in Burma largely to the destruction of legitimate traditional authority patterns under the colonial impact. British colonial authority and the authority of the nationalists who succeeded the British "was neither familiar nor acceptable to most politicized Burmese and thus did not contain within it recognized sanctions to the extent that was to be found in the more traditionally based Thai Kingdom."[92]

Results of two recent cross-national studies provide some quantitative evidence. An indirect measure of regime legitimacy-illegitimacy was constructed for 114 nations and related to a measure of magnitude of civil strife in 1961–1965. Highest legitimacy was attributed to regimes whose institutions were primarily of indigenous origin and which had persisted longest without substantial change; legitimacy was assumed to be lowest in countries whose political institutions were short-lived and imposed under foreign tutelage. The combined index based on these two measures correlated −.37 with magnitude of strife: the greater the inferred legitimacy, the less strife. When the 114 polities were divided according to the character of their regimes, distinct differences were found. Legitimacy most strongly minimizes strife

[89] Manfred Halpern, *The Politics of Social Change in the Middle East and North Africa* (Princeton: Princeton University Press, 1963), 210.

[90] Edward Shils, "On the Comparative Study of the New States," in Clifford Geertz, ed. *Old Societies and New States: The Quest for Modernity in Asia and Africa* (New York: The Free Press, 1963), 1–26, quotation 21.

[91] Clifford Geertz, "The Integrative Revolution: Primordial Sentiments and Civil Politics in the New States," *Old Societies and New States*, 105–151.

[92] Von der Mehden, 8–14, quotation 13.

in pluralist, democratic nations ($r = -.45$), and in personalist nations, mostly Latin American nations with leaders of the *caudillo* type ($r = -.58$). Among elitist nations, however, including most of the new states, the correlation is weaker, −.26, and among highly authoritarian states it is an inconsequential −.08. One interpretation is that, in the latter two groups of nations, coercion may be considerably more important in inhibiting political violence than the internalized inhibitions associated with feelings of legitimacy.[93] In another study Bwy, using a set of measures of legitimacy for Latin American countries based on estimates of their degree of "democracy," found that legitimacy correlated −.71 with organized violence but insignificantly (−.14) with anomic violence (turmoil).[94]

* * *

Dispositions to violence, and to peace, are deeply rooted in human culture and vary markedly among cultures. People acquire basic attitudes about the desirability of acting out their aggressions as children, and then and later in life develop attitudes about the responsibilities of rulers for their well-being. These attitudes fundamentally influence responses to depriving political circumstances. People also may be taught about the gains their ancestors won or liberties they protected through violence, teachings that often provide enduring justifications for violence in new circumstances. The hypotheses that state these relations precisely are summarized at the conclusion of the next chapter. The crucial implications of this chapter are that there *are* violent societies, that we know something about how they originate and perpetuate themselves, and that the discontents that precede violence in them are probably more amenable to change than the attitudes that justify it.

[93] Results of the analysis for all politics are reported in Gurr, "A Causal Model." Comparisons by types of political systems appear in Gurr, "A Comparative Survey."

[94] Douglas P. Bwy, "Political Instability in Latin America: The Cross-Cultural Test of a Causal Model," *Latin American Research Review*, III (Spring 1968), 17–66.

7. Perspectives on Violence and Politics: Ideologies, Utilities, and Communication

> New truths are always being prepared in the cellars of violence.
>
> Antoine de St. Exupéry

WE ACQUIRE OUR norms about violence partly from how we are taught to deal with aggressive impulses, partly from our cultural heritages of civil peace or conflict. If we have shared discontents, our attitudes about the legitimacy of our rulers and political institutions either focus that discontent on or deflect it away from political targets. These attitudes are remote rather than immediate causes of political violence. The more immediate psychological determinants of how we respond to specific deprivations are our cognitive maps of social causality and responsibility, by which we attribute blame, and our beliefs about the justifiability and consequences of specific kinds of actions in response to those situations. If intensely discontented, we are susceptible to new ideologies, and less complex beliefs, that assert the righteousness and usefulness of political violence. We also are likely to make calculations, whether shrewd or self-deceiving, about the gains we can achieve through violence. The most potent attitudes about political violence are those most widely shared in a society. Almost any group in any society can express new and reinforce old beliefs justifying violence; such beliefs are most widely and effectively disseminated among discontented people in societies with many and uncensored communication media. This chapter provides an analysis and hypothetical summary of the role of these ideological, utilitarian, and communication factors in the justification of political violence.

Doctrinal Justifications for Political Violence

Frames of reference for interpreting and acting on discontent vary markedly in both content and elaboration. In content they range from Gandhian doctrines of nonviolence to Sorelian glorification of violence per se. They vary in complexity from elaborate, consciously propagated intellectual structures which provide a comprehensive *Weltanschauung*, like Maoist revolutionary ideology, to the temporary juxtaposition of cognitive elements of prejudice and tumor, like the Watts rioters' antipathy toward white police and acceptance of the rumor that the police beat up a pregnant woman. These ideas about violence can be examined in terms of their specific content, or their psychological functions for the discontented, or according to the kinds of social structures in which they are embedded, or the group interests manifest in them, as well as other perspectives. This section focuses on the functions of ideas about violence for deprived groups, taking their content into account to illustrate how they appear to correspond to the situations of particular groups.

SOME FUNCTIONS OF IDEOLOGY, REVOLUTIONARY AND OTHERWISE

Ideologies are "frameworks of consciousness" which provide men with an interpretation of the world for purposes of acting in it.[1] Political ideology, in Dion's view, "is a more or less integrated system of values and norms, rooted in society, which individuals and groups project on the political plane in order to promote the aspirations and ideals they have come to value in social life."[2] When men's ideational systems prove inadequate to their purposes, and particularly when they become intensely and irremediably discontented because goals are unattainable by old norms, they are susceptible to new ideas which justify different courses of action. "Generalized beliefs" is Smelser's term for the new ideas that develop in situations of social strain which cannot be managed within the existing framework for action. Such beliefs mobilize people for collective action by explaining ambiguous situations and creating a "'common culture' within which leadership, mobilization, and concerted action can take place."[3]

Men's ideational systems, including their political ideologies, usually incorporate norms about the desirability of political violence. They may prohibit the use of violence as an instrument of political competition, or prescribe violence as an historically justified response to political oppression. Under conditions of strain or discontent, however, new ideas circulate among the discontented which are more likely to offer normative justifications for violence. Dion maintains that the disruptive content of new political ideologies is an expression of preexisting social tensions and conflicts, given political expression and channeled into po-

[1] The phrase is from David Apter, "Ideology and Discontent," in Apter, ed., *Ideology and Discontent* (New York: The Free Press, 1964).

[2] Léon Dion, "Political Ideology as a Tool of Functional Analysis in Socio-political Dynamics: An Hypothesis," *Canadian Journal of Economics and Political Science*, XXV (February 1959), 49.

[3] Neil J. Smelser, *Theory of Collective Behavior* (New York: The Free Press, 1963), chap. 5, quotation 82.

litical activity. He hypothesizes that "the more acute the social tensions and conflicts, the more likely to be extreme the political ideologies that express them."[4] Other interpretations of revolutionary ideology attribute its normative justification of political violence to the tactical requirements of a revolutionary movement, and especially to the need to obtain mass support for violence. Naess argues that greater justification and rationalization is needed for attaining "aggressive intentions" than for attaining "benevolent intentions." "The technique of building up impressive superstructures of principles and means-ends doctrines is to a large degree used for the rationalization of demands which seem most easily satisfied by fighting or oppressing other peoples."[5] Leiden and Schmitt emphasize the guidance and justification that revolutionary ideologies provide for the revolutionaries. "Every revolution proceeds upon whatever guidance—plans, philosophies, martyrology, doctrines—is available and compatible to its functionaries; but every revolution also produces a plethora of justification." The justification is often post hoc. "All revolutionaries find it necessary to defend what they have done and to consolidate their achievements. . . . The justification that is produced is rarely candid."[6] To the extent that revolutions are accomplished through violence, justificatory ideologies are therefore likely to stress the desirability of political violence as an instrument for the revolutionaries' attainment of power.

Most participants in political violence, revolutionary or otherwise, do not carry complex ideologies around in their heads. The subtleties of justification articulated by revolutionary leaders penetrate to many of their followers in a congeries of phrases, vague ideas, and symbols. Studies of a variety of communist movements, using many research techniques, "show that hard core ideologues are primarily middle-class professionals and intellectuals, few in number, who were attracted primarily by the ideological appeal of Marx; lower-class communists seem little affected by ideology."[7] The slogans which suffice to justify violence for most participants in strife may be derived from complex ideologies,

[4] Dion, 56.

[5] Arne Naess, "The Function of Ideological Convictions," in Hadley Cantril, ed., *Tensions that Cause Wars* (Urbana: University of Illinois Press, 1950), 275–276.

[6] Carl Leiden and Karl M. Schmitt, *The Politics of Violence: Revolution in the Modern World* (Englewood Cliffs: Prentice-Hall, 1968), 97, 99–100.

[7] Samuel H. Barnes, "Ideology and the Organization of Conflict: On the Relationship between Political Thought and Behavior" (Paper read at the Annual Meeting of the American Political Science Association, Washington, D.C., 1965), 8.

but their operative force lies not in the ideology itself but in the relevance of the slogans to the actors' perceptions of their situation and the cues the slogans provide for violent action. Berkowitz shows, on the basis of experimental evidence, that the mere utterance of hostile words—words that subjects previously associated with aggression—tends to increase the subjects' levels of aggression. "A person making hostile statements, or who uses words connoting hostility, may actually be providing himself with internal stimuli which can increase the probability of subsequent aggression."[8] Repetition of slogans like, "Liberty, equality, and fraternity!" "Workers of the world arise, and you have nothing to lose but your chains!" and "Burn, baby, burn!" serve this function for the angry man. They are mental reminders of the nature and causes of his discontent, and internal cues, based on recollection and observation of others using the slogans, for violent response. Sorel's advocacy of the general strike was designed to provide this kind of energizing slogan for violence by the working classes. He regarded the general strike as a myth, "a body of images capable of evoking instinctively all the sentiments which correspond to the different manifestations of the war undertaken by Socialism against modern society."[9] Fanon attempted to create a revolutionary myth out of the advocacy of purifying violence by peasant revolutionaries against colonial masters. "Violence is a cleansing force. It frees the native from his inferiority complex and from his despair and inaction; it makes him fearless and restores his self-respect."[10]

Slogans invested with recollection of grievance and violence can serve as well or better than ideology to justify political violence. Such ideas may be created by ideologues, as they were by Sorel and Fanon, or be adopted by the discontented to symbolize their actions, as they were by black rioters, or they can arise from intergroup hostility of the kind conventionally called prejudice. Hostile attitudes along lines of ethnic, political, or class cleavage can originate in a variety of ways: from a history of group conflict, from threatening demands of a subordinated group for greater privileges, or simply from frequent contact between people ad-

[8] Leonard Berkowitz, "Some Experiments on Automatism and Intent in Human Aggression" (Paper read at University of California at Los Angeles, Brain Research Institute, November 1965), 6–8, quotation 6.

[9] Georges Sorel, *Reflections on Violence*, tran. T. E. Hulme (New York: Peter Smith, 1915, 1941), 137.

[10] See Frantz Fanon, *The Wretched of the Earth* (New York: Grove Press, 1966). The quotation, and a critical review of Fanon from this viewpoint, appear in Lewis A. Coser, *Continuities in the Study of Social Conflict* (New York: The Free Press, 1967), 214.

hering to different ideational systems and life styles (see chapter 5). Given the existence of such intergroup hostilities, a report of an actual or fancied attack by members of one group on another can provide sufficient justification for collective violence. An analysis of the precipitants of seventy-six American race riots shows that fifty-two followed actual or reported interracial assaults.[41] On the basis of his study of eighteenth- and nineteenth-century crowd behavior in England and France, Rudé suggests that even in the most spontaneous outbreaks some unity was provided by underlying beliefs and by slogans. Pervasive beliefs, for example about the evil purposes of opposing groups or governmental responsibility for failure to remedy deprivations, were essential in preparing a militant climate of opinion. More directly slogans such as "Wilkes and Liberty" and "No Popery and Wooden Shoes" "served to unify the crowd itself and to direct its energies toward precise targets and objectives."[12] The massacre of Communist Party (PKI) supporters in Indonesia in 1965–66 is a contemporary and specifically political example. Its remote antecedents were several historical attempts by the PKI to seize power. Its more immediate cause was the encouragement the PKI gave to its followers in 1964–65 to enforce land redistribution legislation at the village level, which crystallized hostility against the PKI. The attempt of PKI leaders to seize power on September 30, 1965, and their widely publicized torture and murder of government officials, combined with preexisting hostility to provide justification for the slaughter of three to five hundred thousand communist sympathizers over the next five months.[13] Other examples could be cited. These are sufficient to illustrate that, when group prejudices or hostility exist, the report of any additional grievance can activate norms justifying collective violence.[14]

RECEPTIVITY TO DOCTRINAL JUSTIFICATIONS FOR POLITICAL VIOLENCE

Diverse ideologies, slogans, and rumors can mobilize people for political violence. They are most likely to do so if people are intensely discontented, as is argued in chapter 4. Intensely dis-

[11] Stanley Lieberson and Arnold R. Silverman, "The Precipitants and Underlying Conditions of Race Riots," *American Sociological Review*, XXX (December 1965), 889. For other examples see Smelser, 247–253.

[12] George Rudé, *The Crowd in History, 1730–1848* (New York: Wiley, 1964), 245.

[13] See Tarzie Vittachi, *The Fall of Sukarno* (New York: Praeger, 1967).

[14] For a review and interpretation of the social psychological evidence on intergroup hostility see Leonard Berkowitz, *Aggression: A Social Psychological Analysis* (New York: McGraw-Hill, 1962), chaps. 6, 7.

contented people are most susceptible to new doctrines when they are uncertain about the origins of their discontent, and more generally are anxious about the lack of certainty in their social environment. Because of their discontent, they are inherently disposed to doctrinal justification of aggressive action. Some arguments and evidence in support of these assertions follow.

Some scholars suggest that new doctrinal justifications for political violence themselves create discontent. Heckscher says that the "propaganda auction" among competing groups making vast promises in prerevolutionary situations has the effect "of creating general unrest and dissatisfaction."[15] Hoffer says that ideologues prepare the ground for mass movements "by discrediting prevailing creeds and institutions and detaching from them the allegiance of the people" and "by indirectly creating a hunger for faith in the hearts of those who cannot live without it," thus facilitating the spread of new beliefs.[16] However, revolutionary doctrines can be widespread yet have little apparent effect. Walzer shows that English Protestants who went into continental exile in the mid-sixteenth century, after Mary gained the English throne, developed and directed at England a remarkably vituperative ideology advocating violent revolution, but to no apparent effect.[17] The ideology's lack of success in mobilizing popular support may have been due partly to inadequate communication channels; it may also have been due to a lack of discontent to provide a basis for action. Pettee, for example, asserts that "revolutionary myths" develop "only in response to felt need, and therefore only in an emotional context."[18] Toch similarly says that people are susceptible to the appeals of social movements only if they are both aware of a problem and believe change is possible. "Although appeals themselves cannot create problems, they can call attention to problem situations, or reinterpret potential problem situations so as to create susceptibility."[19] These interpretations are consistent with the arguments summarized in hypothesis VE.1 (chapter 4): new beliefs can heighten and intensify expectations, and justify violence as a means to their attainment, but men's susceptibility to these beliefs is a function of the intensity of their discontent.

[15] Gunnar Heckscher, *The Study of Comparative Government and Politics* (New York: Macmillan, 1957), 167.

[16] Eric Hoffer, *The True Believer* (New York: Harper, 1951), 129–139, quotation 139.

[17] Michael Walzer, "Revolutionary Ideology: The Case of the Marian Exiles," *American Political Science Review*, LVII (September 1963), 643–654.

[18] George S. Pettee, *The Process of Revolution* (New York: Harper, 1938), 67.

[19] Hans Toch, *The Social Psychology of Social Movements* (Indianapolis: Bobbs-Merrill, 1965), chap. 1, quotation 20.

The existence of intense discontent alone is not enough to justify violence. Experimental evidence indicates that discontented people act aggressively only when they become aware of the supposed source of frustration, or something or someone with whom they associate frustration. In psychological terminology, whether aggression results from frustration depends largely on the presence of aggression-releasing cues. Berkowitz proposes that "drives such as anger do not lead to the drive-specific behaviors (aggression in this case) unless there are appropriate cues or releasers," and that "the strength of the aggressive reaction to some thwarting is a joint function of the intensity of the resulting anger and the degree of association between the instigator and the releasing cue."[20] Applying the argument to collective discontent, people are most likely to be receptive to new ideational systems when they are intensely discontented and the sources of deprivation are obscure. Ambiguity and unfocussed discontent are widely identified with the spread of beliefs justifying violence in the literature on aggressive movements. Cantril emphasizes the need of people to organize mentally their experiences. Critical situations "arise when an individual is confronted by a chaotic external environment which he cannot interpret and which he wants to interpret," a psychological condition in which people are quite likely to be suggestible.[21] Schwartz examines the functions of revolutionary appeals in the context of cognitive dissonance theory. The target of such appeals, he says, are passively alienated people who perceive threat, futility, and loss of community in their political environment and as a consequence harbor feelings of tension and rage. The revolutionary organizations most effective in mobilizing the alienated use revolutionary appeals that explain "loss of community" or other societal crises and encourage the expression of rage.[22]

A variety of evidence relates people's cognitive uncertainty to their receptivity to new doctrines. It has been postulated, for example, that when the perceived complexity of the individual's environment is either very low or very high, behavior has a low degree of complexity.[23] When the environment appears complex or chaotic, as well as when it is simple and unvarying, conceptual

[20] Berkowitz, *Aggression*, 32ff, quotation 33, italics omitted.

[21] Hadley Cantril, *The Psychology of Social Movements* (New York: Wiley, 1941), 63.

[22] David C. Schwartz, "A Theory of Revolutionary Behavior," in James C. Davies, ed., *When Men Revolt and Why* (New York: The Free Press, 1970).

[23] See O. J. Harvey, D. E. Hunt, and H. M. Schroder, *Conceptual Systems and Personality Organization* (New York: Wiley, 1961). The theory relates primarily to simplicity/complexity of information handling.

discrimination tends to be low, ambiguity is not easily tolerated, and response hierarchies tend to be few and rigid. An example of experimental evidence is Sudefeld's finding that subjects under sensory deprivation were more susceptible to propaganda than less confined subjects.[24] Other experimental evidence suggests that emotional arousal, specifically heightened anxiety, facilitates attitude change.[25] Lifton conducted psychiatric interviews with people who had been exposed to Chinese Communist "thought reform," whom he found had varying potential for an all-or-nothing emotional alignment that he calls "ideological totalism," characterized by "personal closure, self-destructiveness, and hostility toward outsiders." The degree of individual susceptibility to totalism "depends greatly upon . . . early lack of trust, extreme environmental chaos, total domination by a parent or parent-representative, intolerable burdens of guilt, and severe crises of identity." Whether people of this disposition are converted to closed ideological systems depends on the extent of their exposure to such ideologies, and the degree of control that advocates of those ideologies exercise over them.[26] On the basis of evidence on collectivities, Kornhauser concludes that "mass" individuals become available for mobilization by mass movements because of anxieties arising from uncertainty and self-alienation. "The activist response underlies much of the participation in mass movements, as individuals seek to substitute external identities for inner ones, to replace an unwanted or unknown self with a collective image." [27]

THE EFFECTIVES OF ALTERNATIVE DOCTRINES ABOUT POLITICAL VIOLENCE

Groups in unfamiliar and depriving social circumstances are usually exposed to many new doctrines. The number and elaboration of such beliefs depends on the nature and intensity of deprivation, the inventive skills of the articulate, the prior experiences

[24] Peter Sudefeld, "Attitude Manipulation in Restricted Environments: I. Conceptual Structure and Response to Propaganda," *Journal of Abnormal and Social Psychology*, LXVIII (March 1964), 242–247. "Sensory deprivation," a situation in which the intake of sensory data is minimized, is distinct from the RD concept.

[25] J. A. McNulty and J. A. Walters, "Emotional Arousal, Conflict, and Susceptibility to Social Influence," *Canadian Journal of Psychology*, XVI (September 1962), 211–220.

[26] Robert Jay Lifton, *Thought Reform and the Psychology of Totalism: A Study of "Brainwashing" in China* (New York: Norton, 1961), chap. 22, quotation 436.

[27] William Kornhauser, *The Politics of Mass Society* (New York: The Free Press, 1959), chap. 4; quotation from 112. Many examples are cited by Smelser, 80–81, 86–89, 104–105.

and conceptual abilities of the potential audience, and the access of articulators to communication channels. Willer and Zollschan remark that in prerevolutionary eras, which are characterized by the existence of many groups whose "exigencies," or grievances, are not articulated, "ideologies are first formulated which may have to compete on an 'idea market' for acceptance."[28] Marxism was but one of many revolutionary doctrines current in Russia before 1917; those of Kropotkin and Milyukov, among others, were widely held and embodied in a variety of organizations.[29] In nineteenth-century Europe generally, the discontented could choose from many ideational frameworks for action, among them liberalism, nativism, socialism, syndicalism, anarchism, and their several dispensations.[30] Appeals to the discontents of black Americans in the 1960s included the advocacy of revolutionary terrorism, programs of defensive withdrawal and separatism, assertions of black pride and cultural autonomy, and more muted appeals to the integrationist doctrine that is a derivative of American egalitarianism.

The relative effectiveness of such doctrines varies with the extent to which they provide rationales for men to act on their discontent; this they do insofar as they are consonant with the interests and experiences of the deprived, focus their anger on likely agents of responsibility, and facilitate a sense of mutual awareness among them. (A fourth factor, specification of attractive objectives and means to their attainment, is examined separately in the section on utilitarian justifications.) Not all new beliefs and ideational systems satisfy these functions equally well. Those which do so best are most likely to persuade discontented men; to the extent that they call for violence against political targets, they increase normative justifications for political violence. A summary hypothesis is proposed:

Hypothesis JV.6: The intensity of normative justifications for political violence varies strongly with the extent to which symbolic appeals offer plausible explanations of the sources of

[28] David Willer and George K. Zollschan, "Prolegomenon to a Theory of Revolution," in George K. Zollschan and Walter Hirsch, eds., *Explorations in Social Change* (Boston: Houghton-Mifflin, 1964), 140. Similar statements are made by Heckscher, 167, and Louis Gottschalk, "Causes of Revolution," *American Journal of Sociology*, L (July 1944), 5–6.

[29] See for example Franco Venturi, *Roots of Revolution: A History of the Populist and Socialist Movements in Nineteenth Century Russia*, trans. Isaiah Berlin (New York: Knopf, 1960).

[30] An account of the origins and effects of nineteenth-century European ideologies of protest is Jacob S. Schapiro, *Movements of Social Dissent in Modern Europe* (Princeton: Van Nostrand, 1962).

> relative deprivation, identify political targets for violence, and provide symbols of group identification.

The hypothesis applies only to the effects of new beliefs about political violence on the *intensity* of normative justifications. Their *scope*, i.e. the proportion of a population likely to accept new ideas sanctioning violence, is a function of the scope of RD (see hypothesis VE.1 and corollary V.3.1), and of the extent and openness of communication networks by which new ideas can be disseminated (hypothesis JV.11, below). Much of the supporting evidence for the hypothesis, below, relates to doctrines and beliefs about collective violence generally, but the underlying relationships are applicable to beliefs justifying political violence as well.

Appropriateness. New ideational justifications for violence are effective to the extent that they make sense to discontented people in terms of their specific deprivations and their past experiences. The more specific new ideas are in identifying the sources of deprivation and prescribing remedial action, the greater their likely appeal to groups who experience highly specific deprivations, but the less appeal they are likely to have for other discontented groups. Toch, for example, says that social movements succeed in attracting members to the extent that the movements' appeals suggest solutions which are appropriate to the particular situations of their audience. He cites the Nazi movement as an example of a movement using a "saturation" method, presenting diverse appeals for diverse needs.[31]

Evidence from case and comparative studies illustrates the relationship between the appropriateness of new ideas about violence to the conditions of those who seize upon them, and also the parallels among the doctrines adopted by the discontented in diverse eras and cultures. During times of plague and famine, waves of chiliastic excitement swept medieval Europe, and rumors, portents, and preachers of heresies abounded. But, as Cohn points out, the heresies which most effectively mobilized the discontented were those which suited or could be moulded to their states of mind.

> The various "heresies" could and did appeal in many different ways and to many different needs. For instance, some of the great ladies who turned to Catharism were clearly moved by emotional conflicts such as nowadays would have led them to theosophy or maybe psycho-analysis. . . . But when these and

[31] Toch, 13–19, 87–88. Another theoretical statement is Willer and Zollschan, 137–138.

similar eschatological doctrines penetrated to the uprooted and desperate masses in town and country they were re-edited and reinterpreted until in the end they were capable of inspiring revolutionary movements of a peculiarly anarchic kind.[32]

The doctrines of the French Enlightenment similarly were capable of modification or emendation to suit the needs of their adherents. "Each class seized upon these doctrines and interpreted its own particular situation in terms of them. The aristocracy . . . invoked the rights of man and citizenship to protect its members from royal impingement," [33] the middle class and clergy similarly interpreted their condition in this language, and for the poor people of Paris the same views justified mob violence. Nazi ideology was successful in part because it justified ethnic prejudice and scapegoating through a theory of racial superiority and provided a social and economic program that promised something for all discontented groups. But its effectiveness in identifying Jews as scapegoats did not rest primarily on the immediate plausibility of the argument or an inherent psychological need for victims. The doctrine was acceptable largely because, as Pulzer has shown, anti-Semitic sentiment developed and was given organizational expression from 1867 to 1918; the Nazi movement merely exploited a prejudice already firmly established in the minds of many Germans.[34]

Doctrines of apocalyptic or supernatural change that will be accomplished through violence are most likely to take root among people accustomed to stable lifeways who experience intense and diverse deprivations of obscure origins. Johnson writes that

> When the sources of dysfunction are obscure, or when the individual having an effective sense of the system's dysfunctions possess no clear understanding of their own social role vis-à-vis other roles, one way of articulating the changes that are required in order to relieve the dysfunctions is to accept a belief that change will occur by means of supernatural forces.[35]

The consequence of the acceptance of such doctrine is likely to be "millennarian rebellion." The pervasiveness of anarchic millennarian doctrines of nineteenth-century southern Europe, with

[32] Norman Cohn, *The Pursuit of the Millennium*, 2nd edn. (New York: Harper, 1957, 1961), 31.

[33] Smelser, 348–351, quotation 349.

[34] Peter G. J. Pulzer, *The Rise of Political Anti-Semitism in Germany and Austria* (New York: Wiley, 1964).

[35] Chalmers Johnson, *Revolution and the Social System* (Stanford: Hoover Institution on War, Revolution and Peace, 1964).

their promises of a Day of Change to initiate the new world in which goods would be shared by all, Hobsbawm attributes to their correspondence to the mood of the peasants, and suggests that the discontents underlying such primitive reformist movements can also serve to propel modern social revolutionary movements.[36] Cohn sees parallels between the popular apocalyptic lore of medieval Europe and the ideologies of Communism and Nazism, all of which endow "social conflicts and aspirations with a transcendental significance," and in doing so provide both a justification and a prophecy of violence.[37] Similar are the millennial beliefs of the wandering, poverty-stricken pilgrims of northeastern Brazil in the mid-twentieth century, whose faith in the return of King Sebastian has periodically led to extensive rural violence.[38]

A brief comparison of the effectiveness of Marxism-Leninism and Gandhian doctrine provides one last illustration of the thesis that the effectiveness of ideologies depends on the circumstances of the audience. Marxist doctrine, in its original formulation, corresponded rather closely to the condition of urban workers in industrializing societies. It located the source of their grievances in the economic system and the class structure and political institutions based on it; facilitated mutual awareness; and asserted the inevitability of revolutionary remedies. The doctrine gained the adherence of a substantial minority of European workers during the past century; its appeal to most peasants, subjugated ethnic minorities, and subjects of colonial rule was negligible prior to the reinterpretations of Lenin, Mao, and Guevara. Reinterpretations do not make it inevitably effective either. It has been rejected by almost all moderate and most militant black Americans—among the former probably because of fundamental acceptance of the belief system of the dominant culture, among the latter because of a preemptive preference for counter-racist doctrines created in reaction against one set of white cultural themes.[39] As another example, Marxism-Leninism has not yet been widely accepted as a revolutionary doctrine in Latin America, even in the Maoist or Guevara interpretations. The reason may

[36] E. J. Hobsbawm, *Social Bandits and Primitive Rebels,* 2nd edn. (New York: The Free Press, 1959), 64–65, 90–99.

[37] Cohn, 308ff., quotation 308.

[38] On Antonio Conselheiro's revolutionary millennarian movement in northeastern Brazil in the 1890s, a precursor of mid-twentieth-century millennarianism in this region, see Euclydes da Cunha, *Rebellion in the Backlands,* trans. S. Putnam (Chicago: University of Chicago Press, 1902, 1960).

[39] Empirical evidence is reported by John Kosa and Clyde Z. Nunn, "Race, Deprivation and Attitude Toward Communism," *Phylon,* XXV (December 1964), 337–346.

be that, as an operative doctrine, it is antithetical to some pervasive Latin cultural themes. The Marxian theoretical emphasis is on the subordination of the individual's interests and productive capacities to the interests of the community, whereas Latin culture stresses the desirability of strong formal authority that provides wide leeway for individual self-assertion and pride, but provides no support for strong communal or community sentiment. Consequently, communist doctrine in Latin America has been a plaything of intellectual radicals. Cuba is an exception after the fact. Marxist doctrine was imposed after power was seized, and as an operating doctrine has been drastically reinterpreted.

By contrast the Gandhian doctrine of attaining double revolution, human and social, through nonviolence seems to have had greatest appeal to subordinated groups who sensed their relative powerlessness against clearly identifiable oppressors. For colonial subjects, and for American Negroes in the early stages of the civil rights movement, passive resistance provided a technique of mass manifestation of discontent that promised success consonant with group norms about the undesirability of overt violence against hostile, powerful rulers. Marxian and nonviolent doctrines have both had successes and failures. But the contemporary appeal of of doctrines of nonviolence has been weakened by the dramatic evidence in Algeria, Cuba, and Vietnam that violence can be more effective, however rare the successes are compared with the failures. Since the discontented have a fundamental disposition to aggression, *ceterus paribus*, doctrines justifying violence are likely to seem more appropriate and hence to gain wider currency.[40]

Specification of Sources of Deprivation. If the sources of deprivation are obscure, the effectiveness of new doctrinal justifications for violence is increased to the extent that they provide a plausible identification of those sources. The justification of political violence increases to the extent that political agents of responsibility are identified; the more concrete the source identified, the more effectively is anger focussed on it. "The establishment" is an elusive opponent, and so are disembodied entities like "evil spirits" and "atheistic communism." Abstractions justify violence mainly for revolutionary intellectuals; real villains are needed to mobilize mass support and to provide actual targets for violent action. Edwards wrote that the articulation

[40] A remarkable and neglected analysis of the sociological nature, ideas, and historical practice of nonviolent collective opposition is Clarence Marsh Case, *Non-Violent Coercion: A Study in Methods of Social Pressure* (New York: Century, 1923).

of revolutionary ideologies created an "oppression psychosis" which

> turns the previous more or less passive discontent of the repressed group into the active emotion of hate of the repressors. Hatred of a common enemy is the most powerful known agency for producing group unity. The publicists, by their previous attack, have pointed out the repressors as the common enemy. The discontent of the repressed at their lot turns into hatred of the repressors. . . .[41]

Revolutionary activists recognize the principle equally well. "In any revolution there must be an immediate, well-known enemy for everyone to hate, and in our revolution it is the French police," a student told a reporter in June 1968. "Our aim is to destroy the Government, and to change society, but we fight the police to remind France of who we are, and what we want."[42]

One requirement for effective specification is that the targets be vulnerable to attack, in a normative and physical sense. If the discontented identify closely and strongly with those they believe responsible, or if they believe that their oppressors are infinitely powerful, they are unlikely to attack them. In such circumstances the discontented are prone to devise, and to be receptive to, alternative interpretations of evil circumstances. The nobility of medieval states often justified their rebellions against the impositions of royal authority on grounds that the king was misled by wicked advisers. For the nobles this attribution of evil was partly tactical: they had a vested interest in preserving a political structure associated with the institution of hereditary nobility. It also had a normative function for them and their followers. The monarchy was a divinely sanctioned institution in medieval thought, and to attack the king's person or position was tantamount to an attack on God. But there were no consequential theological prohibitions against attacking his advisers.[43] The theme is a persistent one in Western history. Six mid-seventeenth-century revolutions analyzed by Merriman occurred at times of widespread discontent, but the precipitating grievances were in most cases fiscal and were popularly attributed to unpopular ministers rather than to the monarchs they served. The revolutionaries persuaded themselves that the king and ancient rights were with them, thus jus-

[41] Lyford P. Edwards, *The Natural History of Revolution* (Chicago: University of Chicago Press, 1927), 55.

[42] *New York Times*, June 13, 1968, 3.

[43] Joel T. Rosenthal, "The King's 'Wicked Advisers' and Medieval Baronial Rebellions," *Political Science Quarterly*, LXXXII (December 1967), 599–604.

tifying attacks against the ministers.[44] French and American revolutionaries were equally prone to such beliefs, opposing misguided policies of the king's agents in the name of the king. But, when a ruler is not shielded by an aura of divinity or power, he is likely to be held responsible for a great many deprivations: people tend to attribute responsibility for deprivations of uncertain origin to those whom they believe have the power to alleviate them.

People also are susceptible to beliefs that identify ethnic, religious, political, or tribal minorities as sources of deprivation, hence as justifiable targets of attack. During the 1930s Hitler is said to have been asked whether he thought that the Jew had to be destroyed. In retrospect his reply is grotesquely ironic. "No," he said. "We should have then to invent him. It is essential to have a tangible enemy, not merely an abstract one."[45] Some of the intergroup violence facilitated by such beliefs is attributed to displacement of aggression from other objects. Much recent psychological research suggests that a number of other factors influence the effectiveness of beliefs justifying "scapegoating." One is the previous association of the outgroup with hostility, for example as a source of past frustrations or as previous targets of aggression. If men already dislike an outgroup for these or other reasons, they are susceptible to rumors and beliefs that associate their present discontents with the group.[46] Another is the visibility of outgroups. The more visible or "different" they are, the more readily discontented people learn external and mental cues that associate such groups with their discontent. Anticipations of rewards or punishment also are crucial in selecting outgroups as targets; the more defenseless an outgroup appears to be, the more readily is blame attributed to it and aggression directed against it.[47] Finally, occurrence of overt hostility *within* an outgroup can also encourage violence against it.[48] Although most research on the subject has concerned hostility towards minority groups, the same characteristics are likely to apply generally to specification of attackable sources of deprivation.

[44] Robert B. Merriman, *Six Contemporaneous Revolutions* (Oxford: Clarendon Press, 1938), 212.

[45] Hermann Rauschning, *Hitler Speaks* (New York: Putnam, 1940), 234, cited in Hoffer, 90.

[46] See Berkowitz, *Aggression*, 152–160 for a summary of evidence.

[47] See Richard H. Walters, "Implications of Laboratory Studies of Aggression for the Control and Regulation of Violence," *Annals of the American Academy of Political and Social Science*, CCCLXIV (March 1966), 69–70.

[48] Ralph Epstein, "Aggression Toward Outgroups as a Function of Authoritarianism and Imitation of Aggressive Models," *Journal of Personality and Social Psychology*, III (No. 5, 1966), 574–579.

The Sense of Community. The effectiveness of new justificatory beliefs about political violence also varies with the extent to which they provide the discontented with a sense of community. That sense can be created or reinforced by use of symbols that make men aware of their common discontents, of the worthiness of their group or organization, and of their potential for cooperative action against their oppressors. Schwartz says that revolutionary appeals are successful to the extent that they provide a sense of "prideful historical community," even if it is a fictionalized one; explain alienation in terms of a loss of that community; and assert that the community can be reestablished through a revolutionary movement.[49] Gottschalk asserts that the second "cause of revolution" is solidified public opinion," that is, the awareness of the discontented that others "are equally discontented and likely to unite with me in the expression of my discontent. General awareness of resentment . . . creates that kind of demand for change which becomes effective in making revolutions."[50]

Such mutual awareness is fostered by symbols of inclusiveness, like the Marxist dictum that all workers are exploited. A persistent theme of Nazi ideology, ritually emphasized in innumerable Nazi ceremonies, was the historical community and accomplishments of the Germanic people. Traditions symbolizing German unity were revived or created out of whole cloth, Germanic culture was glorified, and the evils in German society projected onto non-Germanic groups—the Jews, the international bankers, the Communists, hostile international forces. Rudé suggests that the philosophy of the French Enlightenment provided a basis for a comparable sense of unity among diverse groups in French society:

> it needed more than economic hardship, social discontent, and the frustration of political and social ambitions to make a revolution. To give cohesion to the discontents and aspirations of widely varying social classes there had to be some unifying body of ideas, a common vocabulary of hope and protest. . . . In this case, the ground was prepared, in the first place, by the writers of the Enlightenment.[51]

Hobsbawm provides a comparative example, emphasizing the practical function of millennarian beliefs in mobilizing rural people for violence through mutual awareness. Such beliefs

> helped to organize masses of hitherto unorganized people on a

[49] Schwartz.
[50] Gottschalk, 5.
[51] George Rudé, *Revolutionary Europe, 1783–1815* (Cleveland: World, 1964), 74–75.

> national scale, and almost simultaneously. . . . An atmosphere of high exaltation greatly facilitates the spreading of news. . . . It invests even the smallest organizational advance with an aura of invincibility and future triumph, and nothing is more contagious than success. By these means a movement can almost simultaneously mobilize masses over a wide area.[52]

Revolutionary symbolism has seldom been analyzed comparatively, or related to the development and outcomes of revolutionary movements. Shubs, in a pioneering study, has made a content analysis of some 2,000 speeches, pamphlets, and other documents issued during the genesis of the American revolutionary movement, 1760–76, and the Swaraj movement in India, 1925–45. Three kinds of symbols were counted and their content rated: symbols of group inclusion like "fraternity" and "comrade"; "noble affiliation" symbols, like "nation" and "Gandhi," which were associated with strongly held cultural norms, and hence gave the supporter of a revolutionary movement a feeling of belonging to a worthy group; and goal symbols like "peaceful assembly" and "unity." Changes over time in the frequency and content of such symbols were then analyzed. Remarkably similar patterns in the development of revolutionary appeals characterized both movements. The "inclusion" content of symbols increased markedly and regularly from low to very high levels during both periods, suggesting a need either to activate marginal groups in support of the movement, or to reinforce the feelings of inclusiveness of those already supporting the movement, or both. "Noble affiliation" content was initially quite high, declined in the middle period in both cases, and increased again in the years immediately prior to the period of mass revolutionary action. Shubs suggests that this pattern probably reflects leaders' desires to maintain as broad an umbrella as possible. Moreover the frequency of all the symbols increased marked over the 15–20 year periods of revolutionary preparation; their numbers approximately tripled in both cases.[53] This kind of analysis necessarily makes assumptions about how certain kinds of symbols were perceived by their audiences. Nonetheless, it indicates that two successful revolutionary movements made extensive use of symbols apparently chosen to generate feelings of cohesion and group worthiness among their poten-

[52] Hobsbawm, 105–106.

[53] Peter Shubs, "Symbols of Revolution" (Paper, Foreign Policy Research Institute, University of Pennsylvania, 1968). A later paper on the study is Shubs, "Revolutionary Symbology: Comparative Case Studies of the American and Indian Independence Movement" (Paper read at the Annual Meeting of the American Political Science Association, New York, 1969).

tial supporters, and did so with increasing frequency and intensity as they moved toward mass action.

The Utility of Violence [54]

"By and large, all violence has a rational aspect, for somebody, if not for the perpetrator." [55] In qualified form, this assertion by Nieburg is as axiomatic a principle about political violence as the proposition that intensely discontented men are innately disposed to aggression. The qualified assertion is that most participants in collective protest and violence have utilitarian as well as aggressive motives: they believe that they stand a chance of relieving some of their discontent through violence. Conflict theorists frequently assume that men are rational or at least rationalistic in conflict situations: they tend to choose the courses of action that they think maximize their chances of getting what they want. Evidence examined here suggests that many participants in strife perceive violence in a utilitarian way, but that their perceptions of utility are not often "rational" in the sense of being based on accurate calculations about the effects of alternative courses of action. Instead they tend to be derived from ideological assumptions or perceptions that violence has been successful in other situations.

Utilitarian motives often are contingent upon and secondary to the "nonrational" motivation to act violently out of anger. Labeling utilitarian motives for violence as "rational" and emotional motives as "nonrational" or "irrational" is of course a value judgment imposed by the observer. If the angry man values the emotional satisfaction he gets from satisfying his rage more than the satisfaction he would get from alleviating the situation that caused his rage, then it may be more "rational" in his terms to act violently for its own sake than to use violence to remedy his situation. There also are psychoanalytic arguments that the interpersonal value deprivations associated with status discrimination can be directly relieved by self-assertion through violence.[56] Angry men are probably most susceptible to justifications for action that promise simultaneous satisfaction of all such motives. Consequently this analysis of utilitarian perspectives on violence makes no assumptions about the rationality or irrationality of violence per se. Men are said to

[54] I am indebted to Mancur Olson, Jr., for his persistent and ultimately persuasive arguments that utilitarian justifications for political violence are highly consequential and can be integrated into a theoretical model that emphasizes nonrational motivations for strife. Responsibility for the treatment given them here is mine, however.

[55] H. L. Nieburg, "The Threat of Violence and Social Change," *American Political Science Review,* LVI (December 1962), quotation 867.

[56] See Fanon.

have utilitarian motives about political violence to the extent that they believe violent action will improve overall value positions.

The utilities of political violence are not likely to be perceived in all-or-nothing terms, neither by individuals nor by all members of a collectivity. Men make more or less explicit calculations about the prospective benefits vis-à-vis the prospective costs of violence as a tactic. Such calculations are likely to be more explicit among leaders, more implicit among potential followers. The greater they believe the potential gains to be, the more justifiable violence is likely to appear to them. This relationship is stated formally in hypothesis V.3 (chapter 6).

The value positions men hope to improve may be their own, or those of the present or future collectivity with which they identify. Rank-and-file participants are likely to be motivated most strongly by anticipation of personal gains: removal of an onerous governmental policy or repressive official, increased wages or reduced inflation, cheaper bread or stolen television sets. Leaders are somewhat more likely to cast their utilitarian motives in collective form and to accept the likelihood of personal sacrifice in anticipation of future gains for the organization, the community, or the society as a whole. For example, assassins and terrorists run extraordinarily high risks in the service of what they regard as the collective interest. Revolutionary leaders often justify their actions by reference to the gains of future generations. This is not to suggest that revolutionary idealists find no personal utility in organizing and directing violence. The initial discontents that motivated them may have been economic privation or frustrated desires for membership in the political elite. The act of revolutionary leadership is unlikely to alleviate these deprivations immediately but *is* likely to provide them with extensive substitute satisfactions: a greater sense of self-actualization, status and power in the revolutionary organization itself, and feelings of communality and ideational coherence derived from membership in a close-knit group of like-minded men.

TACTICAL USES OF VIOLENCE

There also are consequential differences among the utilitarian functions attributed to political violence. One variation is the extent to which violence is regarded as a direct tactic of value enhancement. Another is the relative emphasis between demonstrative threats of violence and the actual use of violence. The most direct utilitarian use of violence is to seize a desired value, as rioters do when they pillage warehouses and as conspirators do in a coup d'etat. Less direct uses of violence are protests, like antigovernment riots and strikes, designed to induce rulers to change undesirable policies, and military engagements between dissidents and regime forces for the purposes of securing base areas or fatally weakening a regime. In the former kinds of events the threat of violence is often more potent than the actuality, in the latter violence itself is required. A primary determinant of the directness and extent of tactical violence is the balance of force its strategists perceive between themselves and those they oppose. The greater the disparity, the more likely strategists are to emphasize the indirect and threatened uses of violence.

A common indirect use of violence is to demonstrate symbolically the demands of those who use it and their capacity to disrupt society if their demands are not satisfied. Nieburg writes that "The 'rational' goal of the threat of violence is an accommodation of interests" and that "the 'rational' goal of actual violence is demonstration of the will and capability of action, establishing a measure of the credibility of future threats." The occurrence of violence within the state, even if it is sporadic and unplanned, and even if it has nonpolitical targets, can be used by leaders and regarded by rulers as evidence of the intensity of the discontenteds' demands for change, and as threat of further disorder if those demands are not satisfied.[57] This kind of tactical use and threatened use of political violence is characteristic of participants and leaders who perceive a potential for alleviating deprivation within the existing political system. But if dissidents believe their objectives can be obtained only by transforming the system, they are likely to use terroristic tactics to publicize their existence and objectives, and to widen popular support by providing symbolic models for aggression and by demonstrating the regime's incapacity to provide protection, hoping ultimately to overthrow it. Thornton, in an analysis of terror as a rebel weapon, refers to this as an "advertising" function: terror calls attention to the dissidents' activities, program, and goals.[58] Kropotkin, an ardent advocate of terrorism, emphasized the conversion effect of such acts: "Through the [terrorist] deeds which attract general attention, the new idea insinuates itself into peoples' heads and makes converts. Such an act does more propagandizing in a few days than do thousands of pamphlets."[59]

[57] Nieburg, quotation 865.

[58] Thomas Perry Thornton, "Terror as a Weapon of Political Agitation," in Harry Eckstein, ed., *Internal War: Problems and Approaches* (New York: The Free Press, 1964), 82.

[59] Pierre Kropotkin, *Paroles d'un Révolté* (Paris: C. Marpon et E. Flammerion, no date), 286, quoted in Thornton, 82–83.

If people are intensely discontented and are fundamentally sympathetic to rebel objectives, symbolic violence against a hated regime is likely to have a conversion effect of the kind Kropotkin identifies. But the most common consequence of terror, especially if it is widespread and random, is mass disorientation and anxiety. Whether a disoriented, terrorized public will withdraw support from the incumbents is problematic; they may give greater support to the regime in hope of protecting themselves. If terrorism is severe and the regime weak they can be coerced into providing support for the dissidents, but support given under coercion is unlikely to develop into a more enduring allegiance unless it can be systematically maintained over a long period.[60] Boulding makes an analogous point about the effects of nonviolent protest against unpopular governmental policies. "Protest is most likely to be successful where it represents a view which is in fact widespread in the society, but which has somehow not been called to people's attention." If there is not widespread dissatisfaction about the issue around which protest is organized, however, or if the society is divided or ambivalent on the issue, protest movements are likely to stimulate counter-protest movements that may be larger than the original movement.[61]

Another indirect tactical function of overt violence in the service of revolutionary movements is to trigger governmental repression that will increase support for the insurgents. Evidence is cited in chapter 8, below, that inconsistent repressive measures by a regime in response to political violence tend to alienate those who supported the regime and impel many who were passively discontented into active resistance. The importance of this factor in the Cuban revolution was evident not only to academic observers but to Che Guevara and Regis Debray, whose writings on revolutionary tactics emphasize, among other factors, the usefulness of terroristic regime responses to revolutionary action in mobilizing popular support.[62] In Venezuela, radical insurgents of the *Movemiento de Izquierda Revolucionaria* used such tactics against the Betancourt regime, beginning in 1960. Gude attributes their lack of success in attracting popular support to the fact that the regime minimized the use of troops in urban areas, minimized the overt use of large-scale police

[60] See Thornton, passim, and the discussion of legitimacy in chap. 6; and also E. V. Walter, "Violence and the Process of Terror," *American Sociological Review*, XXIX (April 1964), 248–257.

[61] Kenneth E. Boulding, "Reflections on Protest," *Bulletin of the Atomic Scientists*, XXI (October 1965), 18–20, quotation 18.

[62] For a useful review of the tactical and ideological justifications for violence proposed by Guevara, Regis Debray, and also by Mao Tse-tung and Vo-nguyên-Giap, see Henry Bienen, *Violence and Social Change* (Chicago: University of Chicago Press, 1969).

tactics, and created the impression that it was completely in control and using legitimate means in dealing with the situation.[63]

Leaders and followers of violent political movements probably vary a great deal in the utility they attribute to different modes of violence, whether threatened or actually employed, direct or indirect. Rational, value-maximizing thinking about the uses of violence is more characteristic of leaders than followers. To the extent that leaders do think in these terms, and can ensure that their followers act on directives designed to implement revolutionary strategy, it is useful to analyze revolutionary behavior in the framework of game theory or strategy of conflict theory. Such theories assume rational motives and interdependence of adversaries' decisions and expectations about each other's behavior.[64] A major contention of this analysis is that this axiomatic base is inadequate for the interpretation of the motives of revolutionary actors. In Rapoport's terms, political violence has elements of both "fights" and "games," and the former predominate in the psyches of participants and in their collective behavior. Even if the two assumptions are accepted for purposes of analysis, actors' calculations about the effects of their actions are widely disparate. Janos, for example, attributes a great many unsuccessful rebellions and coups to what he describes as "putschism," an approach to the seizure of power by leaders who make rational calculations based on erroneous assumptions.

> Putschism does not stem from mere lack of information and intelligence, but from a misunderstanding of the fundamental precepts of politics and psychology. Putsches are the products of rational calculation based on erroneous premises, such as the theory of the "life force," a metaphysical idea of the state, or a romantic concept of political mobilization.

Among many illustrations, he notes that Louis Auguste Blanqui called out the people of Paris thirteen times in the mid- and late-nineteenth century, never successfully. In 1870 "the workers of Paris stood by apathetically while Blanqui and his storming party were arrested after an unsuccessful appeal to the masses, yet only

[63] See Edward W. Gude, "Batista and Betancourt: Alternative Responses to Violence," in Hugh Davis Graham and Ted Robert Gurr, eds., *Violence in America: Historical and Comparative Perspectives* (Washington, D.C.: National Commission on the Causes and Prevention of Violence, 1969), 577–589.

[64] See Thomas C. Schelling, *The Strategy of Conflict* (Cambridge: Harvard University Press, 1960, 1963), especially chap. 1, and Anatol Rapoport, *Fights, Games, and Debates* (Ann Arbor: University of Michigan Press Press, 1960), Part II.

three weeks later the same masses spontaneously rose to overthrow the government of Louis Napoleon." [65]

Janos' argument applies to the instrumental calculations of dissident leaders. Ordinary participants are likely to have diverse instrumental beliefs, one contemporary example of which is provided by interviews with peace demonstrators. Samples of British and Danish peace marchers in 1965 were asked what they thought the effects of the demonstrations were. The largest proportion, though less than half, thought that the demonstrations would help sway public opinion directly. A few thought the primary impact would be on politicians directly. Some Danes (11 percent) and more Britons (17 percent) thought that the impact would be made not by the demands themselves but the show of strength. Nearly half the Danish marchers, and a quarter of the Britons, felt that the demonstrations would strengthen the peace movement itself. Moreover, a few Danes and nearly a third of the Britons volunteered that they were marching to demonstrate their dissatisfaction with their governments, i.e. were acting on their discontent for its own sake rather than, or in addition to, pursuing utilitarian motives.[66] In other words, the participants had diverse though not necessarily implausible perceptions of their political environment and of the impact of their demonstrative action on that environment. Though peace demonstrators are by and large articulate and well-informed, their utilitarian justifications rested on untested beliefs about the efficacy of action. Comparably diverse assumptions are likely to underlie the utilitarian justifications of participants in violent as well as peaceful protests.

ORIGINS OF UTILITARIAN JUSTIFICATIONS FOR POLITICAL VIOLENCE

Hypothesis V.3 (chapter 6) relates potential for political violence to a perceptual variable, namely perceptions of its value-enhancing potential. There are evident difficulties in determining directly what utilitarian values men attribute to political violence.

[65] Andrew Janos, *The Seizure of Power: A Study of Force and Popular Consent*, Research Monograph No. 16 (Princeton: Center of International Studies, Princeton University, 1964), quotations 40–41, 81, 84.

[66] Anders Boserup and Claus Iversen, "Demonstrations as a Source of Change: A Study of British and Danish Easter Marchers," *Journal of Peace Research*, No. 4, 1966, 333–335. The questions were open-ended, responses were subsequently classified. The N's of respondents were 137 in Denmark, 155 in Britain. A study by Nicos E. Devletoglou, "Responsibility and Demonstrations: A Case Study," *Public Opinion Quarterly*, XXX (No. 2, 1966), 285–289, suggests that demonstrators' information relevant to the issue of protest also may be low.

The problem is to identify conditions that establish and reinforce perceptions of its utility. If rationality of participants in political violence could be assumed, the objective observer might infer rebel perceptions of utilities from cost-benefit calculations about the consequences of various rebel-regime interactions. But the foregoing evidence suggests that perceptions of utility usually reflect questionable assumptions about the efficacy of threatened or actual violence. A more feasible approach avoids assumptions about rationality by focusing on directly observable social phenomena which can be inferred to influence directly utilitarian justifications.

One of the most potent and enduring effects of "revolutionary appeals" is to persuade men that political violence can provide value gains commensurate to or greater than its costs in risk and guilt. Revolutionary appeals typically provide justification for new or intensified value expectations, and enhance men's value capabilities by specifying appropriate kinds of actions (value opportunities) which make it possible to attain those value expectations. The long-range goals of revolutionary movements often are given utopian expression. "A new social order is envisioned; institutional chaos will give way to harmony and stability; the evil will be eradicated; and human happiness will result." [67] Such utopianism helps generate the extraordinary efforts which make possible the overthrow of entrenched regimes. Those caught up in the revolutionary vision believe that no change is beyond their reach, that the perfection of mankind can be attained within the movement today and in the world tomorrow. To the same point is Hoffer's statement that "For men to plunge headlong into an undertaking of vast change, they must be intensely discontented yet not destitute, and they . . . must also have an extravagant concept of the prospects and potentialities of the future." [68]

There is no inherent relationship between the prescription of revolutionary utopias and the rationalization of violence. But revolutionary appeals often include, and almost necessarily include once a revolutionary organization is established, prescriptions about tactics and practical operations. The kinds of action prescribed—the value opportunities established for participants for the attainment of revolutionary goals—usually include the use of violence. The relative emphasis on violent means varies. Cohn,

[67] Smelser, 348.

[68] Hoffer, 11. Also see Gottschalk, 5, and Rex Hopper, "The Revolutionary Process: A Frame of Reference for the Study of Revolutionary Movements," *Social Forces*, XXVIII (March 1950), 274.

stressing the parallels between the transcendentalism of medieval and modern revolutionary millennarianism, emphasizes that groups as diverse as the Flagellants, the Anabaptists, and Communists believed that terrestrial, collective salvation could be attained only through violent means. "A social struggle is imagined as uniquely important, different in kind from all other struggles known to history, a cataclysm from which the world is to emerge totally transformed and redeemed."[69] The Communist Manifesto specifically prescribes force: "The Communists . . . openly declare that their ends can be attained only by the forcible overthrow of all existing social conditions."[70] Conventional communist doctrine also places emphasis on organizational preparation and on waiting for the development of appropriate "objective conditions" for revolution. The most violent doctrines of contemporary revolutionary struggle, such as the left communist doctrines of Chinese and Latin American revolutionaries, and the less doctrinal appeals of some New Left militants and black radicals in the United States, give less attention to nonviolent tactics, emphasizing instead the need for continuous, violent opposition as a means for creating the conditions that make revolutionary change possible. At the opposite end of the spectrum are Gandhian doctrines of nonviolent resistance (see above). Most revolutionary appeals, however, prescribe violence as one means among many. Chinese history provides two examples. The "T'ai-P'ing" movement, which ruled most of South China from 1850 to 1865, was based on a derivative Christian ideology that prescribed a social, economic, and political restructuring of Chinese life. Its doctrinally prescribed tactics seem to have emphasized organizational factors, however; violence was justified principally in the service of military expansion and later in defense of the territory under the movement's jule.[71] The doctrine of "Cultural Revolution" in modern China advocates uninterrupted revolution in the creation of a new kind of man and a new kind of society in China, but emphasizes social engineering and the persuasive rather than violent purging of revisionists as means to this end. The political clashes associated with the "Cultural Revolution" have not been a manifestation of tactics prescribed in the official versions of the doctrine but of reinterpreta-

[69] Cohn, 308.

[70] Karl Marx and Friedrich Engles, *The Communist Manifesto,* cited in Leiden and Schmitt, 105.

[71] See Li Chien-nung, *The Political History of China, 1840–1928* (Stanford: Stanford University Press, 1956), chap. 2. The death toll of the ensuing civil war was nonetheless enormous.

tions of the doctrine by Red Guard groups and their opponents.[72]

The greater the emphasis of revolutionary appeals on violent rather than nonviolent means for the attainment of utopian goals, the greater the utility that those who subscribe to revolutionary goals are likely to attribute to violence. Since revolutionary doctrines usually penetrate the rank and file in fragmentary rather than coherent form, and since the discontented have an inherent disposition to aggression, it is likely that any violent means prescribed will be more salient to the revolutionary audience than nonviolent tactics. The relationship is nonetheless sufficiently important to be put in hypothetical form.

Hypothesis JV.7: The intensity of utilitarian justifications for political violence varies moderately with the degree to which new symbolic appeals prescribe political violence as an effective value opportunity for increasing value positions.

The concepts of *value opportunity* and *value position* were developed in chapter 2. The proposed relationship applies to the intensity of utilitarian justifications only, not to their scope. The primary determinants of the proportion of a collectivity likely to be influenced by revolutionary appeals of any kind are the scope of RD (hypothesis VE.1) and the characteristics of communication networks (hypothesis JV.11).

Probably the most potent determinant of the perceived utility of political violence is people's previous success in attaining their ends by such means. Psychological and comparative evidence cited above suggests that people who obtain their demands through aggression are likely to use it as a tactic in the future. Intermittent rewards for aggression lead to establishment of very persistent aggressive habits. If aggression always succeeded in an individual's past, a few failures are often sufficient to extinguish the habit. But if aggression succeeded only occasionally, it is likely to be tried repeatedly, despite failures, in hopes that it eventually will succeed again. Comparably, if men believe that collective violence by their predecessors succeeded, they will be disposed to use it themselves in similar circumstances.[73] "Revolutionaries do come to power, machine-breakers do slow the introduction of labor-saving devices, rioters do get public officials removed," writes Tilly. "The local grain riot, so widespread in western Europe from the seventeenth

[72] See S. H. Ahmad, "China's 'Cultural Revolution,'" *International Studies* (Bombay), IX (July 1967), 13–54, and Hans Granqvist, *The Red Guard: A Report on Mao's Revolution* trans. Erik J. Friis (New York: Praeger, 1967).

[73] See Walters, 66–67, and the discussion of "Cultural traditions of collective violence," chap. 6.

through the nineteenth centuries, often produced a temporary reduction of prices, forced stored grain into the market, and stimulated local officials to new efforts at assuring the grain supply." The implication is not that violence is inherently more efficient than nonviolence. Rather, "it works often enough in the short run, by the standards of the participants, not to be automatically dismissed as a flight from rational calculation." [74]

One of the bases of cultural traditions of collective violence is their relative success, as Tilly's grain-riot example suggests. The recurrence of coups d'etat in many Latin American countries may be largely attributable to the success of previous plotters in seizing power and, through it, status and wealth. Between 1907 and 1966 there were ninety-five successful coups in the twenty Latin American countries, half of them concentrated in five of those countries (Argentina, Haiti, and Peru, eight each; Bolivia, nine; Ecuador, thirteen).[75] Putnam found substantial correlations between the extent of military intervention in these twenty nations at various points in time, taking into account not coups per se but variations in degree of military influence on politics. The degree of intervention by country, 1951–55, correlates .71 with the degree of intervention in 1961–65, for example. The pattern is weaker but still significant over much longer periods: intervention levels in the decade 1906–15 correlate .46 with intervention in 1956–65.[76]

The role of military coups d'etat in Argentine and Colombian politics provides contrasting illustrations of the development of such patterns in specific countries. By 1930 Argentina had experienced more than seventy-five years of civilian rule and its military had become increasingly apolitical. The incapacity of civilian leaders to deal with the depression crisis led to a military coup in that year, from which the military benefited both in terms of political influence and budgetary allotments. The failure of a subsequent civilian regime to maintain these benefits led to the coup and power struggle of 1943 that brought Perón to power. His attacks on the Catholic Church and the threat his regime posed to the upper and middle classes led to his overthrow by the military in 1955, with civilian support. A decade of increasingly frequent military interventions followed (eight coups or attempted coups between mid-1959 and mid-1963, for example), culminating in a triumph in 1966

[74] Charles Tilly, "A Travers le Chaos des vivantes Cités" (Paper read to the Sixth World Congress of Sociology, Evian-les-Bains, September 1966), quotation 5.

[75] Egil Fossum, "Factors Influencing the Occurrence of Military Coups d'Etat in Latin America," *Journal of Peace Research*, No. 3, 1967, 229.

[76] Robert D. Putnam, "Toward Explaining Military Intervention in Latin American Politics," *World Politics*, XX (October 1967), 104–105.

for the growing Colorado or *gorila* faction of the military, which believed that indefinite military rule rather than a caretakership for civilian politicians was the only solution to the nation's ills.[77] In broad terms what seems to have happened is that the military, which originally intervened out of reluctant necessity, found coups an increasingly satisfactory means of resolving their own discontents and those of segments of the upper and middle classes that supported them. More and more Argentineans became resigned to the occurrence of coups, especially after 1955, and growing numbers of officers became convinced by their relative success in national management that intervention was justifiable in utilitarian terms.

Colombia also had a long history of military nonintervention. A civilian government survived the depression crisis of the early 1950s, but succumbed in 1953 in the context of a rural civil war that civilian politicians seemed to inflame rather than control. General Rojas Pinilla assumed power; his four-year incumbency has been called "perhaps the most inept military dictatorship in the annals of contemporary Latin American despotism." Rural violence did abate during this period, but the economic and political consequences of his regime were so disastrous, not only for civilians but for the military as well, that his fellow officers sent him into exile and returned power to civilian leaders.[78] This military coup inflicted more harm than benefit on the participants, military and civilian politicians alike, and appears to have generated little utilitarian justification for future coups d'etat in Colombia. They may of course occur, but in spite of the model provided by the events of 1953–57, not in emulation of them. Not all who plan coups succeed, of course. The ratio of failures to successes in coup attempts in Latin America is quite high, indeterminately so because many abortive attempts go unreported and because fictitious attempts are sometimes reported for political purposes. The value gains of successful plotters have been sufficiently great in some countries, however, that many ambitious, frustrated men are willing to take the risk.

The effects of success, even if it is infrequent, are evident in

[77] See James W. Rowe, "Argentina's Restless Military," in *Latin American Politics: Studies of the Contemporary Scene*, Robert D. Tomasek, ed. (Garden City: Doubleday, 1966), 439–466, and Reuben de Hoyos, "Church and Army in the Argentine Revolution of 1955" (Ph.D. dissertation, Department of Politics, New York University, 1969).

[78] John D. Martz, "Colombia: Qualified Democracy," in Martin C. Needler, ed., *Political Systems of Latin America* (Princeton: Van Nostrand, 1964), quotation 215. For a somewhat less critical—but scarcely favorable—interpretation of the Rojas regime see Robert H. Dix, *Colombia: The Political Dimensions of Change* (New Haven: Yale University Press, 1967), chap. 5.

the development of patterns of chronic turmoil in Latin America and elsewhere. In Peruvian politics, Payne argues, political conflict is intense and bipolar, a more or less continuous confrontation between civilian incumbents and their civilian opponents. The more intense collective violence becomes, however, the more likely the armed forces are to intervene against the incumbent president. Consequently, opposition groups regularly work through interest organizations, particularly labor unions, to get wage increases and other benefits from the government, using demonstrative violence to back up the demands. The president, to minimize the threat of military intervention, is obliged to make generous concessions to the assaulting groups. "The President acts as he must, as do the workers in employing violence. For them violence is a highly successful weapon." [79] A similar pattern is said to have developed in India since independence. As the Congress Party has gradually weakened, its administration has had to become increasingly responsive to the demands of political opponents, which have been frequently expressed through antigovernment demonstrations and riots. Because of the increasing success of public protest, agitational politics has become a substitute for institutional means of exercising influence and in fact has tended to supplant them. Bayley writes, "A vicious cycle may be at work. To the extent that agitational activity is perceived to be efficacious it will contribute to the decline in the perceived usefulness of formal democratic mechanisms, and this in turn will renew the temptation to utilize agitation." He suggests that protests and the threat of violence are now partly institutionalized, and will become more routinized in the future.[80]

To the extent that political violence and protest demonstrations prove useful—to their leaders, rank-and-file participants, or both—collective action is likely to be regarded in utilitarian terms. In hypothetical summary.

Hypothesis JV.8: The intensity and scope of utilitarian justifications for political violence vary strongly with the extent to which a collectivity has increased its average value position in the past through political violence.

The independent variable is the extent, not the frequency, of past success, on the inference from psychological evidence that occasional success seems to reinforce an activity at least as much as

[79] James Payne, "Peru: The Politics of Structured Violence," *Journal of Politics*, XXVII (May 1965), 362–374, quotation 374.

[80] David H. Bayley, "Public Protest and the Political Process in India" (Paper read to the Annual Meeting of the Asian Studies Association, Philadelphia, March 1968), quotation 11.

consistent success. Scope as well as intensity is said to be affected, on the assumption that the greater the average value gain through political violence, the greater the proportion of people in the collectivity who are likely to have gotten direct benefit. No specific timespan is suggested for the operation of the effect. Value gains in the immediate past are probably recalled more clearly than more remote gains. But the dramatic successes of previous generations are likely to be enshrined in group traditions, more than losses or failures, and to be invoked to justify future rebellions decades and even centuries hence.

A related source of utilitarian perspectives on violence is provided by the demonstration effect of other groups' successful use or threat of violence. Psychological evidence is cited above that people who see others gain satisfaction through aggression are likely to emulate them. The extrapolation to collective violence is easily made. If the residents of one black ghetto see members of another looting successfully, or protesting successfully to local officials about their grievances, they will readily see the advantages of doing so themselves. In 1966 a national survey showed that a third of American Negroes believed that riots had helped the cause of Negro rights, whereas only a fifth thought they had hurt.[81] Successful food riots in Europe during the industrial revolution had such an effect on people in adjacent towns, student uprisings for greater influence in university affairs have comparable effects within and across national boundaries in the post-industrial era. The resurgence of regional separatist movements in the Western nations similarly is linked to the success of colonial independence movements. French separatists in Quebec draw such a parallel, for example, advocating objectives of greater economic autonomy and development analogous to the objectives more or less successfully attained by African and Asian peoples through independence. Wilson says that "Perhaps the most important cause of the rise of separatism in Quebec was the impact of the end of colonialism." [82] The effect is likely to be greatest if the perceiving group sees substantial comparability between its status and that of the group it might emulate. (See the similar qualification in hypothesis VE.3, chapter 4.) The success of conspirators overthrowing incompetent regimes in one tropical African state presumably has more meaning to dissatisfied military and political leaders in other African states than it does for blacks subject to colonial rule in southern Africa. The sources of their anger, their means, and their opponents are all

[81] Brink and Harris, 264.

[82] Frank L. Wilson, "French-Canadian Separatism," *Western Political Quarterly*, XX (March 1967), 121.

different. The successes of rioters in Watts in 1965—successful at least in asserting their pride—seems to have had greater impact on men in other ghettos than the success of Africans in freeing themselves from European rule. The lessons of African independence in turn seem to have been more persuasive than attempts by revolutionary spokesmen to get the black American to identify with the struggles of Asian and Latin American peasants. The demonstration effect of other groups' successful use of violence is probably sufficiently pervasive and consequential to be summarized in a formal hypothesis.

Hypothesis JV.9: The intensity and scope of utilitarian justifications for political violence in a collectivity vary moderately with the extent to which similar collectivities elsewhere are thought to have increased their average value positions through political violence.

The Communication of Aggressive Symbols

The characteristics of communication systems are in many indirect ways connected with the genesis of collective violence. The development of dense, pervasive communications networks has quickened life throughout the world. The development of modern communications systems is said to be "both index and agent of change in a total social system." [83] Exposure to more attractive modes of life and the consequent intensification of value expectations is facilitated by system-wide communication networks (chapter 4). Perceptions of regime responses to discontent, and to disorder, are acquired through communication media (chapters 5 and 8). Communication among discontented but dispersed individuals may substitute for physical proximity in the development of organizations committed to violence. Effective revolutionary leadership requires open communication channels between leaders and followers (chapter 9).

There are several more direct facilitating effects of communication systems on the dissemination of aggression-sanctioning information and doctrines. The two hypotheses developed below

[83] Daniel Lerner, "Communication Systems and Social Systems: A Statistical Exploration in History and Policy," *Behavioral Science*, II (October 1957), 267. On the role of communications media in modernization in the Middle East see Lerner, *The Passing of Traditional Society* (Glencoe: The Free Press, 1958), chap. 2. On the relation of communications processes to political development generally see Lucian W. Pye, ed., *Communications and Political Development* (Princeton: Princeton University Press, 1963). An evaluation of empirical research on the effects of mass communication is Joseph T. Clapper, *The Effects of Mass Communication* (New York: The Free Press, 1960).

apply to the dissemination of several kinds of aggressive political symbols: those embodied in cultural traditions of political violence, in new doctrinal justifications for political violence, and in reports of violent collective action itself, which can have a demonstration effect for discontented people elsewhere. The hypotheses thus are relevant to the assessment of the intensity and scope of both normative and utilitarian justifications for violence.

The characteristics of communication systems that most directly affect the dispersion of aggressive political symbols in a collectivity are the number of channels or media, the density of information flow over them, and the proportion of the population reached by the media. The greater the number of media, the more likely that means can be found for articulating aggressive symbols. Lifton points out that political control of communication can be used to facilitate ideological conversion, and demonstrates the effectiveness with which the Chinese Communists used communication control to create what he calls a "thought reform environment."[84] The greater the density of aggressive symbols communicated through these media, the more likely people are to attend to and be affected by them. The greater the audience of communication media, the greater the proportion of discontented who are likely to receive such messages. Few political elites tolerate the communication of beliefs directly hostile to themselves, though they may encourage aggression against others. Some elites, particularly in communist systems, have sufficient control over news media that major outbreaks of political violence go unreported, a tacit recognition of their potential cue value for precipitating violence elsewhere. Another tactic is to report such events but to attribute them to "undesirable others": reactionaries, hoodlums, Communists, Jews, bandits. If the articulators of revolutionary symbolism lack access to existing media, or find them closed by censorship, they may establish new media like newspapers and journals. If these are suppressed they may resort to clandestine or foreign communication media, face-to-face agitation, or the generation of rumors. Experimental studies indicate that discontented people tend to give selective attention to aggressive messages, which suggests that even if the aggressive content of communication is small it can reach its potential audience.[85] Clandestine communication nonetheless is generally inefficient and its messages likely to reach fewer of the discontented and with lesser frequency. The following hypotheses are suggested:

[84] Lifton, especially 420–422.
[85] See Berkowitz, *Aggression*, chap. 9.

Hypothesis JV.10: The intensity of normative and utilitarian justifications for political violence varies moderately with the density of aggressive political symbols in communication content.

Hypothesis JV.11: To the extent that the density of aggressive political symbols in communication content is high, the scope of normative and utilitarian justifications for political violence varies strongly with the number and scope of communication media.

Aggressive political symbols are verbal or graphic representations of violence against political targets, including descriptions of actual violence, past or present, and assertions about the desirability or lack of desirability of violence against such targets. The proposed effects are probably strongest for symbols of collective political rather than individual violence, and for symbols that depict political violence in normatively neutral or positive rather than negative terms. The discontented do not necessarily accept the norms of the communicator, however, and even if they do the aggressive symbols themselves may carry the implication that political violence is possible and, for some groups, acceptable. Consequently the relationships should hold for any aggressive political symbols, though more strongly for some than others. The *density* of aggressive symbols is the proportion of such symbols among all symbols in communication content. It can be examined with reference to total communication content, weighted according to variations in audience attention to the media examined, or ideally by reference to the communication intake of particular audiences. The *scope* of communication media refers to the relative size of their audience.

Communication media thus can facilitate specific outbreaks of violence. In the absence of other media, wandering preachers and propagandists can serve as communication agents, s they did in the diffusion of anarchist sentiment in rural Spain in the late nineteenth and early twentieth centuries.[86] In pre- and post-revolutionary Egypt both Communists and the Muslim Brotherhood recruited cadres from unemployed college graduates who were "capable of diffusing throughout Egypt a uniform set of messages" advocating extremist political solutions to national problems.[87] Petras and Zeitlin have shown that the political radicalism of

[86] Hobsbawm, 84 ff.

[87] Lerner, *The Passing of Traditional Society*, 256–257. For a detailed account of the Brotherhood's activities see Christina P. Harris, *Nationalism and Revolution in Egypt: The Role of the Muslim Brotherhood* (Stanford: Hoover Institution on War, Revolution and Peace, Stanford University, 1964).

Chilean mining municipalities has the effect of radicalizing the peasantry of adjoining rural areas, as manifest in relatively high rates of voting support for radical parties in agricultural communities adjoining mining towns. The politicization of the peasantry by the miners is said to be both a conscious effort and a "natural process," i.e. both formal and information communication of radical ideas occurs.[88] Communication of political messages is more efficient and reaches larger audiences when tracts or newspapers can be printed and distributed, or radio speeches delivered. Diáz has written of Andalusian peasant anarchism during 1918–19 that

> Everyone read at all times. There was no limit to the men's curiosity and to their thirst for learning. . . . Admittedly 70 to 80 per cent were illiterate, but this was not an insuperable obstacle. The enthusiastic illiterate bought his paper and gave it to a comrade to read. He then made him mark the article he liked best. Then he would ask another comrade to read him the marked article and after a few readings he had it by heart and would repeat it to those who had not yet read it.[89]

The circulation of clandestine pamphlets among potential civilian and military opponents to Perón's regime in 1955 was instrumental in undermining his legitimacy and generating the support, or at least neutrality, needed for his overthrow.[90] Foreign propaganda broadcasts can incite the discontented to violence as readily as propaganda tracts. Egyptian broadcasts have been held responsible for inciting antigovernment riots in much of North Africa and the Middle East, for example the simultaneous riots that erupted throughout Jordan in 1955 over its prospective membership in the Baghdad Pact.[91]

Formal communication channels also facilitate the "demonstration effect" whereby a call to arms or news of an outbreak of violence provides the discontented with cues or models for resistance.[92] Invocation of a tradition of violence by a spokesman can, by recalling past collective action, set men to violence. Dahlke shows that before both the Kishinew (Russia) anti-Jewish riot of 1903 and the Detroit race riot of 1943 there were organizational

[88] James Petras and Maurice Zeitlin, "Miners and Agrarian Radicalism," *American Sociological Review,* XXXII (August 1967), 578–586.

[89] Juan Diáz del Moral, *Historia de las Agitaciones Campesinas Andaluzas* (Madrid: Alianza Editorial, 1929, 1967), translated in Hobsbawm, 87–88.

[90] De Hoyos, *op.cit.*

[91] Lerner, *The Passing of Traditional Society,* 255.

[92] For theoretical comments on the communication of incidents and the creation of "social epidemics" see Schelling, 74, 90, 146, and Rapoport, 47–59.

advocates of violence against an intensely disliked minority group.[93] Slogans imbedded in revolutionary ideologies can be sufficiently explicit in their prescription of violence that their dissemination provides sufficient cues for violence, though it seems unlikely that such slogans can precipitate a wholly new, unfamiliar type of collective action. Sorel's advocacy of the general strike was designed to invoke images of violent conflict with such clarity that workers would be moved to action by strike appeals. Its effectiveness as a cue for action nonetheless depended upon workers' prior experience with strikes as a form of protest. It is unlikely that slogans advocating, say, lynching of entrepreneurs by the Parisian proletariat would have had even the limited effects of the myth of the general strike.

A call to arms or appeals to traditions of political violence seem less effective as stimuli for violence than news of the occurrence of violence elsewhere, or at best are effective only in conjunction with such news. The demonstration effect of news of revolutionary violence is apparent in the revolutionary contagion that spread from the North American colonies to Western Europe to Hispanic America between 1776 and 1820;[94] in the series of unsuccessful communist revolutions in Europe after 1918; and in the infectious anticolonial nationalism of Africa and Asia after 1945, whose primary models seem to have been the successful Indian and perhaps Indonesian attainment of independence. Hobsbawm cites European examples of the interaction between group traditions of violent protest and news of violence elsewhere in precipitating new outbreaks. Among the chronically rebellious Sicilian peasantry of the nineteenth century, he writes, "when the signal came from one of the great and perennially riotous cities of the island—Palermo, Catania, Messina—they would launch blind and savage insurrections occupying the common lands, sacking town halls, excise stations, communal archives, and the houses and clubs of the gentry." In Andalusia, peasant general strikes began to occur in the 1880s, apparently as a result of the juxtaposition of a tradition of peasant rebellion with advocacy of the new doctrine of general strike. Such strikes recurred in waves, often precipitated

[93] H. O. Dahlke, "Race and Minority Riots: A Study in the Typology of Violence," *Social Forces*, XXX (May 1952), 419–425.

[94] The principal exponents of the thesis linking European and American Revolutions of the eighteenth century are Jacques Godechot, *France and the Atlantic Revolution of the Eighteenth Century, 1770–1799*, trans. H. H. Rowen (New York: The Free Press, 1965), and Robert R. Palmer, *The Age of the Democratic Revolutions: A Political History of Europe and America 1760–1800* (Princeton: Princeton University Press, 1959).

by word of uprisings elsewhere: in 1920, for example, they occurred in response to belated news of the Russian Revolution.[95]

The effects of different kinds of communication media are apparent from comparisons of the number and simultaneity of outbreaks in different eras and cultures. Merriman suggests that improved communication was partly responsible for the precipitousness with which some fifty European uprisings and revolutions followed immediately on the French revolution of 1848, compared with the lack of simultaneity of mid-seventeenth-century revolutions.[96] Newspapers were the principal medium by which news of popular uprisings spread in 1848; their primary audience was dissatisfied intellectuals, the bourgeoisie, and those few urban workers who were literate. Among nonliterate rural people, news of violence spread more slowly. Rudé shows graphically the time lag in the geographic expansion of such disturbances as the English food riots of 1766, the French grain riots of 1775, and Luddite machine-breaking riots in 1811–12 from the place of the initial outbreak. The riots spread to surrounding areas no more quickly than a man could travel on foot or horseback.[97]

In the late-twentieth century the demonstration effect of unrest occurs almost immediately throughout national populations and across national boundaries. A study of the contagion of individual anti-Jewish acts in the United States provides one example. A time-distribution analysis of 559 incidents in the "swastika epidemic" in the United States in 1959–60 shows them rising to a peak within three weeks of the first reported incident and persisting at a diminishing rate for five more weeks. The initial outburst was primarily anti-Jewish, but the majority of incidents at the peak had non-Jewish targets. The demonstration effect through mass media was evidently operative, since the perpetrators were located throughout the country and presumably not in direct communication with one another; moreover the preponderance of non-Jewish targets at the peak of the epidemic indicates that the first incidents suggested a mechanism for expressing anger having a variety of attributed sources. Smelser characterizes this as the "derived," as distinct from the "real," phase of hostile outbursts.[98]

[95] Hobsbawm, 78–79, 96, quotation 96.

[96] Merriman, 209–210. The estimate of the number of attempted revolutions in 1848 is from Priscilla Robertson, *Revolutions of 1848: A Social History* (Princeton: Princeton University Press, 1952), vii.

[97] Rudé, *The Crowd in History,* maps on 25, 40, 82.

[98] D. Caplovitz and C. Rogers, "The Swastika Epidemic: A Preliminary Draft of a Report for the Anti-Defamation League," 1960, summarized and interpreted in Smelser, 257–259.

As a second example, nation-wide news coverage of American ghetto riots, especially through television, provided potent cues for violent action in other ghettos. Five hundred men imprisoned during the Detroit riots of 1967 were asked about their sources of information on other riots. Thirty-five percent had learned of them from television, 33 percent from newspapers, and 20 percent from radio. Most significantly, 80 percent had seen riots on television, and when they were asked what they saw most people doing in these riots, the most commonly reported category of activity was looting, burning, and fighting.[99]

It does not appear justifiable to infer from such findings that a blackout of news coverage would have eliminated the demonstration effect. The Chinese "Cultural Revolution" of 1966–68 was accompanied by nation-wide turmoil despite tight censorship. Roving bands of Red Guards and their poster campaigns effectively disseminated news of violence. If intensely discontented people are members of a literate and mobile society, they will learn of violence by others by informal means if not through formal communication media. Controls on aggressive political symbols in media content may minimize the immediate demonstration effects of turmoil, and thereby lead to protracted and sporadic rather than near-simultaneous violence among the discontented elsewhere, but are unlikely to eliminate it.

Summary

The fundamental relationship between intensity and scope of relative deprivation and the potential for collective violence (hypothesis V.1) is related in this and the preceding chapter to the kinds of perspectives men have on politics and violence. The causal connection between potential for collective violence (discontent) and the potential for violence against political targets is strong (hypothesis V.4), but not absolute. The two cognitive variables that affect whether discontent is transformed into collective political action are the degree to which men believe that violence and the threat of violence against political targets are justifiable in a normative sense (hypothesis V.2), and as a utilitarian means to value satisfaction (hypothesis V.3).

Justifications, like discontent, are psychological variables. A number of more readily observable societal conditions affect their intensity and scope. Two independent variables that facilitate the development and acquisition of perspectives justifying violence

[99] Manpower Administration, U.S. Department of Labor, *The Detroit Riot: A Profile of 500 Prisoners* (Washington, D.C.: author, March 1968), 21.

are general characteristics of society. The intensity of normative justifications for violence varies with the relative emphasis on extrapunitiveness in cultural or subcultural socialization practices (hypothesis JV.1). The scope of both normative and utilitarian justifications for political violence varies jointly with the number and scope of communication media, and the density of aggressive symbols in their content (hypothesis JV.11).

Three general characteristics of political systems have a pronounced impact on men's perspectives on specifically political violence. Discontent tends to be politicized—i.e. blamed on the regime—and to contribute to the normative and utilitarian justification for political violence, to the extent that government has in the past responded effectively to discontent (hypothesis JV.3), and to the extent that it favors one group over another in responding to current demands (hypothesis JV.4). In other words, the more a government has done in the past for its citizens, and the more it does currently for other groups of citizens relative to what it is doing for one's own group, the more it is expected to do, and the more hostile people are if it fails. The argument does not imply that regimes can minimize violence by limiting their sphere of action. If action is reduced from current levels, political violence will increase. If it is maintained at a traditionally low level, collective violence is no less likely to occur but is less likely to be directed against political targets, at least in the short run. But there are potent and widespread doctrines in the modern world that the political system is and should be ultimately responsible for social problems. If those doctrines take root in the minds of discontented citizens their likely response to regimes performing minimal functions is not protest to increase attention to their needs, but revolution. The legitimacy of regimes is a third characteristic that normatively inhibits political violence. The more intensely citizens feel about the worthiness of their political community, institutions, and rulers, the less likely they are to feel justified in attacking them (hypothesis JV.5). They are likely to tolerate value sacrifices for their government and, if intensely discontented with its actions, are more likely to use peaceful protest and limited violence to have policies changed and incumbents removed than to resort to revolutionary violence against the system as a whole.

These societal and political properties have relatively indirect effects on justifications for violence. More direct are some effects of political violence itself. If violent conflict has been common in the history of a collectivity, traditions justifying subsequent violence are likely to develop: the greater the historical magnitude of political strife in a community, the greater the intensity and scope of normative justifications for future political violence (hypothesis JV.2). The effect is partly due to the development of anticipations that political violence will recur (corollary JV.2.1); if discontent is widespread and intense, anticipations are likely to become beliefs that political violence is justified as well (corollary JV.2.2). The success of past strife in improving a community's conditions of life similarly contributes to the development of beliefs about the utility of violence as a response to future deprivation (hypothesis JV.8). A community may have a nonviolent tradition itself, but if its members see similar groups elsewhere making gains through political violence they are likely to see utilitarian justifications for violent tactics for themselves (hypothesis JV.9). In the modern world this demonstration effect of one group's successful use of violence can have almost simultaneous, worldwide consequences.

The content of new doctrines articulated by, and appeals directed at, the discontented also provide evidence about the intensity of men's justifications for violence. The revolutionary appeals potentially most effective in giving men normative justifications for political violence, and hence most likely to be accepted by the discontented, are those that provide explanations of the sources of RD, identify political targets for violence, and stress symbols of group identification among the deprived (hypothesis JV.6). The acceptability of these appeals depends finally on the degree to which they are consistent with the immediate circumstances of the discontented. The effect of revolutionary appeals on utilitarian justifications for violence is a function of the relative importance they attribute to tactics of political violence for increasing men's value positions (hypothesis JV.7). Finally, the intensity of both normative and utilitarian justifications can be inferred from the density of aggressive symbols in communication content. The greater the number of representations of political violence in men's communication intake, the more likely they are to accept such violence as a mode of behavior (hypothesis JV.10).

These relationships do not fully determine the intensities and scope of men's justifications for political violence. The most direct means to that determination is to ask them, an approach seldom feasible, its results not wholly reliable and always subject to change as new events occur and doctrines change. But at least these two chapters should demonstrate that we need to examine more than "television violence" or prevailing revolutionary ideologies to know how men think about violence in politics.

8. The Coercive Balance

> Force empowers its own adversaries. It raises up its own opposition. It engenders its own destruction.
>
> Roy Pearson,
> "The Dilemma of Force"[1]

THE MOST FUNDAMENTAL human responses to the use of force is counterforce. Force threatens and angers men, especially if they believe it to be illicit or unjust. Threatened, they try to defend themselves; angered, they want to retaliate. Regimes facing armed rebellion usually regard compromise as evidence of weakness and devote additional resources to military retaliation. The presumption justifying counterforce is that it deters: the greater a regime's capacity for force and the more severe the sanctions it imposes on dissidents, the less violence they will do. This assumption is often a self-defeating fallacy. If a regime responds to the threat or use of force with greater force, the effect is likely to be an intensification of resistance: dissidents will resort to greater force.

There are only two inherent limitations on the escalating spiral of force and counterforce: the depletion of either group's resources for coercion, or the attainment by one of the capacity for genocidal victory over its opponents. There are societal and psychological limitations as well, but they require tacit bonds between opponents: the acceptance by one of the ultimate authority of the other, submission to arbitration by a neutral authority, recognition of mutual interest that makes bargaining possible, perception that acquiescence will be less harmful than resisting certain annihilation. In the absence of such bases for cooperation, regimes and their opponents are likely to engage in violent conflict to the limit of their abilities.

* * *

The following hypothesis provides a formal link between the arguments of previous chapters and those of this and the next chapter. The basic causal relationships advanced thus far are (1) that the intensity and scope of RD determine the potential for collective violence (hypothesis V.1); and (2) that the potential for collective violence, jointly with men's justifications for political violence, determine the potential for specifically political violence (hypotheses V.2,3,4). The potential for political violence

[1] Roy Pearson, "The Dilemma of Force," *Saturday Review* (February 10, 1968), 24.

is in turn a strong but not complete determinant of the magnitude of political violence:

Hypothesis V.5: The magnitude of political violence varies strongly with the potential for political violence.

Magnitude of political violence, discussed in chapter 1, has three component variables: the extent of participation in political violence within the political unit (*scope*), the destructiveness of action (*intensity*), and the length of time it persists (*duration*). It can be assessed in political units of any scale – city, region, or nation – and for various periods, for example on a monthly, annual, or decennial basis. Its occurrence presupposes some potential for political violence, or *politicized discontent,* among members of a political community. But even if their politicized discontent is widespread and intense, it is not a sufficient condition for political violence. The factors that finally determine its extent and its forms are the characteristics of social policy and structure examined in this and the next chapter: the respective balances of coercive control and institutional support between regimes and dissidents. If a regime exercises pervasive and consistent coercive control over its citizens and provides a dense network of supporting institutions, the impetus to political violence is likely to be directed into nonviolent activity. If, on the other hand, dissidents have high coercive capacities and the support of strong organizations, violent political opposition is facilitated.[2]

The Balance of Regime and Dissident Coercion

A common proposition in theoretical writing on political violence is that its magnitude varies inversely with the coercive capabilities of a regime.[3] Usually "absolute" coercive capacity is referred to, but a less common and more accurate proposition recognizes that the effectiveness of a regime's coercive forces and resources is a function of their size relative to those of opponents. Timasheff proposes that "revolution commonly breaks out when both parties have, or seem to have, a fair chance of victory," and implies that the

[2] Relative strengths of the independent variables can be suggested: the intensity and scope of politicized discontent is, in general, likely to be as consequential as the coercive and institutional balances combined in determining magnitudes of political violence. In statistical terms, about half the explained variation in magnitudes of political violence among political communities is likely to be the result of variations in political discontent. The proportion would tend to be higher for turmoil, lower for internal war.

[3] Some of these propositions and evidence for them are reviewed and interpreted below, 243–246.

relationship applies to turmoil as well as revolution. In the case of riots inspired by dissident leaders, for example, the aim may not be winning but "holding political oppression in tolerable limits." The initiators in other words believe they have "a fair chance of at least partial success."[4] Janos states the hypothesis explicitly in terms of the balance of opponents' capacities:

> The character, intensity, and duration of violence are, above all the function of the relative strength of the parties involved. . . . As the relative capabilities of opponents tend toward an equilibrium, so will the intensity and duration of the conflict increase, assuming more and more the conventional character of warfare between two nations. . . .[5]

Janos' argument applies to both the magnitude and form of political violence. The first relationship is restated here, the others below:

Hypothesis V.6: The magnitude of political violence varies strongly and directly with the ratio of dissident coercive control to regime coercive control to the point of equality, and inversely beyond it.

Dissidents and regimes have *coercive control* to the extent that they can obtain consistent compliance (not fleeting compliance) with their demands and directives through the use or threat of negative sanctions. The most immediately compelling of such negative sanctions is force itself; more generally, a negative sanction is any value-depriving act used in the expectation that it will modify behavior. "The sanction might consist in the manipulation of symbols (praise or censure), or in a redistribution of goods and services, or in the use of violence, or . . . in reward or punishment by way of any value whatever."[6] The following discussion of the determinants of coercive control will be concerned primarily with the effects of force, i.e. the threat and use of violent sanctions, on coercive control; nonviolent sanctions are often predicated on violent ones in any case.

[4] Nicholas S. Timasheff, *War and Revolution* (New York: Sheed and Ward, 1965), 156–158, quotations 156, 158.

[5] Andrew C. Janos, *The Seizure of Power: A Study of Force and Popular Consent* (Princeton: Center of International Studies, Princeton University, Research Monograph No. 16, 1964), quotation 91. For a similar argument see Peter A. R. Calvert, "Revolution: The Politics of Violence," *Political Science*, xv (No. 1, 1967), 6ff.

[6] Harold D. Lasswell and Abraham Kaplan, *Power and Society: A Framework for Political Inquiry* (New Haven: Yale University Press, 1950), 48. For a psychological definition see John Dollard et al., *Frustration and Aggression* (New Haven: Yale University Press, 1939), 34.

Three elaborations of the basic hypothesis are necessary. First, coercive control varies in both scope and degree. A regime may exercise some coercive control over most of its nominal citizens (high scope) but be able to control only a small segment of their activities (low degree). The extent of its coercive control thus may be no greater than that of dissidents whose scope of control is quite small but who can enforce almost absolute compliance with almost any kind of directive. Second, to forestall misunderstanding, "dissident coercive control" refers to the enforcement capacities of any group of politically discontented leaders, whether revolutionary cadres, leaders of opposition parties and trades unions, or disaffected military officers. Finally, force by regimes and by dissidents usually is exerted in different ways and consequently has different effects. Regimes ordinarily employ "internal" force—exercised by their military and internal security forces, judicial and penal systems—against the regime's own "constituencies." In other words, regime force serves primarily an internal policing function. Dissidents also often employ force to ensure their followers' compliance, but its primary use is against opponents outside the group. The brunt of regime force thus falls on its citizens, with the consequent risk of alienating them if used inconsistently or harshly. Dissident force, being directed primarily at opponents, is less ambivalently valued by dissidents.

The Janos quotation above suggests that the form of political violence as well as its magnitude is affected by the balance of coercive control. If the regime and dissidents have approximately equal strength, internal war is more likely than other forms of political violence:

Hypothesis I.1: The likelihood of internal war increases as the ratio of dissident to regime coercive control approaches equality.

If dissident coercive control is substantially less than regime coercive control in both scope and degree, dissidents are not likely to be able to organize and sustain an internal war. If their decisions are mainly utilitarian, they may resort to limited violence—turmoil—in hopes of exerting some influence on government policy. Even in the absence of utilitarian motivations, and in the face of greatly superior force, intensely discontented dissidents sometimes initiate violent clashes or respond riotously to repressive measures. Turmoil thus is more likely to occur when dissidents are weak relative to the regime. Sorokin makes the same point. If the social groups who defend the existing order are strong, he writes, the result of "repressed instincts"—absolute deprivation—is "only a series of spontaneous suppressed riots. But when the groups which stand for order are unable to exercise that restraining influence, a revolution is inevitable."[7] Turmoil also occurs frequently when a regime weakens, but if the lack or ineffectiveness of regime response to turmoil suggests to the dissidents that they have equal or greater coercive control, then riots, localized rebellions, and general strikes tend to be transformed quickly into revolutionary movements, as they were in France in 1789, in Mexico in 1912, and in Hungary in 1956; or they provide the basis for a successful coup d'etat, as in Russia in 1918 and in Egypt in 1953. Chronic turmoil is most likely, therefore, when the balance of coercive control markedly favors the regime.

Hypothesis T.1: The likelihood of turmoil increases as the ratio of dissident to regime coercive control approaches zero.

Conspiracy—plots, coups d'etat, terrorism—is also systematically related to the balance of coercive control. If dissidents are very weak relative to the regime, they may decide that their best chance of success is to develop clandestine organizations, expecting to increase their coercive capabilities and the popular support over the long run or, less likely, anticipating the seizure of power without protracted conflict. They are especially likely to resort to clandestine operations if the regime makes repressive rather than adjustive responses to demands made through conventional channels or by public protest. Inflexible, repressive responses intensify the hostility of dissidents and reduce their hopes of obtaining reform except through revolutionary transformation. On the other hand, if dissidents have, or think they have, a high ratio of coercive control relative to the regime, they also are likely to resort to conspiracy: there is no need to organize an internal war when power can be seized in a precise thrust at a weakened regime. This is the classic pattern of the successful coup d'etat: its leaders correctly estimate that incumbents can compel neither military nor popular support, and consequently ask or force them to resign, often with only minimal use of force. Conspiratorial activity thus is likely if the coercive balance strongly favors either the regime or the dissidents, but not if the coercive balance approaches equilibrium.

Hypothesis C.1: The likelihood of conspiracy varies with the degree of discrepancy between dissident and regime coercive control.

The relationship is linear: the greater the discrepancy, whether it favors the dissidents or the regime, the more likely is conspiracy.

[7] Pitirim A. Sorokin, *The Sociology of Revolution* (Philadelphia: Lippincott, 1925), 370.

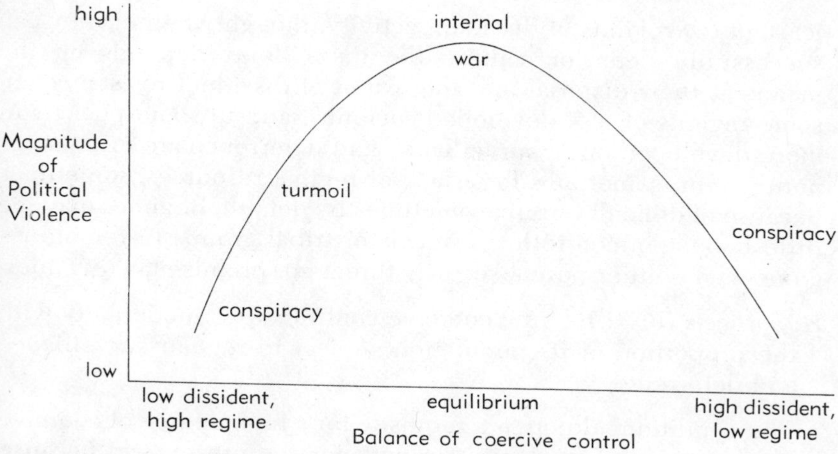

Figure 8. Effects of varying ratios of dissident to regime coercive control on magnitudes and characteristic forms of political violence.

The relationships specified in the above four hypotheses are illustrated schematically in figure 8, the curve representing magnitudes of political violence.

There are other determinants of the likelihood of the three forms of political violence, including the distribution and types of RD in a collectivity, historical experience with particular types of political violence, and the balance of institutional support between regimes and dissidents. Some of these interact with and some are independent of the balance of coercive control. Institutional factors are identified in the next chapter, other determining variables in chapter 10.

Regime Coercion

Many determinants of the extent of regime coercive control have been identified in the literature on political violence: the principal variables examined here are the proportion of a population directly subject to the security and judicial apparatus of a regime; the size and resources of military and security forces; the loyalty of those forces to the regime; and the severity and consistency of sanctions.

THE SCOPE OF CONTROL

A necessary condition for regime coercive control is the active presence of regime agencies, security and judicial, throughout its population. In most modern nations the scope of regime control includes the entire population: security forces are highly likely to learn of overt kinds of dissident activity, though whether they can successfully deter or capture the dissendents depends on the means at their disposal and the extent of dissident resistance. In some regions of less developed societies, and in some pockets in more developed ones, surveillance and deterrence are minimal or nonexistent, sometimes for a lack of regime resources, sometimes because of difficult terrain, sometimes by default. Regimes may see little benefit in controlling nomads or tribal groups in remote regions who neither pose a security threat nor promise tax revenues.

Hypothesis RC.1: Regime coercive control varies moderately with the proportion of its population subject to regular surveillance and deterrence.

The condition, although a requisite for a high degree of coercive control, is only of moderate strength for the present era because most regimes do have a fairly dense network of control agencies throughout their more densely populated areas. The crucial determinant of regime coercive control in this century is the *quality* of coercive activities in the areas within a regime's network of control.

DETERRENCE AND SANCTIONS

"Can anything be more infuriating to an American than to be beaten and otherwise mistreated by the very authorities who have been entrusted with a monopoly of physical force for the express purpose of protecting him?"[8] This rhetorical question can be asked of anyone in any era. The informed answer, supported by much psychological, historical, and comparative evidence, is that the threat and use of negative sanctions anger people, the more so the less justified the victims think the sanctions are. Imposed sanctions are deprivations, the threat of sanctions is equivalent to the concept of anticipated deprivation, the innate emotional response to both is anger.

But sanctions also inhibit violent responses to anger. If men anticipate severe and certain retribution for proscribed actions they are likely to restrain their anger in the short run. In the long run, if they think their motives for action are legitimate, they will attempt to get the means—comrades, organization, arms—to counter the severity and certainty of regime sanctions. The inference is that the more severe and certain are unjustified sanctions, the greater the extent of ultimate political violence. In the short run,

[8] Robert M. Fogelson, "From Resentment to Confrontation: The Police, the Negroes, and the Outbreak of the Nineteen-Sixties Riots," *Political Science Quarterly*, LXXXIII (June 1968), 227.

however, threatened and imposed sanctions have a curvilinear relationship with the magnitude of political violence. Men subject to mild sanctions for their actions are little angered by them; men subject to severe sanctions are intensely angered but deterred from the sanctioned acts and, in the short run, from retaliation against the sanctioning agents. But if men anticipate or experience sanctions of intermediate severity, their anger is likely to outweigh their fear. These relationships hold for sanctions invoked for any kind of activity—traffic violations, public criticisms of an authoritarian regime, draft resistance. They have especially strong impact on people with politicized discontent. If they are in a previolent stage, already politically discontented but not enough so to take overt action, additional police or military surveillance, with its implicit threat of sanctions, or new repressive measures, may increase anger to the point that they will riot. If coercive sanctions have been severe enough to inhibit retaliation but then are reduced, violent resistance also becomes increasingly likely. If they are already rioting or rebelling, regime sanctions of intermediate severity intensify their anger but are unlikely to deter them: the effect is to intensify the violence of their opposition.

Two specific hypotheses are suggested by this argument. One is that regime coercive control varies curvilinearly with the degree to which it threatens to use violent sanctions. Violent sanctions are likely to be more immediately feared, and resisted, than nonviolent sanctions administered through routinized judicial processes. Degrees of threat, either in regime intentions or popular perception, are not readily assessed directly. The numbers and mobility of internally available military and security forces are however a major determinant of the extent to which dissidents feel threatened by force, and are more readily determined. The proposed relationship is specified in hypothesis RC.2: intermediate levels of threat, manifest in military and security forces of intermediate size, are more likely to increase the anger and hence the opposition of dissidents within the regime's scope of control than they are to force them into compliance.

Hypothesis RC.2: Regime coercive control varies curvilinearly with the size and resources of its military and internal security forces, control being lowest when size and resources are at intermediate levels.

The *size* of forces should be indexed in relative not absolute terms, as a proportion of total or of adult male population of the community being studied. *Resources* are indexed relative to the equipment and mobility of the best-equipped contemporary forces. Both military and internal security forces are included because military units are used at least occasionally in almost all nations, and frequently in most, for maintaining internal order; they are the ultimate source of force.

The second hypothesis is that regime coercive control varies curvilinearly with the severity of negative sanctions actually imposed: the likely effect of sanctions of intermediate severity, like the effect of intermediate degrees of threat, is to reduce rather than increase compliance. The relationship should apply not only to violent sanctions but to other kinds of sanctions as well.

Hypothesis RC.3: Regime coercive control varies curvilinearly with the severity of regime-administered negative sanctions, control being lowest when severity is at intermediate levels.

The most *severe* sanctions are those that deprive men of all their most salient values. Life itself is the ultimate value for most men in most societies, but for some it may be honor, ideological purity, or freedom (see chapter 2).

The proposed relationships are shown schematically in figure 9. The hypotheses do not imply that *no* political violence will occur when forces are small and sanctions mild. In this situation politicized discontent is likely to lead to political violence in proportion to its intensity. But the use of minimal force does minimize the escalation of violence, especially turmoil, caused by the use or threat of intermediate force. If politicized discontent is so in-

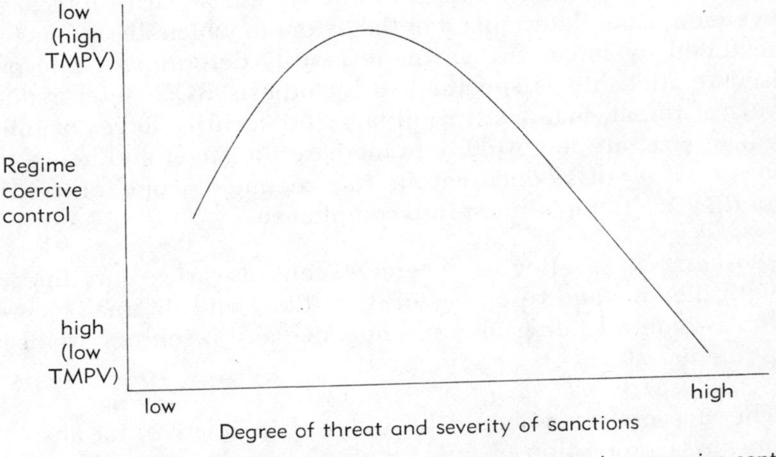

Figure 9. Effects of threatened and imposed sanctions on regime coercive control and total magnitude of political violence (TMPV).

tense and pervasive that the existence of the regime is threatened, the only coercive response likely to be functional for the regime is to increase rapidly to high levels either or both threats and sanctions.

Psychological Bases. A survey of some psychological evidence suggests that negative physical sanctions are at best problematic in their effects on levels of aggression. In the laboratory they tend to increase anger and to inhibit aggressive responses only as long as the punitive agent is present. They increase the likelihood that aggression will be directed at other, less threatening objects, and displace and increase the aggressive response over time, a relationship discussed in chapter 3 and summarized in hypothesis ID.5.

Dollard et al. propose that punishment has two effects, one to inhibit aggressive responses, the other to interfere with aggressive responses and hence increase frustration and the consequent instigation to aggression.[9] Buss suggests more specifically that low levels of punishment do not inhibit aggression and that only high levels of punishment are likely to result in anxiety or flight. Intermediate levels of punishment are frustrating and elicit further aggression, establishing an aggression-punishment-aggression sequence.[10] Maier found in animal studies that under conditions of severe frustration, punishment increased the intensity of aggressive and other fixated behavior. Similarly, the greater the punishment for human subjects the more likely they were to manifest repetitious behavior that was highly resistant to change. Both kinds of studies suggest that if people are repeatedly punished for aggressive behavior, and if they have no positive alternatives, they will become increasingly and nonfunctionally aggressive, and find it increasingly difficult to respond in other ways.[11] Berkowitz summarizes other experimental evidence to the effect that "the arousal of strong aggressive tendencies in a person may delay the time at which he comes to anticipate punishment or disapproval for his aggression." [12] That is, if anger is strong enough it overrides the inhibitions associated with anticipated punishment; if anger

[9] Dollard et al., 39–40.

[10] Arnold H. Buss, *The Psychology of Aggression* (New York: Wiley, 1961), 58.

[11] Norman R. F. Maier, *Frustration: The Study of Behavior Without a Goal* (New York: McGraw-Hill, 1949), Part I. For reviews of psychological theory and evidence about the effects of punishment see for example Russell M. Church, "The Varied Effects of Punishment on Behavior," *Psychological Review*, LXX (September 1963), 369–402, and Richard L. Solomon, "Punishment," *American Psychologist*, XIX (April 1964), 239–253.

[12] Leonard Berkowitz, *Aggression: A Social Psychological Analysis* (New York: McGraw-Hill, 1962), 96.

is partly or wholly the result of previous experience or threat of punishment, the effects of anticipation of future punishment may thus be neutralized. Another study suggests that mild punishment can be more effective in deterring people from nonaggressive acts than severe punishment. Children were dissuaded from playing with an attractive toy with threats of mild punishment for some, more severe punishment for others. All of them obeyed. Some weeks later they were asked about the toy's attractiveness. Those threatened with severe punishment still found it attractive, the others did not.[13] Whatever interpretation is put on the findings, they are consistent with the thesis that mild sanctions can have a greater deterrent effect than more severe ones.

A number of studies show that punishment only temporarily inhibits aggression and that it facilitates displacement. For example, two groups of children played with dolls in four sessions, children in one group being reprimanded for hostile acts during the second session. The reprimanded children showed less aggression in the third session but were just as aggressive as the control group in the fourth.[14] In a study more relevant to collective political behavior, Lewin, Lippitt, and White compared the aggressive behaviors of ten-year-old boys under autocratic, democratic, and laissez-faire leadership. Aggression by boys who were consistently under autocratic leadership was eight times as frequent as among those under democratic leadership, but the aggression was largely directed at scapegoats, never at the autocratic leader. Other boys were exposed to all three kinds of leadership on successive days. They were largely passive under autocratic leadership but showed a sharp rise in aggression when the autocrat left the room, and were highly aggressive on days when they were in a freer atmosphere.[15]

Relatively subtle social pressures such as anticipated disapproval and high status of frustrators also inhibit aggression. Cohen demonstrated experimentally that people of low status who have a chance of improving their status inhibit aggression against superiors more than those who have no upward mobility.[16] Thibaut and Riecken

[13] E. Aronson, "Threat and Obedience," *Trans-Action*, III (1966), 25–27, summarized in Jerome D. Frank, *Sanity and Survival: Psychological Aspects of War and Peace* (New York: Vintage Books, 1967, 1968), 69.

[14] E. H. Chasdi and M. S. Lawrence, "Some Antecedents of Aggression and Effects of Frustration in Doll Play," in David McClelland, ed., *Studies in Motivation* (New York: Appleton-Century-Crofts, 1955), summarized in Berkowitz, 75, 87.

[15] Kurt Lewin, Ronald Lippitt, and Ralph K. White, "Patterns of Aggressive Behavior in Experimentally Created Social Climates," *Journal of Social Psychology*, X (May 1939), 271–299.

[16] Arthur R. Cohen, "Upward Communication in Experimentally Created Hierarchies," *Human Relations*, XI (1958), 41–54.

had Air Force reservists listen to pompous, unpleasant orders from people they believed to be of various ranks. When given an opportunity to communicate back, they were much more aggressive to supposedly low-ranked people.[17] Such findings do not bear directly on the curvilinearity hypotheses; they do suggest that social sanctions can be as effective as physical sanctions in inhibiting aggression. Walters cites considerable evidence that social rewards (positive sanctions) for nonaggressive behavior are more effective than punishment in dissuading children from aggressive responses. Many studies of child-raising indicate that if parents use physical punishment they both provide children with aggressive models and increase their aggressiveness outside the family. But if children are awarded for cooperative or "prosocial" responses when they are frustrated, they become less and less aggressive.[18]

Evidence for a Negative Relationship Between Force and Violence. The common argument that if police forces and armies are large and force firmly employed by a regime, disorder will be minimized, seems inconsistent with the curvilinearity hypotheses. Chorley, for example, states as a general principle that "Insurrections cannot be permanently won against a professional army operating its technical resources at full strength. They can be won only when the introduction of some extraneous factor cripples the striking power of the professional fighting forces." [19] Smelser stresses the importance of the effectiveness of "agencies of social control" in minimizing the occurrence of "hostile outbursts" (turmoil) and in suppressing "value-oriented movements" (including revolutionary movements). Effectiveness can be reduced if social change weakens the police and military control apparatus, if authorities become unwilling to employ those forces, or if they are disloyal. If a government refuses to respond to demands for reform but subsequently weakens its control of the coercive forces, a value-oriented revolutionary movement is likely.[20] In Janos's view the decay of authority begins a revolutionary cycle. Disap-

[17] J. W. Thibaut and H. W. Riecken, "Authoritarianism, Status, and the Communication of Aggression," *Human Relations,* VIII (No. 2, 1955), 95–120. Other studies to this effect are summarized in A. J. Yates, *Frustration and Conflict* (New York: Wiley, 1962), 73.

[18] Richard H. Walters, "Implications of Laboratory Studies of Aggression for the Control and Regulation of Violence," *Annals,* CCCLXIV (March 1966), 68–69.

[19] Katherine Chorley, *Armies and the Art of Revolution* (London: Faber and Faber, 1943), 23, quoted in Chalmers Johnson, *Revolution and the Social System* (Stanford: The Hoover Institution on War, Revolution and Peace, Stanford University, 1964), 16.

[20] Neil J. Smelser, *Theory of Collective Behavior* (New York: The Free Press, 1963), 231–236, 261–268, 332, 365–379.

pearance of law-enforcement agencies stimulates "general disorder, inordinate concrete demands by various groups, and the rise of utopian aspirations."[21] Gottschalk says the immediate cause of revolution is "the weakness of the conservative forces. . . . Unless those who wish to maintain the status quo are so weak that they cannot maintain themselves, there is little likelihood of a successful revolution."[22]

These and comparable interpretations attribute increases in political violence not to limited force per se but to *weakening* coercive control, often following periods of repression. One can suggest that the relationship is assumed to be linear because it is based on examination of cases on the right side of the curve in figure 9: the weakening regimes most susceptible to revolutionary movements are those that lose the capacity to carry out their threats to impose relatively severe sanctions, shifting toward the point of intermediate sanctions. Such regimes are exposed not only to the uninhibited anger caused by the new pattern of sanctions but to the accumulated hostility displaced from the previous era of more repressive control. Two other factors also may be operative. The weakening of regime force may lead to a reduction in the scope of its control, which facilitates the growth of dissident control and a consequent shift in the balance of coercive control toward equilibrium. Another kind of weakness is declining loyalty of armed forces to the regime, an analytically distinct relationship examined in the following section.

Many of the examples cited in support of generalizations about regime coercive control can be interpreted in these same terms. The immediate antecedents of the French Revolution included ineffective governmental attempts at reform, the capitulation of the King to the demands of the Third Estate in June 1789, and the unwillingness or inability of the King's troops to suppress rioting in July and October of the same year.[23] A unified army and bureaucracy systematically suppressed Russian revolutionaries in 1905; a disintegrating bureaucracy and defeated army were powerless to control the riots of February 1917 or later to defend the Kerensky regime when it ineffectually attempted to prosecute both internal reform and the war.[24] Weakened political authority and

[21] Janos, 5.

[22] Louis Gottschalk, "Causes of Revolution," *American Journal of Sociology*, L (July 1944), 7.

[23] For interpretations of the relative importance of these factors see Smelser, 377–379; Gottschalk, 7; and Crane Brinton, *The Anatomy of Revolution* (New York: Norton, 1938), 45–46, 51–52.

[24] Such interpretations are suggested by Feliks Gross, *The Seizure of Power in*

inadequate police and military control preceded the Fascist victory in Italy and the Nazi victory in Germany. The loss of coercive control contingent on military defeat has often led to political violence. Hunter cites nineteen cases of revolutionary upheavals following defeat in war.[25] Briefly comparing the military effectiveness of the British in Malaya and Cyprus, Paret and Shy remark that "terror was effective in Cyprus against a British government without sufficient political strength or will; it failed in Malaya against a British government determined and able to resist and to wait." [26] Declining French, British, and Belgian coercive capacity in Africa during and after World War II was one of the background conditions that encouraged African demands for political participation and led the metropolitan governments first to grant concessions and ultimately to agree to independence. Riot, mutiny, and secession in the Congo from 1960 to 1962 were preceded by abrupt decline of almost every aspect of coercive control: chaotic transfer of power from a strong to a weak regime, departure of Belgian troops, discontent among Congolese troops and their disloyalty to either their white officers or the new regime.

In most of these cases—and many others could be cited—political violence followed the transition from high threat and severe sanctions to looser, more sporadically applied control. In almost all of them there was massive and widespread political hostility, engendered by previous repression, the deprivations imposed by military defeat, or both. The effects of terrorism against British rulers in Cyprus and Malaya is a contrast between patterns of coercive control characteristic of the midpoint of figure 9 and of the right-hand side of the curve, respectively. The Congo in 1960 was characterized by an abrupt shift from maximum to minimum force, i.e. from the right to the left extremes of the figure. The release of repressed hostility was manifest in considerable violence, but with United Nations and bilateral foreign assistance the Congolese regime was able to increase the effectiveness of its military apparatus to the point at which intermittent sanctions could be applied; accounts of events in 1961 through 1963 indicate that the army engaged in extensive terrorism against the civilian population but in many regions was unable to establish a regular presence or employ systematic force. The rebellions of the "second in-

---

a Century of Revolutions (New York: Philosophical Library, 1958), 63–79, 151–186; Johnson, 14–15; and Smelser, 376–377.

[25] Robert Hunter, *Revolution: Why, How, When?* (New York: Harper, 1940).

[26] Peter Paret and John W. Shy, *Guerrillas in the 1960's*, rev. edn. (New York: Praeger, 1964), 34–35.

dependence" that began in 1964 were more pervasive and of much greater intensity than the outbreaks of 1960–61, at least partly because the degree of threat and the severity of sanctions were at the most dysfunctional, intermediate level.[27]

Other examples relate the adequacy of police control to the occurrence of turmoil. Extensive rioting in England during the late-seventeenth century has been attributed in part to the inadequacy of local constables and delays in using military personnel to restore order—the armed forces being in any case of questionable loyalty to the government. Luddite violence during Regency England occurred in a setting in which urban concentrations had grown vastly but often lacked any effective authority. The police were almost nonexistent, voluntary defense associations were usually ineffective, and the yeomanry and militia were trained for military rather than for civil duty.[28] These waves of English riots seem characteristic of the left-hand side of the curve in figure 9: they were more or less direct manifestations of popular discontent, facilitated but not intensified by low levels of police presence and response. It is noteworthy that although turmoil was chronic in England until the middle of the nineteenth century, it was seldom countered with massive force and never after the 1640s was it transformed into popular revolutionary movements.

Tacit approval of violence by authorities also can facilitate violence. Police tolerance for white violence against blacks and civil rights workers in the American South is an obvious example. Dahlke found the same pattern in a comparative study of anti-Jewish riots in Kishinew (Russia) in 1903 and anti-Negro riots in Detroit in 1943.[29] The effect is to increase normative justifications for violence.

Evidence for Positive and Curvilinear Relationships Between Force and Violence. Other theoretical views and empirical evidence provide more direct support for the curvilinearity hypotheses. Eckstein, Parsons, and Passos describe conditions in which increasing reliance on force increases the potential for, or magnitude of, violence. None require psychological assumptions about the frustrating effects of threat or coercive sanctions; all are consistent with the positive relationship underlying the left side of the curve in figure 9. Eckstein points out that in societies with

[27] See the references in chap. 4, note 82.

[28] See Max Beloff, *Public Order and Popular Disturbances 1660–1714* (London: Cass, 1938, 1963), chap. 7; Frank O. Darvall, *Popular Disturbances and Public Order in Regency England* (London: Oxford University Press, 1934); and George Rudé, *The Crowd in History, 1730–1848* (New York: Wiley, 1964), 79–91.

[29] H. O. Dahlke, "Race and Minority Riots: A Study in the Typology of Violence," *Social Forces*, XXX (1952), 419–425.

a potential for political violence, repression is "little more than a narcotic, intensifying the conditions it seeks to check and requiring ever larger doses to keep affairs in balance. . . ."

> Unless it is based upon extremely good intelligence, and unless its application is sensible, ruthless, and continuous, its effects may be quite opposite to those intended. Incompetent repression leads to a combination of disaffection and contempt for the elite. Also, repression may only make the enemies of a regime more competent in the arts of conspiracy; certainly it tends to make them more experienced in the skills of clandestine organization and sub rosa communication.[30]

Parsons proposes that some types of political systems are prone to "vicious circles of power-deflation," precipitated when increased and unsatisfiable public demands make it necessary for the system to use threatened or actual sanctions to deter those making the demands. One of the two most common responses to such policies "is the active, aggressive attempt to *enforce* demands against the inclinations of the collective leadership. This response clearly leads in the direction of seeking capacity to implement countersanctions of severity equal to or exceeding that of those commanded by the collective leadership."[31] Passos argues that political instability in Latin America is a consequence of the reluctance of traditional elites to follow developmental policies, which makes it necessary for them to rely on the coercive apparatus to minimize attack. This in turn obliges the elites to reach accommodation with the military by increasing their social privileges, political influence, and resources, thus reducing the resources available for satisfying demands for development and increasing the potential for violence.[32]

Galtung explicitly argues that the application of negative sanctions among nations increases rather than decreases resistance, illustrated by a case study of the effects of international economic sanctions against Rhodesia. The conventional, "naive" theory of economic warfare assumes that there is a linear relationship between the severity of economic sanctions and declining political support or "political disintegration." He proposes that, in fact, "value-deprivation creates the social conditions under which

[30] Harry Eckstein, "On the Etiology of Internal Wars," *History and Theory*, IV (No. 2, 1965), 154.

[31] Talcott Parsons, "Some Reflections on the Place of Force in Social Process," in Eckstein, ed., quotations 64, 65.

[32] Alaor S. Passos, "Development Tension and Political Instability: Testing Some Hypotheses Concerning Latin America," *Journal of Peace Research*, No. 1, 1968, 70–73.

much more sacrifice is possible so that the limit for political disintegration will be reached much later." Sanctions increase, not minimize, resistance because they antagonize. The evidence of the first two years of application of sanctions to Rhodesia indicates that sanctions did lead to increased political integration and determination by whites to resist. Such a response is especially likely if the sanctions are seen as an attack on the group as a whole, innocent as well as "guilty"; if the group has low or negative identification with the sanctioning agent; and if members of the group believe their own goals are better than any alternatives offered by the attacker.[33] These three conditions are precisely those that hold in most conflicts between regimes and revolutionary movements.

Thompson has analyzed the effects of regime repression on insurgencies in South Vietnam and Malaya, and identifies a number of reasons for the ineffectiveness of the South Vietnamese army. Because of its sheer size, it commanded the services of the most talented men in the country, reducing the efficiency and resources of civil government. Moreover it was organized for defeating an anticipated foreign invasion and for occupying and administering foreign territory. When directed against internal rebellion, it acted as an invader in its own country, terrorizing and alienating the population it was to protect. Its large size and the multitude of paramilitary forces with comparable objectives contributed to "a situation in which the rule of force rather than the rule of law prevailed." Thompson recommends the use of police forces in populated areas and small, mobile armies to counteract insurgency. Large armies generate dissident military response. He also recommends mild sanctions against dissidents and argues against hate campaigns directed at insurgents. Severe sanctions and hate campaigns, the latter equivalent to threats, encourage troops to terrorize the population in insurgent-controlled areas, force dissidents to fight to the death rather than accept accommodation or surrender, and alienate all those who must be reincorporated into the polity if the government wins.[34] The curvilinear relationships are implicit throughout this analysis: small, efficient military and security forces are more effective than any but the largest ones; mild sanctions are more effective than severe sanctions.

[33] Johan Galtung, "On the Effects of International Economic Sanctions, with Examples from the Case of Rhodesia," *World Politics*, XIX (April 1967), 378–416, quotation 389.

[34] Sir Robert Thompson, *Defeating Communist Insurgency* (New York: Praeger, 1966), 60–62, 94, 104–105, 110, quotation 104.

Many specific cases illustrate the positive relationship of the left-hand side of the curve in figure 9. Invading foreign armies almost always meet popular resistance, partly because they create discontent by disrupting valued patterns of rule, partly in response to their tactics of coercive control. The most intense and widespread resistance seems to occur in territories in which foreign control is at an intermediate level: in China, Yugoslavia, and western Russia during World War II, for example, but not in countries like the Netherlands, France, and Denmark where foreign troops were numerous and very severe sanctions were rather consistently employed.[35] The enforcement activities of military and security forces often have a comparable effect on their own populations. Several frontier rebellions occurred in eighteenth- and nineteenth-century America as a defensive response to the expansion of federal regulatory and police powers.[36] In France in 1789 the decision of the Court party to resort to force rather than accept the demands of the Estates-General contributed directly to the organization of resistance by the bourgeoisie and skilled workers.[37] Almost all the urban riots in the United States in the 1960s were precipitated by routine police actions in the ghetto, and throughout most riots the police were among the principal targets. Moreover, increased police response to the initial incidents usually transformed them into major disorders.[38] Several non-Western examples also are illustrative. The Second Maroon War in Jamaica began when, in 1795, a colonial governor insisted on punitive military and judicial action against Trelawny Town Maroons (former slaves) who had threatened violence in the course of an anti-government protest. Although the Maroons were satisfied by promises of remedial measures and took no hostile action, the governor insisted on judicial punishment for all of them, sent troops to enforce the decision when most refused to surrender, and in doing so precipitated a five-month guerrilla war.[39] In Thailand in the

[35] On World War II resistance movements see, for example, Chalmers A. Johnson, *Peasant Nationalism and Communist Power: The Emergence of Revolutionary China, 1937–1945* (Stanford: Stanford University Press, 1962); John A. Armstrong, ed., *Soviet Partisans in World War II* (Madison: University of Wisconsin Press, 1964); and *European Resistance Movements 1939–45*, Vols. 1 and 2 (Oxford: Pergamon Press, 1964).

[36] This interpretation is developed at length in Richard Rubenstein, *Rebels in Eden* (Boston: Little, Brown, 1970).

[37] See for example Georges Lefebvre, *The Coming of the French Revolution*, trans. R. R. Palmer (Princeton: Princeton University Press, 1947), chap. 6.

[38] See Fogelson, 218–219, and Morris Janowitz, *Social Control of Escalated Riots* (Chicago: University of Chicago Center for Policy Study, 1968), passim.

[39] See Clinton V. Black, *The Story of Jamaica* (London: Collins, 1965), chap. 13.

mid-1960s, a small-scale insurgency in the northwestern provinces was intensified when the government increased the level of administrative, police, and military activity in the area. On the one hand, expansion of the government presence provided more targets for dissidents to attack; on the other, military and police retaliation stimulated greater dissident resistance.[40]

These examples are based on examination of one or at most a few cases, not all unambiguously relevant. Several quantitative, comparative studies have been made of the relationship between various measures of military capability or the inferred severity of sanctions, on the one hand, and level of political violence on the other. All of them show distinct curvilinear relationships. Walton devised a rating scale to evaluate the relative coerciveness or permissiveness of national political systems, based on such conditions as degree of protection of civil rights, extent of toleration of political opposition, and degree of representativeness and responsiveness of government. Scores for eighty-four nations were compared with measures of their political stability, 1955–61. Almost all the most stable countries were highly permissive, most of the most unstable countries had intermediate levels of coerciveness; the most highly coercive regimes were either stable or moderately unstable, seldom highly unstable.[41] The other studies related defense expenditures or size of military and security forces to collective violence. Bwy plotted the defense expenditures of Latin American countries (as a percentage of Gross National Product) for 1959–60 against a measure of anomic violence (turmoil) in 1958–60. Countries with either low or high proportional expenditures on defense had little anomic violence; most countries with intermediate levels, including Venezuela, Argentina, Cuba, Panama, Brazil, and Ecuador, had relatively high anomic violence.[42] A third study compared a composite measure of military and internal security force size to magnitude of civil strife for 114 polities in 1961–65. The relationship proved to be curvilinear. To test the possibility that either external conflict or protracted internal wars affect coercive force size, and hence the relationship,

[40] See Louis E. Lomax, *Thailand: The War That Is, The War That Will Be* (New York: Vintage Books, 1967), and articles on Thailand in the *New York Times*, May 17, 1965; June 26, 1966; and August 18, 1966.

[41] Jennifer G. Walton, "Correlates of Coerciveness and Permissiveness of National Political Systems: A Cross-National Study," (M.A. thesis, San Diego State College, June 1965). For similar results see Betty A. Nesvold et al., "Regime Coerciveness and Political Instability" (Paper read at the Annual Meeting of the American Political Science Association, New York, 1969).

[42] Douglas Bwy, "Political Instability in Latin America: The Cross-Cultural Test of a Causal Model," *Latin American Research Review*, III (Spring 1968).

nations engaged in such conflict were eliminated and the relationship plotted again for sixty-nine "low-conflict" countries. Curvilinearity was still pronounced.[43]

These comparative studies also raise problems of interpretation. The measures of degree of threat and severity of coercive sanctions are indirect. There also are substantial unmeasured variations within countries as well as among them in the pattern of coercion. None of these studies takes into account the relative coercive control of dissidents. When all the evidence examined here is juxtaposed, however, including theoretical speculation, psychological findings, case studies, and large-scale comparative studies, the curvilinearity hypotheses seem to offer the most parsimonious and convincing explanation.

MILITARY LOYALTY

The capacity of a regime to exercise any kind of persistent coercive control over its citizens, at any level of threat or severity of sanctions, depends ultimately on the loyalty of its military and internal security forces. The greater their loyalty, the more effective the regime is likely to be, other things being equal, in exercising coercive control. The less their loyalty, the more likely they are to use their force against the regime itself, and the more likely civilian dissidents are to think they can succeed in attacks on the regime.

Hypothesis RC.4: Regime coercive control varies strongly with the loyalty of coercive forces to the regime.

The proposed linearity of the relationship does not assume that elites know what the most functional uses of force are. They quite often may not. Insofar as they do know, however, they can implement that knowledge only to the extent that the armed forces and police are loyal. The extent of loyalty varies in both scope and degree, like the extent of compliance in the collectivity generally. Some officers and units may be generally loyal, others not. All may be willing to obey orders to defend the regime against external aggression or armed insurrection but unwilling to fire on unarmed civilians. Maximum coercive control is likely to require maximum loyalty in both scope and degree.

A hypothetical regime strategy for maximizing control is to use

[43] Ted Gurr, "A Causal Model of Civil Strife: A Comparative Analysis Using New Indices," *American Political Science Review,* LXII (December 1968), 1117–1118. Also see Ted Gurr with Charles Ruttenberg, *The Conditions of Civil Violence: First Tests of a Causal Model* (Research Monograph No. 28, Princeton: Center of International Studies, Princeton University, 1967), 82–83.

maximum threat and mild but consistent sanctions; this is essentially the policy attempted by New York City in response to racial disorders during the Lindsay administration. A very high degree of loyalty (compliance) is needed to implement such a policy, since it requires military and police personnel to have a high degree of contact with dissidents but to use minimum force despite their frequent hostility toward dissidents and despite verbal and physical provocation. A less compliant military or police establishment is likely to react out of anger in the way the Chicago police responded to student and antiwar demonstrators, namely with inconsistently applied force of intermediate severity—i.e. more or less random arrests and beatings, tactics which are highly dysfunctional for long-range coercive control.[44] Wolf similarly discusses dysfunctional consequences of infractions of military discipline during internal wars. Military discipline needs to be maximized for two reasons: first "to avoid capricious and unnecessary additions to the already large inventory of grievance and discontent," and more important "to amplify the signals that the government is trying to convey to the people" about what actions are desirable and which not. He also recognizes that conflict with insurgents "inevitably increases the likelihood of misbehavior by government military forces as a frustration reaction," their misbehavior strengthening the insurgency. In the Philippines, the Magsaysay government instituted a military complaint office which dispatched investigators by aircraft to investigate complaints about military brutality within a few hours of their receipt; severe penalties were quickly meted out to offenders, with striking effects on military discipline and minimization of popular hostility.[45]

The bases of loyalty vary. The loyalty of officers, if not of enlisted men, is likely to be greatest if based on feelings that the regime is legitimate rather than on threat of negative sanctions. Only other forces can enforce compliance based on threat; consequently a common practice in states in which the regime doubts the loyalty of its officers is the creation of several countervailing military and paramilitary units, for example a regular army, a strong air force or navy, a militia, and one or several national police forces. Disaffection in one can be countered by force from others. A third motive for loyalty, one that seems most characteristic of nations in the third world, is provided by the regime's manipulation of positive sanctions. Military and police in many Latin, African,

[44] See Daniel Walker, *Rights in Conflict* (Washington, D.C.: Chicago Study Team, National Commission on the Causes and Prevention of Violence, 1968).

[45] Charles Wolf, Jr., "Insurgency and Counterinsurgency: New Myths and Old Realities" (Paper P-3131-1, Santa Monica: RAND Corporation, July 1965), 22.

and Asian countries tend to remain loyal to civilian leaders so long as it is in their best interests to do so. Under threat of disorder, social change (or lack of social change), or diminishing allocations of resources, status, or influence to the military, they are disposed to intervene to protect their own interests and the interests of the groups or classes with which they identify. The incompetence of civilian regimes to maintain growth or order is one of the most common justifications for military intervention among these regimes.[46]

There is also a strong inverse relationship between the loyalty of the military to civilian regimes and the likelihood of conspiracy, as distinct from other forms of political violence. The military as an institution of force can easily intervene against a civilian regime, and if its officers are both disloyal and discontented, a coup d'etat is likely to seem the most convenient means to resolve their discontents. Less directly, if dissidents think that factions of the military are not completely loyal, they may enlist their support for conspiratorial activity rather than resorting to turmoil or internal war. In the 1961–65 cross-national study of civil strife cited previously, for example, military or police personnel were reported to have participated in 48 percent of those conspiracies in which participants were identified, in 30 percent of internal wars, but in only one percent of turmoil events. Moreover they participated in 53 of 58 coups and coup attempts identified in the 114 countries studied.[47]

Hypothesis C.2: The likelihood of conspiracy varies inversely with the loyalty of coercive forces to the regime.

The importance of the loyalty of coercive forces for maintaining regimes against revolution and conspiracy is widely argued or assumed. Some attributions of revolution to declining loyalty are examined in the preceding section. Johnson has emphasized "the central position of armed forces in revolutions," proposing that "the success or failure of any revolution depends upon the role of the armed forces."

> Practically speaking, revolution involves armed insurrection, and this implies a clash with professionally trained and equipped troops at the command of the extrinsic elite. Both the success

[46] See for example Henry Bienen, ed., *The Military Intervenes: Case Studies in Political Development* (New York: Russell Sage, 1968); Morris Janowitz, *The Military in the Political Development of New Nations* (Chicago: University of Chicago Press, 1964); John J. Johnson, *The Military and Society in Latin America* (Stanford: Stanford University Press, 1964); and Edwin Lieuwen, *Generals vs. Presidents: Neo-Militarism in Latin America* (New York: Praeger, 1964).

[47] Based on previously unpublished analyses of data.

> or failure of armed insurrection and, in the age of committed professional revolutionary brotherhoods, commonly even the decision to attempt revolution rest, therefore, upon the attitude (or the revolutionaries' estimate of that attitude) that the armed forces will adopt toward the revolution.[48]

Lasswell and Kaplan similarly propose that the elite's control over the instruments of violence is a fundamental determinant of regime stability. The stability of the elite's power position does not vary with the actual use of violence, however, but only with its ability to use it. "Exclusive reliance on violence for maintenance of rule is an index of weakness rather than of strength" because in such a situation "defection of the instruments of violence . . . would mean collapse. The strongest army may be subverted in its support for the regime."[49]

If a regime does rely primarily or exclusively on force to maintain itself in power, any condition which weakens military loyalty is likely to precipitate revolution. Johnson identifies four "accelerators of dysfunction" that influence the armed forces. One is fraternization with the population, which can weaken army unity and lead to conversion of some of its members to revolutionary doctrines. Such fraternization led a few Soviet troops and officers to fight on the side of the Hungarian revolutionaries in 1956. Army mutinies over such issues as pay, promotion, or involuntary retirement of officers similarly can weaken the apparent loyalty of the military to a regime, as can factional competition within the armed forces. Elite indecisiveness in its control of the military has comparable effects; the army and police may be loyal but restrained from taking action against dissidents. The most common solvent of the bonds of military loyalty, however, is defeat in war, which alienates the officer corps to the extent that they believe the regime responsible for defeat, and which may signal the populace that the military is too weak to maintain internal order.[50] A major source of disaffection in post-World War I Germany, for example, was the pervasive belief among officers and enlisted men that the surrender in 1918 was the responsibility of incompetent civilian politicians, not the result of relatively minor reverses on the battlefield.[51]

[48] Johnson, *Revolution and the Social System*, 14, 16–17; also see Chalmers Johnson, *Revolutionary Change* (Boston: Little Brown, 1966), chap. 5.

[49] Lasswell and Kaplan, 265–266.

[50] Johnson, *Revolutionary Change*, 102–104. On the fraternization of Soviet troops with the local populace in Hungary and Poland in 1956 see Feliks Gross, *The Seizure of Power in a Century of Revolutions* (New York: Philosophical Library, 1958), 316–323.

[51] See Theodore Abel, *The Nazi Movement: Why Hitler Came to Power* (New York: Atherton, 1938, 1966), especially chap. 2, and F. L. Carsten, *The Rise of Fascism* (Berkeley: University of California Press, 1967), chap. 3.

THE CONSISTENCY OF COERCION

A fifth determinant of regime coercive control is the *consistency* with which sanctions are applied. Sanctions are consistently applied to the extent that all those who engage in proscribed activity are subject to sanctions in proportion to their "guilt," and nonparticipants not sanctioned. The concept is analogous to "justice" in its conventional meaning.

Force and nonviolent sanctions can be imposed on rebellious people in a variety of ways. For example, police typically arrest some rioters but not others. The smaller the proportion arrested, the more likely the others are to think that they can participate in future riots with a fair chance of impunity; the threat of sanctions for them is reduced. Another common pattern is the indiscriminate arrest of both rioters and nonparticipant observers or, in the context of an internal war, the destruction of a village only some of whose inhabitants support the dissidents. The innocent people who suffer from such retaliatory measures are highly likely to be angered by such action, and alienated from the regime that uses such techniques. Indiscriminate repression antagonizes more men than it deters, as the curvilinearity hypothesis implies. In a third pattern the agencies of force selectively apprehend participants, capturing all of a band of terrorists or plotters, or arresting only the leaders or most active members of a riotous mob, but are inconsistent in applying sanctions. Some riot leaders may be beaten and released, others released without penalty, still others beaten, imprisoned, and subject to legal penalties as well. Some terrorists, or plotters, may be shot to deter others, and some released as a gesture of leniency. The basis for inconsistency may be the status of those arrested, their relative influence with the regime, or simply the whim of their captors. Whatever the reasons, those suffering the inconsistently severe penalties and those who sympathize or identify with them are likely to be increasingly hostile, and those who escaped with minimum harm not significantly deterred from future participation, and perhaps encouraged to take the risk.

The typical pattern of police and military response to political violence throughout the world combines all three kinds of inconsistency. Faced with hostile demonstrators or rioters, police are likely to seize the participants and bystanders closest to hand, beat or arrest some, release others, and ignore the majority who were able to get away. The description applies with some accuracy to the American police response to many ghetto riots and antiwar demonstrations, to the reactions of French, Spanish, and Italian riot police to student demonstrations, to South African, Malayan, and Venezuelan response to some workers' protests, and to hundreds of other cases. Military forces committed to the control of insurgency may shoot or capture a few of the dissidents and many of their supposed sympathizers, decimate suspect rural areas, shoot some captives on the spot, send others to rehabilitation centers or resettlement camps, let some escape. The contemporary examples are legion: Algeria, Angola, South Vietnam, Cuba under the Batista regime, the Congo during the wars of the "second independence," Guatemala, the Kurdish areas of northern Iraq, Tibet under Chinese rule. The more inconsistent the use of force in response to political violence in any respect, the greater the anger and, often, the lower the apparent risk, for the affected survivors, and consequently the less effective the coercive control exercised by the regime that uses such policies.

Hypothesis RC.5: Regime coercive control varies strongly with the consistency of regime-administered negative sanctions.

The relationship should hold irrespective of the degree of threat or the severity of coercive sanctions. If threat and severity are both high but sanctions consistently imposed, the sum of repressed hostility in the population is likely to be less than if sanctions are inconsistent. Relaxation of control by regimes that employ severe but consistent sanctions seems less likely to precipitate civil disorder than relaxation of control when sanctions were inconsistent. Yugoslavia in the 1960s, Malaya after the end of the "Emergency" in 1960, and possibly South Korea in the late 1960s offer examples of the former pattern. History offers many more examples of the latter pattern, among them revolutionary France and Russia, Mexico in 1912, East Germany in 1953, and Hungary in 1956. Comparably, even if threat and severity of sanctions are at the most dysfunctional intermediate level, they will if consistently employed cause less hostility than if inconsistently used.

Consistency is not an absolute but is subject to some cross-cultural variability. In some societies, in rural China and among some East African tribes for example, the kin or community of a deviant or rebel have been assumed to share responsibility for his actions, hence sanctions against some who are personally innocent may be thought justified. But it is highly likely that sporadic government terrorism against a population that harbors rebels, or the shooting of randomly chosen hostages, is thought by its victims to be less just or consistent, and creates more hostility, than action directed specifically against known dissidents.

Several studies discuss the need for consistency of coercion to minimize political violence. Thompson, deriving "principles of counter-insurgency" from the experience of Malaya and South Vietnam, puts major emphasis on the need for the challenged regime to use consistent, legal means: "each new law must be effective and must be fairly applied. It is no good enacting laws which cannot be enforced . . . or which fall unfairly on particular groups in the population." In Malaya punitive laws against Chinese were withdrawn because they penalized the innocent as well as the guilty.

> On the other hand, laws imposing strict curfews, a mandatory death penalty for carrying arms, life imprisonment for providing supplies or other support to terrorists, restricted residence or detention for suspected terrorist supporters and so on were introduced and effectively used. The main point about them was that they were seen by the population to be effective and were applied equally to all.[52]

Another theme of his recommendations is that the harshness of sanctions is less consequential than their consistency. "People will stand very harsh measures indeed, provided that they are strictly enforced and fairly applied to all, are effective in achieving their purpose and are seen to be so." Such policies can be followed only in areas within the scope of regime control, however. If they are sporadically applied to people in areas under insurgent control, the people have little choice but to support the insurgents in self-defense.[53] Wolf similarly suggests that counterinsurgency efforts are crippled if military and paramilitary forces wantonly abuse power. Such abuse are "counterproductive" because they are "either randomized or arbitrary. Hence it becomes impossible for the populace to infer anything about the relationship between the harsh conduct of the government forces and the behavior of the villagers themselves."[54]

The Philippines offer an illustration. From 1946 through 1950 the policy of successive Philippine governments toward the Hukbalahap rebellion vacillated from Roxas' "mailed fist" policy to negotiation to renewed police action, compounded by increasing economic malaise. Beginning in 1950 a more consistent set of military and police policies was put in effect, simultaneously with the beginnings of programs of socioeconomic and political reform. Military action against the rebels was harsh but increasingly

[52] Thompson, 53. For a study of the motives and reactions of participants see Lucian W. Pye, *Guerrilla Communism in Malaya: Its Social and Political Meaning* (Princeton: Princeton University Press, 1956).
[53] Thompson, 146–147.
[54] Wolf, 22.

effective, policies toward surrendering rebels lenient. In effect, increased severity and consistency of sanctions, plus inducements for compliance, largely suppressed the movement by 1954.[55] Venezuela provides a Latin American example. Gude suggests that the Communist insurgent movement that began in 1960 failed because of the cautious governmental use of force in response to its initial phases, and the use of intensive force only in response to the most serious rebel terrorism. The Betancourt regime minimized both the use of troops in urban areas and the overt use of large-scale police tactics to avoid alienating groups potentially susceptible to dissident influence. At the same time the regime successfully made public capital of the rebel's indiscriminate uses of terror and their foreign support to minimize their legitimacy. Reform policies also were followed and most normal channels of political participation remained open. In summary,

> By undertaking major moves in response to major insurgent acts, the government was able to maintain a sense of legitimacy. Contributing to this was the largely successful attempt to stay within the legal code. The insurgents, on the other hand, continually committed acts that were considered illegitimate. They were unable to shift the focus to the illegitimacy of governmental acts and the legitimacy of their own.[56]

Other suggestive evidence also could be cited. Many of the revolutions that followed weakening of government control seem to have been associated either with inconsistency of coercive measures during the preceding periods or with growing inconsistency of coercion during the period of relaxation, or both. The ghetto riots that followed Dr. King's assassination in April 1968 were countered with massive threat of force, often the relatively neutral force of the National Guard rather than local police, but with consistently minimal use of force. Their duration, pervasiveness, and human cost were substantially less than the riots of the summer of 1967, in which much greater but also much less consistent force was used. But there is no precise, systematic evidence on the effects of consistency of sanctions on the magnitude of political violence, a conclusion that is not only intellectually dissatisfying

[55] Two detailed studies of the Philippines during this period are Alvin H. Scaff, *The Philippine Answer to Communism* (Stanford: Stanford University Press, 1955), and Frances Lucille Starner, *Magsaysay and the Philippine Peasantry: The Agrarian Impact on Philippine Politics, 1953–1956* (Berkeley: University of California Press, 1961).

[56] Edward W. Gude, "Political Violence in Venezuela: 1958–1964" (Paper read at the 1967 Annual Meeting of the American Political Science Association, Chicago, September 1967), 13–18, quotation 18.

but very disquieting, considering that regimes have for millennia relied on force as the last and often the first resort for maintaining civil peace.

A Note on Rational Conflict Models and Negative Sanctions

An assumption of policy makers, and of scholars employing rational conflict and game theory models, is that threats and actual sanctions are evaluated and responded to on the basis of cost-benefit or value-maximization calculations. The greater the credible threat "player" X poses to an opponent Y, the greater the potential costs to Y for noncooperation, unless Y can increase the credibility and level of counterthreats. If the costs of counterthreats for Y are greater than the costs of cooperation, or if no counterthreats can be made, cooperation or compliance is likely. A series of exchanges of threats and counterthreats, sometimes accompanied by actual use of sanctions to demonstrate credibility, are likely as the opposing parties assess one another's intentions and capacities. Inadequate communication between the parties, miscalculation, or inconsistent value hierarchies among one or both may lead to less than optimum outcomes, but the ultimate objective of both parties is to get maximum value out of the situation at minimal cost. If this kind of analysis is applied to conflict between a regime and dissidents, *ceteris paribus* they should arrive at a compromise based on their relative coercive capacities.[57]

If the curvilinearity arguments proposed above are correct, this kind of conflict model should be substantially revised. The essence of the required revision is that the threat and use of negative sanctions changes the value hierarchies of opponents. The greater the threat and the greater the sanctions imposed by one party, the greater the value the other party is likely to attribute to retaliation. The argument is of course based on the evidence that aggression is self-satisfying for angered men, and that threats and negative sanctions induce anger. Assume a hypothetical situation in which dissidents resort to a general strike to improve their economic and participatory value positions. If the regime responds with force and imposes sanctions on strike leaders, retaliation is likely to become an increasingly salient value for dissidents; if force is massive and sanctions severe, retaliation may become more salient than the economic and participatory values for which the strike was initiated. To the extent that this kind of value shift

[57] See for example George Kent, *The Effects of Threats* (Columbus: Ohio State University Press, 1967), and Thomas C. Schelling, *The Strategy of Conflict* (Cambridge: Harvard University Press, 1960, 1963).

occurs, dissidents are increasingly likely to use retaliatory force without reference, or with only secondary reference, to their initial objectives. For the regime, the primary value in such conflict situations is presumably the maintenance of internal order. But the same kind of value shift may occur among its incumbents in response to dissident use of sanctions, and especially among the commanders and rank-and-file of its military and police forces who bear the brunt of dissident counterforce.[58]

The argument is applied here to dissident vs. regime conflict. If it is plausible within nations, it may also be plausible for international conflict. It may apply to the insistent demands of the American military for more troops in South Vietnam, despite the evidence that by 1967 the power considerations that dictated intervention were not sufficient to justify the costs of that intervention. If there is a tendency for retaliation to become an increasingly salient, self-satisfying goal in conflict situations, then strategic and tactical decisions based on cost-benefit calculations applied only to the initial objectives of actors can have serious and unintended consequences.

Dissident Coercion

The major determinants of dissident coercive control differ substantially from those of regime control, in part because some variable conditions of regime control tend to be invariant for dissidents. For example, there is wide variability in the loyalty of military and police force to regimes, whereas the military formations of dissidents, if they have them, are almost always intensely loyal to dissident leaders. There are exceptions, especially in civil wars in which dissidents control substantial territory and can use force to induct men into their forces, but they are too few for variations in loyalty to be regarded as a major cause of variations in dissident coercive control.

The degree of threat and severity of negative sanctions exercised by dissident leaders over their followers are likely to have the same curvilinear relationship to dissident control as they do to regime control, but they also tend to be invariant for dissidents, variable among regimes. Like dissident troops, most rank-and-

[58] A useful review of the uses and limitations of game theory in the study of real conflict situations, emphasizing the need for modifying the game-theoretic notion of "rationality" and for introducing dynamic components, is William A. Welsh, "A Game-Theoretic Conceptualization of the Hungarian Revolt: Toward an Inductive Theory of Games," unpublished ms. (Athens: Department of Political Science, University of Georgia, n.d. [1968]), mimeo.

file followers of dissident leaders are followers by choice, against whom few negative sanctions need to be employed. They are likely to obey directives not in response to threat but because of the chance to oppose their enemies, the hope of success in relieving deprivation, the satisfactions of belonging to a supportive group of like-minded individuals, united in defense of its interests. There are unwilling supporters of internal wars, and dissident or undisciplined individuals in the ranks of guerrilla and terrorist movements. When their dissidence or lack of discipline becomes apparent, however, sanctions are usually certain and severe; or else they defect. In other words, the pattern of dissident coercive control over followers is likely to be predominantly mild or nonexistent for most acts of most of them, very severe for a few acts of a few; only in relatively rare cases, usually in the context of internal war, does the pattern of dissident coercive control substantially alienate many followers.[59]

The four dimensions of dissident coercion examined below are the scope of their control, the concentration of their supporters in inaccessible terrain, and their military resources, both the capacity of their own forces and the extent to which they can command the loyalties of regime forces. Though most of the examples and illustrative materials describe the coercive capacities and actions of organized rebels, the relationships apply generally to all dissidents. If antigovernment strikers, rioters, and their sympathizers are numerous and concentrated in the capital city, for example, their coercive control is greater vis-à-vis the regime than if they were fewer and dispersed in several cities. If they have arms and the sympathy of some of the military and police as well, their coercive control may equal or surpass that of the regime. Combinations of such factors sometimes make it possible for dissidents to overthrow governments or obtain major concessions without having full-fledged revolutionary organizations or even revolutionary motives. A few cases in point are the Costa Rican revolution of 1948, the Bolivian revolution of 1952, the general strike that unseated the Martinez regime in El Salvador in 1944, the demonstrations that ousted President Youlou in the Congo (Brazzaville) in 1963, and the demonstrations, strikes, and riots that accomplished the Sudanese revolution of 1964. Unorganized or partly organized dissidents are most likely to acquire sufficient coercive control to overthrow regimes in smaller and less-de-

[59] Counter insurgency theorists place greater emphasis on the use of coercion by rebels to obtain popular support. A detailed presentation of this point of view is Nathan Leites and Charles Wolf, Jr., *Rebellion and Authority: An Analytic Essay on Insurgent Conflicts*, (Santa Monica: RAND Corporation, January 1969).

veloped countries, but even in such countries the chances of success are small. Should they temporarily gain ascendency, regimes are likely to muster enough force, sometimes with foreign support, to put down the rebels. Examples of such temporary successes are the revolt of the lower classes of Naples against Spanish rule in 1647, suppressed by Spanish troops; the revolutionary risings of workers in Paris and Berlin in 1848, both put down by government forces after a period of hesitation; and the uprisings of Hungarians in 1956 and Dominicans in 1965, suppressed with the assistance of foreign troops. Nonetheless, a high degree of organization is not a necessary condition for dissidents to acquire substantial control, though it may be for maintaining it. Organization facilitates securing control, as the following chapter demonstrates, but should be analytically distinguished from the balance of coercive control.

THE SCOPE AND ECOLOGY OF DISSIDENT CONTROL

Dissidents do not necessarily need regular administrative control over a portion of a population to maintain some degree of coercive control, or to mount effective attacks. Their capacity for coercion may depend on clandestine or overt organization, the loyalties of followers and sympathizers scattered throughout a population, or their ability to move like "fish in the water" of a sympathetic or neutral population. Their coercive control, and their institutional support, are nevertheless greatly facilitated if they exercise administrative control in some rural regions or population centers.

Hypothesis DC.1: Dissident coercive control varies moderately with the proportion of a population subject to their regular surveillance and deterrence.

More important than the scope of control is the availability of inaccessible terrain in which dissidents and their supporters can take refuge, arm and train military formations, and mount attacks against the regime. One of Clausewitz's five general conditions for successful guerrilla warfare is that the country in which it is fought be irregular, difficult, and inaccessible.[60] Thompson points out that insurgents do not need to control extensive areas; control of limited, remote areas can provide a sufficient base for a successful internal war.[61] A military expert observes that the rugged interior of Greece, the base of operations of the Communist in-

[60] Summarized in Paret and Shy, 13.
[61] Thompson, 29–35, 115.

surgency during 1946–49, provided almost optimum conditions for waging guerrilla warfare.[62] The list of dissidents who have used difficult terrain—jungles, mountains, marshes, urban slums—to shield themselves is very long; the Maroons in the Cockpit Country of northwestern Jamaica in the eighteenth century; the Maya in the Yucatecan bush during the Caste War, 1847–1855; the EOKA in the mountains of Cyprus after World War II; practitioners of *machetismo* in Colombia's mountain valleys from 1948 to the present; in Algeria since 1954, the FLN in the mountains and desert, the OAS in the warrens of the cities, the opponents of the Ben Bella regime in the Kabylia mountains in the north and the Aures mountains in the south. Remote mountainous regions have traditionally been the locales of autonomy and irredentist movements. Cases in point are the Caucasus Mountains during the nineteenth century and after the Russian Revolution of 1917; eastern India's Naga Hills; the tribal districts of Western Pakistan; northern Iraq; northwestern Eritrea; and even the Swiss Jura. Generally, any area that is relatively inaccessible by reason of terrain can shelter groups committed to violent political opposition, providing them a base of operations from which to attack hated officials and more or less safe refuge from retaliation.

Guerrilla war is common in underdeveloped countries because of poor transportation and communication networks and the isolation of rural areas, which facilitate guerrilla incursions. Free access to rural people enables guerrillas to propagandize, control, and secure support from them.[63] The relatively dense road and rail networks of the Congo helped make it possible for United Nations and Congolese forces to suppress a number of regional rebellions between 1961 and 1966; the lack of comparable facilities has contributed to the inability of the Sudanese army to control the Anya-nya rebellion in the southern Sudan. The insulation of the American colonies from Britain by 2,000 miles of ocean facilitated a successful revolt; a comparable geographic separation has been of little value to rebels in Portuguese Angola and Mozambique. The Castro guerrillas were able to sustain themselves in the Sierra Maestra against a much larger army that lacked surface or aerial mobility; Spanish-American dissidents in the more rugged

[62] Edward R. Wainhouse, "Guerrilla War in Greece, 1946–49: A Case Study," in Franklin M. Osanka, ed., *Modern Guerrilla Warfare: Fighting Communist Guerrilla Movements, 1941–1961* (New York: The Free Press, 1962), 211–218.

[63] James Eliot Cross, *Conflict in the Shadows: The Nature and Politics of Guerrilla War* (Garden City: Doubleday, 1963), chaps. 2, 3; Mancur Olson, Jr., "Economic Development and Guerrilla Warfare: The War of the Country Against the City," (Princeton Center of International Studies, Princeton University, no date [1966], mimeo).

terrain of northern New Mexico had no such chance, in June 1967, against police helicopter patrols. Given the technological capabilities of the best-equipped modern military forces, the terrain that offers the most effective physical protection for dissidents must be mountainous, without roads or tracks, and almost continuously cloud-covered. By these criteria guerrillas in the Western Hemisphere would best be directed to the southernmost Andes or the coast of Western Canada and Southern Alaska.

The impracticability of the last suggestion—there are neither dissidents nor sources of supplies in these areas—directs attention to another and equally relevant ecological variable that facilitates dissident action, namely the geographical concentration of dissidents and their supporters. If most or all the population of an area is dissident, or at least neutral between the dissidents and the regime, dissidents are relatively free to organize and, if they are in armed rebellion, to obtain supplies and move with relative freedom and anonymity. Guevara, for example, pointed out that though guerrillas are most secure in comparatively difficult terrain, they rarely find sufficient supplies or profitable targets in such areas. His own failure and death in Bolivia were partly a consequence of the fact that the terrain was favorable but the population unsupportive.[64] Mao has repeatedly emphasized the need for such popular support, writing for example that "guerrilla warfare is basically organized and maintained by the masses, and once it is deprived of these masses, or fails to enlist their participation and cooperation, its survival and development is not possible."[65] The principle is generally applicable, whether the dissidents are concentrated in urban slums, mining camps, or an ethnically homogenous rural area. But some kind of protective terrain is almost essential if dissidents, even if concentrated, are to maintain persistent opposition to a strong regime. German-speaking separatists in the Italian Tyrol have been able to carry on a prolonged terrorist campaign in Italian Alpine valleys; Walloon separatists in the flat, densely settled farm country of southern Belgium have resorted to strikes and demonstrations but would find it almost impossible to use small-scale guerrilla tactics for any length of time. Protective terrain and concentration of dissidents are complementary ecological variables in the facilitation of dissident coercive control. Neither is necessary for the occurrence of turmoil; both are necessary in some degree for sustaining guerrilla and civil wars.

[64] See especially Ernesto Guevara, *Che Guevara on Guerrilla Warfare* (New York: Praeger, 1961).

[65] Quoted in George B. Jordan, "Objectives and Methods of Communist Guerrilla Warfare," in Osanka, ed., 403.

Hypothesis DC.2: Dissident coercive control varies strongly with the extent to which dissidents are geographically concentrated in areas to which regime forces have limited access.

These ecological factors also affect the form of political violence, as several of the above examples suggest. If dissidents are members of a geographically cohesive group, coordinated large-scale action is facilitated. If the dissident group is also compact, the crowd setting provides its members with a shield of anonymity that temporarily can be as effective for increasing dissident coercive capacities as the availability of protective terrain. Nineteenth- and early twentieth-century theorists speculated at length on the "unconscious" nature of crowd behavior and its "deindividuating" effects as facilitators of aggressive behavior.[66] Some of the effect can be attributed to the anonymity of the crowd setting. To the extent that a crowd consists of individuals of similar motivations engaged in similar actions, it reinforces members' feelings that their perceptions, emotions, and impulses are valid and that they are justified in expressing them. Evidence to this effect is examined in the following chapter. To the extent that those impulses are aggressive, they are likely to think that they can get away with expressing them because they cannot readily be identified by security personnel. Schelling mentions "the immunity that goes with action in large numbers."[67] In an experiment by Festinger and others, students were found to exhibit more verbal hostility towards their parents when they felt anonymity in a group.[68] Myers' study of an anti-Communist mob in Trenton, New Jersey, demonstrates that the anonymity of group action, among other factors, led to a political clash that neither individual members nor leaders would have attempted alone.[69]

Crowds must form before such processes occur, and crowds of dissidents are most likely to form in cities, not in rural areas. Olson writes that "the concentration of population in cities can sometimes make agitation cheaper and the spread of new ideas faster" and that "riots and revolts are often technically easier to

[66] For a summary of the views of Freud, Le Bon, Floyd Allport, William McDougall, and others on crowd behavior see Roger W. Brown, "Mass Phenomena," in Gardner Lindzey, ed., *Handbook of Social Psychology,* Vol. 2 (Reading, Mass.: Addison-Wesley, 1954), 842–847.

[67] Schelling, 14.

[68] Leon Festinger, A. Pepitone, and Theodore M. Newcomb, "Some Consequences of Deindividuation in a Group," *Journal of Abnormal and Social Psychology,* XLVII (1952), 382–389.

[69] R. C. Myers, "Anti-Communist Mob Action: A Case Study," *Public Opinion Quarterly,* XII (Spring 1948), 57–67. Another relevant case study is George Wada and James C. Davies, "Riots and Rioters," *Western Political Quarterly,* X (December 1957), 864–874.

organize in cities."[70] Peasant revolts are thus less likely to succeed than urban uprisings, as Marx pointed out:

> the agricultural population, in consequence of its dispersion over a great space and of the difficulty of bringing about an agreement among any considerable portion of it, never can attempt a successful independent movement; they require the initiatory impulse of the more concentrated, more enlightened, more easily moved people of the towns.[71]

In France and England during the industrial revolution, country riots were as common as urban riots, but with few exceptions they began not in the fields or at isolated farmsteads but in the marketplaces of towns and villages.[72] Towns and cities have a special attraction for people who are discontented with rural ways of life and urban deprivations may add to their discontent, further increasing the likelihood of political protest by urban crowds. But police and military forces are also concentrated in cities, and unless the dissidents include most of the urban population and have the sympathy of the security forces, an uncommon set of conditions, they are usually quickly dispersed. The urban environment facilitates turmoil, but not internal war. Six generations of Parisians have been unable to defend their street barracades against determined military opposition. The war of the country against the city is most likely to succeed through attrition and and disaffection, not armed assault. Hence:

Hypothesis T.2: The likelihood of turmoil varies with the concentration of dissidents in areas in which regime forces are concentrated.

The geographical concentration of dissidents facilitates internal war rather than turmoil if they occupy defensible terrain. The classic modern case is the Chinese Communist movement after 1927. Faced with their almost fatal failure to control the cities, Mao and his military associates established an autonomous enclave, the Chinese Soviet Republic, in mountainous Kiangsi province from 1928 to 1934. After the success of Chiang Kai'shek's fifth "bandit extermination campaign," the Communists were able to retreat some 6,000 miles through terrain sufficiently difficult that they could avoid annihilation and reestablish themselves in Shensi province in the northwest. Once a territorial base has been estab-

[70] Mancur Olson, Jr., "Rapid Growth as a Destabilizing Force," *Journal of Economic History*, XXIII (December 1963), 535.

[71] Karl Marx, *Revolution and Counter-Revolution*, cited in Pettee, 87.

[72] See Rudé, 19–45.

lished and secured, political violence tends to assume the character of war between nations. Such bases "provide food, refuge, and area in which military equipment may be manufactured, and training bases; and they weaken the status quo by removing territory from the system's productive substructure."[73] Base areas can be established even in relatively modern societies if the population is wholly dissident and regime coercive capabilities only moderate, as Irish rebels were able to do in southern and western Ireland by 1920. Holt writes that in these areas "the administration of British justice had virtually ceased. . . . Even when policemen were killed in public no witnesses would come forward, and the general work of the British Courts had been largely taken over by the Sinn Fein courts set up by Dail Eireann."[74] Debray is highly critical of dissident recourse to zones of self-defense and advocates reliance on mobile guerrilla forces rather than fixed bases, but his critique is based on two assumptions that may hold for contemporary Latin America but not necessarily elsewhere: first that the regime has such preponderance of force that it will not tolerate, and can crush dissident control of, base areas; and second that dissidents will concentrate on defense of base areas rather than intensifying attacks on regime forces.[75] The Debray doctrine seems most applicable to guerrilla operations in settings in which the terrain is favorable but the population generally neutral, i.e. it is a generalization based primarily on Cuban, Colombian, and Bolivian experience. The general relationship proposed here is that internal war is most likely if dissidents are both geographically concentrated and situated in protective terrain, whether their control of that terrain is permanent or temporary.

Hypothesis I.2: The likelihood of internal war varies with the geographical concentration of dissidents in areas to which regime forces have limited access.

THE MILITARY RESOURCES OF DISSIDENTS

The above determinants of dissident coercive control are more relevant to defensive than offensive capabilities. The anonymity of urban crowds temporarily increases dissident coercive capacity because it provides a sense of security from regime sanctions. Rural isolation is primarily effective because it provides protection from retaliation; it facilitates offensive action only if dissidents

[73] Johnson, *Revolution and the Social System*, 82.

[74] Edgar Holt, *Protest in Arms: The Irish Troubles 1916–1923* (New York: Coward-McCann, 1961), 211.

[75] Régis Debray, *Revolution in the Revolution? Armed Struggle and Political Struggle in Latin America* (New York: Grove Press, 1967), especially 27–46.

have or can create military means in their base areas. There are two variable sources of dissident offensive capacity: the size and resources of their own military formations, and the extent regime forces can be persuaded to defect to the dissident side.

Hypothesis DC.3: Dissident coercive control varies strongly with the size, training, and resources of its military formations relative to the size, training, and resources of regime forces.

Military formations comprise all dissidents who regularly carry and can use weapons, whether or not they are members of organized units. Few dissidents except those fighting internal wars have regular military units. Some exceptions are paramilitary organizations of conservative political movements like the anti-Semitic *Camelots du Roi* in France after 1908, the *Stahlhelm* and similar groups in Germany during the 1920s, the Fascist Militia in 1919–22, and the Minutemen in the United States in the 1960s. Examples of paramilitary organizations among left-wing dissidents include communist worker militias in interwar Germany, workers' brigades in pre-civil war Spain, and miner and peasant militias in Bolivia in the 1950s. The establishment of such organizations is often a precursor of internal war, but is by no means a necessary condition for internal war or for the establishment of dissident coercive control. Widespread availability of arms among dissidents, for example, can increase coercive control even in the absence of military organization. The relationship between the military capacity of dissidents and their coercive control is linear rather than curvilinear, as pointed out above, because they are used primarily to oppose regime forces rather than to control dissident followers.

Dissident military formations are ordinarily much smaller than those of regime forces, but often are equally or better trained and more appropriately equipped than regime forces for the hit-and-run tactics that are so effective in internal wars. Equipment and training are especially important. They may be acquired before and facilitate the onset of political violence, for example among the arms-bearing farmers and local militiamen of the American colonies in the 1760s. In England, Monmouth's rural rebellion and the subsequent Great Rebellion, beginning in 1642, were facilitated by the prior military experience of most of the English yeomanry. Serious peasant insurrections, Mosca suggests, are possible "only in places where they have had a certain habit of handling arms, or at least where hunting or brigandage, or family and neighborhood feuds, have kept people familiar with the sound of gunfire."[76] In Indonesia and Vietnam the Japanese unwittingly promoted postwar anticolonial wars by sponsoring mass political organizations and providing military training and equipment to their more committed members. In Malaya, China, and the Philippines, members of anti-Japanese resistance movements obtained arms and a high degree of skill in guerrilla warfare that dissidents subsequently used against other regimes.

Once armed conflict has begun, dissidents can increase their military capacity by concentrating attacks on barracks and armories or isolated patrols to obtain needed weapons, as the Irish did after 1916. If they control suitable base areas they can make their own weapons: large quantities of very sophisticated weapons were made in the Confederacy during the American Civil War, for example, and cruder but effective ones in remote regions of South Vietnam. The control of populated areas greatly facilitates dissident organization of military formations and recruitment of members. If the dissident cause is popular in areas outside their control, recruits and supplies will come to them as they did from Algerian cities to FLN bases and as they do from Guatemalan towns and cities to rural rebel bands.

The greatest potential increment to dissident military capacity is external support. Of relatively least consequence is the availability of safe refuge for guerrilla bands across national borders, which Latin American nations like Guatemala, Nicaragua, and Honduras have from time to time provided for armed opponents of neighboring regimes. More important is training in tactics of clandestine opposition: Ghana, during the last years of the Nkrumah regime, provided such training for dissidents from half-a-dozen nearby countries; Algeria has trained recruits for a number of African and Near Eastern dissident movements; Cuba gives such training for many Latin and North Americans; China for rebels in more than a dozen countries throughout the world. Little more than refuge and training can be provided for dissidents unless they control base areas to which military supplies can be shipped; such base areas are most easily provisioned if they border a country whose regime favors the dissidents. If this condition holds, dissidents can be equipped to the extent of their capacity to make use of the equipment, subject only to limitations on the resources of and international restraints on the supplying nations. Maximum foreign support includes not only training and military equipment but military units as well. Contemporary examples of foreign military support for dissidents are so well known that none need be

[76] Gaetano Mosca, *The Ruling Class*, trans. Hannah D. Kahn (New York: McGraw-Hill, 1939), 210–212, quotation 212.

cited. Such support is not a modern communist invention: the French provided military support for the rebellious American colonies and the British, Americans, French, and others for the White Russians from 1919 to 1922, for example.

Much theoretical attention has been given to the international implications of internal war, less to the specific effects of intervention; Rosenau is representative of scholars who have focused on internal war as "cause" and then analyzed its effects on the international system.[77] Deutsch has raised a number of questions about the effect of various kinds and degrees of external support on the duration, extent, character, and outcome of internal war, but few empirical studies have dealt with those questions.[78] Within the framework of this analysis, we would expect that the greater the extent of foreign support for dissidents, the greater their military capacity vis-à-vis the regime, hence the greater the magnitude of political violence to the point of dissident equality with the regime. If external support rapidly increases dissident coercive control well beyond that of the regime, dissidents will win quickly and magnitude of violence will be low. Most regimes threatened by internal war also have foreign supporters, however, who frequently respond by increasing military assistance to the regime. Consequently, foreign support is likely to be dysfunctional for terminating internal wars. It is much more likely to increase the scale of conflict to a high level and to prolong it. Mutual escalation in Vietnam is an obvious case in point. Empirical evidence is provided by the 114-nation study of civil strife discussed earlier. The extent of foreign military support for dissidents and for regimes challenged by internal war was roughly measured, taking into account the degree of support and the number of nations providing it. The greater the support for dissidents, the longer and more pervasive was civil strife during 1961–65 (r's = .37 and .22); external support for regimes was similarly related to duration and pervasiveness (r's = .30 and .28). The close connection between support for dissidents and countervailing support for the regime (and vice versa) is evident from the fact that their correlation is

[77] See James N. Rosenau, "Internal War as an International Event," in Rosenau, ed., *International Aspects of Civil Strife* (Princeton: Princeton University Press, 1964), 45–91. The contributions to this volume are a compendium of recent theorizing on the linkages between internal war and the international system. A set of case studies of United Nations involvement in political violence is Linda Miller, *World Order and Local Disorder: The United Nations and Internal Conflicts* (Princeton: Princeton University Press, 1967).

[78] Karl W. Deutsch, "External Involvement in Internal War," in Harry Eckstein, ed., *Internal War: Problems and Approaches* (New York: The Free Press, 1964), 100–110.

.83.[79] The nature of the relationship is subsumed by hypothesis DC.3, above. But foreign support also is likely to affect the form of political violence. To the extent that external support for dissidents increases their coercive control relative to the regime, internal war is increasingly likely (hypothesis I.1). We found, for example, that external support was provided the dissidents in thirty of fifty-four internal wars identified, whereas external support was reported in only 12 percent of conspiracy events and one percent of turmoil events. The following hypothesis is suggested:

Hypothesis I.3: The likelihood of internal war varies with the degree of foreign support for dissidents.

The second determinant of dissident offensive capacity, in addition to the military resources it directly commands, is the extent regime forces are willing to support the dissidents. Forces disloyal to a regime are not necessarily loyal to dissidents; they are more likely to be neutral. If and when they do go over to the dissidents, however, they can drastically shift the balance of coercion, directly because they increase rebel military capacity at the expense of the regime, indirectly because they signal that the regime is weak and sometimes precipitate defection by other regime forces. There are two kinds of situations in which such shifts are likely to occur. At the outset of antigovernment rioting, troops and their commanders may decide that their sympathies lie with the opposition and join them. If only a few do so, as in the Polish and Hungarian uprisings of 1956, violence can still be readily suppressed. If many but not all defect, internal war may result; if almost all defect, the regime will almost certainly collapse. Mosca points out that the Poles were able to mount a major rebellion against Russian rule in 1830–31 because they had the support of a Russian-trained Polish army, whereas the Polish insurrection of 1863–64 was more quickly suppressed for lack of such support.[80] The second situation is the competition for influence that accompanies elite conspiratorial movements before the outbreak of hostilities. Dissidents planning a coup d'etat may include or solicit the cooperation of military commanders. If the loyalty of part of the military can be secured, the conspirators increase their coercive capacity and are increasingly likely to take overt action. They are most likely to do so, and most likely to succeed, if most or all the military is either loyal to them or takes a neutral position. The delicate negotiations that precede coup attempts, especially in

[79] The measures used are described in more detail in Gurr, "A Causal Model." The correlation coefficients are from previously unpublished analyses.

[80] Mosca, 210–211.

Latin America, in fact resemble bargaining sessions; the purpose of the participants is to ascertain and if possible to alter the balance of coercive control. If the dissidents gain the ascendency, incumbents are so informed and, if gentlemen, are usually willing to be displaced with a minimum of open conflict. If dissidents fail to gain a sufficient advantage, by their estimation, they are likely to refrain from action until they can do so.[81] The substitution of bargaining for more violent means of assessing the balance of coercion is most likely in countries in which elite conspiracies have been chronic. The general relationship, of which this pattern is an example, is:

Hypothesis DC.4: Dissident coercive control varies strongly with the loyalty of regime coercive forces to dissident leaders.

The condition is infrequent in most cases of turmoil and internal war: regime forces ordinarily cannot be converted to the dissident cause. But when they are, as in conspiracies, they fundamentally affect the outcome. It is noteworthy that such conversion is particularly unlikely once an internal war has been in progress for some time. Regime forces that have suffered many casualties at the hands of dissidents are more hostile towards them, less likely to cooperate with them. Major shifts of loyalty are most likely to occur at the outset of conflict, not later. South Vietnam during the early 1960s offers a striking case in point. The loyalty of the army as a whole to any particular civilian or military leader has never been great; that lack of loyalty has been manifest in many coups and attempted coups. But because of the conflict-induced hostility between the army and the National Liberation Front, no major defections have occurred, and if they do occur in the future are most likely among newly recruited troops who have experienced little or no combat.

* * *

On balance, the use of coercion by a regime poses more risks than the use of coercion by dissidents. The extensive use of force by either side is likely to be dysfunctional to their initial goals, nonetheless. Force, as Pearson says in the quotation at the beginning of the chapter, "raises up its own opposition." Moreover,

[81] For some illustrative case studies see Lieuwen; Martin C. Needler, *Anatomy of a Coup d'etat: Ecuador 1963* (Washington, D.C.: Institute for the Comparative Study of Political Systems, 1964); and James W. Rowe, "Argentina's Restless Military," in Robert D. Tomasek, ed., *Latin American Politics: Studies of the Contemporary Scene* (Garden City: Doubleday, 1966), 439–466.

it tends to become an end in itself both for those who employ it and for those who seek to protect themselves against it. It is symptomatic of the tendency, both among those who govern and those who oppose, to fail to recognize that force is a two-edged sword and to blame the gods or scapegoats when, resorting to it, they find they have wounded themselves.

9. The Balance of Institutional Support

> If at any former time the mob were inflamed with sedition, they were a headless multitude, bound together only by the momentary union of blind passion; they are now an organised association, with their sections, their secret commissions, and their treasury.
>
> Robert Southey [1]

THE USE OF COERCION to control discontent and maintain stable patterns of social action has complex and potentially self-defeating consequences. The thesis of this chapter is that political elites and dissidents can best establish and maintain enduring social support by providing patterns of action that have predictably rewarding consequences for their followers. Regimes can minimize support for dissidents and channel political discontent to constructive, or at least nondestructive, purposes insofar as they offer stable, effective institutional alternatives to violent dissent. But if regimes rely primarily on force, dissidents can increase the scope of their support and their effectiveness by creating the rewarding patterns of action that regimes fail to provide.

The chapter analyzes some sources of institutional support and its effects on the outcomes of politicized discontent. The basic relationship proposed is that, given the existence of politicized discontent, magnitudes and forms of political violence vary with the balance of institutional support between regimes and dissident organizations. The extent of institutional support is determined by such structural characteristics of regime and dissident organizations as scope, cohesiveness, and complexity; and by the organizations' capacity to provide their members with value opportunities, satisfactions, and means for expressive protest.

The Balance of Regime and Dissident Institutional Support

The consequences of organized association among the discontented are the subject of somewhat contradictory propositions. Lasswell and Kaplan propose that the greater the degree of organization among a counterelite, the greater is political instability.[2] Mosca writes that "one of the principal agencies by which revolutionary traditions and passions have been kept alive in many countries in Europe has been the political association, especially

[1] *Essays, Moral and Political* (London: John Murray, 1832), 125–126.

[2] Harold Lasswell and Abraham Kaplan, *Power and Society: A Framework for Political Inquiry* (New Haven: Yale University Press, 1950), 267.

the secret society."[3] Templeton concludes a survey study of alienation in the United States with the statement that the stability of the American political system "seems to rest . . . upon the absence of institutionalized channels through which discontent can be effectively expressed."[4] However Kerr argues that institutionalization of labor protest is associated with decreasingly disruptive forms of protest.[5] B. R. Wilson maintains that the sometimes aggressive fervor of the early stages of religious movements tends to be transformed over time by practical and organizational exigencies into formal, nonspontaneous denominationalism.[6]

Whether or not different degrees of organization affect the extent of instability, civil strife does in fact originate among members of almost any kind of association or institution. We identified the group context for action in about 1,000 strife events that occurred between 1961 and 1965. Initiators most frequently acted as members of legal political parties or movements—in 42 percent of all cases, including half of turmoil events and about a quarter each of conspiracies and internal wars. Clandestine organizations were responsible for 15 percent, including about 40 percent of conspiracies and internal wars. Factions within the governmental hierarchy itself, usually among the military, initiated 10 percent of all events, mostly conspiracies. Communal groups—regional, ethnic, linguistic, and religious—initiated 20 percent of all cases, including 22 out of 54 internal wars. Economic associations (7 percent) and nonpolitical student groups (4 percent) also provided frequent bases for collective protest and violence.[7]

Neither the extent nor the kinds of organization in a society have an invariant relationship with the extent or forms of political violence. The effects of a given pattern of organization on violence de-

[3] Gaetano Mosca, *The Ruling Class*, trans. Hannah D. Kahn (New York: McGraw-Hill, 1896, 1939), 219.

[4] Frederick Templeton, "Alienation and Political Participation: Some Research Findings," *Public Opinion Quarterly*, XXX (Summer 1966), 249–261.

[5] Clark Kerr et al., *Industrialism and Industrial Man: The Problems of Labor and Management in Economic Growth* (Cambridge: Harvard University Press, 1960).

[6] B. R. Wilson, "An Analysis of Sect Development," *American Sociological Review*, XXIV (February 1959), 3–15.

[7] Ted Robert Gurr, "A Comparative Study of Civil Strife," in Hugh Davis Graham and Ted Robert Gurr, eds., *Violence in America: Historical and Comparative Perspectives* (Washington, D.C.: National Commission on the Causes and Prevention of Violence, 1969), 443–495. Coding instructions were to "specify the type of social grouping in which the initiators carried out the action or series of actions," using a set of operationally defined categories of group type. The categories and instructions appeared in Ted Gurr with Charles Ruttenberg, *Cross-National Studies of Civil Violence* (Washington, D.C.: Center for Research on Social Systems, American University, 1969), Appendix B.

pend first on the prior existence of some politicized discontent (hypothesis V.5). A population can be categorized according to the intensity of its members' politicized discontent into three simple groups: those whose discontents are intense, moderate, and low or nonexistent. The population also can be categorized on the basis of members' political orientations, distinguishing among loyalists, neutrals, and active dissidents. The loyalists are those committed to using regime-approved means for remedying or protesting deprivation; the actively dissident are those committed to the use of illegal means; and the neutrals, probably the majority of most populations, are apathetic or ambivalent about the means of action, committed neither to the regime nor to active, illegal opposition. The correspondence between discontent and orientation is not likely to be precise: some loyalists are likely to be moderately, even intensely, discontented; a few of the active dissidents may have little politicized discontent. A hypothetical distribution of the two sets of groups in a population is shown in figure 10.

The initial determinant of the effects of organization on the magnitude of political violence is the actual size and distribution of these groups in a population. The second determinant is the extent to which they are organized in support of the regime or dissidents. Not all dissidents are necessarily members of dissident-oriented organizations, nor are all loyalists members of regime-oriented organizations. Many people, especially in transitional societies, may belong only to neutral organizations, those which

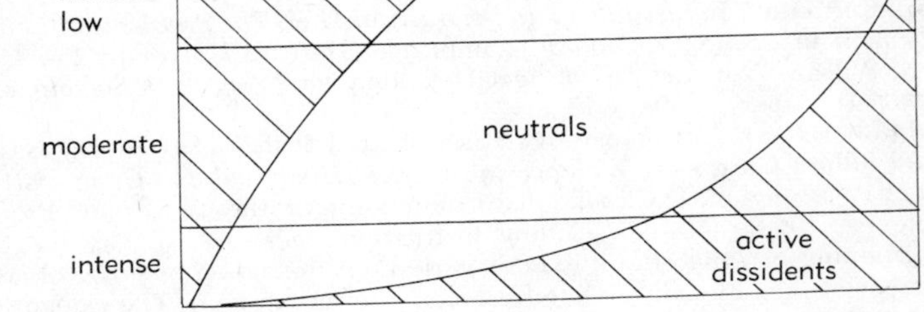

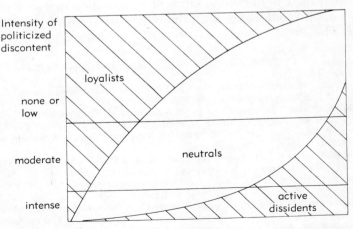

Figure 10. Hypothetical distribution of a population by level of politicized discontent and political orientation.

actively support neither a regime nor its opponents. The crucial question for those who are members of regime- or dissident-oriented organizations is the degree of support they are prepared to provide those organizations. If members respond willingly to requests for almost any kind of material or personal sacrifice, the organizations have a high capacity for fighting, or any other activity. If members willingly provide only token support, the organization will either be paralyzed in a conflict situation or will have to rely on coercion to gain compliance, a strategem that consumes scarce resources and has inconsistent effects (chapter 8).

To determine the effects of organizations on political violence, therefore, it is necessary to evaluate the balance of institutional support between regimes and their opponents. The following general hypothesis is proposed:

Hypothesis V.7: The magnitude of political violence varies strongly and directly with the ratio of dissident institutional support to regime institutional support to the point of equality, and inversely beyond it.

Dissidents, and regimes, have *institutional support* to the extent that they direct organizations through which they obtain consistent compliance with their demands and directives without resort to coercive sanctions. Levels of institutional support are a function of the relative scope of dissident and regime organizations, and of the degree to which leaders can demand and receive sacrifices from members in the service of the organizations; hypotheses about these and other determinants of institutional support are developed beginning on p. 282. The relationship is analogous to that proposed for the balance of coercive control. If regime institutional support is high vis-à-vis dissident institutional support, political violence is likely to be limited in scope, duration, and intensity. If dissident institutional support approaches that of the regime, both are likely to have the capacity to maintain prolonged conflict. If dissidents have markedly greater institutional support than does the regime, they are likely to win, or secure desired concessions, with relative ease.

Dissidents can establish organizational bases for active opposition in several ways. One is to create new organizations for themselves and potential sympathizers. If the scope of regime institutional support is low, and if discontent is so intense and pervasive that belief and normative systems have lost their coherence, the organizations are likely to be what Wallace terms "revitalization movements": organized, essentially religious attempts to construct a more satisfying culture, which may take the form of revolutionary, millennarian, or nativistic movements.[8] If discontent is less severe or widespread, dissident organizations may resemble more conventional political and economic associations. However, if regime institutional support is high, the most feasible kind of organization is clandestine: secret societies, revolutionary cells, and terrorist organizations.

A second possible organizational basis for dissident institutional support is the "capture" of regime-oriented organizations. Dissidents' chances of doing so are best if such organizations are not directly controlled by the regime and if their members are intensely discontented. Active dissidents may "seize control" of regime-oriented economic and political organizations, and of military units, by a sort of internal coup d'etat; but once in authority they are restricted in their capacity to direct the organization into overt opposition by their ability to persuade its members of the legitimacy of opposition. This is not to minimize the importance of dissident leaders in focusing discontent, however. For example, the Dravidian separatist movement in southern India is said to be based on the discontent of lower-caste Tamils at the regional elite, which has been focused by the movement's leaders on "foreign," i.e. north Indian, scapegoats.[9] In his study of the riotous Japanese opposition to the Security Treaty with the United States in 1960, Packard suggests that Communist members of the leadership of labor, student, and popular associations channeled a variety of grievances into an attack on this particular issue.[10] Dissident leaders can direct members' discontents into a variety of activities; they are not likely to gain or maintain control of regime-oriented organizations unless there is substantial discontent among the rank-and-file.

The same generalization applies to the third organizational basis for dissident institutional support, the conversion of a neutral association to active dissidence. Traditionally governed local and regional communities often are neutral vis-à-vis the regime in modernizing societies, as are many labor, religious, student, and ethnic associations in plural societies. Shifts by organizations to active dissidence usually occur either in response to governmental intervention or as a second-stage response, after attempts at participation through conventional channels meet inadequate or re-

[8] Anthony F. C. Wallace, "Revitalization Movements," *American Anthropologist*, LVIII (April 1956), 264–281.

[9] Selig S. Harrison, "Hindu Society and the State: The Indian Union," in Kalman H. Silvert, ed., *Expectant Peoples: Nationalism and Development* (New York: Random House, 1963), 286–289.

[10] George R. Packard, III, *Protest in Tokyo: The Security Treaty Crisis of 1960* (Princeton: Princeton University Press, 1966), especially chap. 3.

pressive responses. Coal miners in eastern Pennsylvania resorted to violent strikes and terrorism during the 1870s after a series of legal, political, and economic obstacles were raised to their efforts to organize.[11] A messianic Congolese religious cult, *kimbanguisme*, was suppressed by the Belgian government in the 1920s. The successors of its imprisoned leader are said to have been "much more organizational and nationalistic in intention"; the movement provided the basis for several politically dissident movements in subsequent decades.[12] An important factor in the *Peronistas'* ability to base a mass movement on the industrial proletariat of Greater Buenos Aires during the 1940s was the hostility engendered by regime suppression of labor unions during the preceding decade.[13] The French government's coercive response to demands for academic reforms by Parisian students in May 1968 helped push student organizations into revolutionary activity.

However dissident leaders acquire institutional support, its scope and degree pose limits on the kinds of action they can take. If followers are intensely hostile to the regime and prepared to make great sacrifices to the dissident cause, leaders can organize conspiratorial or revolutionary movements. If followers are few in number, conspiratorial activity is more feasible than revolutionary activity. But if followers are not so intensely committed, whatever their numbers, overt action probably will be limited to turmoil, for example antigovernment riots and general strikes. Three general hypotheses about the forms of political violence are suggested:

Hypothesis I.4: The likelihood of internal war increases as the level of dissident to regime institutional support approaches equality.

Figure 11 shows a hypothetical distribution of regime and dissident institutional support that is likely to facilitate internal war. Regime support is restricted largely to loyalists and is of relatively low degree, symbolized by the lightness of the cross-hatching. Although dissident support is of smaller scope, it encompasses most of the active dissidents and is of greater degree. The pattern is typical of noncentrist states at intermediate levels of develop-

[11] See J. Walter Coleman, *The Molly Maguire Riots: Industrial Conflict in the Pennsylvania Coal Region* (Richmond: Garrett and Massie, 1936).

[12] See James W. Fernandez, "African Religious Movements: Types and Dynamics," *Journal of Modern African Studies*, II (December 1964), 531–50; and Crawford Young, *Politics in the Congo: Decolonization and Independence* (Princeton: Princeton University Press, 1965), 284–286. Quotation from Fernandez, 243.

[13] See Gino Germani, *Integration Politica de las Mesas y el Totalitarismo* (Buenos Aires: Colegio Libre de Estudios Superiores, 1956).

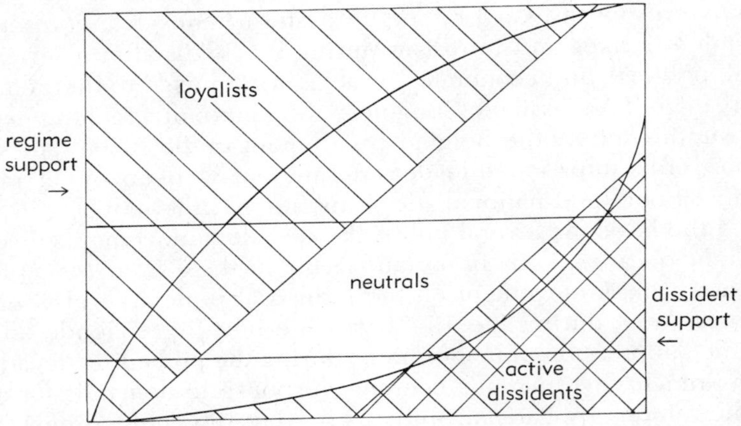

Figure 11. A hypothetical pattern of institutional support facilitating internal war.

ment. Moreover, the existence of many discontented but unorganized people offers potential for the expansion of dissident institutional support at relatively low cost. The optimum pattern of dissident institutional support, for the purposes of prosecuting an internal war, is close organization of all active dissidents and relatively loose organization of neutrals (who are likely to be alienated by close organization). It is not necessarily desirable, however, for dissidents to seek the active support of all groups under regime control who are moderately or intensely discontented. Disaffection within the regime may inhibit the regime's capacity to resist dissidence more than it would help the dissidents if directly at their service.

Hypothesis T.3: The likelihood of turmoil varies inversely with the degree of dissident institutional support.

Figure 12 provides an illustration of a pattern of the type likely to facilitate turmoil. Both regime and dissident institutional control cut across all three categories of discontent and regime orientation. Such a pattern is likely among societies in the early stages of modernization, in which patterns of organizations have not yet been aligned with the distribution of changing group interests and RD; and among plural modern societies in which large numbers of cross-cutting associations have developed. The low degree of dissident support may be a consequence of lack of skills and resources for organization, as is likely in the former case, or of the lack of responsiveness of neutrals and loyalists in dissident organizations to appeals for oppositional activities, likely in the

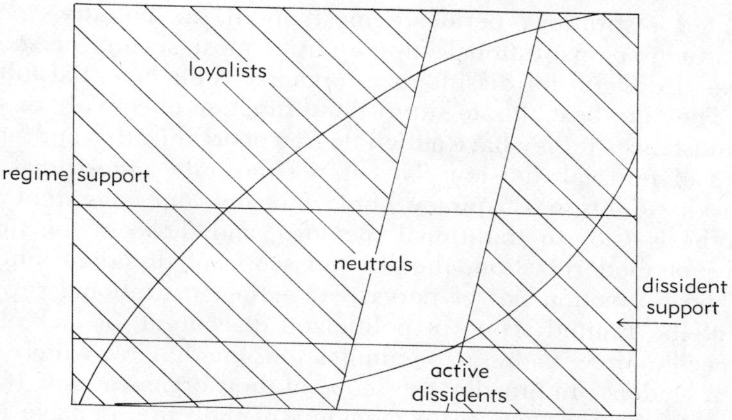

Figure 12. A hypothetical pattern of institutional support facilitating turmoil.

latter case. In either event, dissidents are rather unlikely to have the degree of support necessary for intense, protracted conflict. If the degree of support is low but its scope relatively wide, turmoil is likely to be widespread and chronic; if scope is also narrow, turmoil is likely to be isolated and sporadic.

Hypothesis C.3: The likehood of conspiracy varies with the extent to which the degree of dissident institutional support is high and its scope low.

A hypothetical pattern favoring conspiracy is shown in figure 13. The pattern is most common in centrist states, in which regime-

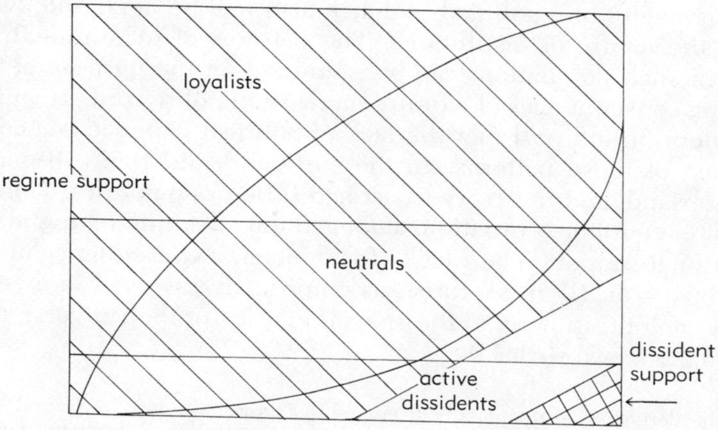

Figure 13. A hypothetical pattern of institutional support facilitating conspiracy.

oriented institutions permeate most or all the country's social area. Regime institutional support from most sectors of society makes it difficult for dissidents to organize their potential followers. They are best able to survive and function effectively in such circumstances if they have a high degree of organization and a minimum of internal division. This is not the only pattern that disposes dissidents to conspiracy, nor is it the only one consistent with hypothesis C.3. In traditional societies, and those in the initial stages of modernization, the limited scope of dissident support may be a function not of pervasive regime institutional support but of the limited scope of politicized discontent, or lack of resources (money, cadres, communications media) by which dissident leaders can broaden the scope of their organizations. If dissidents in such societies are members of the elite, or have elite skills, conspiracy may therefore be their most effective means of opposition.

Some Structural Determinants of Institutional Support

Several kinds of determinants of the scope and degree of regime and dissident institutional support are mentioned above, including the incidence of politicized discontent and oppositional attitudes in a population; organizational resources; and the organizing skills of leaders. This and the following section specify more precisely and generally some structural and functional determinants of institutional support that are applicable to both regime and dissident organizations. Variations in the scope of politicized discontent and opposition attitudes are not taken into account in this analysis, but if politicized discontent in a population is negligible, political violence also will be negligible, whatever the nature of institutions. The patterns of institutional support in such populations can be examined for the purpose of forecasting consequences of a future increase in politicized discontent; it cannot be inferred that the lack of political violence is a consequence of those patterns. In the early and mid-1960s, Rumania, Switzerland, and the Ivory Coast had little or no political violence despite enormous variation among them in kinds of regime institutional support. Their lack of violence is a consequence of very low levels of RD in all three, as empirically assessed in a recent study, not a testimony to the special efficacy of their diverse institutional characteristics.[14]

[14] The derivation of this data is discussed in Ted Robert Gurr, "A Causal Model of Civil Strife: A Comparative Analysis Using New Indices," *American Political Science Review*, LXII (December 1968), 1104–1124.

Structural and functional determinants of institutional support are distinguishable. The structural characteristics—the scope, complexity, and cohesiveness of organization—determine the capacity of organizations for carrying out any kind of concerted action or satisfying any functions for their members. Three functions of organizational activity are crucial for the discontented: the provision of societal value opportunities, political value opportunities, and channels for expressive protest. The first two functions are instrumental, the third expressive. The social-psychological bases on which they are predicated are described in chapters 2 and 3. These functions are crucial in two senses. First, the ways they are satisfied determine whether discontent has destructive or constructive consequences for the individual, the institution of which he is a member, and the larger society of which that institution is a part. Second, the extent to which they are satisfied by an organization partly determines the extent to which leaders can command the persistent compliance and loyalty of their followers. If the functions are satisfied badly, or less well by one organization than another, organizations tend to lose their cohesiveness and their followers.

ORGANIZATIONAL SCOPE

One of the two general determinants of the level of institutional support discussed above is its *scope*, the proportion of a population that participates in the activities of regime or dissident organization. The scope of such organizations sets the limits within which other structural and functional variables are operative.

Hypothesis RI.1: Regime institutional support varies strongly with the proportion of a population belonging to regime-oriented organizations.

Hypothesis DI.1: Dissident institutional support varies strongly with the proportion of a population belonging to dissident-oriented organizations.

A pervasive assumption in the literature on insurgencies is that dissident strength depends on an organized popular base, and that a prerequisite for governmental success is the extension of governmental organization at the expense of dissident organization. Paret and Shy distinguish between the "governmental base" and the guerrillas' "popular base." [15] Resettlement has been used widely, for example in Algeria, South Africa, Malaya, and the Phil-

[15] Peter Paret and John W. Shy, *Guerrillas in the 1960's*, rev. edn. (New York: Praeger, 1962), 43–46.

ippines, in an effort to reduce the scope of dissident organization and coercive control. The progress of revolutionary war in South Vietnam is assessed by both participants and observers in terms of the proportion of population or number of villages under Saigon and National Liberation Front control.[16] The scope of dissident organization vis-à-vis the regime also affects forms of strife other than internal war. The greater the scope of extremist political parties or opposition labor unions, for example, the greater the likely extent of antigovernment turmoil. Labor unions are regime-oriented in most nations, and their size relative to the nonagricultural labor force tends to vary inversely with levels of civil strife. In tropical Africa, for example, where labor union leaders have ordinarily been intensely loyal to nationalist leaders, the scope of unionization correlated −.53 with magnitude of civil violence in 1961–63. The inference is that the political orientation of the unions kept their members within the regime's sphere of institutional support. In Latin America, however, where labor unions are frequently controlled by dissident leaders, the scope of unionization correlated +.24 with magnitude of strife in that period.[17]

ORGANIZATIONAL COHESIVENESS AND COMPLEXITY

The greater the goal consensus and cooperative interaction among members of an organization, and the greater its internal differentiation, the more effective the organization is likely to be in pursuing members' goals, whatever they are. For regimes and regime-oriented organizations, these characteristics are especially important for establishing effective value opportunities and maintaining nondestructive means for expressing anger. For dissidents, they also facilitate efficient creation and distribution of values, but most important they enable dissident organizations to defend their members against assault and to organize effective opposition.

Hypothesis RI.2: Regime institutional support varies strongly with the cohesiveness and complexity of regime-oriented organizations.

[16] Anthony Russo points out (personal correspondence) that there is close correspondence between the judgments of the combatants about the regional patterns of National Liberation Front control. A map published by the *Los Angeles Times*, January 14, 1968, based on official U.S. sources, agrees closely with a map published by the North Vietnamese government in *Vietnam* (December 1967), 9.

[17] These correlation coefficients were obtained in analyses reported in Gurr with Ruttenberg, Part II. On the political orientations of labor unions in Latin America see, for example, James Payne, "Peru: The Politics of Structured Violence," *Journal of Politics*, XXVII (May 1965), 362–374; and Germani.

Hypothesis DI.2: Dissident institutional support varies strongly with the cohesiveness and complexity of dissident-controlled organizations.

Cohesiveness is the extent of goal consensus and cooperative interaction among members; *complexity* is the extent of hierarchial and functional differentiation within an organization.[18] A high degree of cohesiveness is predicated on consensus about the means and ends of organizational activity; high levels of cooperative interaction are otherwise difficult to achieve except by coercive means. Cohesiveness and complexity do not necessarily coincide. Angry crowds often have a high degree of cohesiveness, seldom much complexity. Aggregative political parties typically have a high degree of organizational complexity but considerably less cohesiveness. Revolutionary movements ordinarily have a high degree of both cohesiveness and complexity. Neither is a necessary condition of the other; they are reinforcing conditions, however , and the degree of institutional support is probably a function of their product rather than their sum.

Regime-Oriented Organizations. Many theoretical arguments attribute the instability of political systems to organizational weaknesses, and state or imply that political stability is enhanced, and may be predicated upon, the establishment of differentiated, cohesive organizations oriented toward the regime. Kornhauser says that a high rate of mass behavior, i.e. popular movements operating against the political order, is most likely "when elites are accessible to direct intervention by nonelites, and when nonelites are available for direct mobilization by elites," a condition he attributes to the lack or weakness of associational groups mediating between elites and nonelites.[19] Huntington proposes that increasing mobilization and participation in politics produces political decay —instability—insofar as they are not associated with organization and institutionalization.[20] Ake says that the politically disintegrative effects of mobilization are best minimized by political systems having four characteristics: they should be authoritarian, exercising

[18] These variables are analogous to two of the four variables that Samuel P. Huntington associates (by definition) with levels of institutionalization, in "Political Development and Political Decay," *World Politics*, XVII (April 1965), 394–404; cohesiveness is defined here more broadly than he defines the similar concept of coherence. The other two variables he specifies are adaptability, which seems to be more a consequence than a cause or defining property of institutionalization; and autonomy, not a quality of organizational structure per se but a characterization of its relationships with other organizations.

[19] William Kornhauser, *The Politics of Mass Society* (Glencoe: The Free Press, 1959), passim.

[20] Huntington, 386.

centralized control over political and other resources; paternalistic, contributing to the followers' sense of purpose and helping them "find coherence and meaning" in a changing society; identific, creating and maintaining mutual identification between rulers and ruled; and consensual within the context of the ruling elite.[21] Apter suggests that the tensions created by the process of social change can be managed through "a high degree of government regulation of social life in order to introduce greater coherence of values and institutions. . . ." The legitimation of close control is best accomplished through "retraditionalization," the validation of current practices by symbolic reference to or use of traditionally familiar patterns of institutional control.[22]

Empirical evidence also supports the regime hypothesis. The stability of the British political system is conventionally credited to the evolution of complex and responsive political institutions, supported by widespread, fundamental agreement on the procedures if not necessarily the purposes of political activity. The instability of French government is similarly associated with a fundamental lack of consensus about forms, procedures, or purposes of political activity and the lack of organizational development of most French political parties.[23] Eckstein attributes the stability and effectiveness of the Norwegian political system to a strong valuation of consensual and cooperative behavior among Norwegians and to the scope and similarity of patterns of organization in all sectors of collective action.[24] An example of comparative evidence is our finding that stability of political party systems was strongly and negatively correlated with levels of civil violence in 119 countries during 1961–63. Party system stability was measured dichotomously, distinguishing between countries with large and persisting party organizations (including one- as well as multiparty systems), and those with parties that were predominantly ephemeral, personalistic, or nonexistent. The measure correlated −.34 with total magnitude of violence. The relationship also held when countries were divided according to type of political system: among polyarchic (pluralist) countries the correlation is −.21,

[21] Claude Ake, "Political Integration and Political Stability: A Hypothesis," *World Politics*, XIX (April 1967), 488–492.

[22] David E. Apter, *The Politics of Modernization* (Chicago: University of Chicago Press, 1965), 66–67, 257, quotation 66–67.

[23] See for example Harry Eckstein, "The British Political System," and Nicholas Wahl, "The French Political System," in Samuel H. Beer et al., *Patterns of Government: The Major Political Systems of Europe*, 2d edn. (New York: Random House, 1958, 1962).

[24] Harry Eckstein, *Division and Cohesion in Democracy: A Study of Norway* (Princeton: Princeton University Press, 1965).

among elitist (newly independent) countries −.27; and among centrist (authoritarian) countries −.47.[25]

Cohesiveness of Dissident Groups. High levels of interaction and mutually reinforcing perceptions of deprivation and demands for action are commonly found among dissidents, often but not necessarily in an organized setting. Much of the literature on crowd behavior and mob violence can be interpreted in terms of the effects of crowds in enhancing group cohesiveness. The nineteenth- and early twentieth-century interpretation was that conventional norms tended to break down in crowd settings. Le Bon said that participants in revolutionary crowds are characterized by "the disappearance of the conscious personality, the predominance of the unconscious personality, the turning by means of suggestion and contagion of feelings and ideas in an identical direction."[26] Martin emphasized the effects of the crowd in reinforcing shared but ordinarily repressed impulses, giving them normative sanction: "The crowd condition is . . . a release of repressed impulses which is made possible because certain controlling ideas have ceased to function in the immediate social environment. . . ."[27] Other writers suggest that crowds facilitate collective action only to the extent that their members have shared perceptions and motives: "The mob acts only to release prepared impulses"; the collectivity facilitates expression of but does not create the aggressive impulses of its members.[28] Some theorists emphasize the importance of behavioral contagion among such groups. Frank writes that the actions of an emotionally aroused person depend partly on the behavior of others in his environment. The presence of others behaving violently is "powerfully stimulating. . . . The contagiousness of any strong emotion, whether joy, grief, or rage, is probably one of the most potent causes of this phenomenon."[29]

Some empirical studies of group behavior show that mutual reinforcement of perception and cohesion facilitate aggression under conditions of frustration. Stotland compared reactions of subjects to a frustrating supervisor when working alone and when

[25] Previously unreported data from analyses described in Gurr with Ruttenberg, Part II.

[26] Gustave Le Bon, *The Crowd: A Study of the Popular Mind* (New York: Macmillan, 1896), and *The Psychology of Revolution,* trans. Bernard Miall (New York: Putnam, 1913).

[27] Everett Dean Martin, *The Behavior of Crowds: A Psychological Study* (New York: Harper, 1920), 48–49.

[28] Roger W. Brown, "Mass Phenomena," in Gardner Lindzey, ed., *Handbook of Social Psychology,* Vol. 2 (Reading, Mass.: Addison-Wesley, 1954), 845.

[29] Jerome D. Frank, *Sanity and Survival: Psychological Aspects of War and Peace* (New York: Vintage Books, 1967, 1968) 79–80.

able to meet others working on the same tasks. The latter expressed stronger overt hostility towards the supervisor, presumably because they had a reference point independent of the frustrator and were more certain of their opinions.[30] Pepitone and Reichling formed highly cohesive and poorly cohesive groups, exposed them to an insulting lecture, and found that the more cohesive groups expressed more, and more direct, hostility than the others.[31] Similarly, French found that organized groups whose members had previously worked together expressed aggression more freely than groups of unorganized strangers.[32] A comparable phenomenon has been observed in recent experiments on decision-making, which suggest that under some conditions groups take considerably more risky decisions than would their members acting separately.[33] Some kinds of frustration apparently increase cohesion: Coser has proposed that hostility towards outgroups also contributes to the cohesion of the ingroup,[34] and Thibaut found that the cohesiveness of low-status groups was significantly increased in the face of continuing frustration.[35]

Evidence about collective action suggests the importance of high levels of interaction and group homogeneity in the facilitation of violence. Behavior in crowds, and in revolutionary organizations, is characterized by high and sometimes exclusive interaction among the members. In the development of revolutionary organizations, Hopper suggests, discontented people become aware of one another by participating in shared activity. "Their negative reactions to the basic factors in their situations are shared and begin to spread. . . . Discontent tends to become focalized and collective." This collective excitement "serves to integrate unrest and discontent, break down old behavior patterns, and prepare the way for new patterns of behavior."[36] The process is epitomized by a

[30] Ezra Stotland, "Peer Groups and Reactions to Power Figures," in Dorwin Cartwright, ed., *Studies in Social Power*, (Ann Arbor: Institute for Social Research, University of Michigan, 1959), 53–68, summarized in Berkowitz, *Aggression*, 81.

[31] A. Pepitone and G. Reichling, "Group Cohesiveness and the Expression of Hostility," *Human Relations*, VIII (No. 3, 1955), 327–37.

[32] J. R. P. French, Jr., "Organized and Unorganized Groups Under Fear and Frustration," *Authority and Frustration* (Iowa City: University of Iowa Studies in Child Welfare, Vol. XX, 1944), 231–308.

[33] See M. A. Wallach, N. Kogan, and D. G. Bem, "Diffusion of Responsibility and Level of Risk-Taking in Groups," *Journal of Abnormal and Social Psychology*, LXVIII (March 1964), 263–274.

[34] Lewis A. Coser, *The Functions of Social Conflict* (Glencoe: The Free Press, 1956), 87.

[35] J. W. Thibaut, "An Experimental Study of Cohesiveness of Underprivileged Groups," *Human Relations*, III (No. 3, 1950), 251–278.

[36] Rex D. Hopper, "The Revolutionary Process: A Frame of Reference for the Study of Revolutionary Movements," *Social Forces*, XXVIII (March 1950), 272–275.

laboring woman of Yerres, arrested as a ringleader in the French grain riots of 1775, who told the police that far from being a leader, "she had been carried away . . . that she got excited like everybody else, and she didn't know what she was saying or doing." [37] Wada and Davies, on the basis of a retrospective study of Japanese-Americans who participated in a riot at the Manzanar relocation camp in 1943, describe the sense of group identification that pervades an angry crowd, reinforcing their sense of the rightness of action:

> An individual in a crowd loses perhaps most of the identity and uniqueness that make him an individual. His role as crowd member provides a protective mask behind which he can join in action he would scarcely perform in a gathering of known friends and acquaintances. Losing a measure of identity, a person in a crowd loses a sense of individual responsibility and at the same time gains a sense of power, in the expression of feelings he shares with others present but which he could not express—or express effectively—by himself. This sense of power, which as a release from tension is one aspect of freedom even though it destroys individuality, may in part serve to explain why crowd action may be so satisfying an experience to many individuals. One participant in the riot we studied said with strong emphasis that he "felt *good*" when it was in progress.[28]

Interaction is facilitated to the extent that the discontented are or see themselves as being alike. Two French historians of labor movements write of the new urban proletariat that

> . . . the spectacle of uniform poverty suffered under identical conditions promoted the mutual awareness of the dispossessed. The working mass, meeting at the factory, met again in the sordid shacks and unhealthy sidestreets of the great industrial cities. . . . That feeling of belonging to the same category of rejects, separated from the rest of the nation, was to help give to all the sense of belonging to a single class of pariahs, living outside the collectivity.[39]

[37] Quoted in George Rudé, *The Crowd in History, 1730–1848* (New York: Wiley, 1964), 251.

[38] George Wada and James C. Davies, "Riots and Rioters," *Western Political Quarterly*, X (December 1957), 864.

[39] Gerard Dehove and Edward Dolleans, *Histoire du Travail*, Vol. I (Paris: Domat-Montchrestien, 1953), 147, translated in Charles Tilly and James Rule, *Measuring Political Upheaval* (Princeton: Center of International Studies, Princeton University, Research Monograph No. 19, 1965).

A comparative study of the interindustry propensity to strike in eleven Western nations over a twenty-five-year period seems to support this interpretation. Kerr and Siegel found that the most strikeprone industries are those whose workers form a relatively homogenous group that is geographically or otherwise isolated from the larger community and "capable of cohesion."[40] In an earlier study, Crook similarly found that many general strikes evolved from disputes in coal, lumber, textiles, and waterfront industries, those most characterized by an "isolated" mass of laborers.[41] The enforced homogeneity of the ghetto poor similarly has facilitated riots by black Americans. Evidence summarized in chapter 4 indicated that there has been differential participation in some ghetto riots between recent immigrants and long-term residents, the latter participating more frequently; long-term residents are not only likely to be more intensely discontented but to have had those feelings reinforced by higher levels of interaction with others. The effects of cohesiveness in facilitating violence are evident among many groups of dissidents other than those in isolated or degrading situations. The frequency of student demonstrations and insurrections is partly attributable to the relative homogeneity and high degree of interaction characteristic of student culture, in juxtaposition with particularly intense discontent about the conditions of larger society. The American Revolution could scarcely have succeeded had it not been for the consensus on goals among young men of the colonial upper-middle classes, based on their common schooling and similar socioeconomic backgrounds, and their interaction in colonial politics and later in the Committees of Correspondence.

Characteristics of Dissident Organization. The development of leadership and cadres, differentiation of organizational functions, and establishment of formal bodies to carry out those functions greatly facilitate the survival and effectiveness of dissident groups. Organizational development is neither a prerequisite nor substitute for cohesiveness; but it can be used to increase and extend it to much larger groups. Organizational differentiation is equally important for mobilizing resources for other group purposes.

Much of the attention given to the leadership of dissident organizations is in tacit or explicit recognition of its role in creating

[40] Clark Kerr and Abraham Siegel, "The Interindustry Propensity to Strike," in Arthur Kornhauser et al., eds., *Industrial Conflict* (New York: McGraw-Hill, 1954), 189–212.

[41] Wilfred H. Crook, *The General Strike* (Chapel Hill: University of North Carolina Press, 1931).

and extending dissident institutional support. Leaders can articulate doctrines justifying political violence and communicate them to followers and potential followers; establish patterned modes of action and provide sanctions for those who use them; provide the means and cues for violent action; and minimize the likelihood of retaliation for their followers. There is no precise correspondence between the existence of leadership and the development of massive political violence. Some revolutions have failed for want of adequate leadership, others have failed in spite of it, yet some successful ones have had no effective leaders until the revolutionary process was well under way.[42] Leadership, and its establishment and direction of resilient organization, are nonetheless essential if political violence is to succeed in the face of organized resistance.

The function most frequently attributed to revolutionary leadership is the articulation of doctrinal justifications for violence. Cantril describes this leadership function in conditions in which discontent is widespread.

> These critical situations . . . furnish fertile soil for the emergence of the mob leader, the potential dictator, the revolutionary or religious prophet. . . . Such leaders arise because they provide people with an interpretation that brings order into their confused psychological worlds. The clever leader will sense the causes of dissatisfaction, will realize which old loyalties remain unshaken and which are being seriously challenged. He will spread among the confused and eager souls a rationalization that, from their points of view, combines the best of the old and the best of the new. . . .[43]

The use of appeals and the development of organizational means make it possible to synthesize a diversity of interests and discontents and put them to the service of the goals of dissident leaders. Rosberg, in a study of the organization of the Mau Mau movement, says that Kikuyu leaders decided to administer the mass oath, on which the movement was based, to create an overarching organization that would overcome intense factionalism within the tribe. Once the organization was in existence, more militant

[42] See for example Louis Gottschalk, "Causes of Revolution," *American Journal of Sociology*, L (July 1944), 6.

[43] Hadley Cantril, *The Psychology of Social Movements* (New York: Wiley, 1941), 66. For similar statements see Lyford P. Edwards, *The Natural History of Revolutions* (Chicago: University of Chicago Press, 1927), 3, and Herbert Blumer, "Collective Behavior," in J. B. Gittler, ed., *Review of Sociology* (New York: Wiley, 1957), 148.

groups were able to obtain control of it.[44] The appeals that are effective in mobilizing support in the short run are not necessarily conducive to the maintenance of dissident activity over the long run. If dissident organizations shift from expressive to instrumental activity, for example, the doctrines that served to justify violent action are likely to require reinterpretation. Bittner argues that radical beliefs have a polemic disadvantage that jeopardizes the continuity of radical movements, and that a principal organizational task of radical movements is to compensate for this disadvantage.[45]

Different kinds of leaders are said to fulfill different organizational functions. Hoffer attributes responsibility for discrediting the prevailing political order to "the militant man of words." Once the regime is discredited, by this or other means, revolutionary movements are consolidated by "men of action." [46] In the earliest stage of revolutionary development, Hopper suggests a distinction between the "calm, dignified" agitator "who stirs the people . . . by what he says" and the activist who stimulates men to action. Leadership in the subsequent "popular stage" is provided by the prophet, who propounds "a special and separate knowledge of the causes of unrest and discontent," and later by the reformer, who proposes a specific program of action.[47] Discussions of charismatic leadership emphasize the symbolic functions of leaders; a charismatic leader symbolizes and may even preclude the need for a doctrine of revolutionary action on the part of his followers.[48] "In all essentials a leader is a symbol," Pettee writes. "In some sense, like any symbol, he mediates for [his followers] some principle of life." [49] Such men are endowed by their followers with extraordinary powers and qualities, qualities that may be as much a function of the psychological state of the led as of the leaders.

Highly competent leadership is necessary for the creation and direction of persistent, organized violence. McAlister proposes

[44] Carl G. Rosberg, Jr., "The Mau Mau as a Political Mobilization Institution" (Paper read at the Seventh Annual Meeting of the African Studies Association, Chicago, October 1964). Also see Carl G. Rosberg, Jr., and John Nottingham, *The Myth of "Mau Mau": Nationalism in Kenya* (New York: Praeger, 1966).

[45] Egon Bittner, "Radicalism and the Organization of Radical Movements," *American Sociological Review*, XXVIII (December 1963), 928–940.

[46] Eric Hoffer, *The True Believer: Thoughts on the Nature of Mass Movements* (New York: Harper, 1951), 129–151.

[47] Hopper, 272, 274–275.

[48] The concept of charisma was developed by Max Weber, *The Theory of Social and Economic Organization*, trans. A. M. Henderson and Talcott Parsons (Glencoe: The Free Press, 1947), especially 358–359, 362. For a contemporary analysis see Ann Ruth Willner, *Charismatic Political Leadership: A Theory* (Princeton: Center of International Studies, Princeton University, Research Monograph No. 32, 1968).

[49] George S. Pettee, *The Process of Revolution* (New York: Harper, 1938), 75.

that there is a close correspondence between the effectiveness of revolutionary violence and the degree of revolutionary organization and unity.[50] A comparative study of rural banditry in Colombia and urban terrorism in Venezuela concludes that effective organizational unity is a prerequisite for the pursuit of goal-oriented revolutionary policy and that highly politicized leadership is necessary if dissidents are to sustain a campaign opposed by both government and the majority of citizens. If leadership is not politically competent, political violence can persist only if there is widespread socioeconomic discontent.[51] If a dissident organization was created as, or is transformed into, a paramilitary body, a leadership hierarchy is a prerequisite for successful military operations. Other dissident organizations, like extremist political parties, may pursue their objectives primarily by nonviolent means. The political and organizational skills of their leaders may help them attain those objectives by enabling them to direct spontaneous violence to their own purposes. The Bolsheviks did so successfully in Russia in 1917; leaders of the French Communist Party chose not to do so in France in 1968.

The latter example makes it clear that there is no exact correspondence between the existence of dissident leadership and organization, and the extent of violence. Competent leadership and complex organization enhance dissident institutional support; that support may be used to minimize rather than increase political violence, depending on the commitments and tactical calculations of leaders. A coup d'état in a prerevolutionary situation can forestall massive violence, for example, by removing hated symbols of political repression and offering hopes for the alleviation of deprivation.[52] Generally, if dissident leaders are committed primarily to the enhancement of their own or members' value position rather than to expressive violence, they will adjust their tactics to the exigencies of the situations they face. If tactical considerations suggest that gains are best achieved with minimal violence, they are likely to control their followers to minimize rather than increase violence. It also is possible that the needs of intensely discon-

[50] See John McAlister, *Vietnam: The Origins of Revolution* (New York: Knopf, 1969).

[51] John D. Martz, "Urban and Rural Factors in Contemporary Latin American Violence," *Western Political Quarterly*, XVIII (September 1965), Supplement, 36–37.

[52] On this point see Andrew Janos, *The Seizure of Power: A Study of Force and Popular Consent* (Princeton: Center of International Studies, Princeton University, Research Monograph No. 16, 1964), 6–39; and Chalmers Johnson, *Revolution and the Social System* (Stanford: The Hoover Institution on War, Revolution and Peace, Stanford University, 1964), 49–57.

tented followers for expressive hostility will force leaders into more violent action than they consider desirable on tactical grounds, on pain of losing control. They may then develop more routinized, less violent means of symbolic protest of the kinds used by regimes to minimize the destructive consequences of protest (see the following section). The ritual use of antigovernment demonstration and strike, accompanied by high levels of verbal hostility, is one possible outcome of this process.

Other organizational functions to which leadership contributes are the provision of normative and physical support for followers, thereby increasing group cohesiveness and reducing the effects of regime coercion A major function of the doctrines articulated by leaders is to provide their followers with normative justifications for opposition. Followers' awareness that they are members of an organized group of like-minded individuals reinforces group cohesion and provides a sense of security in the face of external pressure. "We must all hang together, or most assuredly we shall all hang separately" is a sentiment common to many rebels besides the American colonial leaders who gave it this expression. The mere existence of leadership also may reduce the perceived likelihood of retaliation by a sort of lightning rod effect. The rank-and-file member of a dissident organization may believe that the brunt of negative sanctions will fall on his leaders rather than on him.

The specific organizational characteristics of dissident groups vary widely, depending on the circumstances of group formation, the objectives of leaders and followers, the social and ecological setting of action, and kinds of regime response to their activities among many other factors. Though no analysis of these factors is attempted here, it is noteworthy that dissident organizations usually reflect organizational patterns common in the milieu in which they operate. The most obvious reason is that many dissident organizations, particularly those with limited rather than revolutionary aims, were originally neutral or regime-oriented associations, which were subsequently pushed or led into overt opposition. This is the case with many expressive, millennarian religious movements; political parties and associations that have resorted to violent opposition when conventional means of political activity were closed to them; and radical labor organizations like the International Workers of the World. A more pervasive reason is simply that men do best what they know how to do. Dissident leaders are most likely to act effectively if they use organizational techniques with which they are experienced. They are most likely to attract and gain the loyalty of followers if they exercise authority in ways familiar to those followers. There are many parallels between prevailing patterns of group organization and dissident organization. Mass protest in medieval Europe tended to take the form of religious movements, the only kind of organization other than those of kinship and manor familiar to most rural and many urban people.[53] Many conspiratorial organizations in nineteenth-century Europe resembled the peaceful secret societies of that era.[54] The organization and tactics of guerrilla bands in less-developed countries are often similar to those of traditional bandits. Regional separatists and revolutionaries who control substantial territory often take over existing administrative structures and procedures or, if none exist, create their own following either the model of the regime they oppose or foreign models. The captured files of a district government established by rebels in the Congo's Kwilu province in the mid-1960s demonstrate an almost ritualistic adherence to administrative procedures of national and colonial Congolese governments.[55]

The Communist revolutions have been a principal source of organizational inspiration for other mid-twentieth-century revolutionary movements, and have been described in more detail than any other kind of revolutionary organization. The most appropriate and effective models are provided by Chinese and Vietnamese revolutionary organization, which developed in the course of protracted revolutionary warfare. The Russian Communist organizational experience has been with small-scale clandestine operations, in Russia and Europe before 1918 and outside Russia since then; and with procedures for implementing revolutionary policies once in power. The organizational patterns and procedures appropriate to such operations are less effective, probably dysfunctional in some respects, for the conduct of revolutionary war.[56] The basis for Asian Communist revolutionary movements is provided by the cadre party, "an organization of skills which can serve as the skeletal structure of a complex process of mobilization and action."[57] Mobilization requires both agita-

[53] See Norman Cohn, *The Pursuit of the Millennium*, 2d edn., rev. (New York: Harper, 1957, 1961).

[54] E. J. Hobsbawm, *Primitive Rebels: Studies in Archaic Forms of Social Movement in the 19th and 20th Centuries* (New York: Norton, 1959, 1965), especially chapters 8 and 9.

[55] According to Herbert Weiss, New York University, who has examined many of the documents.

[56] On the characteristics of Western Communist party organizations out of power see the papers in Milorad M. Drachkovitch, ed., *The Revolutionary Internationals, 1864–1943* (Stanford: Stanford University Press for the Hoover Institution on War, Revolution, and Peace, 1966).

[57] David A. Wilson, "Nation-Building and Revolutionary War," in Karl W. Deutsch and William J. Foltz, eds., *Nation-Building* (New York: Atherton Press, 1963), 89.

tion among potential supporters and the creation of complex, integrated structures "capable of committing members to execute orders with unquestioning obedience. . . ."[58] Mao describes the kinds of political and military structures of Communists in areas of China under nominal Japanese control. Each area

> must be subdivided and individual companies or battalions formed to accord with the subdivisions. To this "military area," a military commander and political commissioners are appointed. Under these, the necessary officers, both military and political, are appointed. In the military headquarters, there will be the staff, the aides, the supply officers, and the medical personnel. These are controlled by the chief of staff. . . . In the political headquarters, there are bureaus of propaganda, organization, people's mass movements, and miscellaneous affairs. Control of these is vested in the political chairmen.[59]

The prescribed patterns of relationship between military and political organization vary, as do the administrative procedures actually implemented. Without significant exception, however, the proponents, analysts, and opponents of modern revolutionary warfare attribute the capacity of revolutionary organizations on the Communist model to persist and succeed in the face of massive counterforce primarily to their organizational development.[60]

Some Functional Determinants of Institutional Support

The scope, complexity, and cohesiveness of organized groups affect their capacity to carry out functions of any kind: maintenance of stability, seizure of power, aggrandizement of elites, satisfaction of popular expectations, creation of goods, or enjoyment of their consumption. People who are discontented have two dominant

[58] Robert A. Scalapino, "Communism in Asia: Towards a Comparative Analysis," in Scalapino, ed., *The Communist Revolution in Asia: Tactics, Goals, and Achievements* (Englewood Cliffs: Prentice-Hall, 1965), 19.

[59] *Mao Tse-Tung on Guerrilla Warfare*, trans. S. B. Griffith (New York: Praeger, 1961), 77.

[60] In addition to the works cited above, see for example, Régis Debray, *Revolution in the Revolution? Armed Struggle and Political Struggle in Latin America*, trans. Bobbye Ortiz (New York: Grove Press, 1967), which critically assesses the applicability of Asian Communist techniques to the Latin American situation; Vo-nguyên-Giap, *People's War, People's Army* (New York: Praeger, 1962); Johnson, *Revolution and the Social System*, 57–69; Chalmers A. Johnson, *Peasant Nationalism and Communist Power: The Emergence of Revolutionary China, 1937–1945* (Stanford: Stanford University Press, 1962); and Douglas Pike, *Viet Cong: The Organization and Techniques of the National Liberation Front of South Vietnam* (Cambridge: MIT Press, 1967).

kinds of motivations for participating in organizational activity: they want compensatory values to alleviate RD, and they have an innate disposition to act aggressively against those responsible for their discontent (chapters 2 and 3). If regime or dissident organizations are to obtain persistent and high levels of support from the discontented they must establish means for the satisfaction of such motivations. Three relevant organizational functions examined below are the provision of direct and indirect means for value attainment, and of means for the expression of anger. Both regime and dissident organizations can fulfill all three functions. The relative importance of the functions for their members varies, however, with the extent and nature of their discontent. Moreover the ways the functions are fulfilled vary between and among regime and dissident organizations, and have quite different long-range consequences for the potential for violence.

SOCIETAL VALUE OPPORTUNITIES

The most evident, not necessarily the most important, instrumental function of organizations is to provide members with patterned and predictably successful courses of action for direct value satisfaction. The acts of participation per se can provide intrinsic interpersonal satisfactions, among them companionship, self-definition, and reinforcement of shared beliefs, provided that members follow normative prescriptions for conduct in the organization. Membership also can provide means for attaining power values. Members of stable, effective organizations can be given the sense and fact of security from external interference, i.e. a measure of freedom. To the extent that they can regularly influence the decisions of the organization, they can satisfy desires for participation and at the same time maintain and perhaps increase their spheres of personal freedom. If organizations have material resources members can be given opportunities to share in them: salaries for civil servants and party workers, housing and medical care for union members. To distribute such values, organizations must have substantial resources or at least the capacity to generate them. The generation of welfare values requires physical or monetary resources. Establishment of an organizational context in which power and interpersonal values can be created and shared similarly requires some physical resources, as well as willingness on the part of members and elites to accord rights of participation and status to one another. Two hypotheses are suggested:

Hypothesis RI.3: Regime institutional support varies moderately with the value stocks of regime-oriented organizations.

Hypothesis DI.3: Dissident institutional support varies moderately with the value stocks of dissident-oriented organizations.

The importance of physical resources for enhancing regime institutional control is suggested by one result of the cross-national, 119-nation study of civil violence cited previously. A measure of governmental control of economic resources was constructed, by relating the size of the central government budget to each country's Gross Domestic Product, and correlated with measures of the magnitude of civil violence in 1961–63. For all countries, the correlation was –.34: the greater the governmental share of economic resources, the less the magnitude of violence. The relationship also holds for countries at varying levels of economic development, suggesting, consistently with hypothesis V.7, that it is the relative rather than absolute share of resources that determines regime institutional support. Among the most highly developed countries the correlation is –.25; among moderately developed countries, –.31; among less developed countries, –.36; and among the least developed, –.43.[61] Availability of physical resources similarly enhances dissident institutional support, as examples in chapter 8 suggest. Dissidents who control base areas or have foreign sources of supplies are better able to conduct protracted insurgencies than those who do not. The decreasing strength of the relationship between regime resources and violence as the level of development increases, evident in the above correlations, may indicate that the more wealthy the nation, the more readily can dissident-controlled organizations obtain substantial resources for their own uses, whatever the proportion of resources under governmental control.

The importance of nonmaterial value satisfactions for the maintenance of institutional support is documented by interview and questionnaire studies of relationships among status, participation, and alienation. People who have little opportunity for participation in the organizations that control their affairs, and who have low status in these organizations, tend to feel alienated from the organization and are most disposed to activistic, aggressive "solutions," either within or outside the organization. In a study of workers in the automotive industry, Kornhauser et al. found that those who felt most futile politically were the most highly alienated from the American political system.[62] In a study of 450

[61] Previously unreported results of analyses summarized in Gurr with Ruttenberg.

[62] Arthur W. Kornhauser, Harold L. Sheppard, and Albert J. Mayer, *When Labor Votes: A Study of Auto Workers* (New York: University Books, 1956), 194–195.

workers, including members and nonmembers of work-related organizations, Neal and Seeman found that membership in mediating organizations—notably unions—diminished workers' feelings of alienation and powerlessness.[63] A survey study by Templeton of the relation between alienation and political participation in a general rather than working-class sample showed a similar pattern. Alienation was assessed using questions about Americans' satisfaction or dissatisfaction about living in their society. Those who were highly alienated tended strongly to be of lower socioeconomic status, to have hostile attitudes toward governmental agencies and procedures, to have low levels of participation in politics, and to be hostile toward Negroes.[64] These results are consistent with findings in almost all survey research done on alienation. Cause and effect are not clearly isolated in such studies: the hostility associated with alienation may result from lack of status and participation, or it may be the cause of lack of participation in a society in which participatory channels are formally open. There are probably complex interactions among the emotional state, attitudes, and behavior. The evidence is nonetheless consistent with the proposed relationship that hostile manifestations of discontent tend to be minimized by provision of interpersonal and participatory values.

To the extent that organizations can and do provide values commensurate with the expectations of their members, the potential for political violence is minimized. The assertion is as applicable to dissident as to regime organizations. Insofar as dissident organizations have or obtain the means to provide such satisfactions, political violence decreases. But they seldom can do so, even less than regime and neutral organizations, whose inability to provide adequate opportunities and satisfactions for their members is the primary source of the discontent which provides leaders and recruits for dissident organizations. Moreover the unsatisfied value expectations of members of dissident organizations are usually great, and the fact of membership in dissident organizations increases the need for defense against external retaliation; the first condition further decreases the likelihood that dissident organizations can substantially reduce the deprivation of their members,

[63] Arthur G. Neal and Melvin Seeman, "Organizations and Powerlessness: A Test of the Mediation Hypothesis," *American Sociological Review*, XXIX (April 1964), 216–226.

[64] Templeton, 249–261. For a general review see Joel D. Aberbach, "Alienation and Political Behavior," *American Political Science Review*, LXIII (March 1969), 86–99. On the bases and correlates of working-class hostility, with documentation from survey materials in a number of countries, see Seymour M. Lipset, *Political Man: The Social Bases of Politics* (Garden City: Doubleday, 1960), chapter 5.

the second requires leaders to devote a disproportionate amount of their resources to group defense.

There are some kinds of value satisfactions that dissident organizations are relatively well-suited to providing, including desires for interpersonal values—status, communality, and ideational coherence—and participatory values. Descriptions of revolutionary movements, labor organizations during their formative years, and millennarian movements frequently cite their importance in satisfying such needs. Cohn says that most followers of millennarian movements in medieval Europe were strongly alienated from the Church and found in the movements solutions for their alienation:

> But if these people were alienated from the Church, they also suffered from their alienation. . . . To be uncertain of the consolation and guidance and mediation of the Church aggravated their sense of helplessness and increased their desperation. It is because of these emotional needs of the poor that the militant social movements. . . . were at the same time surrogates for the Church. . . .[65]

The relative success of the National Liberation Front in South Vietnam in securing the loyalties of rural people has been attributed in part to the opportunities it provides for status and participation to ambitious village youth, in contrast to the class and educational barriers to upward mobility within military and administrative hierarchies of the Saigon government. The fact remains that most dissident movements lack the physical resources to satisfy directly the economic deprivations of their members or to provide them with adequate security against external threat. By satisfying psychosocial needs they create the bonds of loyalty that give the organizations the resilience and capacity to fight for other goals.

POLITICAL VALUE OPPORTUNITIES

Most political organizations, and many other associational groups, are used by their members as means as much as ends. Such organizations provide approved courses of action whereby value gains can be gotten from other individuals, groups, and institutions. One major function of political systems and of some communal and associational groups is the mediation and resolution of conflict among members; that is, they provide means by which individuals and groups competing for scarce values can be appor-

[65] Cohn, 316.

tioned more or less equitable shares of them. Members of political parties in a responsive political system are provided opportunities to affect value-distribution policies of the regime, as are other associational groups.

The effectiveness of political value opportunities for members of regime and dissident organizations is determined not by the immediate value gains they provide, but by the sense of increased value capabilities they give to those who make use of them. The same assertion is true of societal value opportunities. (See hypotheses ID.4 and VC.4 in chapters 3 and 5.) The immediate instrumental function of joining a dissident organization for a discontented individual is to increase his value opportunities, an increase likely in the short run to reduce the intensity of his discontent. A regime's establishment of new means of participation has the same effect. Organizations of all types thus can increase institutional support by increasing the number of alternative courses of action open to their members. Two hypotheses are proposed:

Hypothesis RI.4: Regime institutional support varies strongly with the number and scope of value opportunities provided by regime-oriented organizations.

Hypothesis DI.4: Dissident institutional support varies strongly with the number and scope of value opportunities provided by dissident-oriented organizations.

Scope in this context refers to the proportion of the members of such organizations who are eligible to use the means provided. Two qualifications to the hypothesis are needed. If new means are provided that fail to give participants a sense of progress and also fail to provide compensatory satisfactions, for example with respect to participatory, status, and communality values, the intensity of their discontent increases, and along with it organizational divisiveness, conflict, and desertion. The second is that those opportunities be open to all who wish to use them. Those who are excluded from new modes of political activity, or from joining "the vanguard of the workers' movement," are not likely to sense any increase in their prospects and may be increasingly discontented by their discriminatory treatment (corollary VC.4.1).

The two characteristics of political value opportunities that appear most consequential for maintaining regime institutional support are the provision of adequate conflict resolution mechanisms and a considerable degree of feedback in response to demands. Social conflict is ubiquitous and inevitable in social life.

Its institutionalization requires the formalization of rules agreed upon by the parties to the dispute, and the embodyment of these rules and their supportive beliefs in socialization processes and persisting organizations. Galtung identifies fifteen conditions that contribute to the institutionalization of permanent mechanisms of conflict resolution: for example, such mechanisms need to be directed by individuals with elite status, to appear both general and relevant to issues at hand, to provide unambiguous results, to define the point at which conflict terminates, and to distribute values or administer negative sanctions in support of decisions.[66] Effective methods of conflict resolution can be institutionalized at the communal level, especially among traditional societies in which most conflict is localized. Associational groups also can establish procedures for the formal resolution of internal conflicts, as religious bodies and universities often do. But in complex, modern societies conflict often involves large, dispersed, and powerful groups. Only the regime ordinarily has the capacity to develop institutionalized methods for nonviolent resolution of such conflicts.[67]

Most demands channeled through regime-oriented organizations are for additional values, not for resolution of value conflicts with other groups. The distinction between value demands and value conflicts is partly a matter of perspective: value conflicts by definition involve value demands by one party to the conflict. The distinction made here is between the number of parties to the dispute and their respective roles. The distinguishing characteristic of conflict-resolution systems is that, when X demands values of Y, the issue is submitted to Z, an independent or hierarchically superior unit, for adjudication. In simple value demand situations X demands values of Y, expecting Y to make the decision itself, based typically on the relative power of the two parties and shared notions of equity. The effectiveness of such value demands for reducing discontent depends, first, on the openness of channels for expressing demands, and second on the willingness and ability of Y to respond to them. Easton describes the lack or closure of channels as "channel failure," a consequence of which may be the resort to public protest for expressing and communicating

[66] Johan Galtung, "Institutionalized Conflict Resolution: A Theoretical Paradigm," *Journal of Peace Research*, No. 4, 1965, 348–397.

[67] The literature on the nature and resolution of conflict is voluminous. Three theoretical works, representative of sociological, economic, and anthropological perspectives respectively, are Coser, *The Functions of Social Conflict;* Kenneth E. Boulding, *Conflict and Defense: A General Theory* (New York: Harper, 1962); and Alan R. Beals and Bernard J. Siegel, *Divisiveness and Social Conflict: An Anthropological Approach* (Stanford: Stanford University Press, 1966).

demands. "Blockage of demands in these cases has not served to obliterate them. Its consequence has been to transform what might have been a pacific continuous flow of demands into a spasmodically violent, eruptive one."[68] A study of student nationalism in China during the 1920s and 1930s identifies the Kuomintang policy of preventing student participation in politics as one of the sources of growing student support for the Communists.[69] A fundamental issue in the violent Homestead, Pennsylvania steel strike of 1892 was the refusal of the Carnegie Steel Company to continue to deal with the workers' union, the Amalgamated Association of Iron and Steel Workers.[70]

Even if channels are open, lack of adequate response or "feedback" is ultimately dysfunctional. Appell summarizes a variety of experimental and field evidence to the effect that if symbolic feedback in organizations is low, group performance declines and hostility increases. His case study of political communication in a colonially ruled tribe shows that the creation of new channels in the form of political parties and elections reduced stress and hostility only to the extent that the demands made through them led to modification of the policies of the District Administration.[71] Eckstein describes the more concrete kinds of responses to demands of potential dissidents as "concessions," citing as a case in point the truism "that timely concessions have been the most effective weapons in the arsenal of the British ruling class. . . ."[72]

Dissident organizations similarly can strengthen their institutional support by providing mechanisms for internal conflict resolution and channels for making value demands. But many, sometimes all, members of dissident organizations are intensely hostile toward the regime, hence intrinsically value aggressive opposition to it. Provision of means for expressing this hostility thus is a particularly important function of such organizations. Demonstrations and riots against government policies, and revolutionary

[68] David Easton, *A Systems Analysis of Political Life* (New York: Wiley, 1965), 122.

[69] John Israel, *Student Nationalism in China, 1927–1937* (Stanford: Hoover Institution, Stanford University, 1967).

[70] Leon Wolff, *Lockout: The Story of the Homestead Strike of 1892* (New York: Harper and Row, 1965).

[71] G. N. Appell, "The Structure of District Administration, Anti-administration Activity and Political Instability," *Human Organization*, XXV (Winter 1966), 312–320. For an interpretation of feedback in political systems generally see David Easton, *A Framework for Political Analysis* (Englewood Cliffs, N.J.: Prentice-Hall, 1965), 127–130.

[72] Harry Eckstein, "On the Etiology of Internal Wars," *History and Theory*, IV (No. 2, 1965), 156.

warfare, simultaneously satisfy instrumental and expressive functions: they are ways of asserting demands and of acting out hostility. It also is likely, as Coser argues, that internal conflict among dissidents tends to be minimized. Members of groups in conflict tend to unite in response to opposition, to value cohesiveness and conformity as requisites for pursuing their goals, and to impose severe social sanctions on internal dissidents; moreover, discontent arising from internal conflict can be readily displaced onto the opposing group. Thus the fact of conflict between a dissident group and a regime tends to provide solutions for conflict within the group. Elaborate institutionalized mechanisms for conflict resolution are seldom needed. When they are it usually is in the context of an internal war in which dissidents exercise institutional and coercive control over neutral groups, in which case dissidents often establish their own judicial structures, as they did in Ireland in the early 1920s and in rural China during the 1930s and 1940s.

Members of dissident organizations are therefore most likely to want means that satisfy both instrumental and expressive functions. The failure of instrumental means should not necessarily be expected to weaken the organization. Lack of success in obtaining demanded values is more likely to intensify than to reduce dissident opposition, because initial hostility not only persists, it is intensified by the effort expended in what was thought to be value-enhancing action (corollary ID.2.2 and hypothesis ID.4). The fact that external groups—the regime, or political competitors—are responsible for not responding to the demands makes it highly likely that hostility will continue to be focused on them, not on the dissident leaders who specified the unsuccessful mode of action. Expressive protest also is intrinsically satisfying, hence reinforcing for the discontented, even in the absence of other value gains (chapter 2). But what are the consequences of value gains achieved through hostile demands? They are highly likely to increase the degree of dissident institutional support; they also are likely under some circumstances to decrease the intensity of dissident commitment to violent opposition, as is argued subsequently.

CHANNELS FOR EXPRESSIVE PROTEST

Some members of almost every kind or organization are discontented, and the most effective organization is unlikely to provide value opportunities adequate for the elimination of all RD. The more intense discontent is, the more necessary are safety-valve mechanisms—channels for protest—to the maintenance of institutional support. The same structured patterns of action, like channels for political participation, often serve both instrumental and expressive purposes. The identity of structure should not conceal the duality of functions such structures serve for those who use them. When discontent is low, their uses are primarily instrumental; when discontent is intense, they permit the expression of considerable hostility. To the extent that organizations provide institutionalized channels for protest, the potentially destructive consequences of hostility for the organization can be minimized. Dissident organizations channel most of the anger of their members, whatever its sources, into attacks on their opponents, so long as overt hostility is possible. If it is not, for example under conditions of severe repression, discontent may contribute to the divisiveness which is manifested in the splintering of extremist political groups. The lack of capacity for expressing some kinds of external hostility is relatively uncommon among dissident groups, however. Provision of adequate means for expressive internal protest is ordinarily much more critical for the maintenance of regime institutional support than it is for dissidents. The equivalent function for dissident organizations is provision of frequent opportunities for taking hostile action against the regime. Two hypotheses are proposed:

Hypothesis RI.5: Regime institutional support varies strongly with the number and scope of regularized channels for protest provided by regime-oriented organizations.

Hypothesis DI.5: Dissident institutional support varies strongly with the number and scope of means for anti-regime action provided by dissident-oriented organizations.

Scope in these hypotheses refers to the proportion of the members of such organizations who are eligible to participate in these activities. Those who are excluded may find some vicarious satisfaction in seeing others do what they would like to do, but vicarious satisfaction of emotional needs is inherently less rewarding than direct satisfaction.

The expressive functions of political activity are identified in a great many analyses. Lasswell's argument that "political movements derive their vitality from the displacement of private affects upon public objects" is cited above. He suggests that men's "primitive impulses," notably aggression, originate in the family and that politics is the process by which such impulses are publically expressed. Political demands "probably bear but a limited relevance to social needs. The political symbol becomes ladened with the residue of successive positive and negative identifications, and with the emotional charge of displaced private motives."[73] Tannenbaum writes that "American democracy has been strong to the extent to which the national parties have been torn by internal dissension," implying that party activity absorbs and displaces potentially destructive forces.[74] Ellwood makes the point explicitly: "A political or economic system which is felt to be burdensome or repressive by some usually excites little revolt if expressions against it and statements of grievances are permitted and tolerated."[75] Revolutionary movements in pluralistic democratic societies are relatively rare, suggests May, because freedom of speech and press allow for verbal outlet of discontent, because voting against a candidate satisfies some aggressive impulses, and because participation in activities of voluntary associations dissipates much aggression. "Aggressive movements in a democracy seldom reach revolutionary proportions partly because there are so many of them."[76]

Psychological evidence on the displacement of aggression identifies more precisely some of the relationships operative in the collective use of expressive protest. The psychological analysis of displacement assumes that the source of a frustration is known and that the innate response to it is physical aggression against the source. The aggressive response is "displaced" to the extent that it is directed against some other, presumably related, object (object generalization) and to the extent that it takes other than physical form (response generalization). Displacement theory, as developed by Miller, contends that aggressive responses generalize to objects that are perceived as close or similar to the frustrating agent, and that the stronger the anger, the less similar the objects attacked. Such generalization may occur because the frustrator himself is inaccessible, or because of fear of punishment for attacking him. One of Miller's basic propositions is that the stronger the fear of retribution relative to the strength of anger, the more dissimilar the target of aggression and the more indirect the form of aggression. If only external retribution is feared, inhibition is relatively narrow in its effects on object generalization: relatively similar objects are still likely to be attacked, and in rather

[73] Harold Lasswell, *Psychopathology and Politics* (Chicago: University of Chicago Press, 1930), 173–196, quotations from 173, 193.

[74] Frank Tannenbaum, "On Political Stability," *Political Science Quarterly*, LXXV (June 1960) 168.

[75] Charles A. Ellwood, *The Psychology of Human Society: An Introduction to Sociological Theory* (New York: Appleton, 1925), 254.

[76] Mark A. May, *A Social Psychology of War and Peace* (New Haven: Yale University Press, 1943), 188–191, quotation 191.

direct form. If internalized, normative prohibitions are operative, inhibitions extend to a wider range of objects and forms. If attacks occur at all they are likely to be quite indirect in both object and form.[77]

Varied empirical evidence demonstrates the occurrence of generalization. Comparative studies of relatively aggressive and nonaggressive boys provide evidence of response generalization. The nonaggressive boys, who had learned to inhibit aggressive responses, exhibit higher levels of indirect forms of aggression—for example fantasy aggression—than did the overtly aggressive boys.[78] In an experimental study by Miller and Bugelski, boys' attitudes towards Mexicans and Japanese were measured, the boys were later prevented from going to a movie, and were subsequently found to have increased hostility towards Mexicans and Japanese.[79] Berkowitz has proposed and demonstrated that hostility tends to generalize from a frustrator not to any object or group but to previously disliked individuals or groups.[80] One major qualification suggested by experimental evidence is that only a narrow range of objects provides satisfying targets for men's aggressive responses to frustration, but that almost any *form* of aggression can be satisfying so long as the angered person believes that he has in some way injured his supposed frustrator.[81]

Many examples of object generalization in collective violence can be cited. During a food shortage in Paris in 1720, hungry Parisians threatened violence on the residence but not the person of the king's Regent, whom they blamed for failing to prevent the shortage, and lynched the coachman of a speculator who was more directly responsible. When the livelihood of English hand-weavers was threatened by the introduction of new weaving machines, they destroyed thousands of the machines in the Luddite riots of 1811–16, but almost never attacked directly the employers who installed

[77] The generalization theory of displacement is proposed by Neal E. Miller, "Theory and Experiment Relating Psychoanalytic Displacement to Stimulus-Response Generalization," *Journal of Abnormal and Social Psychology*, XLVIII (April 1948), 155–178. A summary of the theory and some experimental evidence is given in Leonard Berkowitz, *Aggression: A Social Psychological Analysis* (New York: McGraw-Hill, 1962), 106–129.

[78] See for example Albert Bandura and Richard H. Walters, *Adolescent Aggression: A Study of Child-Training Practices and Family Interrelationships* (New York: Ronald Press, 1959), and Berkowitz, *Aggression*, 128–29.

[79] Neal E. Miller and R. Bugelski, "Minor Studies of Aggression: II. The Influence of Frustrations Imposed by the In-Group and Attitudes Expressed toward Out-Groups," *Journal of Psychology*, XXV (April 1948), 437–442.

[80] *Aggression*, chapter 6.

[81] Some such evidence is summarized in Leonard Berkowitz, "The Concept of Aggressive Drive: Some Additional Considerations," in Berkowitz, ed., *Advances in Experimental Psychology*, Vol. II (New York: 1965), 325–327.

the machines and discharged superfluous workers.[82] Lynchings of Negroes in the South between 1882 and 1930 were most frequent in years when economic conditions were poor. Negroes presumably were not held responsible for economic malaise; most of those lynched had in fact been arrested for or accused of crime. The inference is that anger over economic adversity was displaced onto marginally acceptable objects of attack.[83]

One implication of this kind of evidence is that regimes and regime-oriented organizations can minimize destructive consequences of hostility towards the organization by blaming RD on other targets and providing sanctioned means for acting out hostility against those targets. Internal scapegoats like Communists, reactionaries, and Jews may offer plausible targets. External enemies may seem to offer better ones because the disruptive domestic consequences are less. The argument that war serves to displace internal aggressions is common. Alexander says that war is a safety-valve necessary for a nation's self-preservation, providing release for a postulated hostility instinct.[84] Lasswell asserts that "wars and revolutions are avenues of discharge for collective insecurities and stand in competition with every alternative means of dissipating mass tension."[85] Huntington says that declining interstate conflict is likely to result in increased levels of intrastate violence.[86] Specific cases are sometimes cited. Eckstein says that England twice seemed on the brink of large-scale civil strife but was spared by the occurrence of external war, during the Napoleonic wars and in 1914 after the mutiny in the Curragh.[87] The Spanish-American War of 1898 may have provided an outlet for tensions generated by the closing of the American frontier; the Mexican-American War some fifty years earlier may have diverted Southern anger over the limitation on slave-holding in the new Western territories and states. Antiforeign demonstrations, a popular form of outdoor recreation since the end of World War II, seem widely regarded by rulers as having a similar function. Rummel, and Wil-

[82] Rudé, 49, 79–91.

[83] Carl Iver Hovland and Robert R. Sears, "Minor Studies of Aggression: VI. Correlation of Lynchings with Economic Indices," *Journal of Psychology*, IX (April 1940), 301–310.

[84] Franz Alexander, "The Psychiatric Aspects of War and Peace," *American Journal of Sociology*, XLVI (1941), 504–520.

[85] Harold Lasswell, *World Politics and Personal Insecurity*, in *A Study of Power* (Glencoe: The Free Press, 1934, 1950), 25.

[86] Samuel P. Huntington, "Patterns of Violence in World Politics," in Huntington, ed., *Changing Patterns of Military Politics* (New York: The Free Press, 1961), 40–41.

[87] Eckstein, 155.

kenfeld, found evidence of a limited relationship between the occurrence of external and internal conflict in the 1950s, based on data for a large number of nations. But the relationships are not consistent: various kinds of internal political violence sometimes tend to precede, sometimes to follow, external conflict, with the types and sequences varying from one group of nations to another.[88] In any case, even if it is possible for a regime to channel internal hostility towards foreign objects, the costs of doing so are potentially high. Antiforeign demonstrations may lead to a reduction of aid and diplomatic sanctions; the costs of war are often devastatingly high.

Response generalization—the channeling of discontent into symbolic rather than destructive hostility—is more easily institutionalized, can be more frequently used, and is more predictable in its consequences. It has one other advantage as well: when it takes the form of rights of petition and recall, elections, and peaceful demonstrations it may contribute to its own solution, by communicating the substance of discontents to rulers and threatening them with replacement if they do not respond. The evidence that response generalization occurs in political activity is indisputable. Every sensate politician in a competitive political system is aware of the "turn-the-rascals-out" syndrome that accompanies periods of popular discontent. Over a sixty-year period, Nebraska politicians were rather consistently voted out of office when rainfall was less than normal, whereas whatever party was in power was very likely to continue in power when rainfall was greater than normal.[89] From 1825 to 1924, the Northeastern states voted against the incumbent national administration after low rainfall in eleven out of thirteen instances, suggesting that "scant rainfall means poor crops, poor crops mean hard times, and hard times mean discontent," [90] to which can be added that discontent means a search for scapegoats, and that even New England's rugged individualists apparently have a preference for political scapegoats. Simon's analysis of voting support for the Nazi Party, 1927 to 1933, suggests that mass voting represents primarily a nonspecific expression of discontent. For example, the Nazi share of the vote fell from 40 to 32 percent

[88] Rudolph J. Rummel, "Testing Some Possible Predictors of Conflict Behavior within and between Nations," *Peace Research Society, Papers*, I (1963), 79–111; Jonathan Wilkenfeld, "Domestic and Foreign Conflict Behavior of Nations," *Journal of Peace Research*, No. 1, 1968, 56–69.

[89] J. D. Barnhart, "Rainfall and the Populist Party in Nebraska," *American Political Science Review*, XIX (August 1925), 527–540.

[90] Robert Marshall, "Precipitation and Presidents," *The Nation*, CXXIV (March 23, 1927), 315–316, quotation 16.

between July and November, 1932, a period of economic recovery.[91]

These electoral examples suggest that voting and other forms of political participation provide for the expression of discontent in relatively nondestructive ways. It is likely, but not demonstrated by this evidence, that discontent is more violently expressed in the absence of such procedures. One bit of evidence in support of this contention is the finding that civil rights campaigns are accompanied by a substantial reduction in aggressive crimes by Negroes. Negro assaults vs. other Negroes declined 31 percent in one Southern city during a year of extensive civil rights demonstrations, for example, and comparable declines have been reported from other cities.[92]

Instrumental vs. Expressive Functions of Associational Groups

Channels for expressive protest are not likely to provide an adequate outlet for intense discontent. When politicized discontent is widespread and intense, organizations that ordinarily serve instrumental functions tend to be used by their members to channel protest and, if they are not under direct regime control, as an organizational base for political violence. Moreover, in the absence of regular means for protest, almost any kind of associational group can provide means for organizing expressive protest and violence. In other words, the primary functions of associational groups for the mediation of members' discontent tend to vary with its intensity, as shown in figure 14. Under conditions of mild and moderate discontent, the instrumental functions of the organization tend to be most important for their members. If discontent increases in severity, the displacement function increases in importance; if discontent is very severe, the organization is likely to provide means for political violence. If people are unorganized, as many are in a mass society, they tend to create new associations. The influx of rural migrants into modernizing cities in Africa and Asia has been accompanied by the luxuriant growth of voluntary associations of every variety—traditional, religious, and modern secular. Some such associations serve primarily to preserve the old communal order and maintain traditional societal value opportunities, for example patterns of mutual assistance. Others have resorted to political activ-

[91] W. B. Simon, "Motivation of a Totalitarian Mass Vote," *British Journal of Sociology*, X (December 1959), 338–345. The 1932 data are from Frederick L. Schuman, *The Nazi Dictatorship: A Study in Social Pathology and the Politics of Fascism* (New York: Knopf, 1935), 182.

[92] F. Solomon et al., "Civil Rights Activity and Reduction in Crime Among Negroes," *Archives of General Psychiatry*, XII (March 1965), 227–236.

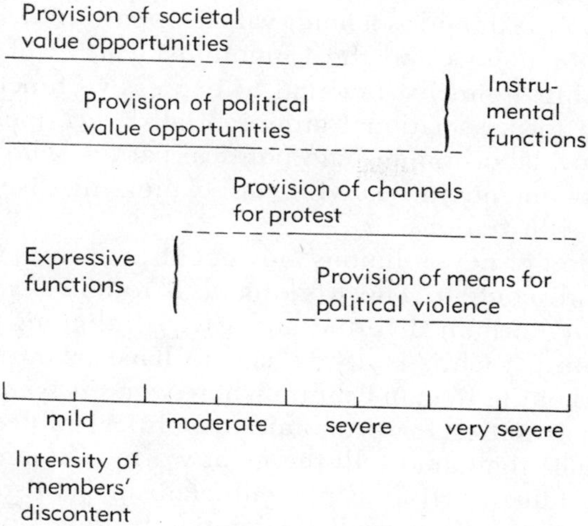

Figure 14. Predominant functions of associational groups in response to varying intensities of discontent.

ism, i.e. have been established or modified to provide political value opportunities and channels for protest.[93] Black organizations in the United States in the late 1960s represented every point on the spectrum. Cooperatives in the rural South and some community action programs in Northern ghettos attempted to provide direct value satisfactions for their members. Traditional civil rights organizations like the NAACP and the Urban League emphasized political value opportunities. Newer organizations like SCLC, CORE, and SNCC were initially established to provide means for political action, but began placing increasing emphasis on expressive protest and opposition for its own sake. Groups like the Deacons for Defense, the Black Muslims, and the Black Panthers were partly concerned with mobilizing their members for defensive and in some cases offensive violence.

Generally, under conditions of intensifying discontent, existing organizations will tend to be transformed to satisfy expressive functions. To the extent that they are inflexible, new organizations are likely to be created to provide means for more overt expressions of discontent. The reverse pattern occurs under conditions of declining discontent. If RD is reduced, organizations established for expressive purposes either decline, like some extremist political parties in Western Europe, or shift their emphasis toward the pro-

[93] See for example Kenneth Little, "The Organisation of Voluntary Associations in West Africa," *Civilisations*, IX (No. 3, 1959), 283–300.

vision of political and societal value opportunities, like most Western labor unions and the Communist Parties of France and Italy. The shift from instrumental to expressive functions can be documented for associational groups of all kinds, including communal groups, labor unions, and political parties. The functions of religious movements in resolving and expressing discontents provide a set of illustrations.

The creation of new religious movements and sects is a common response to discontent. The working-class religious sects of nineteenth-century Britain diverted and gave a religious form to proletarian protest.[94] Christianity is said to have taken root particularly in areas of the Roman Empire where workers were restive and had no opportunities for economic or political protest.[95] Sorokin offers evidence that almost all the great world religions, including Judaism, Buddhism, Hinduism, Confucianism, Jainism, and some ancient Egyptian cults, as well as Christianity, developed and were most successful in gaining converts in times of social crisis.[96] In Ashanti and elsewhere in tropical Africa a great many religious shrines have been established in the last several decades "to give supernatural protection and help to people increasingly preoccupied with a sense of insecurity." Field analyzed some 2,500 complaints and requests made at Ashanti shrines. The most common concerns related to economic goods and personal prosperity, which Field attributes to the insecurity contingent on the expansion of the cocoa industry and the money economy.[97]

The primary motives of participants in such religious movements were presumably instrumental. But if discontent is intense and wide in scope, existing religious bodies frequently shift to expressive activities and new, violently millennarian religious movements may develop. Pre- and protonationalistic protest in colonial Africa often took a religious form, for example. Fernandez attributes both nationalism and religious protest movements in colonial Africa to feelings of dependence and inferiority imposed by colonial rulers. Some African religious movements have been primarily instrumental. The separatist West African Church of the

[94] Hobsbawm, chap. 7. Also see Sydney G. Dimond, *The Psychology of the Methodist Revival* (London: Oxford University Press, 1926), chap. 2.

[95] S. Dickey, "Some Economic and Social Conditions of Asia Minor Affecting the Expansion of Christianity," in S. J. Case, ed., *Studies in Early Christianity* (New York: Century, 1928), 393–416, summarized in Neil J. Smelser, *Theory of Collective Behavior* (New York: The Free Press, 1963), 326.

[96] Pitirim A. Sorokin, *Man and Society in Calamity* (New York: Dutton, 1942), 200–226.

[97] M. J. Field, *Search for Security: An Ethno-Psychiatric Study of Rural Ghana* (Evanston: Northwestern University Press, 1960), 87, 105–133, quotation 13.

Lord Aladura and the reformative Bwiti movement of Gabon are said to have been characterized by "fairly pragmatic attempts to compensate for the deprivations and other frustrations involved in the situation of subordination, without endangering the continuity and survival of the religious group, since it is seen as the only institution that can achieve its goals." Examples of expressive religious movements include xenophobic, messianic cults such as *kimbanguism* in the lower Congo and nativist elements in the Mau Mau movement. Such groups emphasize "escape by symbolic displacement from the situation which is causing frustration." [98] The symbolic aggression in such expressive activity is often high, as studies of nativistic Amerindian religious protest in the nineteenth century show.[99] If discontent is severe and the external response is repressive, overt violence is likely. In Africa *kimbanguism* had its violent episodes and the Mau Mau movement mounted a full-scale rebellion. So did John Chilembwe's Protestant Industrial Mission in Nyasaland after its founders largely failed in efforts to create a European mode of existence; in 1915 the sect attempted an abortive rebellion against colonial rule.[100] Western examples include the millennarian violence of medieval Europe, the Hussite rebellion in fifteenth-century Czechoslovakia, the religious wars of the Reformation, and, in the modern era, the personally destructive violence of the Dukhobor sect of Canada. Even so well-institutionalized an organization as the Catholic Church of Argentina supported and provided one of two organizational foci—the other being the Army—for the anti-Perón movement in 1954 and 1955. The Church shifted from its neutrality toward the regime to active opposition, by the rank-and-file and activists if not the hierarchy, after the suppression of religious schools, the burning of several churches, and verbal attacks on the Church by Perón. In June 1955, 250,000 members of Catholic Action demonstrated against the regime in Buenos Aires, and Church members were widely active in the conspiratorial activity that laid the groundwork for the coup d'etat in September.[101]

The tendency of social movements, including many revolutionary ones, to shift in the other direction, from expressive to instru-

[98] Fernandez, quotation 535.

[99] For a summary discussion and citations see Smelser, 365–366.

[100] See George Shepperson and Thomas T. Price, *Independent African: John Chilembwe and the Origins, Setting, and Significance of the Nyasaland Native Uprising of 1915* (Edinburgh: Edinburgh University Press, 1948), especially 127–187; and Fernandez, 539, 542.

[101] Reuben de Hoyos, "The Catholic Church and the Army in the Argentine Revolution of 1955" (Ph.D. Dissertation, Department of Politics, New York University, 1969).

mental activities, is a widely observed trait of dissident organizations. The most obvious examples are successful revolutionary movements, whose accession to power, according to Brinton, is likely to be followed by the brief rule of moderates, the triumph of extremists, a reign of terror, and finally thermidor, a "convalescence from the fever of revolution." [102] Smelser labels the process institutionalization, and attributes it to the exigencies of group persistence. "The movement must generate new types of leadership to sustain the organization of the movement itself; it must seek permanent bases of financing; it must accommodate new and more specialized activities within the movement; it must routinize its modes of recruitment." [103] Toch similarly says that if social movements of any kind are to survive they must "undergo adaptive transformations that are designed to enhance their attractiveness in competition with the outside." [104] In this process leaders may come to value the organization and the satisfactions it provides more than do their followers. If leaders do so, and if they become unresponsive to the interests and new discontents of their followers, the cycle of dissident opposition and withdrawal is likely to begin again within the organization.

Many kinds of dissident organizations experience the transition to nonviolent, instrumental activities, not only those that have passed successfully through so convulsive a process as revolution. It is a frequently documented characteristic of religious sects, for example.[105] The participation of industrial workers in associational activity similarly tends to reduce their alienation and to transform protest from violent to nonviolent forms. A comparative study of patterns of industrial conflict in fifteen European, North American, and Asian countries shows the virtual disappearance of disruptive conflict in many countries in which collective bargaining is practiced, and the common transformation of the strike from a violent confrontation into a brief demonstration of protest.[106] Another broad survey of industrial societies concludes that "worker protest in the course of industrialization tends to peak relatively early and to decline in intensity thereafter," partly because workers' value positions rise, partly because new and more effective channels for expressing grievances develop concurrently with industrialization.[107] This is Kerr's summary of the process:

[102] Crane Brinton, *The Anatomy of Revolution* (New York: Norton, 1938).
[103] Smelser, 359.
[104] Hans Toch, *The Social Psychology of Social Movements* (New York: Bobbs-Merrill, 1965), 214, 227–228.
[105] Smelser, 359–361; Wallace; and Wilson.
[106] Arthur M. Ross and George W. Hartmann, *Changing Patterns of Industrial Conflict* (New York: Wiley, 1960).
[107] Kerr et al., 208–210, quotation 208–209.

> At first, the worker is so little connected with industrial life and so bereft of power and the basis for organizing power that he has neither a great desire nor sufficient means to protest. As his involvement in and experience with industrial life increases, his power to influence the industrial environment also increases, and his tendency to protest rises. Industrial life is now his life, and he wishes to mold it closer to his heart's desire. Later on, as machinery is established to meet his grievances and as the cost of the conflict begins to bulk larger, industrial protest may tend to fade away. . . . What protest remains tends to be highly structured and formally expressed.[108]

Labor conflict in the United States was more violent than that of any other industrial nation, its most violent episodes occurring between the 1870s and 1930s. A typical sequence in these conflicts was a nonviolent strike, combining instrumental and expressive motives, followed by forceful attempts by employers to break the strike, leading to retaliatory, predominantly expressive violence by workers. Such outbreaks were almost always quickly suppressed, at considerable cost and little benefit for the workers involved, but they persisted for nearly three generations. Economic prosperity unquestionably contributed to the decline of labor violence after the 1930s, but in the judgment of Taft and Ross the most consequential factor was the federally regulated recognition of workers to organize and bargain collectively. Once this step toward formal institutionalization occurred, violent labor conflict quickly declined to a negligible level.[109]

These examples of the transformation of labor conflict make it clear that the shift from expressive to instrumental activity by dissident organizations is not solely, and probably not primarily, an imperative of organizational persistence. The Viet-Minh and its predecessor and successor organizations have become increasingly institutionalized, and increasingly effective in the prosecution of political violence, over a span of more than thirty years, without evidence of any decline in revolutionary commitment. Rebel bands in the Burma hills, in central Luzon, in India's Naga Hills, and in the Colombian state of Tolima have maintained insurgencies for

[108] Clark Kerr, "Changing Social Structures," in Wilbert E. Moore and Arnold S. Feldman, eds., *Labor Commitment and Social Change in Developing Areas* (New York: Social Science Research Council, 1960), 353. For similar views and documentation of the transformation of industrial protest see Reinhard Bendix, *Work and Authority in Industry* (New York: Wiley, 1950), 434–437; W. Kornhauser, 150–156; Rudé, chap. 4; and Neil J. Smelser, *Social Change in the Industrial Revolution* (Chicago: University of Chicago Press, 1959), 245–263.

[109] Philip Taft and Philip Ross, "American Labor Violence: Its Causes, Character, and Outcome," in Graham and Gurr, eds., 221–302.

twenty years or more. The Irish Republican Army under one name or another has been engaged in terrorism for more than forty years. Basque separatists have been violently opposing foreign rulers quite literally from the beginning of recorded history, though ordinarily in the context of persisting communal rather than associational organization. Transformation to peaceful activity is less a function of organizational age than of the alleviation of discontent. If political violence is defensive, which it is for many collectivities that seek to retain or regain their autonomy, violence is likely to subside when the threat is removed. Political, labor, and religious sects are most likely to shift toward instrumental activity once they obtain the means to satisfy the value expectations of their members, either from their own resources or by the development of regularized and effective means of bargaining and participation. Political violence by a group is likely to become chronic only when it leads to transient success. When dissidents acquire through violence the means to work constructively toward the permanent resolution of their discontent, violence has contributed to its own demise rather than its recurrence.

10. Causes and Processes of Political Violence: A Conclusion

> If we eschew violence it is not because of any moral imperative, but it is because violence cannot change human beings.
>
> Jayaprakash Narayan [1]

POLITICAL VIOLENCE is episodic in the history of most organized political communities and chronic in many. No country in the modern world has been free of it for as much as a generation. But it is not an ineluctable manifestation of human nature, nor is it an inevitable consequence of the existence of political community. It is a specific kind of response to specific conditions of social existence. The capacity, but not a need, for violence appears to be biologically inherent in men. The disposition to collective violence depends on how badly societies violate socially derived expectations about the means and ends of human action. This disposition to violence, discontent, can be tempered by socially implanted attitudes that condemn violence, facilitated and focused on the political system by similarly derived doctrines and experience that suggest its justifiability and utility. Civil violence can occur in the context of any kind of political community. It is most likely to occur in societies that rely on coercion to maintain order in lieu of providing adequate patterns of value-satisfying action. The use of coercion in the service of any collective purpose tends to antagonize and increase the resistance of those against whom it is directed, a principle that applies equally to political elites and those who oppose them. By contrast, if discontented people have or get constructive means to attain their social and material goals, few will resort to violence. Only men who are enraged are likely to prefer violence despite the availability of effective nonviolent means for satisfying their expectations.

This approach to the explanation of political violence is documented in the preceding chapters with a variety of evidence, theoretical and empirical, rigorous and impressionistic, psychological and societal. It is summarized using a set of analytic distinctions about the psychological and societal causes of violence and syn-

[1] "The Nature of the Revolutionary Situation Around the World" (Address delivered to the National Conference on the United States in a Revolutionary World, Princeton University, April 2, 1968), 3.

thesized in a set of interrelated hypotheses. The hypotheses moreover are probabilistic, not deterministic. Estimates of the relative importance of each independent variable have been made; their relationships with their immediately dependent variables are said to be either linear or curvilinear. It should be possible, on the basis of further comparative study, to estimate more precisely the relative weights of the variables and the nature of their interrelationships. It can be inferred from psychological evidence, for example, that the potential for collective violence is a power rather than a linear function of the intensity of RD.[2] If relationships are found to be constant, or, more likely, to vary over a relatively small range, it should be possible to state parts of the theory as probabilistic laws.

My objective in this chapter is to synthesize the proposed relationships. The hypothetical relationships are first integrated in the form of causal models, of a kind that can be evaluated empirically.[3] Complex causal models show the determinants of each of the three primary variables in the basic theoretical model: the potential for collective violence, the potential for political violence, and the magnitude of political violence. Simple models are then deduced from relationships among the independent variables. Additional hypotheses about the forms of political violence are proposed and similarly summarized in simple causal models. Then a process model of political violence is developed deductively from some of the proposed relationships. Much of this discussion is necessarily abstract and technical. In a lighter and more policy-relevant section, the process model is used illustratively to outline optimum strategies for attaining three kinds of social objectives:

[2] See Robert L. Hamblin et al., "The Interference-Aggression Law?" *Sociometry*, XXVI (June 1963), 190–216.

[3] Causal models of the kinds developed here are subject to evaluation and revision using causal inference analysis of correlation data. Basic techniques are described in Hubert M. Blalock, Jr., *Causal Inferences in Non-experimental Research* (Chapel Hill: University of North Carolina Press, 1964); Herbert A. Simon, *Models of Man* (New York: Wiley, 1957); and Otis Dudley Duncan, "Path Analysis: Sociological Examples," *American Journal of Sociology*, LXXII (July 1966), 1–16. For political applications see Hayward R. Alker, Jr., "Causal Inference and Political Analysis," in J. Bernard, ed., *Mathematical Applications in Political Science* (Dallas: Southern Methodist Press, 1967) and H. D. Forbes and Edward R. Tufte, "A Note of Caution in Causal Modelling," *American Political Science Review*, LXII (December 1968), 1258–1264. Some applications to data on political violence and instability are Manus Midlarsky and Raymond Tanter, "Toward a Theory of Political Instability in Latin America," *Journal of Peace Research*, No. 3, 1967, 209–227; Robert D. Putnam, "Toward Explaining Military Intervention in Latin American Politics," *World Politics*, XX (October 1967), 83–110; Ted Gurr, "A Causal Model of Civil Strife: A Comparative Analysis Using New Indices," *American Political Science Review*, LXII (December 1968), 1104–1124; and Ted Gurr, "Urban Disorder: Perspectives from the Comparative Study of Civil Strife," *American Behavioral Scientist*, XI (March-April 1968), 50–55.

maintaining political stability, achieving violent revolution, and maximizing the value satisfactions of discontented groups. Finally, some common misinterpretations of the causes and consequences of violence are mentioned, and hopefully dispelled.

Determinants of the Magnitude of Political Violence: A Summary

The basic causal relations in the genesis of political violence are shown schematically in figure 15. A summary list of all hypotheses and corollaries developed in this study appears in Appendix I, pp. 360–367. The social-psychological potential for collective violence is a diffuse disposition toward aggressive action, a primary variable whose immediate determinants in a collectivity are the intensity and scope of RD. RD is defined in psychosocial terms as a perceived discrepancy between men's value expectations and their value capabilities, i.e. a discrepancy between the goods and conditions of life they believe are their due, and the goods and conditions they think they can in fact get and keep. The motivational consequence of such a discrepancy is a disposition to aggressive action, not inherently remedial, called discontent or anger in this analysis. The potential for violence in a collectivity varies jointly with the intensity of discontent, which ranges from mild dissatisfaction to rage, and the proportion of its members (scope) who are intensely discontented (hypothesis V.1).

Discontent has potential political consequences to the extent that men believe violence against political actors is justified in a normative sense, and potentially useful in enhancing or defending their value positions. The potential for political violence, the second primary variable, is a focused disposition to use or threaten violence against political actors who are held responsible, by their errors of commission or omission, for depriving conditions. In the causal model, the potential for political violence (in motivational terms, politicized discontent) is a result of general discontent (hypothesis V.4), and a set of secondary, cognitive variables: the intensity and scope of normative and utilitarian justifications for political violence (hypotheses V.2 and V.3). The cognitive variables, normative and utilitarian justifications, are formally dependent on the motivational one, discontent. Belief in the utility and desirability of violence can motivate men to organize and participate in political violence only if they are already in some degree discontented.

The actualization of politicized discontent in political violence is modified by the patterns of coercive control and institutional support. The magnitude of political violence, the third primary varia-

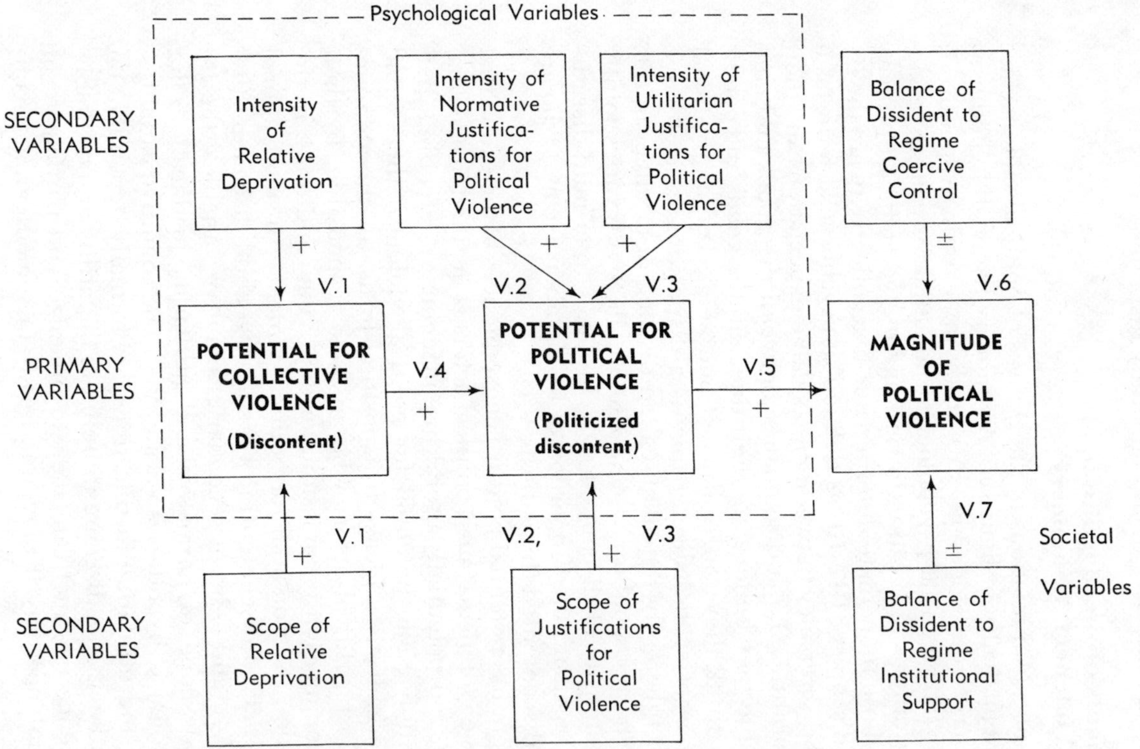

Figure 15. A causal model of the primary and secondary determinants of magnitude of political violence.

Note: All variables are defined and discussed in preceding chapters. Hypotheses (denoted V.1, V.2, etc.) identify all causal relationships shown, some of which are positive (+), some curvilinear (±). See Appendix I, 360–361, for chapters in which hypotheses are developed.

ble, is defined in terms of the proportion of a collectivity that participates in it, its destructiveness, and its duration. At this final stage of the causal model the potential for political violence is a necessary but not sufficient condition for political violence. Magnitude of violence varies strongly with the scope and intensity of politicized discontent (hypothesis V.5), but is minimized to the extent that the regime has either a very high or very low degree of coercive control and institutional support vis-à-vis dissidents (hypotheses V.6, V.7). Dissidents are those actively committed to political violence. If they have widespread organizational support and a high degree of coercive capacity compared with the regime, they ordinarily can seize power or attain more limited political aims with minimal violence. Coups d'état typically occur and political concessions are most readily granted by elites under threat of violence when the balance of social control and support so favors the dissidents. If dissident control and support approximate that of the regime, however, political violence is likely to be protracted and intense.

The primary relationships specified in these seven hypotheses can sometimes be studied directly but are too general for most kinds of analysis and interpretation. The scope and intensity of the psychological variables can be ascertained in contemporary nations using survey techniques, for example, and magnitudes of political violence measured using standard coding procedures. Political elites are notoriously sensitive about inquiries into the disloyalties of their citizens, however, and historical scholarship must deal with many different kinds of information. Moreover, one determinant of the adequacy of theoretical generalization is the degree to which it integrates more specific explanations and observed regularities. The usefulness of the basic causal model for synthesizing information on political violence and facilitating explanation depends on precise specification of the psychological and societal conditions that determine such secondary variables as the intensity of RD and the balance of institutional support. Most of this study has been devoted to identifying these conditions, summarizing the evidence for them, and specifying why and to what extent they affect the secondary variables. In the next three sections each of the primary variables shown in figure 15 – potential for collective violence, potential for political violence, and magnitude of political violence – is treated as a dependent variable in a causal model; the secondary variables are treated as intervening variables; and their respective determinants, specified in preceding chapters, are shown schematically. More parsimonious, simple models are deduced from relationships among the determinants.

Some general questions of empirical application also are considered.

Two different levels of analysis, the psychological and the societal, are represented by the tertiary variables in figures 15 and 16. For some analytic purposes the state-of-mind variables may be regarded as intervening variables and causal linkages drawn directly among the societal variables. For theoretical explanation, however, both levels are taken into account throughout this analysis. Neither can be fully interpreted without reference to the other, as has been demonstrated repeatedly, and neither alone gives an explanation of the causes and processes of political violence that is "adequate" in the sense that it accounts at all simply for observed regularities.

DETERMINANTS OF THE POTENTIAL FOR COLLECTIVE VIOLENCE

All the determinants of the intensity of RD, psychological and societal, are shown in figure 16. For those impatient with its complexity, the simplified model is shown in figure 17; it is justified below. RD is conventionally treated as a social variable. Defining it here as a discrepancy between collective value expectations and value capabilities makes it possible to specify some major determinants of the strength of the consequent impulse to action, by reference to psychological theory and evidence on the frustration-aggression relationship. These psychological determinants are discussed in chapter 3 and their effects on the intensity of RD shown schematically on the top portion of figure 16. The effects of these variables in collectivities are interpreted in distributional terms: the greater the *average* degree of discrepancy between value expectations and capabilities among members of a group (ID.1), for example, the greater the average intensity of RD.

One method for assessing the psychological variables is survey research; another is systematic inference from narrative and aggregate statistical data. An alternative or supplementary approach to studying particular societies or cases is the analysis of class or group configuration, using the societal variables specified. The value expectation and capability hypotheses, derived in chapters 4 and 5, identify some general consequences of relative levels and changes in groups' shares of social goods on the RD of their members. Groups or classes in a society can be distinguished—analytically, structurally, or subjectively—and their likely degree of RD inferred from such conditions as the total goods available for distribution in the society, changes in each group's means for obtaining those goods, and their changing levels of value attainment vis-à-vis their own past and the experience of other classes.

A simpler formulation of the societal determinants of the potential for collective violence is derived by combining the parallel societal variables and relating them directly to the dependent variable, as shown in figure 17. For example, upward value mobility of other, socially significant groups tends to increase the level and salience of expectations in one's own group (VE.3). To the extent that an upwardly mobile group increasingly monopolizes social goods that are thought to be fixed in quantity, like political power and status, one's own group's value capabilities simultaneously decline (VC.2). A more general relationship that comprises both is that any differential increase in value position by one group tends to increase RD among other groups. One drawback of such a hypothesis is that it does not take account of the two major qualifications introduced in the separate hypotheses, and supported by a good deal of evidence. These are, first, that the upward mobility of one group, for example a rising professional class, appears to increase the value expectations only of those other classes or groups that identify with it. This is a classic problem in the sociological literature on RD: Which groups do others choose as reference groups? Second, upwardly mobile groups are perceived as a threat to one's own group's capabilities only if the total stock of goods is thought inflexible. Evidence was summarized to the effect that perspectives on value flexibilities vary widely among cultures (chapter 5); in some societies some of the good things of life are thought to be infinitely expandable, in others all are thought immutable. The more general relationship thus is likely to explain less than the two relationships separately. But simplicity of explanation is usually gained at the expense of accuracy in specific cases.

Another parallel between the determinants of expectations and capabilities is between two postulated effects of a group's past experience of change. Past increases generate expectations about further increases (VE.5), past decreases reduce perceived capabilities (VC.3). A general relationship that comprises both is that RD varies with the rate of change in a group's value position: the higher the rate of past change, in whatever direction, the greater the likely RD; the lower the rate, *ceteris paribus*, the lower the RD. A third parallel that seemingly offers possibility for more parsimonious generalization is the apparently contradictory effects proposed for value opportunities. If opportunities are few, capabilities are said to be low (VC.4); opening of new ones hypothetically increases expectations (VE.2). If these two relationships cancel out, then an increase in value opportunities has inconsequential effects on RD, neither intensifying nor reducing it. But the former

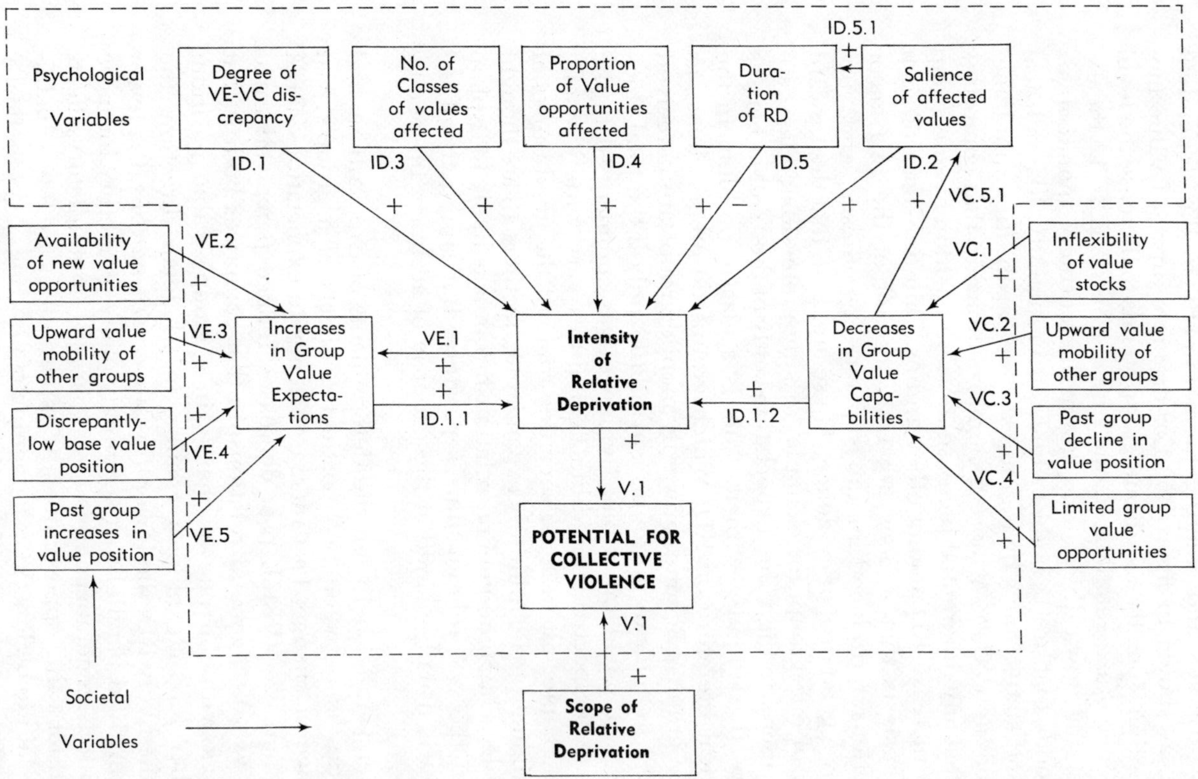

Figure 16. A complex causal model of the psychological and societal determinants of the potential for collective violence.

Note: All variables are defined and discussed in preceding chapters. Hypotheses (denoted V.1, VE.5, etc.) and corollaries (denoted ID.1.1, etc.) identify all causal relationships shown. See Appendix I.

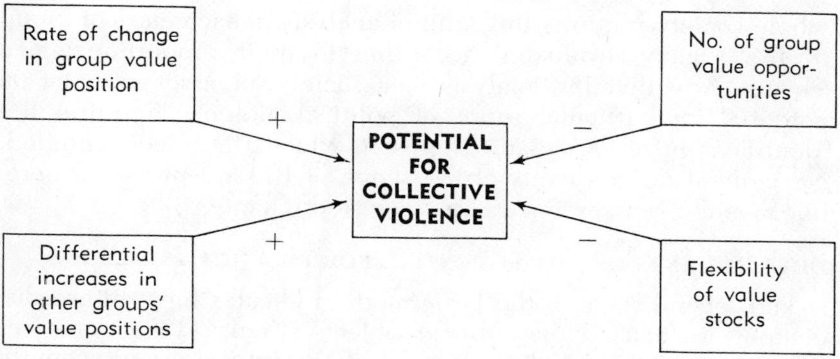

Figure 17. A simplified causal model of the societal determinants of the potential for collective violence (discontent) in any subnational group.

Note: This model is deduced from relationships inferred among the determinants of changes in group value expectations and capabilities shown in figure 16 (see text). Variables are defined and discussed in preceding chapters. Hypotheses summarizing the relationships are not formally proposed but can be stated in terms analogous to the hypotheses developed in chapters 4 and 5.

relationship (VC.4) is a strong one, the latter moderate. Moreover, the hypothetical increase in expectations that follows the opening of opportunities holds only in the special case of "conversion," the shift of group perspectives from an old to a new way of life; and such a shift is likely to occur only under conditions of intense preexisting discontent. In the most general case, expansion of value opportunities is likely to increase more substantially perceived chances for attaining those expectations; on balance, the intensity of RD is likely to be lower if a group has many rather than few value opportunities, and to be reduced if value opportunities are increased.

The simplified causal model in figure 17 takes into account these three generalized relationships plus the inflexibility of value stocks. The effects of discrepancies among a group's relative attainment of different values (VE.5) are excluded because their effect is only moderate (see chapter 4). The interaction effect between the intensity of RD and increases in value expectations (VE.1) cancels out. Thus, a general assessment of any group's potential for collective violence theoretically can be made by determining the rate of change in its absolute share of each class of values; the extent to which other groups in its society are experiencing a more rapid increase in value position; the extent to which values are, or are thought to be, expandable; and the number of alternative courses of value-enhancing action open to members of the group. Estimating the potential for collective violence in a whole society requires this kind of analysis of each class or group in the society, evaluated according to their proportional size (scope). Any detailed analysis of a society, or assessment of its potential for particular forms of political violence, requires the identification of classes or groups in which RD is concentrated. No general determinants of the scope of RD are proposed here, but means for assessing it are suggested (chapter 3).

DETERMINANTS OF THE POTENTIAL FOR POLITICAL VIOLENCE

The second stage of the basic model indicates how diffuse discontent is focused on political objects. Figure 18 summarizes diagrammatically the determinants of the intensity and scope of justifications for political violence identified in chapters 6 and 7; figure 19 shows a much-simplified model. The determinants are societal ones, although the effects of several of them—regime legitimacy, and the affective and utilitarian content of symbolic appeals—make assumptions about intervening psychological variables, and can be studied using psychological (interview and survey) techniques as well as social and historical techniques (content analysis of doctrinal appeals, evaluation of political support for the regime). Two of the secondary variables—the intensities of normative and utilitarian justifications for political violence—also are most directly determined by those expensive and infrequently practicable survey techniques. But some of their societal determinants are specified to facilitate assessment by nonsurvey methods. The apparent complexity of the causal relationships shown is a consequence of arguments in chapters 6 and 7 that normative and utilitarian attitudes towards violence are related, and that several of their societal determinants strongly affect both rather than one primarily. Explanation would be simpler if both kinds of justifications were treated as one. Such a reduction is not theoretically justified for detailed analyses, however: discontent provides an innately nonrational (but widely rationalized) impetus to violence, empirically and analytically distinguishable from actors' estimations of the utilities of violence. Different psychological processes are involved and their collective effects are manifestly different—the difference between riotous eruptions and revolutionary seizures of power. The distinction between their determinants makes it possible to study their separate effects.

Several important causal connections exist among the independent variables that one is mathematically obliged to take into account to evaluate the theoretical model quantitatively, and which common sense dictates be considered in less rigorous studies. They also permit a substantial simplification of the causal model.

The closest of these relations is among the historical magnitude of political violence (JV.2) and past or present group success with political violence (JV.8, JV.9). Successful violence increases the likelihood of its recurrence; the greater the extent of historical violence, the more likely it is that some groups have found it effective. A similar connection can be inferred between the extrapunitiveness of socialization practices in a culture or subculture (JV.1) and its past experience of political violence. These two conditions presumably reinforce one another over time; extrapunitive attitudes tend to increase men's willingness to participate in political violence; the widespread occurrence of such violence probably leads its participants and supporters to implant attitudes favorable to some kinds of violence in their children. The group success and socialization variables thus can be deleted in the generalized model.

It also is likely that the greater the success groups have had in using political violence, the greater the utilitarian content of symbolic appeals justifying violence (JV.7). Most such appeals have both utilitarian and affective content; these two variables, JV.6 and JV.7, thus can be formally combined as a single, more general determinant of the potential for political violence. The density of aggressive political symbols in media (JV.10) and the scope of the media that carry them (JV.11) are also related; the existence of media of substantial scope is a prerequisite for the communication of such symbols. The more general relationship is that potential for political violence varies with the scope and density of symbols communicated.

Three other nominally independent but causally linked variables are past regime effectiveness in alleviating RD (JV.3), differential regime responses to the discontents of different groups (JV.4), and regime legitimacy (JV.5). One source of high governmental legitimacy is its effectiveness in resolving RD. The argument for the first relationship (JV.3) is that the greater the past scope of governmental action, the greater the specifically political hostility of discontented groups if the regime fails to act to improve their present situation. Given such historically derived expectations, inadequate regime response is likely to reduce legitimacy. Similarly, if a regime makes differential contemporary responses to RD (JV.4), its legitimacy is likely to be reduced among members of the less-favored groups. Generally, therefore, the more effective regimes are in responding to RD, the greater is regime legitimacy and the less the potential for political violence. These generalized relationships are summarized in the simplified causal model in figure 19. Parsimony again is gained at the ex-

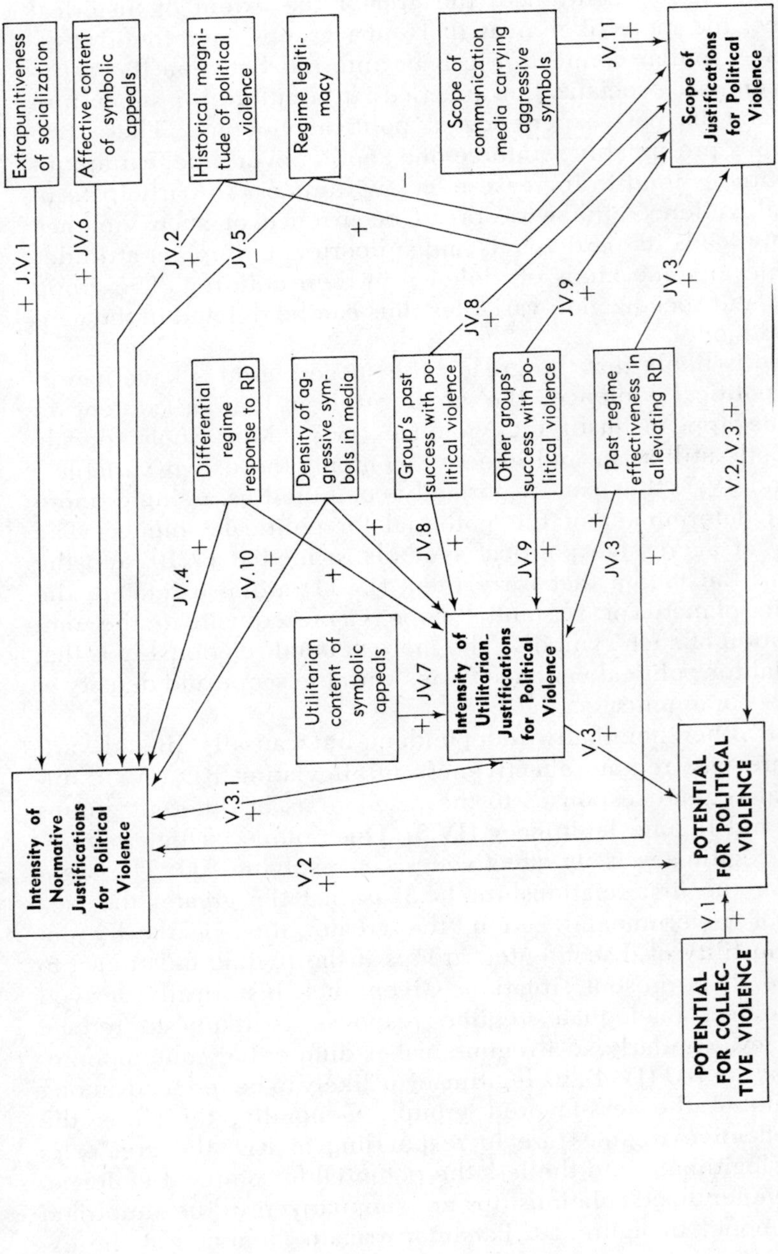

Figure 18. A complex causal model of the determinants of the potential for political violence.

Note: All variables are defined and discussed in preceding chapters. Hypotheses (denoted V.1, JV.3, etc.) and corollaries (denoted V.3.1, etc.) identify all causal relationships shown. See Appendix I.

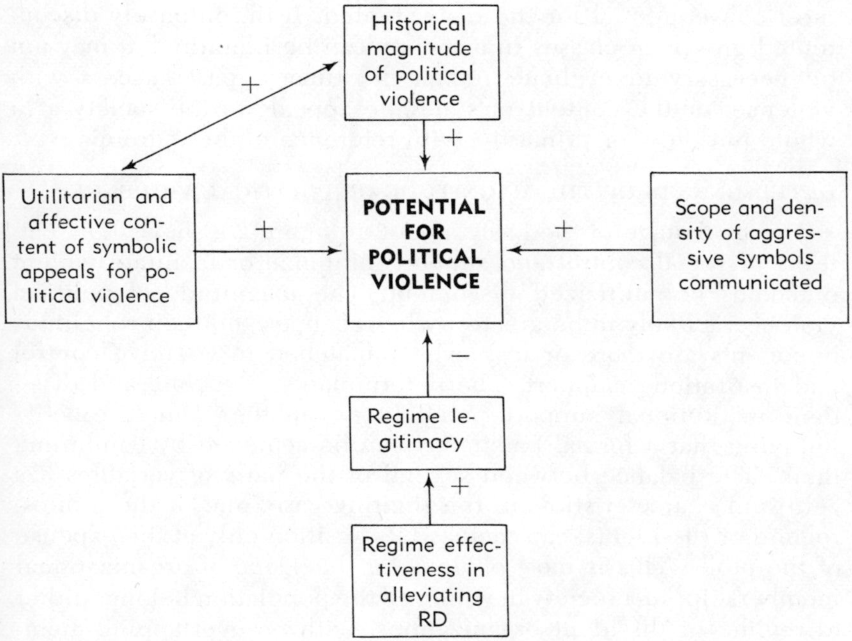

Figure 19. A simplified causal model of the societal determinants of the potential for political violence.

Note: This model is deduced from relationships inferred among the determinants of the scope and intensity of normative and utilitarian justifications for political violence, shown in figure 18 (see text). Variables are defined and discussed in preceding chapters. Hypotheses summarizing the relationships are not formally proposed but can be stated in terms analogous to the hypotheses developed in chapters 6 and 7. Potential for collective violence, a necessary precondition, is not shown; see Figure 18.

pense of information necessary for the interpretation of specific kinds of events.

The assessment of scope of justifications for political violence is crucial, whether the detailed or the generalized models are used as guides to analysis. The potential for political violence is greatest if discontented groups are also those who hold the greatest attitudinal justifications for violence. An understanding of the *forms* political violence takes in any society requires specific attention to the utilitarian attitudes of specific groups. Determining the scope of such attitudes is helped by specification of some of its determinents (figure 18) and by the fact that most of these determinants are also causes of the intensity of justifications; both can be evaluated simultaneously. Assessment may be further simplified if it is assumed, following corollary V.4.1, that justifications are most consequential for the discontented. If the intensely discontented groups or classes in a society can be identified, it may not be necessary to evaluate regime legitimacy, past success with violence, or the content of symbolic appeals in the society as a whole but only, or primarily, with reference to these groups.

DETERMINANTS OF THE MAGNITUDE OF POLITICAL VIOLENCE

The final stage of the basic model, in figure 20, shows how patterns of social control and support minimize or facilitate violent outcomes of politicized discontent. The magnitude of political violence is likely to be greatest when regimes and their rebellious opponents are more or less evenly matched in coercive control and institutional support. The determinants of regime and dissident institutional support parallel one another almost exactly, implying that a formal parsimony can be achieved by combining them. The balance between several of the pairs of variables has zero-sum characteristics: in the limiting case, one of the groups, regime or dissidents, can increase its position only at the expense of the other. This is most obvious for the scope of organizational membership: in a society in which all the population belongs either to regime or dissident organizations, with no overlapping memberships, the scope of dissident organizations is the obverse of regime organizations. The condition does not exist in the real world, however. There are always some, usually many, men whose primary and secondary memberships are in neutral or crosscutting institutions. The same limiting case holds for some scarce and inflexible types of goods (value stocks) like weaponry and transportation equipment. Dissidents and regimes can ordinarily increase their absolute and relative positions on the remaining three pairs of variables without direct effect on the position of the other—though by doing so, for example by expanding the number and scope of value opportunities, one side may indirectly affect the other by converting some of its followers, from loyalty to dissidence or vice versa.

There is less parallelism between the determinants of regime and dissident coercive control, because of the different functions and effects of coercion for regimes and for dissidents. The most important difference is that the higher the level of regime coercive activity and the more severe the sanctions it imposes, the greater the hostility of citizens affected. If coercive forces are very large and effective, and sanctions very severe, hostility tends to be repressed in the short run, thereby enhancing regime coercive control (RC.2,3). Dissidents, by contrast, ordinarily use their coercive capacities in group defense and in assaults on the regime and political opponents; consequently, dissident coercive capacity (DC.3) has a more or less uniformly positive effect in enhancing dissident coercive control. Two pairs of the determinants of coercive control are relatively direct counterparts of one another: the scope of population under regime and dissident surveillance (RC.1, DC.1) and the loyalty of regime forces to the political elite or to dissident leaders (RD.5, DC.4). One is not simply the obverse of the other, however. Some segments of a population may be subject to the control of neither side. Similarly, regime forces may be more or less disloyal to the ruling elite but neutral or even intensely hostile toward dissidents.

Important relationships hold among the two sets of determinants of regime control and support, and the determinants of dissident control and support. The complexity and cohesiveness of organizations (RI.2, DI.2) and the value opportunities (RI.4, DI.4) they provide their members are partly determined by their resources (value stocks, RI.3, DI.3). For dissident organizations, their means for antiregime action (DI.5) and the capacity of their military formations (DC.3) similarly depend in part on their resources (DI.3). The geographical concentration of dissidents in isolated areas (DC.2) tends to increase the scope of population in dissident organizations (DI.1) and under dissident surveillance (DC.1). For the regime, the size and resources of regime forces (RC.2) are partly a function of regime value stocks (RI.3). The capacity of those forces affects in turn the scope of population under regime surveillance (RC.1) and the consistency of regime sanctions (RC.5).

If these linkages among regime and dissident social control variables are combined with the zero-sum linkages between several pairs of regime and dissident variables specified above, it is possible to derive a simplified six-variable model of the structural determinants of magnitude of political violence, shown in figure 21. This parsimony is achieved at the expense of precision, of course. Such variables as the complexity and cohesiveness of organization and their value opportunities are only partly determined by organizational resources; eliminating them because of their partial dependency on value stocks precludes assessment of their independent effects. Similarly, the size of value stocks is only a limiting condition on coercive capacities; actual allocation of resources by ruling elites and dissidents to military activity varies widely within this limit. The simplified causal model may facilitate general comparative analysis; it is less appropriate for detailed comparative and case studies. Note that one independent variable, the severity of regime sanctions, is neither directly nor indirectly represented in the simplified model because its effects are curvilinear.

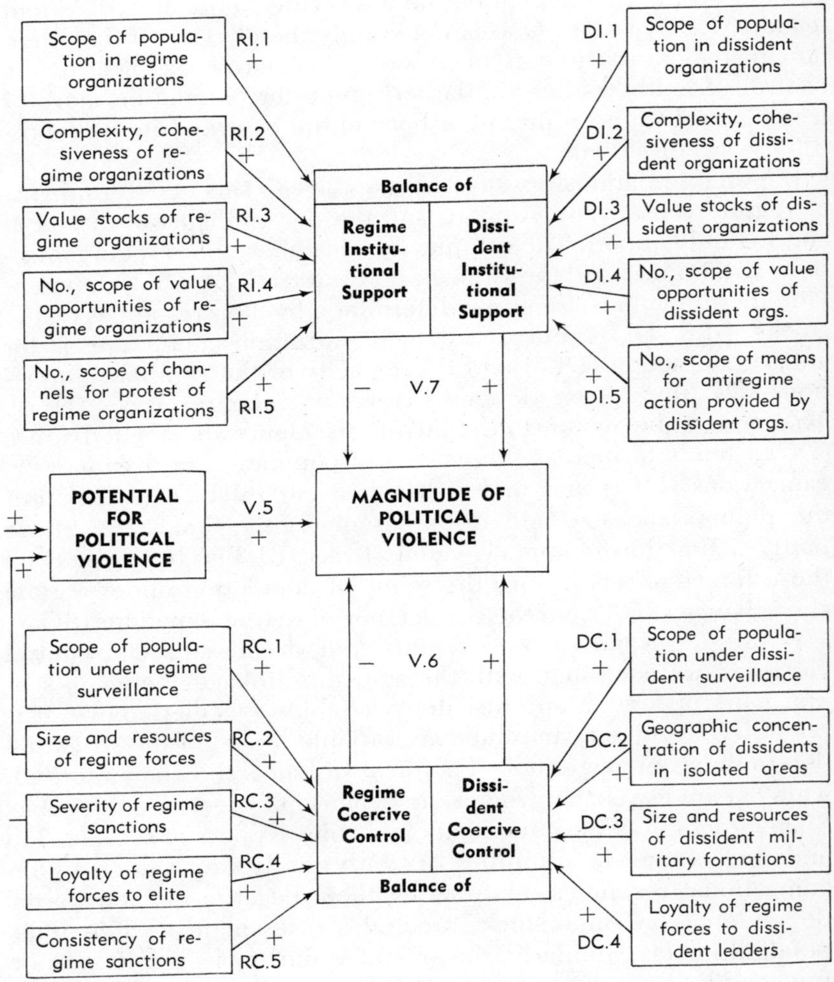

Figure 20. A causal model of the societal determinants of magnitude of political violence.

Note: All variables are defined and discussed in preceding chapters. Hypotheses (denoted RI.1, DI.1, etc.) identify all causal relationships shown, some of which are positive (+), some negative (—). See Appendix I.

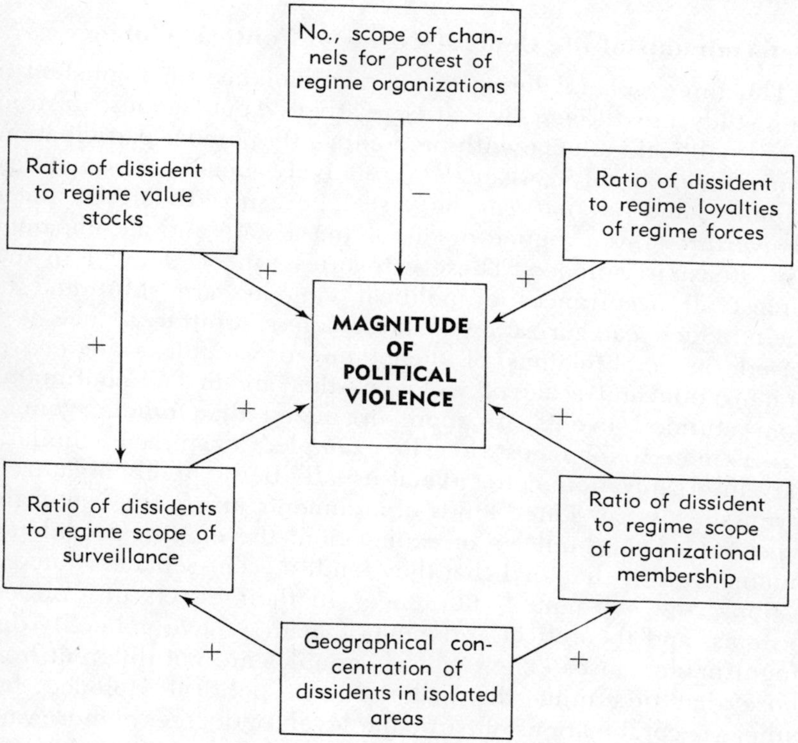

Figure 21. A simplified causal model of societal determinants of the magnitude of political violence.

Note: This model is deduced from relationships inferred among the determinants of the balance of regime and dissident institutional and coercive control, shown in figure 20 (see text). Variables are defined and discussed in preceding chapters. Hypotheses summarizing the relationships are not formally proposed but can be stated in terms analogous to the hypotheses developed in chapters 8 and 9.

One other simplification also is made; the ratios are shown to have linear rather than curvilinear effects on the magnitude of political violence. The assumption is that in the great majority of cases the scope of regime control and proportional regime value stocks equal or exceed those of dissidents. In those rare cases in which dissidents do have a substantial advantage over the regime, the relationships are reversed: magnitude of political violence is likely to decrease as the regime's capacity to resist declines. Here again, simplification is gained at the expense of applicability to some specific cases.

Determinants of the General Forms of Political Violence

The three general forms of political violence distinguished in this study are *turmoil*, which is relatively spontaneous, unstructured political violence with predominantly popular participation; *conspiracy*, highly organized, relatively small-scale political violence; and *internal war*, large-scale, organized violence aimed at overthrowing a regime or dissolving a state and accompanied by extensive violence. These categories can be defined so that almost all occurrences of political violence are subsumed by them.[4] Such categorization is nonetheless arbitrary, since it is based on combinations of dichotomized variables—degrees of organization and scale of violence—that are in fact continuous. Some turmoil events are more organized than others, general strikes more so than most riots, for example. Conspiracies similarly vary in organization, coups d'etat usually being highly organized, terrorism less so. Three kinds of arguments justify the use of the types as separate objects of explanation: the empirical evidence summarized in chapter 1 that they tend to occur separately among nations; the substantial differences in their effects on political systems; and theoretical arguments that they have generally distinguishable causes. Their causal variables are not different from those that determine the magnitude of political violence, but rather are combinations of particular levels or degrees of those variables. Some general effects of the balance of coercive control and institutional support on the likelihood of one or another form of violence are specified in chapters 8 and 9. The types and class incidence of RD also are systematically related to the forms of political violence, as the following arguments and hypotheses suggest. The determinants of the likelihood of the three forms are then summarized schematically and illustrated with several recent cases.

THE INCIDENCE OF RELATIVE DEPRIVATION AND THE FORMS OF VIOLENCE

Comparative studies summarized in chapter 1 suggest that in contemporary nations the three types of violence tend to occur independently. Nations in which internal wars are being fought usually have relatively little turmoil, for example, and nations with high levels of turmoil have relatively little conspiratorial

[4] A mutually exclusive set of subcategories of each of the three basic forms for use in empirical studies is reported in Ted Gurr with Charles Ruttenberg, *Cross-National Studies of Civil Violence* (Washington, D.C.: Center for Research on Social Systems, American University, 1969), Appendix A.

able to meet others working on the same tasks. The latter expressed stronger overt hostility towards the supervisor, presumably because they had a reference point independent of the frustrator and were more certain of their opinions.[30] Pepitone and Reichling formed highly cohesive and poorly cohesive groups, exposed them to an insulting lecture, and found that the more cohesive groups expressed more, and more direct, hostility than the others.[31] Similarly, French found that organized groups whose members had previously worked together expressed aggression more freely than groups of unorganized strangers.[32] A comparable phenomenon has been observed in recent experiments on decision-making, which suggest that under some conditions groups take considerably more risky decisions than would their members acting separately.[33] Some kinds of frustration apparently increase cohesion: Coser has proposed that hostility towards outgroups also contributes to the cohesion of the ingroup,[34] and Thibaut found that the cohesiveness of low-status groups was significantly increased in the face of continuing frustration.[35]

Evidence about collective action suggests the importance of high levels of interaction and group homogeneity in the facilitation of violence. Behavior in crowds, and in revolutionary organizations, is characterized by high and sometimes exclusive interaction among the members. In the development of revolutionary organizations, Hopper suggests, discontented people become aware of one another by participating in shared activity. "Their negative reactions to the basic factors in their situations are shared and begin to spread. . . . Discontent tends to become focalized and collective." This collective excitement "serves to integrate unrest and discontent, break down old behavior patterns, and prepare the way for new patterns of behavior."[36] The process is epitomized by a

[30] Ezra Stotland, "Peer Groups and Reactions to Power Figures," in Dorwin Cartwright, ed., *Studies in Social Power*, (Ann Arbor: Institute for Social Research, University of Michigan, 1959), 53–68, summarized in Berkowitz, *Aggression*, 81.

[31] A. Pepitone and G. Reichling, "Group Cohesiveness and the Expression of Hostility," *Human Relations*, VIII (No. 3, 1955), 327–37.

[32] J. R. P. French, Jr., "Organized and Unorganized Groups Under Fear and Frustration," *Authority and Frustration* (Iowa City: University of Iowa Studies in Child Welfare, Vol. XX, 1944), 231–308.

[33] See M. A. Wallach, N. Kogan, and D. G. Bem, "Diffusion of Responsibility and Level of Risk-Taking in Groups," *Journal of Abnormal and Social Psychology*, LXVIII (March 1964), 263–274.

[34] Lewis A. Coser, *The Functions of Social Conflict* (Glencoe: The Free Press, 1956), 87.

[35] J. W. Thibaut, "An Experimental Study of Cohesiveness of Underprivileged Groups," *Human Relations*, III (No. 3, 1950), 251–278.

[36] Rex D. Hopper, "The Revolutionary Process: A Frame of Reference for the Study of Revolutionary Movements," *Social Forces*, XXVIII (March 1950), 272–275.

for high value positions, whether or not they ha
those positions. In Western societies those char
include high degrees of intelligence, technical tra
ability, ambition, and skill in interpersonal dealings
prises those who have these characteristics in lesse
RD is perhaps most common among men who have
teristics but not high value positions—the intrinsic elite
term—for example the underemployed intelligentsia
veloped countries, and competent men and women ba
advancement by discriminatory barriers in Western s
Elite RD is also common among many members of extrinsi
political leaders barred from electoral activity, entrepr
subject to restrictive legislation, military officers given what
regard as inadequate resources.

The three hypotheses are based on the assumptions that le ership is essential for the development of organization, and th leadership skills are more likely to be found among elites, or a least among men with substantial experience in directing others' activities, than among others. The first assumption is all but true by definition, the second requires some documentation. Empirical studies of revolutionary leadership suggest that the substantial majority of leaders and cadres have come from the middle and upper socioeconomic strata of their societies. In a study of peasant participation in internal wars, AlRoy says that a pervasive characteristic is "their dependence upon nonpeasants for political, military, and other leadership skills, a dependence which increases with the increase in the scope of insurgencies." Almost no "peasant wars" or rural revolutionary movements have been led by peasants. Although some of their leaders had rural origins, like Jack Cade (leader of the English insurrection of 1450), Pugachev (leader of the Russian peasant's rebellion of 1772), and Mao Tse-tung, they had acquired substantial military or organizational experience before becoming revolutionary leaders.[5] Extensive studies of participation and leadership in the French Revolution show a dominance of professional people among the leaders, and of skilled workers and shopkeepers among the activists. Viles, analyzing the leadership of four revolutionary governments of Paris between 1789 and 1792, shows that between 70 and 100 percent of each were professionals, businessmen, or skilled trades-

[5] Gil Carl AlRoy, *The Involvement of Peasants in Internal Wars* (Princeton: Center of International Studies, Princeton University, Research Monograph No. 24, 1966), 16–19, quotation 16.

men, the professionals predominating.[6] Of some 1,300 members of Civil and Revolutionary Committees throughout France, and militants in other local revolutionary organizations, the great majority were minor merchants, shopkeepers, or artisans. Less than 7 percent were factory workers. "Grocers, publicans, cabinetmakers, tailors, shoemakers, hairdressers—these were the neighborhood revolutionaries." [7] The revolutionary millennarian leaders of medieval Europe were mostly members of the lower clergy and laymen with a cleric's education, "a frustrated and rather low-grade intelligentsia." [8] Revolutionary activists in Bengal during the first two decades of the twentieth century were almost all of high caste origin; 90 percent of persons convicted of or killed in the commission of "revolutionary crimes" between 1907 and 1917 were members of the three highest castes, which together formed less than 6 percent of the total population.[9] In Burma and Indonesia during the 1930s, the activists in Communist movements were drawn largely from the younger, nationalistically inclined members of the indigenous elite.[10]

Revolutionary leaders may be marginal, in the sense that they feel their social position and prospects for advancement precarious, but they seldom emerge from the lowest classes. A distinctive characteristic of revolutionary movements, and internal wars generally, is substantial participation by higher classes, especially at the leadership level. Brinton and the other scholars who have examined the classic European revolutions have emphasized that discontent was widespread not only among the common people but among large segments of the middle and upper classes. The "desertion of the intellectuals" has been repeatedly cited as a harbinger of revolution. Tilly shows that the armed crowds who participated in the Vendée counterrevolution of 1793 included peasants and artisans roughly in proportion to their distribution in the rural population, but also enlisted many members of the

[6] Perry Viles, "Participants and Elites in French Revolutionary Politics, 1789–1795" (Philadelphia: Foreign Policy Research Institute, University of Pennsylvania, 1968), dittoed.

[7] Data summarized in Charles Tilly, "Reflections on the Revolutions of Paris: An Essay on Recent Historical Writing," *Social Problems,* XII (Summer 1964), 113.

[8] Norman R. C. Cohn, *The Pursuit of the Millennium,* 2nd edn., rev. (New York: Harper, 1957, 1961), 318.

[9] Leonard A. Gordon, "Portrait of a Bengal Revolutionary," *Journal of Asian Studies,* XXVII (February 1968), 207.

[10] Ruth McVey, "The Southeast Asian Insurrectionary Movements," in Cyril E. Black and Thomas P. Thornton, eds., *Communism and Revolution: The Strategic Uses of Political Violence* (Princeton: Princeton University Press, 1964), especially 147–154.

bourgeoisie as well as some of the old elite.[11] Seton-Watson, in a general survey of twentieth-century revolutionary and conspiratorial movements, concludes that their leadership has come primarily from the intelligentsia, whatever their bases of popular support.[12] He also suggests, consistently with the preceding theoretical argument, that conspiratorial movements are most likely when the masses are "backward," by which he means their lack of consciousness of the modern world.

> As the masses become more prosperous, more skilled and more educated, broadly based mass movements became more possible, the leadership of intellectuals became less essential. . . . It is the combination of backward masses, extremist intellectuals and despotic bureaucrats which creates the most conspiratorial movements.[13]

Comparative evidence on differential class participation in types of political violence is provided by 1961–65 data on some 1,000 strife events. Working class groups were reported to have participated in about three out of four turmoil events and in all internal wars. "Middle class" groups participated in three out of five turmoil events (in most cases these participants were students), two of five conspiracies, and two of three internal wars. "Regime classes," including security forces and members of the political elite, almost never engaged in turmoil but took an active role in seven of ten conspiracies and half of the internal wars. In effect, turmoil in contemporary nations mobilizes the lower classes, but with a substantial leaven of middle-class participants. Conspiracy is very largely a regime and middle-class form of political opposition, internal war is likely to engage people from all socioeconomic classes.[14]

TYPES OF RELATIVE DEPRIVATION AND THE FORMS OF POLITICAL VIOLENCE

Revolutions and insurgencies typically are preceded by popular discontent over many issues: absolute or relative decline in economic conditions, breakdown of established patterns of com-

[11] Charles Tilly, *The Vendée* (Cambridge: Harvard University Press, 1964), 326–327. For a general survey of evidence on the nature of revolutionary leadership see Carl Leiden and Karl M. Schmitt, *The Politics of Violence: Revolution in the Modern World* (Englewood Cliffs, N.J.: Prentice-Hall, 1968), 75–89.

[12] Hugh Seton-Watson, "Twentieth Century Revolutions," *Political Quarterly*, XXII (July 1951), 263.

[13] *Ibid.*, 258.

[14] Based on data reported in greater detail in Ted Robert Gurr, "A Comparative Study of Civil Strife," in Hugh Davis Graham and Ted Robert Gurr, eds., *Violence*

munity organization and belief, the demonstrated incapacity of governments either to maintain social order or to take remedial action. Mosca writes that revolution is possible only if "the masses are stirred" by "great spiritual unrest,"[15] Johnson that multiple dysfunctions or disequilibria are necessary preconditions for revolutionary war.[16] I proposed in chapter 3 that the intensity of RD varies with the proportion of values affected (hypothesis ID.3). The suggestion here is that internal war is most likely if RD is intense with respect to a variety of values. A corollary relationship proposed in chapter 3 is that the salience or importance of a value tends to vary with the effort invested in it (corollary ID.2.2); unsatisfied expectations for values never attained contribute to discontent of less intensity than interference with an attained value position. The decremental and progressive patterns of deprivations described in Chapter 2 are thus likely to increase the potential for collective violence more than aspirational RD. The point is commonly made in the literature. Davies attributes revolution to progressive RD, i.e. to a decline in a nation's output of goods and services after a period of prolonged and more or less steady growth.[17] The central thesis of Soule's theory of revolution is that during periods of social change, rising classes attain increasing power of which the old elite attempts to deprive them; "revolutionary violence of importance occurs when those who have been thrust from power strive to regain it. It comes in defense of a revolution which has been made, or virtually made."[18] Chaplin, commenting on an unsuccessful peasant rebellion in Peru in 1965, observes that "peasants can be radicalized more easily by the threat of losing acquired gains than by simply raising their aspirations beyond their achievements."[19] These observations suggest two hypotheses about the types of RD that are likely to lead to internal war.

Hypothesis I.6: The likelihood of internal war varies with the proportion of value classes affected by intense relative deprivation.

---

in America: Historical and Comparative Perspectives (Washington, D. C.: National Commission on the Causes and Prevention of Violence, 1969), 443–495.

[15] Gaetano Mosca, *The Ruling Class*, trans. Hannah D. Kahn (New York: McGraw-Hill, 1896, 1939), 220.

[16] Chalmers Johnson, *Revolution and the Social System* (Stanford: Hoover Institution on War, Revolution and Peace, Stanford University, 1964).

[17] James C. Davies, "Toward a Theory of Revolution," *American Sociological Review*, XXVII (February 1962), 5–19.

[18] George Soule, *The Coming American Revolution* (New York: Macmillan, 1935), 70.

[19] David Chaplin, "Peru's Postponed Revolution," *World Politics*, XX (April 1968), 411.

Hypothesis I.7: The likelihood of internal war is greatest if relative deprivation is decremental or progressive, less if it is aspirational.

Hypothesis I.6 is supported by evidence gathered on the reported primary motives of participants in internal wars during 1961–65, in the cross-national study cited in preceding chapters. Multiple motives—political, economic, and social—were characteristic of almost all internal wars (see table 4, chapter 6). Initiators of turmoil events like riots, demonstrations, and political strikes ordinarily had fewer and more specific motives, for example taking action to oppose particular governmental policies or leaders, or to defend their community against an external threat.

One major qualification is needed to this argument. An analysis of the specific motives attributed to or voiced by conspirators suggests that they have an even narrower range of motives than participants in turmoil. Conspirators are substantially less likely to have publicly articulated economic or social motives than rioters, and are quite likely (in more than half of 343 conspiracy events identified) to be motivated primarily or exclusively by a desire for political power.[20] They may not necessarily want power for its own sake but as a base value for enhancing their status or economic well-being; Kling suggests that this is a principal motive for Latin American coups.[21] RD with respect to power values nonetheless seems empirically more common among conspirators than among participants in either of the other general forms of political violence. Moreover, the desire for participatory values, and specifically for control, is an especially salient one for elites, not for most other men. Evidence summarized in chapter 3 suggests that most men are more immediately concerned with attaining a minimally adequate standard of material well-being and maintaining stable familial and community relationships than they are with acquiring power (corollary ID.2.1). When they seek political participation it is seldom for its own sake but to defend their material and communal interests. Elites and those who aspire to formal elite status are most likely to seek control for its own sake; to the extent that conspirators have elite characteristics (hypothesis C.4), they are more likely than other groups to be motivated by frustrated desires for power. Two hypotheses about the forms of political violence are derived from these arguments.

[20] See Gurr, "A Comparative Study."

[21] Merle Kling, "Towards a Theory of Power and Political Instability in Latin America," *Western Political Quarterly*, IX (March 1956), 21–35.

Hypothesis T.5: The likelihood of turmoil varies inversely with proportion of value classes affected by intense relative deprivation.

Hypothesis C.5: The likelihood of conspiracy varies with the intensity of participatory value deprivation.

CAUSAL MODELS OF THE DETERMINANTS OF FORMS

The general conditions that maximize the likelihood of political turmoil are shown schematically in figure 23. If intense discontent is found among ordinary people but not the elite, and if that discontent extends to only a few conditions of life, the potential for riots and demonstrations is high but the potential for conspiracy or internal war is low (T.4, T.5). Whatever the incidence of RD, the likelihood of turmoil is high if the politically discontented are poorly organized (T.3) and the regime has high coercive capacities vis-à-vis them (T.1). If dissidents are concentrated in areas under close regime surveillance, for example in urban working-class districts, their opportunities either for developing effective opposition organizations or acquiring countervailing coercive capacities are low (T.2).

The potential for conspiratorial attacks on the regime is greatest, as shown in figure 24, if groups with elite characteristics are intensely discontented about their lack of political influence, but popular discontent is mild (C.4, C.5). Conspiratorial activities are best prosecuted if these dissatisfied elites can develop tight-knit organizations (C.2). Insofar as popular discontent is low (C.4) and regime suppression of oppositional activities severe (C.1), conspirators are unlikely to be able to expand the scope of their

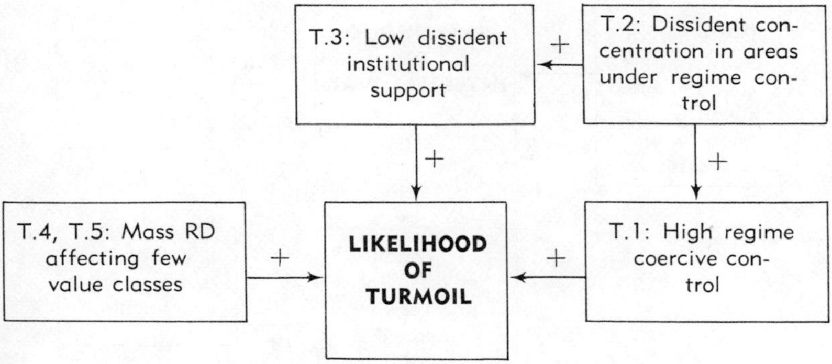

Figure 23. Conditions maximizing the likelihood of turmoil.

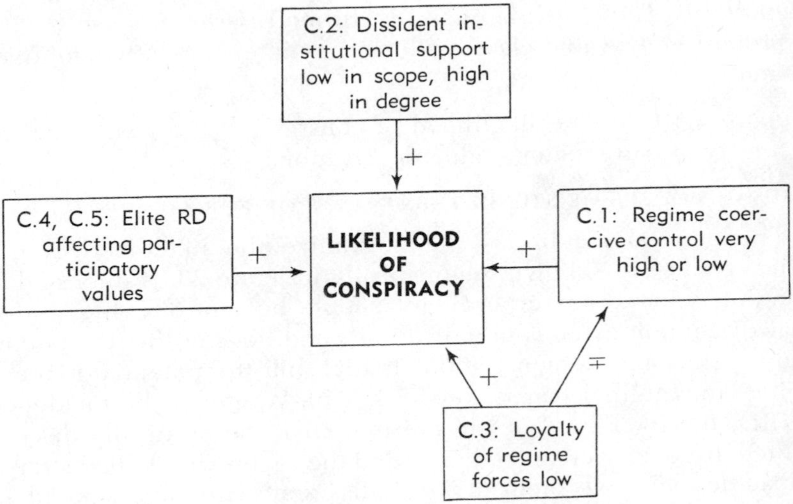

Figure 24. Conditions maximizing the likelihood of conspiracy.

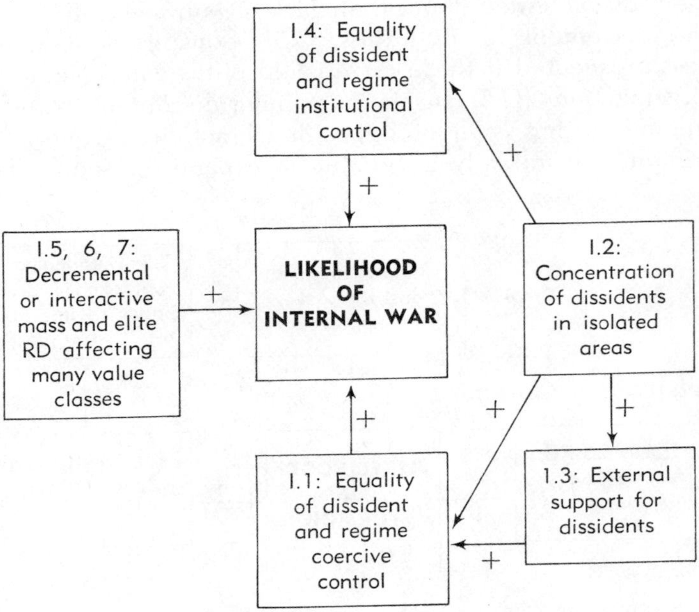

Figure 25. Conditions maximizing the likelihood of internal war.

institutional support. Their best chance for success in such circumstances is to convert regime forces to their cause (C.3). If they can enlist the loyalties of most or all those forces, or at least ensure their neutrality, regime coercive control is reduced to a low level and a successful coup d'etat is possible. If the regime forces are unshakably loyal to the ruling elite, the conspirators may resort to terrorism or small-scale guerrilla warfare with the tactical objectives of eroding regime strength over the long run and of increasing popular discontent, thus increasing the likelihood of internal war.

Mass revolutionary and secessionist movements are most likely to develop (figure 25) if discontent is widespread and intense among both elite and mass, the result of relative or absolute deterioration of many conditions of social existence (I.5, I.6, I.7). Turmoil and conspiratorial activity are likely to occur simultaneously during the period immediately after the development of such patterns of discontent; over the longer run there are likely to be concerted efforts by dissidents to establish or assume leadership of large-scale organizations, and to acquire military capacities that make concerted revolutionary action possible. The more closely their coercive and institutional capacities approach those of the regime, the more protracted and intense political violence is likely to be (I.1, I.4). Two structural conditions identified in chapter 8 have indirect effects on the likelihood of internal war. The concentration of dissidents in areas outside the sphere of effective regime control facilitates the expansion of both institutional support and coercive control by dissidents (I.2). The availability of foreign military and material support for dissidents is most easily provided if they control isolated base areas; if provided, it facilitates expansion of their coercive capacities (I.3).

These models are probabilistic, like all the models developed in this chapter: the variables specified do not wholly determine the likelihood that a particular form of political violence will occur. The differences among the forms are of degree—of organization and scale—not kind, as pointed out above. Moreover there are relatively few societal situations in which all the conditions specified for a particular form of violence hold. Mixed patterns are likely to characterize a given society at any given point in time. Insofar as those conditions vary over time, the probabilities of occurrence of a particular form of political violence can change. Several examples of pure and intermediate patterns of societal conditions illustrate the models, and some processes by which one form of violence can be transformed into another.

The conditions of black Americans in the early and mid-1960s approximated the "turmoil" model. Intense discontent was confined largely to the people of the urban ghettos and was a result principally of relative economic and status deprivation. Discontent was most intense among lower-class black Americans, less among the black bourgeoisie, most of whom were oriented toward white society and had more opportunities for personal mobility than less advantaged Negroes. Most Negro associations were concerned with the provision of value opportunities for their members; organizations whose leaders were committed to violent political opposition were nonexistent. The concentration of Negroes in the ghettos facilitated police control, which was relatively high despite its inconsistency (chapter 8). During the mid- and late 1960s the patterns of RD among blacks changed substantially, shifting toward those conditions necessary for internal war. Newly articulated beliefs in black pride and unity intensified the discontent of the black elite, as did the partial failure of political action through conventional channels. The failure of attempts to obtain prompt and adequate regime action to alleviate RD added political grievances to the economic and status discontents of all classes of Negro society. The initial pattern of police response to riots—lenient and vicious in turn, inconsistent throughout—further intensified discontent. None of the structural conditions that facilitate internal war have yet developed, however. Although many black organizations have been radicalized, regime coercive and institutional control remain high. A few clandestine radical organizations have been established, very small in membership but with the high degree of organization that facilitates defensive and offensive conspiratorial violence. But it appears highly unlikely that militant black organizations can obtain substantial foreign support, or develop a substantial degree of coercive control. The fact that black Americans comprise 12 percent of the population precludes the development of sufficient institutional support that might otherwise make protracted internal war possible. The most likely future forms of black political violence, consequently, are chronic turmoil and conspiracy, until and if the underlying discontents are resolved. If blacks do develop a substantial measure of institutional support and resources in the ghettos, as many black and some white leaders advocate, the likely long-range effect is a reduction of deprivation, by processes examined in chapter 9 and in the following section.

Cuba in 1957 provides an example of the "conspiracy" model, and an illustration of processes by which conspiracy can develop into a successful internal war. The most intensely discontented Cubans in the mid-1950s were students and bourgeoisie who had been deprived of political liberties and conventional means of political participation in 1952. Cuba was by no means a worker's paradise, but economic conditions for the people were better than in most of Latin America and improving; popular discontents over economic and political issues were considerable but not intense. Almost all the rebels who landed in Oriente Province in December 1956 were members of the politically discontented bourgeoisie, as were the men who attempted an abortive coup in Havana on March 13, 1957. The guerrilla movement established by the survivors of the Oriente landing was archtypical of conspiratorial organizations: small in membership—very small at first—but highly organized and tightly disciplined. The coercive capacities of the Batista regime were initially very high vis-à-vis the guerrillas, although not high enough to eliminate them. Thus of the five conditions said to determine the likelihood of conspiracy, four characterized Cuba in 1957. Successful guerrilla activity had several direct and indirect effects that shifted societal conditions toward those characteristic of internal war. First, the Batista regime became increasingly repressive in its political policies and terroristic in police and military tactics. The result was a substantial increase in decremental RD among the urban people and the peasants in the Sierra Maestra who bore the brunt of military reprisals. Consequently, more and more urban associations—unions, parties, student groups—shifted from a pro-Batista orientation toward neutrality and overt opposition in 1957 and 1958. The guerrilla movement gradually increased the scope of its control in rural areas. Militarily the guerrillas were never strong, having at most 1,500 men under arms at the end of 1958, but they used that force with such tactical brilliance—relative to the tactics of the regime—that military morale and loyalty declined precipitiously. Thus by the end of 1958, six of the seven conditions associated with internal war were present in Cuba: widespread and intense decremental RD affecting many values; concentration of effective, armed dissidents in areas outside the regime's sphere of control; and a balance of institutional support and coercive control between the regime and rebels that had rapidly shifted toward equality in the last part of the year. Batista, aware of the continuing shift of coercive control against him, fled the country rather than continue the war to its almost inevitable conclusion.[22]

The pattern of conditions preceding the Egyptian "revolution" of 1952 was intermediate between the conditions of conspiracy

[22] For a summary account of events preceding Fidel Castro's victory see Boris Goldenberg, *The Cuban Revolution and Latin America* (New York: Praeger, 1965), part II.

and of internal war. RD was characteristic of prerevolutionary situations: widespread and intense economic discontent, the result of a decaying seven-year cycle of boom and bust; interpersonal RD among the uprooted peasants who had migrated to the cities; and hostility toward an incompetent political regime among both mass and elite. The principal mass oppositional organization was the traditionalist Muslim Brotherhood, but neither it nor any other associational groups mobilized a large segment of the Egyptian people. Both regime and dissident institutional support were low in scope; the most highly organized sectors of Egyptian society were the bureaucracy and the military. The crucial condition in this case was the loyalty of the army. Turmoil was chronic in 1951 and 1952; the unwillingness or inability of the regime to control rioting in January 1952 is suggestive of a decline in regime coercive control. Most of the officer corps appears to have been neutral, their disaffection largely a result of the incompetent management of the Palestinian War of 1948, rather than positively disloyal. Nonetheless their neutrality made possible the success of the July 23 coup d'etat by the clandestine group of Free Officers, led by Colonel Nasser. The coup itself attracted widespread popular support, making it possible for the new regime to begin a largely peaceful socioeconomic transformation that promised solution of a revolutionary situation.[23]

The French general strike of May and June, 1968, provides a final example, this of the presence of conditions intermediate between those leading to turmoil and internal war. The incidence of RD appears more characteristic of turmoil than of internal war. Discontent was most intense among the students, whose primary demands were for massive political change. There was substantial but not generally intense economic discontent among many workers and farmers; the middle and upper classes were for the most part satisfied with if not enthusiastic about political and economic conditions. But the balance of institutional support favored revolution. If the leaders of the twelve million striking workers had been committed to revolutionary objectives and willing to cooperate with the students in pursuing those objectives, internal war could have been attempted. If worker discontent had been more intense, the regime less conciliatory, and revolutionary objectives more clearly formulated, they might have done so. The outcome of an internal war would ultimately have depended on the balance of coercive control. The dissidents had neither

[23] For a brief interpretation of the preconditions of the Egyptian revolution see Davies, 13–14. A fuller account of its preconditions and consequences is given in Leiden and Schmitt, chap. 9.

the base areas nor the external support that facilitate the development of military formations; their only hope of equalizing the coercive balance would have been to secure the loyalty or at least neutrality of the army and security forces. It is unlikely that they could have done so, given the hostility of the police toward the students and the commitment of the army to President de Gaulle. Men talked of revolution in France in the spring of 1968, and students thought they had begun one. Given the conditions of French society at that point in time it was unlikely to have developed beyond the stage of turmoil, even less likely to have succeeded had it done so.

Processes of Political Violence

Various models of the "revolutionary process" have been proposed, for example by Hopper, Brinton, and Schwartz.[24] The ten-stage model proposed by Schwartz is the most rigorously developed. The process is said to begin with political alienation, followed by the development of revolutionary organization, articulation of revolutionary appeals, a period of revolutionary coalition and movement-building, a subsequent period of nonviolent revolutionary politics, and then the outbreak of revolutionary violence. Four subsequent, postviolent stages also are identified.[25] Causal inference analyses of quantitative data have been used in attempts to determine the sequence of conditions contributing to political instability in Latin America. For example, Midlarsky and Tanter find evidence of a sequence in which foreign economic presence leads to increased levels of economic development which in turn leads to revolutionary violence.[26]

The analytic purposes of such models vary. Some, including those of Hopper and Brinton, and the sequences identified in causal inference analyses, are essentially descriptions of observed or inferred regularities. Nadel treats Brinton's statement of the

[24] Rex D. Hopper, "The Revolutionary Process: A Frame of Reference for the Study of Revolutionary Movements," *Social Forces*, XXVIII (March 1950), 270–279; Crane Brinton, *The Anatomy of Revolution* (New York: Norton, 1938); and David C. Schwartz, "A Theory of Revolutionary Behavior," in James C. Davies, ed., *When Men Revolt and Why* (New York: The Free Press, 1970). For other analyses of revolutionary processes see Lyford P. Edwards *The Natural History of Revolutions* (Chicago: University of Chicago Press, 1927); George S. Pettee, *The Process of Revolution* (New York: Harper, 1938); and Louis R. Gottschalk, "Causes of Revolution," *American Journal of Sociology*, L (July 1944), 1–9. A study of coup processes is Charles Wheatley, "Military Coups and Their Effects in Terms of Political Development" (Princeton: Center of International Studies, Princeton University, 1968).

[25] Schwartz.

[26] Midlarsky and Tanter; also see Putnam.

stages of revolution as a definition that can be used to determine whether other events are "revolution" and thereby to explain them.[27] Models like that of Schwartz have the implicit purpose of predicting consequences of particular conditions: if a certain set of conditions holds at time X, then specified consequences are likely at time Y. However they seldom take into account more than one or two conditions that might hold at time X; the conditions relevant at time X are not often said to be relevant at subsequent stages; and "feedback" effects of the occurrence of Y, or conditions associated with Y, on preceding stages are infrequently identified. In effect, they tend to analyze political violence as a one-way process. An attempt is made here to develop an abstract model that overcomes some of these limitations. One of its uses is to identify optimum strategies for regimes and their opponents, a use to which it is put in preliminary fashion beginning on p. 352.

A PROCESS MODEL

The process model shown in figure 26 assumes the existence of some potential for collective violence (discontent) in a political community at any given time. It is based on ten of the causal variables that seem most susceptible to short-term change by the efforts either of dissidents or ruling elites. It is not comprehensive, nor is it necessarily accurate; it is preliminary at best. Unrepresented variables such as the historical magnitude of political violence and rates of group value mobility also are susceptible to planned—and unplanned—change, but ordinarily change only gradually and are seldom the object of social engineering by ruling elites or dissidents. Eight of the ten causal variables used in the process model have simultaneous effects on two of the primary variables. It should be noted that the process model makes it possible both to assess the effects of various policies on the immediate potential for and magnitude of political violence, and to evaluate the effects of those policies on the potential for subsequent violence. The following paragraphs justify the relationships shown in the process model by reference to preceding theoretical arguments.

Given the existence of a potential for collective violence, dissidents can most easily focus it on political targets by articulating new symbolic appeals that offer justifications for political violence (JV.6, JV.7). Generalized discontent can simultaneously be in-

[27] George Nadel, "The Logic of the *Anatomy of Revolution*, with Reference to the Netherlands Revolt," *Comparative Studies in Society and History*, II (July 1960), 475–476.

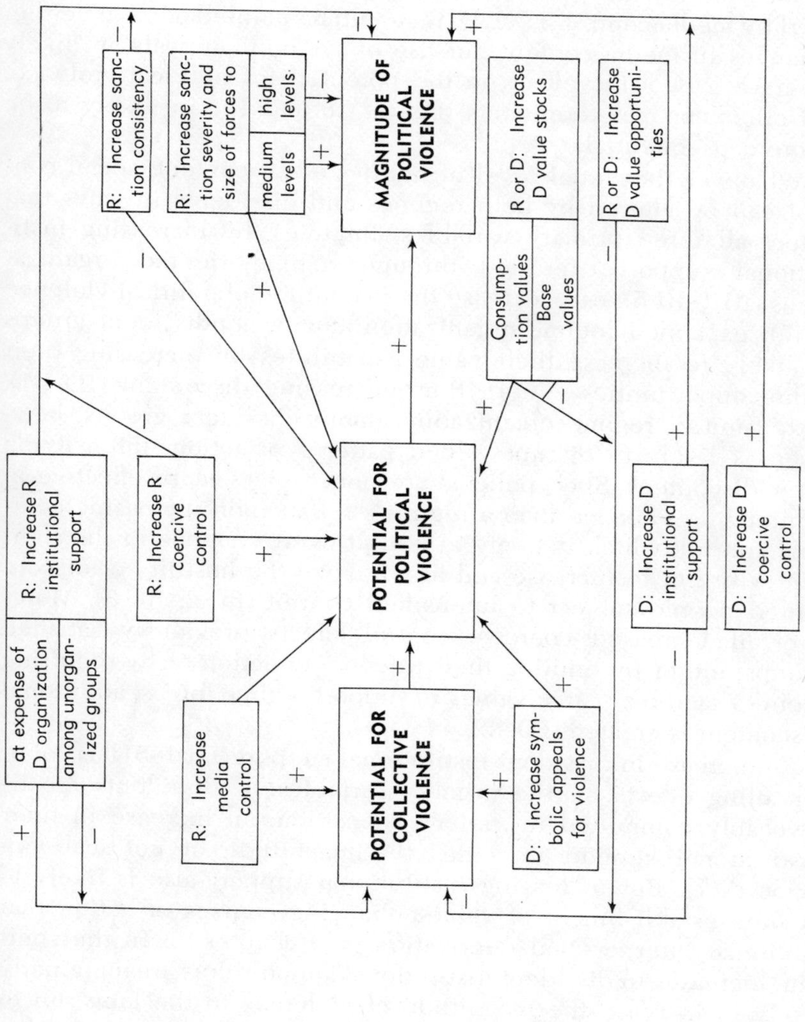

Figure 26. A process model of political violence showing some primary effects of alternative regime and dissident responses to the potential for and occurrence of violence. *Legend:* R = regime D = dissidents

creased to the extent that dissidents' appeals provide justifications for new or intensified expectations (ID.1, ID.2) and specify means for their attainment (VE.2). The most potentially effective short-term tactic at a regime's disposal for minimizing the politicization of discontent is to control the content of communications media (JV.10, JV.11), a policy that will increase discontent if freedom of expression is valued in the society (ID.2) and is significantly limited by media control (ID.1.1). It should be pointed out that neither changes in media content nor use of symbolic appeals are likely to have a decisive effect on the potential for political violence; its other major determinants (figures 18 and 19) are likely to be more consequential.

Whatever the initial level of politicized discontent, social control can be altered by both regimes and dissidents in ways that effect all three primary variables. Regimes, by increasing institutional support exercised through regime-oriented organizations (RI.1–RI.5), can decrease the magnitude of political violence (V.7); expanded regime organization among nondissident groups is likely to increase their value capabilities by increasing their value opportunities (VC.4), thus decreasing discontent (ID.1.1). Extension of regime organization among dissident groups, however, is likely to disrupt valued patterns of action, intensifying their discontent. Such policies are nonetheless more effective in minimizing violence than a regime's reliance on increasing coercive control, which is likely to inhibit overt violence in the short run (V.6) but to increase and to politicize the hostility of discontented people subject to intensified control (RC.2, RC.3). Moreover, if increased coercive control affects previously satisfied groups, either by limiting their freedom of action or by requiring them to sacrifice scarce values to support regime forces, additional discontent is created (ID.1.2).

An increase in dissident institutional support (DI.1–5) has countervailing effects on the primary variables. If dissidents are irrevocably committed to violent opposition, an increase in their institutional support increases the magnitude of political violence (V.7). But increasing institutional support also is likely to include establishment of value-enhancing courses of action that minimize interpersonal deprivation (see chapter 9). In the short run, increases in dissident institutional support thus are marginally likely to increase the magnitude of violence, in the long run to reduce the potential for collective violence. An increase in dissident coercive control (DC.1–DC.4) directly increases the magnitude of political violence (V.6), without significant feedback effects on other variables. (The curvilinear relationships proposed for the effects of the balance of coercive control and institutional support for regimes and dissidents in V.6 and V.7 are not taken into account in the process model, on the basis of the simplifying assumption that dissident control and support seldom exceed that of the regime. The curvilinear effect could readily be incorporated in a more complex process model.)

The actual occurrence of political violence can have disparate effects on the potential for future violence, varying with the degree of dissident success and the kinds of regime response to it. Regimes' basic options in the face of political violence are to increase coercive measures, or to meet some or all dissident demands. If regimes increase their forces and the severity of sanctions to very high levels, they tend to deter men from political violence in the short run but also are likely to intensify and extend the duration of discontent (ID.5), create new discontent among the people directly affected (RC.2, RC.3), increase their will to resist (chapter 8), and provide highly visible objects for attack (chapter 6). If forces and sanctions are increased only to medium levels, the effects are usually dysfunctional for the regime. Medium force levels intensify dissidents' discontent and will to resist but are not likely to deter them (RC.2, RC.3). If regimes increase the consistency with which sanctions are applied, however, the consequent increase in certainty of retribution is likely to deter dissidents (RC.5) and to enhance regime legitimacy, thereby reducing the potential for further political violence (JV.5).

Dissidents may "succeed" through political violence in defending threatened values successfully or seizing new values, or in obtaining concessions and benefits. If the resources (value stocks) dissidents obtain are consumption values, i.e. resources used to satisfy immediate deprivation rather than to generate additional resources, the beneficiaries are reinforced in their disposition to resort to violence again when the resources are exhausted (JV.8). If the resources obtained are base values, ones that the dissidents can use to create new value opportunities and goods, the potential for collective violence is reduced (VC.1, VC.4, ID.1.1). The same argument applies to increases in dissident value opportunities obtained through violence: the effect is an increase in value capabilities and a consequent reduction in discontent.

This exercise in "if-then" can be concluded by suggesting optimum strategies for social action by men with conservative and revolutionary motives. In a society characterized by intense levels of discontent, three rather different kinds of motives with respect to political violence are likely to be found. The primary motive of the incumbent political elite is usually to minimize violence and maximize order in both the short and long run. The most intensely discontented dissidents probably want to maximize violence in satisfaction of their anger, however they may rationalize the impulse. Other dissidents, including many of the less intensely discontented and the moralists, are likely to want to minimize RD more than to act out their anger for its own sake; their motivations are primarily instrumental. The process model and the general causal models suggest optimum policies for each of these groups.

A STRATEGY FOR INCUMBENTS

The objective attributed here to the typical incumbent elite is to maintain stability, whether or not it maximizes the satisfactions of other citizens. To minimize the potential for collective violence, these are the kinds of alternatives open to it: first, to minimize change in group value positions, in other words to maintain the status quo in the distribution of social, economic, and political goods. If the elite is committed to progress, or willy nilly caught up in it, the benefits of that progress should be evenly distributed. No group, at least no discontented group, should gain less rapidly than others. Limited resources may preclude significant progress for all groups; or developmental policy may dictate that an entrepreneurial or bureaucratic class get more of what there is to get. In the face of such necessities, discontent can be reduced by increasing the number and scope of value opportunities for the less advantaged groups. People who have little can be satisfied at least temporarily if they have the means to work toward their goals —if they have a degree of control over their resources and destinies, if they can acquire the skills they need to advance themselves, if they face no discriminatory barriers to progress. The opportunities must have at least some payoff, of course. If they do not, hopes soured have more devastating effects for stability than hopes never pursued.

Even if discontent is widespread, a ruling elite can reduce the likelihood of violence against itself by symbolically reinforcing its legitimacy, censoring those who agitate against it, and providing diversionary means for the expression of hostility. Concessions to the discontented help also, but they must be equitably distributed among all the discontented, on pain of antagonizing those who get little: concessions are most effective if they contribute to the capacity of the discontented to help themselves.

If politicized discontent is relatively mild, the optimum pattern for maintaining coercive control is to minimize the men and resources devoted to internal security, and to apply sanctions with both consistency and leniency. If discontent is severe, consistency of sanctions is even more essential; sanctions applied randomly or inequitably are certain to intensify opposition. The combination of leniency and minimal surveillance will not deter intensely angered men, however, and without close surveillance no consistent sanctions can be imposed against them. The best strategy then is to maximize surveillance but to maintain a policy of relative leniency. Such a policy is likely to increase hostility to a lesser degree than maximum surveillance and severe sanctions in combination. It also is likely to "keep the lid on" long enough so that remedial action can be taken. The courses of remedial action include the judicious distribution of goods and means outlined above. They also include the establishment or expansion of effective organizational frameworks in which those goods and opportunities can be put to work, and provision of regular channels for expressing and remedying grievances.

A STRATEGY FOR REVOLUTIONARIES

The "revolutionary" motive assumed here is the violent destruction of the old order, a motive that is almost always rooted in an irreconcilable hatred of the old that is best satisfied by violence. There may be good utilitarian reasons for such a motive as well: some ruling elites are adamantly opposed to change, responding with unmitigated repression to expressions of popular discontent. In such circumstances dissidents are likely to have only two options: acquiescence or revolution. The regime that responds to their demands only with suppression will intensify their hostility, and is thus likely to speed its own destruction. The tactics outlined here for revolutionaries are those most likely to ensure that destruction.

If discontent is intense and widespread in a society, revolutionary tasks are simplified; if not, there are means by which it can be increased. Ideological appeals offer the best means, to the extent that their content is designed to justify new aspirations and specify means toward their attainment. Any relatively disadvantaged group is a potential audience for such appeals. The existence of objective deprivation is far from being a sufficient condition for the effectiveness of appeals, however. The groups most likely to respond are those that already have been exposed to change and are already discontented with some aspect of their lives. One of the best indicators of a potential for conversion to revolutionary expectations is group experience of absolute decline in value position; such a decline indicates more certainly the existence of discontent than a neo-Marxian judgment that group members ought to be discontented because they have less than others. Relatively disadvantaged people who have recently begun to interact with more prosperous groups, or who have been regularly in contact with such groups and regularly subordinated, also are susceptible to conversion. The closer their association with more advantaged groups, and the less their objective (and subjective) opportunities for improving their own status, the more easily they can be persuaded of the justifiability of aspirations for a better life and the necessity for revolutionary action to attain it. Subordinated urban classes, new migrants to cities, and people on the margins of expanding modern economies make better potential recruits for revolutionary movements than rural peoples still caught in the unchanging web of traditional life.

The most effective revolutionary appeals offer means and justifications that are compatible with the discontents and cultural experience of their potential audience. They facilitate revolutionary violence insofar as they convince their listeners that the ruling elite is responsible for discontent, unwilling and unable to alleviate it, and committed to policies that victimize the oppressed. The symbolic and manifest demonstration that revolutionary violence can be carried out and can be successful reinforces appeals' effectiveness. The revolutionary cause is enhanced if the regime can be induced to take repressive action that confirms such ideological assertions. The fact of violent revolutionary agitation often impels such action: media may be censored, civil liberties restricted, dissident leaders jailed and their organizations suppressed, public benefits diverted from dissident followers. The short-range effect of such policies may be to minimize the dissident capacity for action; the more enduring effect is to confirm the accuracy of revolutionary appeals, thus justifying more intense opposition in the future.

Unless a regime is very weak, it is incumbent on revolutionaries to organize for group defense and eventual assault. Organization should be flexible enough to adapt to and survive regime repression, broad enough in scope so that it can mobilize large numbers of people for action or at least make it difficult for them to support the regime. Organizational resources should be devoted primarily to coercive means and to agitational activities rather than the satisfaction of the material deprivations of leaders and their followers. Dissident organizations otherwise tend to become ends in themselves, providing intrinsic satisfactions that blunt the revolutionary impulse. Participation in revolutionary organization should provide sufficient interpersonal values—especially the sense of comradeship and shared purpose—to ensure the enduring commitment of followers, but require enough sacrifices in the service of its long-range purposes to justify and intensify continued opposition to the regime. It must also provide, of course, some minimum of security for its followers; they must feel that they have a fair chance of survival as well as of success. The coercive capacities of revolutionaries can be enhanced by subversion or demoralization of regime forces, solicitation of external support, and establishment of isolated base areas among sympathizers—to the extent that such tactics are feasible.

The trump card of revolutionaries is violence itself. Even if their coercive capacities are low relative to the regime, selective terrorism can be used to demonstrate the incapacity of the regime to defend its citizens. Such terrorism is dysfunctional to the revolutionary cause if it affects neutral or innocent people; it is more effective if directed against those who are widely disliked. Violence is most effective if it invites severe but inconsistent retaliatory responses by the regime, which have the effect of alienating those who might otherwise support the elite. Open revolutionary warfare is the final tactic of revolutionaries, but is difficult to organize in the modern state, extraordinarily costly, and uncertain of success. It is a last resort against strong regimes, an unnecessary one against weak ones, a first resort only when regimes are already weakening and revolutionary capabilities high.

A STRATEGY FOR THE DISCONTENTED

Most discontented men are not revolutionaries. They may be angry, but most of them probably prefer peaceful means for the attainment of their goals to the privations and risks of revolutionary action. Assuming that their primary motive is to increase their well-being rather than to satisfy anger through violence, their optimum strategy lies intermediate between those of elites who would maintain order and of revolutionaries who would destroy that order to establish a new one. The discontented are not likely to be concerned with minimizing or equalizing rates of group progress, tactics that regimes might choose to use, or with intensifying discontent. Their objective is to improve their own lot as much as possible. To do so they must seek new means and resources. Political violence is not thereby excluded from their repertory of tactics towards that end; given their circumstances, some violence may be necessary. But one of their primary tactical concerns, whether or not they resort to violence, is to minimize retaliatory action in response to their actions.

Given the existence of a potential for collective violence, the optimum policy of the discontented is not to increase the potential for political violence as such but to put the potential to constructive purposes. The symbolic appeals of dissident leaders should be of two kinds, one set designed to mobilize potential followers, another to justify their claims to the regime and the social groups from which they are most likely to gain concessions. Limited political violence in such a context has several uses. It can dramatize claims, provide an outlet for the hostility of followers and thereby enhance institutional support for dissident organizations, and may signal to the regime the threat of more disruptive violence if claims are not met. But it is a risky tactic, more risky in some political systems than others. Violence tends to stimulate counter-violence, a principle that applies to both dissidents and their opponents. The threat of violence has the same effect. A regime so challenged may consequently devote more resources to coercive control than to remedial action. The obligation on dissident leaders is therefore to be as careful and judicious in the use of violence as elites must be in their use of counter-force. Perhaps the best tactic of leaders of dissident groups, if violence occurs at all, is to represent it as the excesses of their followers, whom they are capable of controlling if provided with concessions.

The extent to which leaders can in fact control the actions of their followers, and make effective use of whatever means and resources they obtain, is determined by their degree of institutional support. Whereas the first task of revolutionaries is to intensify discontent and focus it on the political system, the most essential task of pragmatic dissidents thus is to organize: to expand the scope of their organizations, elaborate their internal structure, develop the sense and fact of common purpose, and maximize the use of their collective resources, not for violent action but for value-enhancing action. The establishment of such organizations can provide many intrinsic satisfactions for members: a sense of control over their own affairs, a feeling of community and purpose, status for leaders and security for followers. Such organizations are much more likely than unorganized collectivities to take effective political action, to get whatever can be gotten through conventional political bargaining processes. If token violence is to be used in a calculated risk to increase bargaining power, it can be most effectively used if institutional support is high. Most important, whatever value opportunities and resources are obtained, through bargaining or otherwise, are most efficiently used to satisfy discontents in a well-developed organizational context.

If dissident organizations are effective in devising means and obtaining resources for remedial action, they will seldom remain long in opposition. They are likely to become firmly fixed in the existing political order, their leaders incorporated in its ruling elite. But if regimes are adamantly hostile and repressive in the face of the claims of dissident organizations, as they are in too many nations, those organizational capacities can be turned to revolutionary ends. If revolution is accomplished, the result is ultimately the same: dissident leaders become the elite of the new order they have established, their organizations the backbone of that order, and their followers, those who survive, the new loyalists. The dissidents can best judge if the costs of such a course are worth the gains; theirs are the lives at stake.

Conclusion

The theoretical models developed in this analysis are not intended to provide a ready-made explanation of any given act of political violence. My intention has been to make a reasonably parsimonious synthesis of the diverse speculation and evidence about the origins, extent, and forms of group violence in politics, and to do so in a way that contributes to deductive and empirical inquiry in the service of better theory. From one epistemological point of view, the logical coherence, parsimony, and elegance of a theory are the criteria by which its adequacy is judged; its accuracy is both indeterminate and inconsequential. There is however a compelling need in the real world to be able to anticipate political violence and the consequences of various responses to it, a need common to rebels, incumbents, and those who simply want to live their lives in peace. Where I have faced what seemed to be a choice between "telling it as it seems to be" and the dictates of coherence, parsimony, or elegance, I have chosen the first on grounds that, given the present inadequacy of and need for systematic understanding of violence, it is the more fruitful and useful course. Refinement of the theoretical statements proposed here is as much needed as their deductive extension and empirical evaluation. From this point, however, the processes should proceed together rather than separately, as they have too often in the past.

If the central theoretical arguments are essentially accurate, some kinds of interpretations of the nature of political violence are demonstrably inadequate, in a scientific sense and in the efficacy of policies based upon them. There is not much support here for the view that political violence is primarily a recourse of vicious, criminal, deviant, ignorant, or undersocialized people. Men and women of every social background, acting in the context of every kind of social group on an infinite variety of motives, have resorted to violence against their rulers. Nor is political violence "caused" by pernicious doctrines, or at least by doctrines alone. Discontented men are much more susceptible to conversion to new beliefs than contented men. Not all new beliefs provide justifications for violence, and most that do are derived from peoples' own cultural and historical experience rather than alien sources. The belief that some kinds of social arrangements or political institutions are intrinsically immune from violence or capable of satisfying all human desires is only a partial truth. Disruptive violence can and has occurred in every twentieth-century political community. No pattern of coercive control, however intense and consistent, is likely to deter permanently all enraged men from violence, except genocide. No extant or utopian pattern of social and political engineering seems capable of satisfying all human aspirations and resolving all human discontents, short of biological modification of the species.

Political violence is not uniformly and irretrievably destructive of human well-being. Many groups have resorted to political violence at one stage or another in their historical development with positive long-range results: the resolution of divisive conflicts, defense of threatened interests, and attainment of means by which their members could work effectively and peacefully toward their own security and well-being. There is even less support for the revolutionary view that violence has a special efficacy unmatched by other means, or for the precisely comparable contention of conservative authoritarians that massive force is the best means for maintaining order. Violence inspires counter-violence by those against whom it is directed. It consumes scarce resources that could otherwise be used to satisfy aspirations. Worst of all it consumes men, its victims physically, its practitioners mentally, by habituating them to violence as the means and end of life. The more intense and widespread the use of force the less likely are those who use it, rebels or regimes, to achieve their objectives except through total victory. In view of the resources available to modern governments and modern revolutionary movements, total victory is highly likely to be pyrrhic victory.

Some conventional wisdom about the means to the resolution of violent conflict is also fallacious. Coercion alone is demonstrably ineffective, in the long run if not the short, because on balance it is more likely to inspire resistance than compliance. The assumption that discontent has primarily physical origins, hence that satisfaction of material aspirations is its cure, is no more accurate. Men aspire to many other conditions of life than physical well-being, not the least of which are security, status, a sense of community, and the right to manage their own affairs. If basic physical needs are met, provision for these aspirations is at least as important as increased material well-being for minimizing violence. If men have substantially more physical resources than status or freedom, they may well use the former to gain the latter, by violent means if necessary. There also is a fallacy in the assumption that all wants must be satisfied to minimize discontent. Discontent is not a function of the discrepancy between what men want and what they have, but between what they want and what they believe they are capable of attaining. If their means are few or threatened, they are likely to revolt; if they obtain new means they can work to satisfy their wants. Concessions also can have unintended effects, however. Temporary palliatives are likely to reinforce a return to violence once their narcotic effect wears off. If men fight to preserve what they have, concessions that remove the threat to it are sufficient. If they rebel to satisfy new or intensified expectations, the only effective concession is to provide them with means adequate to those expectations.

Men's resort to political violence is in part unreasoning, but does not occur without reason. Ignorance is almost always among its causes: sometimes ignorance of its consequences by those who resort to it, more often ignorance by those who create and maintain the social conditions that inspire it. But political violence is comprehensible, which should make it neither necessary nor inevitable, but capable of resolution.

Appendix: Summary List of Hypotheses and Corollaries

NOTE: The hypotheses are listed according to their dependent variable corollaries appear after the hypotheses they qualify. Hypotheses specifying relationships among primary and secondary variables, and the determinants of the forms of political violence, are designated by a single-letter prefix, e.g. V.1, T.3. Hypotheses specifying determinants of the secondary variables are designated by a two-letter prefix, e.g. ID.1, DI.2. Corollary relationships are shown by adding a number following the hypothesis number, e.g. C:ID.3.1 is a corollary to hypothesis H:ID.3.

The number in parentheses after each hypothesis and corollary indicates the chapter in which it is proposed.

Linkages Among Primary and Secondary Variables

H:V.1: The potential for collective violence varies strongly with the intensity and scope of relative deprivation (RD) among members of a collectivity. (2)

H:V.2: The potential for political violence varies strongly with the intensity and scope of normative justifications for political violence among members of a collectivity. (6)

H:V.3: The potential for political violence varies strongly with the intensity and scope of utilitarian justifications for political violence among members of a collectivity. (6)

C:V.3.1: The intensity and scope of normative justifications for political violence vary strongly with the intensity and scope of utilitarian justifications for political violence in a collectivity. (6)

H:V.4: The potential for specifically political violence varies strongly with the potential for collective violence generally. (6)

C:V.4.1: The greater the intensity and scope of RD, the stronger the relationship between the intensity and scope of normative and utilitarian justifications for political violence and the magnitude of political violence. (6)

H:V.5: The magnitude of political violence varies strongly with the potential for political violence. (8)

H:V.6: The magnitude of political violence varies strongly and directly with the ratio of dissident coercive control to regime coercive control to the point of equality, and inversely beyond it. (8)

H:V.7: The magnitude of political violence varies strongly and directly with the ratio of dissident institutional support to regime institutional support to the point of equality, and inversely beyond it. (9)

Determinants of the Intensity of Relative Deprivation

H:ID.1: The intensity of RD varies strongly with the average degree of perceived discrepancy between value expectations and value capabilities. (3)

C:ID.1.1: Any increase in the average level of value expectations in a collectivity without an accompanying increase in value capabilities increases the intensity of RD. (3)

C:ID.1.2: Any decrease in the average level of value capabilities in a collectivity without an accompanying decrease in value expectations increases the intensity of RD. (3)

H:ID.2: The intensity of RD varies strongly with the average salience of the value class with respect to which discrepancy is experienced. (3)

C:ID.2.1: In any heterogeneous population, the intensity of RD is greatest with respect to discrepancy affecting economic values, less with respect to security and communality values, least with respect to participation, self-realization, status, or ideational coherence values. (3)

C:ID.2.2: The salience of a value tends to vary with the average effort invested in attaining or maintaining the desired position on that value. (3)

C:ID.2.3: In instances of aspirational deprivation, the salience of a value tends to vary with the perceived closeness of the desired value position at the time discrepancy is first experienced. (3)

H:ID.3: The intensity of RD varies moderately with the proportion of value classes with respect to which discrepancy is experienced. (3)

C:ID.3.1: The greater the intensity of RD with respect to welfare, power, status, and communal values, the greater the likely decline in ideational coherence. (5)

H:ID.4: The intensity of RD varies strongly with the proportion of value opportunities with which interference is experienced or anticipated. (3)

C:ID.4.1: The intensity of RD varies moderately with the number of actively pursued value opportunities with which interference is experienced or anticipated. (3)

H:ID.5: The intensity of RD varies curvilinearly over time following the onset of discrepancy. (3)

C:ID.5.1: The greater the salience of the value affected by discrepancy, the longer RD persists. (3)

Determinants of Group Value Expectations

H:VE.1: The susceptibility of a group to conversion to rising value expectations through symbolic exposure to a new mode of life varies strongly with the intensity and scope of preexisting RD in the group. (4)

H:VE.2: The susceptibility of groups to conversion to rising value expectations varies moderately with the perceived availability of value opportunities for attaining those expectations. (4)

H:VE.3: The rate at which group value expectations rise varies strongly with the rate of value gain of the most rapidly gaining group of similar socioeconomic status. (4)

H:VE.4: The rate at which group value expectations for a discrepantly low value raises varies moderately with the extent to which the discrepant value is a primary base value for other values. (4)

H:VE.5: The rate at which group value expectations rise varies strongly with the rate and duration of the group's past value gains, except for groups with maximum value positions. (4)

C:VE.5.1: Marginal increases in value capabilities among deprived groups tend to increase the salience of the groups' value expectations. (4)

Determinants of Group Value Capabilities

H:VC.1: Perceived value capabilities vary strongly with the extent to which value stocks in a society are perceived to be flexible. (5)

H:VC.2: To the extent that the stock of any value in a society is perceived to be inflexible, perceived group capabilities for that value vary strongly and inversely with upward mobility of other groups on that value. (5)

H:VC.3: Perceived value capabilities vary strongly and inversely with the rate of a group's past experience of value loss. (5)

H:VC.4: Perceived value capabilities vary strongly with the number and range of value opportunities open to a group's members. (5)

C:VC.4.1: The greater the rate of expansion of value stocks in a society, the greater the intensity of RD among groups with differentially low value opportunities. (5)

Determinants of Justifications for Political Violence

H:JV.1: The intensity of normative justifications for political violence varies moderately with the degree of emphasis placed on extrapunitiveness in socialization. (6)

H:JV.2: The intensity and scope of normative justifications for political violence vary strongly with the historical magnitude of political violence in a collectivity. (6)

C:JV.2.1: The more frequent the occurrence of a particular form of political violence in a collectivity, the greater the expectation that it will recur. (6)

C:JV.2.2: If expectancy of violence is great, the intensity and scope of normative justifications for political violence vary strongly with the intensity and scope of RD. (6)

H:JV.3: The intensity and scope of normative and utilitarian justifications for political violence vary moderately with the effectiveness and scope of past regime action in alleviating RD. (6)

H:JV.4: The intensity of normative and utilitarian justifications for political violence varies moderately with the proportional difference in allocation of regime resources to the alleviation of the RD of different groups. (6)

H:JV.5: The intensity and scope of normative justifications for political violence vary strongly and inversely with the intensity and scope of regime legitimacy. (6)

H:JV.6: The intensity of normative justifications for political violence varies strongly with the extent to which symbolic appeals offer plausible explanations of the sources of RD, identify political targets for violence, and provide symbols of group identification. (7)

H:JV.7: The intensity of utilitarian justifications for political violence varies moderately with the degree to which new symbolic appeals prescribe political violence as an effective value opportunity for increasing value positions. (7)

H:JV.8: The intensity and scope of utilitarian justifications for political violence vary strongly with the extent to which a collectivity has increased its average value position in the past through political violence. (7)

H:JV.9: The intensity and scope of utilitarian justifications for political violence in a collectivity vary moderately with the extent to which similar collectivities elsewhere are thought to have increased their average value positions through political violence. (7)

H:JV.10: The intensity of normative and utilitarian justifications for political violence varies moderately with the density of aggressive political symbols in communication content. (7)

H:JV.11: To the extent that the density of aggressive symbols in communication content is high, the scope of normative and utilitarian justifications for political violence varies strongly with the number and scope of communication media. (7)

Determinants of Regime Coercive Control

H:RC.1: Regime coercive control varies moderately with the proportion of its population subject to regular surveillance and deterrence. (8)

H:RC.2: Regime coercive control varies curvilinearly with the size and the resources of its military and internal security forces, control being lowest when size and resources are at intermediate levels. (8)

H:RC.3: Regime coercive control varies curvilinearly with the severity of regime-administered negative sanctions, control being lowest when severity is at intermediate levels. (8)

H:RC.4: Regime coercive control varies strongly with the loyalty of coercive forces to the regime. (8)

H:RC.5: Regime coercive control varies strongly with the consistency of regime-administered negative sanctions. (8)

Determinants of Dissident Coercive Control

H:DC.1: Dissident coercive control varies moderately with the proportion of a population subject to their regular surveillance and deterrence. (8)

H:DC.2: Dissident coercive control varies strongly with the extent to which dissidents are geographically concentrated in areas to which regime forces have limited access. (8)

H:DC.3: Dissident coercive control varies strongly with the size, training, and resources of its military formations relative to the size, training, and resources of regime forces. (8)

H:DC.4: Dissident coercive control varies strongly with the loyalty of regime coercive forces to dissident leaders. (8)

Determinants of Regime Institutional Support

H:RI.1: Regime institutional support varies strongly with the proportion of a population belonging to regime-oriented organizations. (9)

H:RI.2: Regime institutional support varies strongly with the cohesiveness and complexity of regime-oriented organizations. (9)

H:RI.3: Regime institutional support varies moderately with the value stocks of regime-oriented organizations. (9)

H:RI.4: Regime institutional support varies strongly with the number and scope of value opportunities provided by regime-oriented organizations. (9)

H:RI.5: Regime institutional support varies strongly with the number and scope of regularized channels for protest provided by regime-oriented organizations. (9)

Determinants of Dissident Institutional Support

H:DI.1: Dissident institutional support varies strongly with the proportion of a population belonging to dissident-oriented organizations. (9)

H:DI.2: Dissident institutional support varies strongly with the cohesiveness and complexity of dissident-oriented organizations. (9)

H:DI.3: Dissident institutional support varies moderately with the value stocks of dissident-oriented organizations. (9)

H:DI.4: Dissident institutional support varies strongly with the number and scope of value opportunities provided by dissident-oriented organizations. (9)

H:DI.5: Dissident institutional support varies strongly with the number and scope of means for anti-regime action provided by dissident-oriented organizations. (9)

Determinants of Internal War

H:I.1: The likelihood of internal war increases as the ratio of dissident to regime coercive control approaches equality. (8)

H:I.2: The likelihood of internal war varies with the geographical concentration of dissidents in areas to which regime forces have limited access. (8)

H:I.3: The likelihood of internal war varies with the degree of foreign support for dissidents. (8)

H:I.4: The likelihood of internal war increases as the level of dissident to regime institutional support approaches equality. (9)

H:I.5: The likelihood of internal war varies directly with the intensity and scope of elite and mass RD. (10)

H:I.6: The likelihood of internal war varies with the proportion of value classes affected by intense RD. (10)

H:I.7: The likelihood of internal war is greatest if RD is decremental or progressive, less if it is aspirational. (10)

Determinants of Turmoil

H:T.1: The likelihood of turmoil increases as the ratio of dissident to regime coercive control approaches zero. (8)

H:T.2: The likelihood of turmoil varies with the concentration of dissidents in areas in which regime forces are concentrated. (8)

H:T.3: The likelihood of turmoil varies inversely with the degree of dissident institutional support. (9)

H:T.4: The likelihood of turmoil varies directly with the intensity and scope of mass RD and inversely with the intensity and scope of elite RD. (10)

H:T.5: The likelihood of turmoil varies inversely with the proportion of value classes affected by intense RD. (10)

Determinants of Conspiracy

H:C.1: The likelihood of conspiracy varies with the degree of discrepancy between dissident and regime coercive control. (8)

H:C.2: The likelihood of conspiracy varies inversely with the loyalty of coercive forces to the regime. (8)

H:C.3: The likelihood of conspiracy varies with the extent to which the degree of dissident institutional support is high and its scope low. (9)

H:C.4: The likelihood of conspiracy varies directly with the intensity and scope of elite RD and inversely with the intensity and scope of mass RD. (10)

H:C.5: The likelihood of conspiracy varies with the intensity of participatory value deprivation. (10)

Bibliography

THIS BIBLIOGRAPHY IS divided functionally rather than by format of publication. The first section, "Behavioral and Attitudinal Studies," includes experimental studies related to aggression and collective behavior; studies of attitudes toward politics, collective behavior, and violence; and theoretical analyses and interpretations in psychiatry, psychology, and social and political psychology. The second section, "Studies of Group Conflict and Political Violence," includes case, comparative, and theoretical analyses of the sources, nature, processes, and resolution of group conflict and violence within societies. Also included are some related studies of conflict among nations and manuals on the organization and prophylaxis of political violence. Also see the Supplementary Bibliography, beginning on p. 405.

The listings are selective, not comprehensive. The most comprehensive bibliographies on psychological aspects of aggression are included in Leonard Berkowitz, *Aggression: A Social Psychological Analysis* (New York: McGraw-Hill, 1962), 329–347; and Aubrey J. Yates, *Frustration and Conflict* (New York: Wiley, 1962), 204–225. For a useful general bibliography on collective behavior see Neil J. Smelser, *Theory of Collective Behavior* (New York: The Free Press, 1963), 388–427. Extensive bibliography on guerrilla warfare is included in Franklin Mark Osanka, ed., *Modern Guerrilla Warfare: Fighting Communist Guerrilla Movements, 1941–1961* (New York: The Free Press, 1962). For a current bibliography on urban strife in the United States see John R. Krause, "Political Violence: Revolutions, Rebellions and Riots," in Louis H. Masotti and Don R. Bowen, eds., *Riots and Rebellion: Civil Violence in the Urban Community* (Beverly Hills: Sage Publications, 1968), 421–451. Probably the most comprehensive bibliography on conflict and violence is Douglas Bwy, *Social Conflict: A Keyword-in-Context Bibliography on the Literature of Developing Areas, With Supplementary References from Latin America* (Evanston: Prepared in connection with research supported by the National Science Foundation and the Northwestern University Council for Intersocietal Studies, June 1966), which lists 1,200 items.

I. Behavioral and Attitudinal Studies

Aberbach, Joel D. "Alienation and Political Behavior." *American Political Science Review*, LXIII (March 1969), 86–99.

Adorno, Theodor W., et al. *The Authoritarian Personality.* New York: Harper, 1950.

Ainsworth, Mary D. and Leonard H. "Acculturation in East Africa, II. Frustration and Aggression," *Journal of Social Psychology*, LVII (August 1962), 401–407.

Alexander, Franz. "The Psychiatric Aspects of War and Peace," *American Journal of Sociology*, LXVI (1941), 504–520.

Allport, Floyd H. *Social Psychology*. Boston: Houghton-Mifflin, 1924.

Allport, Gordon. "The Role of Expectancy," In Hadley Cantril (ed.). *Tensions That Cause Wars*. Urbana: University of Illinois Press, 1950.

Almond, Gabriel A. and Sidney Verba. *The Civic Culture: Political Attitudes and Democracy in Five Nations*. Princeton: Princeton University Press, 1963.

Aronson, E. "Threat and Obedience," *Trans-action*, III (1966), 25–27.

Baker, George W. and Dwight W. Chapman (eds.). *Man and Society in Disaster*. New York: Basic Books, 1962.

Bandura, Albert, Dorothea Ross, and Sheila A. Ross, "Transmission of Aggression Through Imitation of Aggressive Models," *Journal of Abnormal and Social Psychology*, LXIII (1961), 575–582.

Bandura, Albert and Richard H. Walters. *Adolescent Aggression: A Study of Child Training Practices and Family Interrelationships*. New York: Ronald Press, 1959.

Bandura, Albert and Richard H. Walters. *Social Learning and Personality Development*. New York: Holt, Rinehart and Winston, 1963.

Barton, Allen H. "The Columbia Crisis: Campus, Vietnam, and the Ghetto." *Public Opinion Quarterly*, XXXII (Fall 1968), 334–362.

Bateson, Gregory. "The Frustration-Aggression Hypotheses and Culture," *Psychological Review*, LXVIII (July 1941), 350–355.

Becker, Ernest. "Anthropological Notes on the Concept of Aggression," *Psychiatry*, XXV (November, 1962), 328–338.

Berkowitz, Leonard (ed.). *Advances in Experimental Psychology*, Vol. II. New York: Academic Press, 1965.

Berkowitz, Leonard. *Aggression: A Social Psychological Analysis*. New York: McGraw-Hill, 1962.

Berkowitz, Leonard. "Aggressive Cues in Aggressive Behavior and Hostility Catharsis," *Psychological Review*, LXXI (March 1964), 104–122.

Berkowitz, Leonard. "Repeated Frustrations and Expectations in Hostility Arousal," *Journal of Abnormal and Social Psychology*, LX (May 1960), 422–429.

Berkowitz, Leonard. "Some Experiments on Automatism and Intent in Human Aggression," Paper read at University of California at Los Angeles, Brain Research Institute, November 1965.

Berkowitz, Leonard. "The Concept of Aggressive Drive: Some Additional Considerations," In Leonard Berkowitz (ed.). *Advances in Experimental Psychology,* Vol. II. New York: Academic Press, 1965.

Bettelheim, Bruno. "Individual and Mass Behavior in Extreme Situations," *Journal of Abnormal and Social Psychology,* XXXVIII (October 1943), pp. 417–452.

Billig, Otto, John Gillin and William Davidson. "Aspects of Personality and Culture in a Guatemalan Community: Ethnological and Rorschach Approaches, Part II," *Journal of Personality,* XVI (March 1948), 326–368.

Bramson, Leon and G. W. Goethals (eds.). *War: Studies From Psychology, Sociology, Anthropology.* New York: Basic Books, 1964.

Brearley, H. C. "The Pattern of Violence," In W. T. Couch (ed.). *Culture in the South.* Chapel Hill: University of North Carolina Press, 1934.

Brehm, Jack W. and Arthur R. Cohen. *Explorations in Cognitive Dissonance.* New York: Wiley, 1962.

Brink, William and Louis Harris. *Black and White: A Study of U.S. Racial Attitudes Today.* New York: Simon and Schuster, 1967.

Brown, J. F. "The Theory of the Aggressive Urges and Wartime Behavior," *Journal of Social Psychology,* XV (1942), 355–380.

Brown, Roger W. "Mass Phenomena," In Gardner Lindzey (ed.). *Handbook of Social Psychology,* Vol. 2. Reading, Massachusetts: Addison-Wesley, 1954, 833–876.

Buss, Arnold H. *The Psychology of Aggression.* New York: John Wiley, 1962.

Cantril, Hadley. "*Sentio, Ergo Sum:* 'Motivation' Reconsidered," *Journal of Psychology,* LXV (January 1967), 91–107.

Cantril, Hadley. *The Pattern of Human Concerns.* New Brunswick: Rutgers University Press, 1965.

Cantril, Hadley. *The Politics of Despair.* New York: Collier Books, 1958, 1966.

Cantril, Hadley. *The Psychology of Social Movements.* New York: Wiley, 1941.

Caplan, Nathan S. and Jeffery M. Paige. "A Study of Ghetto Rioters," *Scientific American,* CCXIX (August 1968), 15–21.

Cartwright, Dorwin (ed.). *Studies in Social Power.* Ann Arbor: Institute for Social Research, University of Michigan, 1959.

Chasdi, E. H. and M. S. Lawrence. "Some Antecedents of Aggression and Effects of Frustration in Doll Play," In David McClelland (ed.). *Studies in Motivation.* New York: Appleton-Century-Crofts, 1955.

Church, Russell M. "The Varied Effects of Punishment on Behavior," *Psychological Review,* Vol. LXX (September 1963), 369–402.

Clapper, Joseph T. *The Effects of Mass Communication.* New York: The Free Press, 1960.

Clark, Kenneth B. "Group Violence: A Preliminary Study of the Attitudinal Pattern of its Acceptance and Rejection: A Study of the 1943 Harlem Riot," *Journal of Social Psychology,* XIX (May 1944), 319–337.

Clark, Kenneth B. and James Barker. "The Zoot Effect in Personality: A Race Riot Participant." *Journal of Abnormal and Social Psychology.* XL (April 1945), 143–148.

Clinard, Marshall B. (ed.). *Anomie and Deviant Behavior: A Discussion and Critique.* New York: The Free Press, 1964.

Coe, Rodney M. "Conflict, Interference, and Aggression: Computer Simulation of a Social Process," *Behavioral Science,* IX (April 1964), 186–196.

Cohen, Arthur R. "Social Norms, Arbitrariness of Frustration, and Status of the Agent of Frustration in the Frustration-Aggression Hypothesis," *Journal of Abnormal and Social Psychology,* LI (1955), 222–226.

Cohen, Arthur R. "Upward Communication in Experimentally Created Hierarchies," *Human Relations,* XI (1958), 41–54.

Cohen, Arthur et al. "Commitment to Social Deprivation and Verbal Conditioning," *Journal of Abnormal and Social Psychology,* LXVII (November 1963), 410–421.

Danziger, Kurt. "The Psychological Future of an Oppressed Group," *Social Forces,* LXII (October 1963), 31–40.

Davies, James C. *Human Nature in Politics.* New York: Wiley, 1963.

Devletoglou, Nicos. "Responsibility and Demonstrations: A Case Study," *Public Opinion Quarterly,* XXX (No. 2, 1966), 285–289.

Dollard, John et al. *Frustration and Aggression.* New Haven: Yale University Press, 1939.

Doob, Leonard W. *Becoming More Civilized: A Psychological Exploration.* New Haven: Yale University Press, 1960.

Doob, Leonard W. *Patriotism and Nationalism: Their Psychological Foundations.* New Haven: Yale University Press, 1964.

Durbin, E. F. M. and John Bowlby. *Personal Aggressiveness and War.* London: Kegan Paul, Trench, Trubner, 1939.

Edwards, Allen L. "The Signs of Incipient Facism," *Journal of Abnormal and Social Psychology,* XXXIX (1944), 301–316.

Epstein, Ralph. "Aggression Toward Outgroups as a Function of

Authoritarianism and Imitation of Aggressive Models," *Journal of Personality and Social Psychology*, III (No. 5, 1966), 574–579.

Eron, L. D. et al. "Social Class, Parental Punishment for Aggression, and Child Aggression," *Child Development*, XXXIV (December 1963), 849–867.

Erskine, Hazel. "The Polls: Demonstrations and Race Riots," *Public Opinion Quarterly*, XXXI (Winter 1967–68), 655–677.

Eysenck, H. J. *The Psychology of Politics*. London: Routledge and Kegan Paul, 1954.

Feshbach, Seymour. "The Function of Aggression and the Regulation of Aggressive Drive," *Psychological Review*, LXXI (July 1964), 257–272.

Festinger, Leon. *A Theory of Cognitive Dissonance*. Stanford: Stanford University Press, 1957.

Festinger, Leon, A. Pepitone, and Theodore M. Newcomb. "Some Consequences of Deindividuation in a Group," *Journal of Abnormal and Social Psychology*, XLVII (1952), 382–389.

Field, M. J. *Search for Security: An Ethno-Psychiatric Study of Rural Ghana*. Evanston: Northwestern University Press, 1960.

Frank, Jerome. *Sanity and Survival: Psychological Aspects of War and Peace*. New York: Vintage Books, 1968.

French, J. R. P. Jr. "Organized and Unorganized Groups Under Fear and Frustration," In Kurt Lewin et al. *Authority and Frustration*. Iowa City: University of Iowa Studies in Child Welfare, University of Iowa Press, 1944.

Freud, Sigmund. *Civilization and its Discontents*. Joan Riviere (tr.). London: The Hogarth Press, 1930.

Goldrich, Daniel. *Sons of the Establishments: Elite Youth in Panama and Costa Rica*. Chicago: Rand McNally, 1966.

Gordon, Leonard A. "Portrait of a Bengal Revolutionary," *Journal of Asian Studies*, XXVII (February 1968), 197–216.

Graham, F. K. et al. "Aggression as a Function of the Attack and the Attacker," *Journal of Abnormal and Social Psychology*, XLVI (October 1951), 512–520.

Greenstein, Fred I. *Children and Politics*. New Haven: Yale University Press, 1965.

Gurr, Ted. "Psychological Factors in Civil Strife," *World Politics*, XX (January 1968), 245–278.

Hamblin, Robert L. et al. "The Interference-Aggression Law?" *Sociometry*, XXVI (June 1963), 109–216.

Hamilton, Richard F. "The Marginal Middle Class: A Reconsideration," *American Sociological Review*, XXXI (April 1966), 192–199.

Haner, C. F. and P. A. Brown. "Clarification of the Instigation to

Action Concept in the Frustration-Aggression Hypothesis," *Journal of Abnormal and Social Psychology,* LI (September 1955), 204–206.

Harvey, O. J., D. E. Hunt, and H. M. Schroder. *Conceptual Systems and Personality Organization.* New York: Wiley, 1961.

Hendin, Herbert. *Suicide and Scandinavia.* New York: Grune and Stratton, 1964.

Henry, Andrew F. and James F. Short, Jr. *Suicide and Homicide: Some Economic, Sociological, and Psychological Aspects of Aggression.* New York: The Free Press, 1954, 1964.

Himmelweit, Hilde T. "Frustration and Aggression: A Review of Recent Experimental Work," In T. H. Pear (ed.). *Psychological Factors of Peace and War.* London: Hutchinson, 1950.

Holton, Richard H. "Changing Demand and Consumption," In Wilbert E. Moore and Arnold S. Feldman (eds.). *Labor Commitment and Social Change in Development Areas.* New York: Social Science Research Council, 1950.

Hyman, Herbert H. "The Value Systems of Different Classes," In Reinhard Bendix and Seymour Lipset (eds.). *Class, Status and Power.* Glencoe: The Free Press, 1953.

Janis, I. L. *Air War and Emotional Stress; Psychological Studies of Bombing and Civilian Defense.* New York: McGraw-Hill, 1951.

Jaros, Dean, Herbert Hirsch, and Frederic J. Fleron Jr. "The Malevolent Leader: Political Socialization in an American Sub-Culture," *American Political Science Review,* LXII (June 1968), 564–575.

Kim, Young C. "Authority: Some Conceptual and Empirical Notes," *Western Political Quarterly,* XIX (June 1966), 223–234.

Klineberg, Otto. *Tensions Affecting International Understanding: A Survey of Research.* New York: Social Science Research Council, 1950.

Kosa, John and Clyde Z. Nunn. "Race, Deprivation and Attitude Toward Communism," *Phylon,* XXV (December 1964), 337–346.

Kregarman, John J. and Philip Worchel. "Arbitrariness of Frustration and Aggression," *Journal of Abnormal and Social Psychology,* LXIII (July 1961), 183–187.

Kuper, Leo. *An African Bourgeoisie.* New Haven: Yale University Press, 1965.

Lane, Robert E. *Political Ideology: Why The American Common Man Believes What He Does.* New York: The Free Press, 1962.

Lasswell, Harold. *Psychopathology and Politics.* Chicago: University of Chicago Press, 1930.

Lasswell, Harold. *World Politics and Personal Insecurity.* Glencoe: The Free Press, 1934, 1950.

Lazarsfeld, Marie and Hans Zeisal. "Die Arbeitslosen Von Marienthal," *Psychologische Monographen,* v (1933).

Le Bon, Gustave. *The Crowd: A Study of the Popular Mind.* New York: Macmillan, 1896.

Le Bon, Gustave. *The Psychology of Revolution.* Bernard Miall (tr.). London: T. F. Unwin, 1913.

Leggett, John C. "Uprootedness and Working-class Consciousness," *American Journal of Sociology,* LXVII (May 1963), 682–692.

Lenski, Gerhard. "Status Crystallization: A Non-Vertical Dimension of Social Status," *American Sociological Review,* XIX (August 1954), 405–413.

Lerner, Daniel. *The Passing of Traditional Society.* New York: The Free Press, 1958.

Lewin, Kurt et al. *Authority and Frustration.* Iowa City: University of Iowa Studies in Child Welfare, University of Iowa Press, 1944.

Lewin, Kurt, Ronald Lippitt, and Ralph K. White. "Patterns of Aggressive Behavior in Experimentally Created Social Climates," *Journal of Social Psychology,* X (May 1939), 271–299.

Lifton, Robert Jay. *Thought Reform and the Psychology of Totalism: A Study of "Brainwashing" in China.* New York: Norton, 1961.

Lindzey, Gardner (ed.). *Handbook of Social Psychology.* Vol. 2. Reading, Massachusetts: Addison-Wesley, 1954.

Lorenz, Konrad. *On Aggression.* New York: Harcourt, Brace, and World, 1966.

McClelland, David (ed.). *Studies in Motivation.* New York: Appleton-Century-Crofts, 1955.

McClelland, David C. *The Achieving Society.* Princeton: Van Nostrand, 1961.

McClelland, David C. and F. S. Apicella. "Functional Classification of Verbal Reactions to Experimentally Induced Failure," *Journal of Abnormal and Social Psychology,* XL (July 1945), 376–390.

McCord, William and John Howard, "Negro Opinions in Three Riot Cities," *American Behavioral Scientist,* XI (March-April 1968), 24–27.

McNeil, Elton D. "Psychology and Aggression," *Journal of Conflict Resolution,* III (June 1959), 195–294.

McNulty, J. A. and J. A. Walters. "Emotional Arousal, Conflict, and Susceptibility to Social Influence," *Canadian Journal of Psychology,* XVI (September 1962), 211–220.

Maier, Norman R. F. *Frustration: The Study of Behavior Without a Goal.* New York: McGraw-Hill, 1949.

Maier, Norman R. F. "The Role of Frustration in Social Movements," *Psychological Review,* LXIX (November 1942), 586–599.

Manheim, H. L. "Intergroup Interaction as Related to Status and Leadership Between Groups," *Sociometry,* XXIII (December 1960), 415–427.

Marquart, Dorothy. "The Pattern of Punishment and its Relation to Abnormal Fixation in Adult Human Subjects," *Journal of General Psychology,* XXXIX (July 1948), 107–144.

Martin, Everett Dean. *The Behavior of Crowds: A Psychological Study.* New York: Harper, 1920.

Maslow, A. H. "Deprivation, Threat, and Frustration," *Psychological Review,* XLVIII (July 1941), 364–366.

May, Mark A. *A Social Psychology of War and Peace.* New Haven: Yale University Press, 1943.

Meier, Norman C., G. H. Mennenga, and H. J. Stolz. "An Experimental Approach to the Study of Mob Behavior," *Journal of Abnormal and Social Psychology,* XXXVI (October 1941), 506–524.

Merelman, Richard M. "Learning and Legitimacy," *American Political Science Review,* LX (September 1966), 548–561.

Miller, Neal E. and R. Bugelski. "Minor Studies of Aggression: II. The Influence of Frustrations Imposed by the In-Group and Attitudes Expressed Toward Out-Groups," *Journal of Psychology,* XXV (April 1948), 437–442.

Miller, Neal E. "Theory and Experiment Relating Psychoanalytic Displacement to Stimulus-Response Generalization," *Journal of Abnormal and Social Psychology,* XLVIII (April 1948), 155–178.

Miller, Neal E. et al. "The Frustration-Aggression Hypothesis," *Psychological Review,* XLVIII (July 1941), 337–342.

Morrison, Denton E. and Allan D. Steeves. "Deprivation, Discontent, and Social Movement Participation: Evidence on a Contemporary Farmers' Movement, the NFO," *Rural Sociology,* XXXII (December 1967), 414–434.

Naess, Arne. "The Function of Ideological Convictions," In Hadley Cantril (ed.). *Tensions That Cause Wars.* Urbana: University of Illinois Press, 1950.

Naroll, Raoul. *Data Quality Control: A New Research Technique; Prolegomena to a Cross-Cultural Study of Culture Stress.* New York: The Free Press, 1962.

Neal, Arthur G. and Melvin Seeman. "Organizations and Powerlessness: A Test of the Mediation Hypothesis," *American Sociological Review*, XXIX (April 1964), 216–226.

Palmer, Stuart. "Frustration, Aggression, and Murder," *Journal of Abnormal and Social Psychology*, LX (May 1960), 430–432.

Pastore, Nicholas. "The Role of Arbitrariness in the Frustration-Aggression Hypothesis," *Journal of Abnormal and Social Psychology*, XLVII (July 1952), 728–731.

Pear, T. H. (ed.). *Psychological Factors of Peace and War.* London: Hutchinson, 1950.

Pepitone, A. and G. Reichling. "Group Cohesiveness and the Expression of Hostility," *Human Relations*, VIII (No. 3, 1955), 327–337.

Polansky, Norman, Ronald Lippitt, and Fritz Redl. "An Investigation of Behavioral Contagion in Groups," *Human Relations*, III (No. 3, 1950), 319–348.

Pye, Lucian W. *Politics, Personality, and Nation Building: Burma's Search for Identity.* New Haven: Yale University Press, 1962.

Raven, B. H. and J. R. P. French, Jr. "Group Support, Legitimate Power, and Social Influence," *Journal of Personality*, XXVI (September 1958), 400–409.

Raven, B. H. and J. R. P. French, Jr. "Legitimate Power, Coercive Power, and Observability in Social Influence," *Sociometry*, XXI (June 1958), 83–97.

Riezler, Kurt. "On the Psychology of the Modern Revolution," *Social Research*, X (September 1943), 320–336.

Ringer, Benjamin B. and David L. Sills. "Political Extremists in Iran: A Secondary Analysis of Communications Data," *Public Opinion Quarterly*, XVI (Winter 1952–1953), 689–701.

Rose, Gordon. "Anomie and Deviation: A Conceptual Framework for Empirical Studies," *British Journal of Sociology*, XVII (March 1966), 29–45.

Rosenzweig, Saul. "Need-Persistive and Ego-Defensive Reactions to Frustration as Demonstrated by an Experiment on Repression," *Psychological Review*, XLVIII (July 1941), 347–349.

Rosenzweig, Saul. "Types of Reaction to Frustration: A Heuristic Classification," *Journal of Abnormal and Social Psychology*, XXIX (October-December 1934), 298–300.

Rothaus, Paul and Philip Worchel. "The Inhibition of Aggression Under Nonarbitrary Frustration," *Journal of Personality*, XXVIII (March 1960), 108–117.

Rothstein, D. A. "Presidential Assassination Syndrome," *Archives of General Psychiatry*, XI (September 1960), 245–254.

Runciman, W. G. *Relative Deprivation and Social Justice.* Berkeley: University of California Press, 1966.

Saul, Leon J. *The Hostile Mind: The Sources and Consequences of Rage and Hate.* New York: Random House, 1956.

Solomon, Richard L. "Punishment," *American Psychologist,* XIX (April 1964), 239–253.

Sorokin, Pitirim A. *Man and Society in Calamity.* New York: Dutton, 1942.

Stagner, Ross. "Studies of Aggressive Social Attitudes," *Journal of Social Psychology,* XX (August 1944), 109–140.

Stern, Eric and Suzanne Keller. "Spontaneous Group References in France," *Public Quarterly,* XVII (No. 2, 1953), 208–217.

Stotland, Ezra. "Peer Groups and Reactions to Power Figures," In Dorwin Cartwright (ed.). *Studies in Social Power.* Ann Arbor: Institute for Social Research, University of Michigan, 1959.

Stouffer, Samuel A. et al. *The American Soldier: Adjustment During Army Life,* I. Princeton: Princeton University Press, 1949.

Sudefeld, Peter. "Attitude Manipulation in Restricted Environments: I. Conceptual Structure and Response to Propaganda," *Journal of Abnormal and Social Psychology,* LXVIII (March 1964), 242–247.

Swanson, G. E. "A Preliminary Laboratory Study of the Acting Crowd," *American Sociological Review,* XVIII (October 1953), 522–533.

Templeton, Frederic. "Alienation and Political Participation: Some Research Findings," *Public Opinion Quarterly,* XXX (Summer 1966), 249–261.

Thibaut, J. W. "An Experimental Study of Cohesiveness of Under-Privileged Groups," *Human Relations,* III (No. 3, 1950), 251–278.

Thibaut, J. W. and J. Coules. "The Role of Communication in the Reduction of Interpersonal Hostility," *Journal of Abnormal and Social Psychology,* XLVII (October 1952), 770–777.

Thibaut, J. W. and H. W. Riecken. "Authoritarianism, Status, and the Communication of Aggression," *Human Relations,* VIII (No. 2, 1955), 95–120.

Thomas, Edwin J. "Effects of Facilitating Role Interdependence on Group Functioning," *Human Relations,* X (No. 4, 1957), 347–366.

Toch, Hans. *The Social Psychology of Social Movements.* Indianapolis: Bobbs-Merrill, 1965.

Tomlinson, T. M. "The Development of a Riot Ideology Among Urban Negroes," *American Behavioral Scientist,* XI (March-April, 1968), 27–31.

Townsend, Peter. "The Meanings of Poverty," *British Journal of Sociology,* XIII (September 1962), 210–227.

Turner, R. H. and S. J. Surace. "Zoot-Suiters and Mexicans: Symbols in Crowd Behavior," *American Journal of Sociology,* LXII (July 1956), 14–20.

Wallach, M. A., N. Kogan, and D. G. Bem. "Diffusion of Responsibility and Level of Risk-Taking in Groups," *Journal of Abnormal and Social Psychology,* LXVIII (March 1964), 263–274.

Walters, Richard H. "Implications of Laboratory Studies of Aggression for the Control and Regulation of Violence," *Annals of the American Academy of Political and Social Science,* CCCLXIV (March 1966), 63–66.

Weeler, L. and A. R. Caggiula. "The Contagion of Aggression," *Journal of Experimental Social Psychology,* II (January 1966), 1–10.

Whiting, J. M. V. "The Frustration Complex in Kwoma Society," *Man,* XLIV (November-December 1944), 140–144.

Whiting, John W. M. and Irvin L. Child. *Child Training and Personality.* New Haven: Yale University Press, 1953.

Williamson, Robert C. "University Students in a World of Change: A Colombian Sample," *Sociology and Social Research,* XLVIII (July 1964), 397–413.

Wolfenstein, E. Victor. *The Revolutionary Personality: Lenin, Trotsky, Gandhi.* Princeton: Princeton University Press, 1967.

Wood, Arthur L. "A Socio-Structural Analysis of Murder, Suicide, and Economic Crime in Ceylon," *American Sociological Review,* XXVI (October 1961), 744–753.

Wright, G. O. "Projection and Displacement: A Cross-Cultural Study of Folk-Tale Aggression," *Journal of Abnormal and Social Psychology,* XLIX (October 1954), 523–528.

Yates, Aubrey J. *Frustration and Conflict.* New York: Wiley, 1962.

Young, Frank W. and Ruth C. "Individual Commitment to Industrialization in Rural Mexico," *American Journal of Sociology,* LXXI (January 1966), 373–383.

II. Studies of Group Conflict and Political Violence

Abel, Theodore F. "The Element of Decision in the Pattern of War," *American Sociological Review,* VI (December 1941), 853–859.

Abel, Theodore F. *The Nazi Movement: Why Hitler Came to Power.* New York: Atherton Press, 1938, 1966.

Aberle, David F. "A Note on Relative Deprivation Theory," In

Sylvia L. Thrupp (ed.). *Millennial Dreams in Action: Essays in Comparative Study.* The Hague: Mouton, 1962.

Adam, Brooks. *The Theory of Social Revolutions.* New York: Macmillan, 1913.

Adamic, Louis. *Dynamite: The Story of Class Violence in America.* New York: The Viking Press, 1931.

Ahmad, Eqbal. "Unfinished Revolutions in The Third World," Paper read to the National Conference on "The United States in a Revolutionary World," Princeton University, April 1968.

Ahmad, S. H. "China's 'Cultural Revolution,'" *International Studies* (Bombay), IX (July 1967), 13–54.

Ake, Claude. "Political Integration and Political Stability: A Hypothesis," *World Politics,* XIX (April 1967), 486–499.

AlRoy, Gil Carl. "Revolutionary Conditions in Latin America," *Review of Politics,* XIX (July 1967), 417–422.

AlRoy, Gil Carl. *The Involvement of Peasants in Internal Wars.* Princeton: Center of International Studies, Princeton University, Research Monograph No. 24, 1966.

AlRoy, Gil Carl. "The Peasantry in the Cuban Revolution," *Review of Politics,* XIX (January 1967), 87–99.

Amann, Peter. "Revolution: A Redefinition," *Political Science Quarterly,* LXXXVII (March 1962), 36–53.

Appell, George N. "The Structure of District Administration, Anti-Administration Activity and Political Instability," *Human Organization,* XXV (Winter 1966), 312–320.

Arendt, Hannah. *On Revolution.* New York: Viking Press, 1963.

Arendt, Hannah. "Revolution and Public Happiness," *Commentary,* XXX (November 1960), 413–422.

Armstrong, John A. (ed.). *Soviet Partisans in World War II.* Madison: University of Wisconsin Press, 1964.

Ashford, Douglas E. "Politics and Violence in Morocco," *Middle East Journal,* XIII (Winter 1959), 11–25.

Bauer, Arthur. *Essai sur les Revolutions.* Paris: V. Giard and E. Briere, 1908.

Bailey, Norman A. "Toward a Praxeological Theory of Conflict." *Orbis,* XI (Winter 1968), 1081–1112.

Baldwin, Leland D. *Whiskey Rebels: The Story of a Frontier Uprising.* Pittsburgh: University of Pittsburgh Press, 1939.

Barnes, Samuel H. "Ideology and the Organization of Conflict: On the Relationship between Political Thought and Behavior," Paper read at the Annual Meeting of the American Political Science Association, Washington, D.C., 1965.

Bayley, David H. "The Pedagogy of Democracy: Coercive Public

Protest in India." *American Political Science Review,* LVI (September 1962), 663–672.

Bayley, David H. "Public Protest and the Political Process in India," Paper read to the Annual Meeting of the Asian Studies Association, Philadelphia, March 1968.

Beals, Alan R. and Bernard J. Siegel. *Divisiveness and Social Conflict: An Anthropological Approach.* Stanford: Stanford University Press, 1966.

Beloff, Max. *Public Order and Popular Disturbances 1660–1714.* London: Frank Cass, 1938, 1963.

Belshaw, C. S. "The Significance of Modern Cults in Melanesian Development," *Australian Outlook,* IV (June 1950), 116–125.

Benson, Lee and Cushing Strout. "Causation and the American Civil War: Two Appraisals," *History and Theory,* I (No. 2, 1961), 163–185.

Bequiraj, Mehmet. *Peasantry in Revolution.* Ithaca: Center for International Studies, Cornell University, 1967.

Beshir, Mohamed Omer. *The Southern Sudan: Background to Conflict.* New York: Praeger, 1968.

Bienen, Henry (ed.). *The Military Intervenes: Case Studies in Political Development.* New York: Russell Sage, 1968.

Bienen, Henry. *Violence and Social Change.* Chicago: University of Chicago Press, 1968.

Billington, James H. "Six Views of the Russian Revolution," *World Politics,* XVIII (April 1966), 452–473.

Bittner, Egon. "Radicalism and the Organization of Radical Movements," *American Sociological Review,* XXVIII (December 1963), 928–940.

Black, Clinton. *The Story of Jamaica.* London: Collins, 1965.

Black, Cyril E. and Thomas P. Thornton (eds.). *Communism and Revolution: The Strategic Uses of Political Violence.* Princeton: Princeton University Press, 1964.

Bloombaum, Milton. "The Conditions Underlying Race Riots as Portrayed by Multidimensional Scalogram Analysis: A Reanalysis of Lieberson and Silverman's Data," *American Sociological Review,* XXIII (February 1968), 76–91.

Blumer, Herbert. "Collective Behavior," In J. B. Gittler (ed.). *Review of Sociology.* New York: Wiley, 1957.

Bornstein, Joseph. *The Politics of Murder.* New York: William Sloane Associates, 1950.

Boserup, Anders and Claus Iversen. "Demonstrations as a Source of Change: A Study of British and Danish Easter Marchers," *Journal of Peace Research,* No. 4, 1966, 328–348.

Boulding, Kenneth E. *Conflict and Defense: A General Theory.* New York: Harper, 1962.

Boulding, Kenneth E. "Reflections on Protest," *Bulletin of the Atomic Scientists,* XXI (October 1965), 18–20.

Brant, Stefan. *The East German Rising: 17th June 1953.* New York: Praeger, 1957.

Brenan, Gerald. *The Spanish Labyrinth: An Account of the Social and Political Background of the Civil War.* Cambridge: Cambridge University Press, 1943, 1950.

Bretton, Henry. *The Rise and Fall of Kwame Nkrumah: A Study of Personal Rule in Africa.* New York: Praeger, 1966.

Brinkman, Carl. *Soziologische Theorie der Revolution.* Gottingen: Vandenhoeck & Ruprecht, 1948.

Brinton, Crane. *The Anatomy of Revolution.* New York: Norton, 1938.

Brogan, Denis W. *The Price of Revolution.* London: Hamish Hamilton, 1951.

Brown, Richard M. "Historical Patterns of Violence in America." In Hugh Davis Graham and Ted Robert Gurr (eds.). *Violence in America: Historical and Comparative Perspectives.* Washington, D.C.: National Commission on the Causes and Prevention of Violence, 1969.

Brown, William R. "The Yemeni Dilemma," *Middle East Journal,* XVII (Autumn 1963), 349–367.

Bryson, Lyman, Louis Finkelstein, and Robert MacIver (eds.). *Conflicts of Power in Modern Culture.* New York: Conference on Science, Philosophy, and Religion, Seventh Symposium, 1947.

Burns, R. I. "Social Riots on the Christian-Moslem Frontier (Thirteenth-Century Valencia)," *American Historical Review,* LXVI (January 1961), 378–400.

Busey, James L. "Brazil's Reputation for Political Stability," *Western Political Quarterly,* XVIII (December 1965), 866–880.

Bwy, Douglas P. "Correlates of Political Instability in Latin America: Over-Time Comparisons from Brazil, Cuba, the Dominican Republic, and Panama." Paper read to the Annual Meeting of the American Political Science Association, Washington, D.C., 1968.

Bwy, Douglas. "Political Instability in Latin America: The Preliminary Test of a Causal Model," *Latin American Research Review,* III (Spring 1968), 17–66.

Calvert, Peter A. R. "Revolution: The Politics of Violence," *Political Studies,* XV (No. 1, 1967), 1–11.

Carr, E. H. *Studies in Revolution.* New York: Barnes and Noble, 1950, 1962.

Carsten, F. L. *The Rise of Fascism.* Berkeley: University of California Press, 1967.

Case, Clarence Marsh. *Non-Violent Coercion: A Study in Methods of Social Pressure.* New York: Century, 1923.

Carter, Gwendolen M. *The Politics of Inequality: South Africa Since 1948.* New York: Praeger, 1958.

Chalmers, David M. *Hooded Americanism: The History of the Ku Klux Klan.* New York: Doubleday, 1965.

Chaplin, David. "Peru's Postponed Revolution," *World Politics,* XX (April 1968), 393–420.

Chassin, Lionel Max. *The Communist Conquest of China: A History of the Civil War 1945–1949.* Timothy Osato and Louis Gelas (tr.). Cambridge: Harvard University Press, 1965.

Chorley, Katherine. *Armies and the Art of Revolution.* London: Faber and Faber, 1943.

Clapham, Christopher, "The Ethiopian Coup d'État of December 1960," *Journal of Modern African Studies,* VI (No. 4, 1968), 495–507.

Clark, M. J. *Algeria in Turmoil: A History of the Rebellion.* New York: Praeger, 1961.

Cohn, Norman R. C. *The Pursuit of the Millennium.* 2nd. edn. rev. New York: Harper, 1957, 1961.

Cohn, Norman R. C. *Warrant for Genocide: The Myth of the Jewish World-Conspiracy and the Protocols of the Elders of Zion.* New York: Harper and Row, 1967.

Coleman, J. Walter. *The Molly Maguire Riots: Industrial Conflict in the Pennsylvania Coal Region.* Richmond: Garrett and Massie, 1936.

Connery, Robert H. (ed.). "Urban Riots: Violence and Social Change," *Proceedings of the Academy of Political Science,* XXIX (July 1968).

Corfield, F. D. *Historical Survey of the Origin and Growth of Mau Mau.* London: H. M. Stationery Office, 1960.

Coser, Lewis A. *Continuities in the Study of Social Conflict.* New York: The Free Press, 1968.

Coser, Lewis. *The Functions of Social Conflict.* New York: The Free Press, 1956.

Crook, Wilfred H. *The General Strike.* Chapel Hill: University of North Carolina Press, 1931.

Crook, W. H. "The Revolutionary Logic of the General Strike," *American Political Science Review,* XXIV (August 1934), 655–663.

Cross, James Eliot. *Conflict in the Shadows: The Nature and Politics of Guerrilla War.* Garden City: Doubleday, 1963.

Crow, R. E. "Religious Sectarianism in the Lebanese Political System," *Journal of Politics,* XXIV (August 1962), 489–520.

Crozier, Brian. *The Rebels: A Study of Post-War Insurrections.* London: Chatto and Windus, 1960.

Da Cunha, Euclydes. *Rebellion in the Backlands.* S. Putnam (tr.) Chicago: University of Chicago Press, 1902, 1960.

Dahlke, H. O. "Race and Minority Riots: A Study in the Typology of Violence," *Social Forces,* XXX (May 1952), 419–425.

Dahrendorf, Ralf. *Class and Class Conflict in Industrial Society.* Stanford: Stanford University Press, 1959.

Darvall, Frank O. *Popular Disturbances and Public Order in Regency England.* London: Oxford University Press, 1934.

Davies, James C. "The J-Curve of Rising and Declining Satisfactions as a Cause of some Great Revolutions and a Contained Rebellion." In Hugh Davis Graham and Ted Robert Gurr (eds.). *Violence in America: Historical and Comparative Perspectives.* Washington, D.C.: National Commission on the Causes and Prevention of Violence, 1969.

Davies, James C. "Toward a Theory of Revolution," *American Sociological Review,* XXVII (February 1962), 5–19.

Daniels, R. R. "The Kronstadt Revolt of 1921: A Study in the Dynamics of Revolution," *American Slavic and East European Review,* X (1951), 241–254.

Debray, Régis. *Revolution in the Revolution? Armed Struggle and Political Struggle in Latin America.* New York: Grove Press, 1967.

de Grazia, Alfred. *Politics and Government, Vol. 1: Political Behavior.* New York: Colliers Books, 1952, 1962.

de Grazia, Sebastian. *The Political Community: A Study of Anomie.* Chicago: University of Chicago Press, 1948.

Dehove, Gerard and Edward Dolleans. *Histoire du Travail,* I. Paris: Domat-Montchrestien, 1953.

Dennis, Lawrence. *The Dynamics of War and Revolution.* New York: The Weekly Foreign Letter, 1940.

De Tocqueville, Alexis. *The Old Régime and the French Revolution.* Stuart Gilbert (tr.). New York: Doubleday, 1955.

Deutsch, Karl W. "External Involvement in Internal War," In Harry Eckstein (ed.). *Internal War: Problems and Approaches.* New York: The Free Press, 1963.

Deutsch, Karl W. "Some Quantitative Constraints on Value Allocation in Society and Politics," *Behavioral Science,* XI (July 1966), 245–252.

Dommanget, Maurice. *La Jacquerie: 600 Anniversaire Des "Ef-*

frois." Crell, L'Oise: Syndicat Des Instituteurs De L'Oise, 1958.

Drake, St. Clair. "Some Observations on Interethnic Conflict as One Type of Intergroup Conflict," *Journal of Conflict Resolution,* I (1957) 155–178.

Eckstein, Harry. *Division and Cohesion in Democracy: A Study of Norway.* Princeton: Princeton University Press, 1966.

Eckstein, Harry (ed.). *Internal War: Problems and Approaches.* New York: The Free Press, 1966.

Eckstein, Harry. "On the Etiology of Internal Wars," *History and Theory,* IV (No. 2, 1965), 133–163.

Edwards, Lyford P. *The Natural History of Revolutions.* Chicago: University of Chicago Press, 1927.

Ellwood, Charles A. *The Psychology of Human Society: An Introduction to Sociological Theory.* New York: Appleton, 1925.

Embree, Ainsle T. (ed.). *1857 in India: Mutiny or War of Independence?* Boston: D. C. Heath, 1963.

Endleman, Shalom (ed.). *Violence in the Streets.* Chicago: Quadrangle Books, 1968.

Enos, John L. *An Analytic Model of Political Allegiance and its Application to the Cuban Revolution.* Santa Monica: RAND Corporation, Publication 3197, August, 1965.

Etzioni, Amitai. "Demonstration Democracy." Paper prepared for the National Commission on the Causes and Prevention of Violence. Washington, D.C.: Center for Policy Research, 1968.

Fals Borda, Orlando. "Unfinished Revolutions in Latin America," Paper read to the Conference on "The United States in a Revolutionary World," Princeton University, April 1968.

Fanon, Frantz. *The Wretched of the Earth.* New York: Grove Press, 1966.

Feierabend, Ivo K. and Rosalind L. "Aggressive Behaviors within Polities, 1948–1962: A Cross National Study," *Journal of Conflict Resolution,* X (September 1966), 249–271.

Feierabend, Ivo K. and Rosalind L., and Betty A. Nesvold. "Social Change and Political Violence: Cross-National Patterns," in Hugh Davis Graham and Ted Robert Gurr (eds.). *Violence in America: Historical and Comparative Perspectives.* Washington, D.C.: National Commission on the Causes and Prevention of Violence, 1969.

Feit, Edward. "Military Coups and Political Development: Some Lessons from Ghana and Nigeria," *World Politics,* XX (January 1968), 179–193.

Feldman, Arnold. "Violence and Volatility: The Likelihood of Revolution," In Harry Eckstein (ed.). *Internal War: Problems and Approaches*. New York: The Free Press, 1963.

Fernandez, James W. "African Religious Movements: Types and Dynamics," *Journal of Modern African Studies*, II (December 1964), 531–549.

Fernandez, James W. "The Lumpa Uprising: Why?" *Africa Report*, IX (November 1964), 30–32.

Finer, S. E. *The Man on Horseback: The Role of the Military in Politics*. New York: Praeger, 1962.

Fink, Clinton F. "Some Conceptual Difficulties in the Theory of Social Conflict." *Journal of Conflict Resolution*, XII (December 1968), 412–460.

Fischer-Galati, Stephen. "The Peasants as a Revolutionary Force in the Balkans," *Journal of Central European Affairs*, XXIII (April 1963), 12–22.

Flanigan, William, and Edwin Fogelman. "Patterns of Democratic Development: An Historical Comparative Analysis," Paper read at the Annual Meeting of the American Political Science Association, Washington, D.C., September 1968.

Fluharty, Vernon Lee. *Dance of the Millions: Military Rule and the Social Revolution in Colombia 1930–1956*. Pittsburgh: University of Pittsburgh Press, 1957.

Fogelson, Robert M. "From Resentment to Confrontation: The Police, the Negroes, and the Outbreak of the Nineteen-Sixties Riots," *Political Science Quarterly*, LXXXIII (June 1968), 217–247.

Forrester, D. B. "The Madras Anti-Hindi Agitation, 1965: Political Protest and Its Effects on Language Policy in India." *Pacific Affairs*, XXXIX (Spring-Summer 1966), 19–36.

Fossum, Egil. "Factors Influencing the Occurrence of Military Coups D'État in Latin America," *Journal of Peace Research*, No. 3, 1967, 228–251.

Fox, Renée C. "The Peasant as a Revolutionary Force in Africa: The Case of Congo-Kinshasa," Paper read to the Annual Meeting of the African Studies Association, New York, November 1967.

Fox, Renée et al. " 'The Second Independence': A Case Study of the Kwilu Rebellion in the Congo," *Comparative Studies in Society and History*, VIII (October 1965), 78–109.

Friedrich, Carl J. (ed.). *Revolution*. New York: Atherton Press, 1966.

Friedrich, P. "Assumptions Underlying Tarascan Political Homicide," *Psychiatry*, XXV (November 1962), 315–327.

Furnivall, J. S. "Communism and Nationalism in Burma," *Far Eastern Survey*, XVIII (August 1949), 193–197.

Galtung, Johan. "Institutionalized Conflict Resolution: A Theoretical Paradigm," *Journal of Peace Research*, No. 4, 1965, 348–397.

Galtung, Johan. "On the Effects of International Sanctions, with Examples from the Case of Rhodesia," *World Politics*, XIX (April 1967), 378–416.

Galtung, Johan. "A Structural Theory of Aggression," *Journal of Peace Research*, No. 2, 1964, 95–119.

Geertz, Clifford. "The Integrative Revolution: Primordial Sentiments and Civil Politics in the New States," In Clifford Geertz (ed.). *Old Societies and New States: The Quest for Modernity in Asia and Africa*. New York: The Free Press, 1963.

Germani, Gino. *Integration Politica de Las Mesas y el Totalitarismo*. Buenos Aires: Colegio Libre de Estudios Superiores, 1956.

Geschwender, James A. "Social Structure and the Negro Revolt: An Examination of some Hypotheses," *Social Forces*, XLII (December 1964), 248–256.

Giap, Vo-nguyen. *People's War, People's Army*. New York: Praeger, 1962.

Glick, Edward Bernard. "Isolating the Guerrilla: Some Latin American Examples." *Orbis*, XII (Fall 1968), 873–886.

Gluckman, Max. "Civil War and Theories of Power in Barotse-Land: African and Medieval Analogies," *Yale Law Journal*, LXXII (Summer 1963), 1515–1546.

Gluckman, Max. *Rituals of Rebellion in South-East Africa*. Manchester: Manchester University Press, 1954.

Godechot, Jacques. *France and the Atlantic Revolution of the Eighteenth Century, 1770–1799*. H. H. Rowen (tr.). New York: The Free Press, 1965.

Goldenberg, Boris. *The Cuban Revolution and Latin America*. New York: Praeger, 1965.

Goodspeed, Donald J. *The Conspirators: A Study of the Coup D'État*. New York: The Viking Press, 1962.

Gottschalk, Louis. "Causes of Revolution," *American Journal of Sociology*, L (July 1944), 1–8.

Governor's Select Commission on Civil Disorder. *Report for Action*. Trenton: State of New Jersey, February 1968.

Graham, Hugh Davis and Ted Robert Gurr (eds.). *Violence in America: Historical and Comparative Perspectives*. Washington, D.C.: National Commission on the Causes and Prevention of Violence, 1969.

Granqvist, Hans. *The Red Guard: A Report on Mao's Revolution.* Erik J. Friis (tr.). New York: Praeger, 1967.

Greer, Donald. *The Incidence of the Emigration During the French Revolution.* Cambridge: Harvard University Press, 1951.

Grimshaw, Allen D. "Urban Racial Violence in the United States: Changing Ecological Considerations," *American Journal of Sociology,* LXVI (September 1960), 109–119.

Grimshaw, Allen D. "Lawlessness and Violence in America and Their Special Manifestations in Changing Negro-White Relationships," *Journal of Negro History,* XLIV (January 1959), 52–72.

Gross, Feliks. *The Seizure of Power in a Century of Revolutions.* New York: Philosophical Library, 1958.

Gude, Edward W. "Political Violence in Venezuela: 1958–1964," In James C. Davies (ed.), *When Men Revolt And Why.* New York: The Free Press, 1970.

Guessous, Mohammed. "An Approach to the Study of the Algerian Revolution," Princeton: Center of International Studies, Princeton University, March 1965 (Mimeographed).

Guessous, Mohammed. "On the Institutionalization of Social Conflict," Unpublished Paper, Princeton: Center of International Studies, n.d. (Mimeographed).

Guevara, Ernesto. *Che Guevara on Guerrilla Warfare.* New York: Praeger, 1961.

Gulliver, P. H. "Land Shortage, Social Change, and Social Conflict in East Africa," *Journal of Conflict Resolution,* V (March 1960), 16–26.

Gurr, Ted. "A Causal Model of Civil Strife: A Comparative Analysis Using New Indices," *American Political Science Review,* LXII (December 1968), 1104–1124.

Gurr, Ted Robert. "A Comparative Survey of Civil Strife." In Hugh Davis Graham and Ted Robert Gurr (eds.). *Violence in America: Historical and Comparative Perspectives.* Washington, D.C.: National Commission on the Causes and Prevention of Violence, 1969.

Gurr, Ted. *New Error-Compensated Measures for Comparing Nations: Some Correlates of Civil Strife.* Princeton: Center of International Studies, Princeton University, Research Monograph No. 25, 1966.

Gurr, Ted. "Tensions in the Horn of Africa," In Feliks Gross. *World Politics and Tension Areas.* New York: New York University Press, 1965.

Gurr, Ted. "Urban Disorder: Perspectives from the Comparative Study of Civil Strife," *American Behavioral Scientist,* XI (March-April 1968), 50–55.

Gurr, Ted with Charles Ruttenberg. *Cross-National Studies of Civil Violence.* Washington, D.C.: Center for Research on Social Systems, The American University, 1969.

Gurr, Ted with Charles Ruttenberg. *The Conditions of Civil Violence: First Tests of A Causal Model.* Princeton: Center of International Studies, Princeton University, Research Monograph No. 28, 1967.

Gusfield, Joseph R. "Mass Society and Extremist Politics," *American Sociological Review,* XXVII (February 1962), 19–30.

Guzmán, Germán, Orlando Fals Borda, and Eduardo Umana Luna. *La Violencia en Colombia.* Bogotá: National University, Monografías Sociológias No. 12, 1962.

Hackney, Sheldon. "Southern Violence." *American Historical Review,* LXXIV (February 1969), 906–925.

Haddad, George M. *Revolutions and Military Rule in the Middle East.* New York: Robert Speller, 1965.

Halpern, Manfred. "The Algerian Uprising of 1945," *Middle East Journal,* II (April 1948), 191–204.

Halpern, Manfred. *The Dialectics of Modernization.* Princeton: Princeton University Press, 1970.

Halpern, Manfred. "A Redefinition of the Revolutionary Situation," *Journal of International Affairs,* XXIII (No. 1, 1969), 54–75.

Haring, C. E. "The Chilean Revolution of 1931," *Hispanic-American Historical Review,* XIII (1933), 197–203.

Harris, Christina P. *Nationalism and Revolution in Egypt: The Role of the Muslim Brotherhood.* Stanford: Hoover Institution on War, Revolution and Peace, Stanford University, 1964.

Hatto, Arthur. "Revolution: An Enquiry into the Usefulness of an Historical Term," *Mind,* LVIII (October 1949), 495–517.

Heaps, Willard A. *Riots U.S.A. 1765–1965.* New York: Seabury Press, 1966.

Heaton, John Wesley. *Mob Violence in the Late Roman Republic.* Urbana: University of Illinois Press, 1939.

Heberle, Rudolph. *Social Movements: An Introduction to Political Sociology.* New York: Appleton-Century-Crofts, 1951.

Hempstone, Smith. *Rebels, Mercenaries, and Dividends: The Katanga Story.* New York: Praeger, 1962.

Hobsbawn, E. J. *Social Bandits and Primitive Rebels: Studies in Archaic Forms of Social Movement in the 19th and 20th Centuries.* New York: The Free Press, 1959.

Hobsbawm, E. J. *The Age of Revolution 1789–1848.* New York: Mentor, 1962, 1964.

Hoffer, Eric. *The True Believer: Thoughts on the Nature of Mass Movements.* New York: Harper, 1951.

Holt, Edgar. *Protest in Arms: The Irish Troubles, 1916–1923.* New York: Coward-McCann, 1961.

Hooper, Rex D. "The Revolutionary Process: A Frame of Reference for the Study of Revolutionary Movements," *Social Forces,* XXVIII (March 1950), 270–279.

Hovland, Carl and Robert Sears. "Minor Studies in Aggression, VI: Correlation of Lynchings with Economic Indices," *Journal of Psychology,* IX (April 1940), 301–310.

Humbaraci, Arslan. *Algeria: A Revolution that Failed: A Political History Since 1954.* New York: Praeger, 1966.

Humphrey, Robert A. and John Lynch (eds.). *The Origins of the Latin American Revolutions, 1808–1826.* New York: Knopf, 1965.

Hunter, Robert. *Revolution: Why, How, When?* New York: Harper and Brothers, 1940.

Huntington, Samuel P. "Patterns of Violence in World Politics," In Samuel P. Huntington (ed.). *Changing Patterns of Military Politics.* New York: The Free Press, 1961.

Huntington, Samuel P. "Political Development and Political Decay," *World Politics,* XVII (April 1965), 386–430.

Huntington, Samuel P. *Political Order in Changing Societies.* New Haven: Yale University Press, 1968.

International Conference on the History of Resistance Movements. *European Resistance Movements 1939–45.* Vols. 1 and 2. Oxford: Pergamon Press, 1964.

International Sociological Association (in collaboration in Jessie Bernard, T. H. Pear, R. Aron, and R. C. Angell). *The Nature of Conflict: Studies on the Sociological Aspects of International Tensions.* Paris: UNESCO, 1957.

Israel, John. *Student Nationalism in China, 1927–1937.* Stanford: Hoover Institution, Stanford University, 1967.

Jacoby, Erich H. *Agrarian Unrest in Southeast Asia,* 2nd. edn. London: Asia Publishing House, 1949, 1961.

Janos, Andrew C. "Authority and Violence: The Political Framework of Internal War," In Harry Eckstein (ed.). *Internal War: Problems and Approaches.* New York: The Free Press, 1963.

Janos, Andrew. *The Seizure of Power: A Study of Force and Popular Consent.* Princeton: Center of International Studies, Princeton University, Research Monograph No. 16, February 1964.

Janowitz, Morris. *The Military in the Political Development of New Nations.* Chicago: University of Chicago Press, 1964.

Janowitz, Morris. "Patterns of Collective Racial Violence." In Hugh Davis Graham and Ted Robert Gurr (eds.). *Violence in America: Historical and Comparative Perspectives.* Washington,

D.C.: National Commission on the Causes and Prevention of Violence, 1969.
Jardine, Douglas. *The Mad Mullah of Somaliland.* London: Herbert Jenkins, 1923.
Jellinek, Frank. *The Paris Commune of 1871.* New York: Grosset and Dunlap, 1937, 1965.
Jenkins, Robin. "Who are These Marchers?" *Journal of Peace Research,* No. 1, 1967, 46–60.
Johnson, Chalmers. "Civilian Loyalties and Guerrilla Conflict," *World Politics,* XIV (July 1962), 646–661.
Johnson, Chalmers. *Peasant Nationalism and Communist Power: The Emergence of Revolutionary China 1937–1945.* Stanford: Stanford University Press, 1962, 1966.
Johnson, Chalmers. *Revolution and the Social System.* Stanford: The Hoover Institution on War, Revolution, and Peace, Stanford University, 1964.
Johnson, Chalmers. *Revolutionary Change.* Boston: Little, Brown, 1966.
Johnson, John J. *The Military and Society in Latin America.* Stanford: Stanford University Press, 1964.
Johnson, Kenneth F. "Causal Factors in Latin American Political Instability," *Western Political Quarterly,* XVII (September 1964), 432–446.
Jordan, George B. "Objectives and Methods of Communist Guerrilla Warfare," In Franklin M. Osanka (ed.). *Modern Guerrilla Warfare: Fighting Communist Guerrilla Movements, 1941–1961.* New York: The Free Press, 1962.
Kahin, George McT. *Nationalism and Revolution in Indonesia.* Ithaca: Cornell University Press, 1952.
Kamenka, Eugene. "The Concept of a Political Revolution," In Carl J. Friedrich (ed.). *Revolution.* New York: Atherton Press, 1966.
Kaplan, Morton A. (ed.). *The Revolution in World Politics.* New York: John Wiley, 1962.
Kecskemeti, Paul. *The Unexpected Revolution: Social Forces in the Hungarian Uprising.* Stanford: Stanford University Press, 1961.
Kerr, Clark and Abraham Siegel. "The Interindustry Propensity to Strike," In Arthur Kornhauser et al. (eds.). *Industrial Conflict.* New York: McGraw-Hill, 1954.
Kerr, Clark et al. *Industrialism and Industrial Man: The Problems of Labor and Management in Economic Growth.* Cambridge: Harvard University Press, 1960.
Kim, C. I. Eugene. "Differential Social Mobilization and Political

Instability in Korea." Paper read to the Annual Meeting of the American Political Science Association, Washington, D.C., 1968.

Kling, Merle. "Toward A Theory of Power and Political Instability in Latin America," *Western Political Quarterly,* IX (March 1956), 21–35.

Knowles, William H. "Industrial Conflict and Unions," In Wilbert E. Moore and Arnold S. Feldman (eds.). *Labor Commitment and Social Change in Development Areas.* New York: Social Science Research Council, 1950.

Kopytoff, Igor. "Extension of Conflict as a Method of Conflict Resolution Among the Suku of the Congo," *Journal of Conflict Resolution,* V (March 1961), 61–69.

Korbel, Josef. *The Communist Subversion of Czechoslovakia, 1939–1949.* Princeton: Princeton University Press, 1959.

Kornhauser, Arthur et al. (eds.). *Industrial Conflict.* New York: McGraw-Hill, 1954.

Kornhauser, William. "Rebellion and Political Development," In Harry Eckstein (ed.). *Internal War: Problems and Approaches.* New York: The Free Press of Glencoe, 1963.

Kornhauser, William. *The Politics of Mass Society.* New York: The Free Press, 1959.

Kort, Fred. "The Quantification of Aristotle's Theory of Revolution," *American Political Science Review,* LXVI (June 1952), 486–493.

Kousoulas, D. George. *Revolution and Defeat: The Story of the Greek Communist Party.* New York: Oxford University Press, 1965.

Kropotkin, Pierre. *Paroles d'un Revolte.* Paris: C. Marpon et E. Flammerion (n.d.).

Lambert, Richard D. "Religion, Economics, and Violence in Bengal," *Middle East Journal,* IV (July 1950), 307–328.

Lanternari, Vittorio. *The Religions of the Oppressed: A Study of Modern Messianic Cults.* New York: Knopf, 1963.

Lasswell, Harold and Abraham Kaplan. *Power and Society: A Framework for Political Inquiry.* New Haven: Yale University Press, 1950.

Lasswell, Harold and Daniel Lerner (eds.). *World Revolutionary Elites: Studies in Coercive Ideological Movements.* Cambridge: M.I.T. Press, 1965.

Laue, J. H. "A Contemporary Revitalization Movement in American Race Relations: The 'Black Muslims,'" *Social Forces,* XLII (March 1964), 315–323.

Lee, Alfred McClung and Norman D. Humphrey. *Race Riot: Detroit, 1943.* New York: Octagon Books, 1943, 1968.

Lefebvre, Georges. *The Coming of the French Revolution.* R. R. Palmer (tr. and ed.). Princeton: Princeton University Press, 1947.

Leiden, Carl and Karl M. Schmitt. *The Politics of Violence: Revolution in the Modern World.* Englewood Cliffs, N.J.: Prentice-Hall, 1968.

Lermarchand, René. "Revolutionary Phenomena in Stratified Societies: Rwanda and Zanzibar." *Civilisations,* XVIII (No. 1, 1968), 1–34.

LeVine, Robert A. (ed.). "The Anthropology of Conflict," *Journal of Conflict Resolution,* V (March 1961), 3–108.

LeVine, Robert A. "Anti-European Violence in Africa: A Comparative Analysis," *Journal of Conflict Resolution,* III (December 1959), 420–429.

Li Chien-nung. *The Political History of China, 1840–1928.* Stanford: Stanford University Press, 1956.

Lieberson, Stanley. "A Societal Theory of Race and Ethnic Relations," *American Sociological Review,* XXVI (December 1961), 902–910.

Lieberson, Stanley and Arnold R. Silverman. "The Precipitants and Underlying Conditions of Race Riots," *American Sociological Review,* XXX (December 1965), 887–898.

Lieuwen, Edwin. *Generals vs. Presidents: Neo-Militarism in Latin America.* New York: Praeger, 1964.

Linares Quintana, Segundo V. "The Etiology of Revolutions in Latin America," *Western Political Quarterly,* IV (June 1951), 254–267.

Linton, Ralph. "Nativistic Movements." *American Anthropologist,* XLV (April 1943), 230–240.

Lofchie, Michael F. *Zanzibar: Background to Revolution.* Princeton: Princeton University Press, 1965.

Lomax, Louis E. *Thailand: The War That Is, The War That Will Be.* New York: Vintage Books, 1967.

Lowie, R. H. "Compromise in Primitive Society," *International Social Science Journal,* XV (No. 2, 1963), 182–229.

Marcum, John A. *The Angolan Revolution, Vol. 1: The Anatomy of an Explosion (1950–1962).* Cambridge: M.I.T. Press, 1969.

McAlister, John T. Jr. "The Colonial Background to the Vietnamese Revolutionary War," Unpublished Paper, New Haven: Department of Political Science, Yale University, June 1, 1964.

McAlister, John T. *Vietnam: The Origins of Revolution.* New York: Knopf, 1969.

McVey, Ruth. "The Southeast Asian Insurrectionary Movements," In Cyril E. Black and Thomas P. Thornton (eds.). *Communism and Revolution: The Strategic Uses of Political Violence.* Princeton: Princeton University Press, 1964.

Mack, Raymond W. and Richard C. Snyder. "The Analysis of Social Conflict: Toward an Overview and Synthesis," *Journal of Conflict Resolution,* I (June 1957), 221–248.

Malaparte, Curzio. *Coup D'État: The Technique of Revolution.* New York: E. P. Dutton, 1932.

Mannoni, O. *Prospero and Caliban: The Psychology of Colonization.* Pamela Powesland (tr.). New York: Praeger, 1956, 1964.

Martin, John Bartlow. *Overtaken by Events: The Dominican Crisis from the Fall of Trujillo to the Civil War.* Garden City, N.Y.: Doubleday, 1966.

Martz, John D. "Urban and Rural Factors in Contemporary Latin American Violence," *Western Political Quarterly,* XVIII (September 1965), Supplement, 36–37.

Marx, Karl and Friedrich Engels. *Revolution and Counter-Revolution.* Eleanor Marx Aveling (ed.). New York: C. Scribner's Sons, 1896.

Mason, Henry L. *Mass Demonstrations Against Foreign Regimes: A Study of Five Crises.* New Orleans: Tulane University Studies in Political Science, Volume X, 1966.

Masotti, Louis H. and Don R. Bowen (eds.). *Riots and Rebellion: Civil Violence in the Urban Community.* Beverly Hills: Sage, 1968.

Massell, Gregory J. "Law as an Instrument of Revolutionary Change in a Traditional Milieu: The Case of Soviet Central Asia," *Law and Society Review,* II (February 1968), 179–228.

Mattick, Hans W. "The Form and Content of Recent Riots," *Midway,* Summer 1968, 3–32.

Mbeki, Govan. *South Africa: The Peasants' Revolt.* Baltimore: Penguin Books, 1964.

Means, G. P. and I. N. "Nagaland: The Agony of Ending a Guerrilla War." *Pacific Affairs,* XXXIX (Fall-Winter 1966–67), 290–313.

Meisel, James H. *Counterrevolution: How Revolutions Die.* New York: Atherton Press, 1966.

Mendras, Henri and Yves Tavernier. "Les Manifestations de Juin 1961," *Révue Francaise de Sciences Politiques,* XII (September 1962), 647–671.

Merriman, Robert B. *Six Contemporaneous Revolutions.* Oxford: Clarendon Press, 1938.

Methvin, E. H. "Mob Violence and Communist Strategy," *Orbis,* V (Summer 1961), 166–181.

Metron. *The Coup D'État: Its Political and Military Significance.* Princeton Metron, Inc., 1961 (Mimeographed).

Metron. *The Coup D'État: Modern Techniques and Countermeasures.* Princeton: Metron, Inc., 1961 (Mimeographed).

Midlarsky, Manus. "Mathematical Models of Instability: A Systematic Approach to the Study of Coups." Paper read at the Annual Meeting of the American Political Science Association, Chicago, September 1967.

Midlarsky, Manus and Raymond Tanter. "Toward a Theory of Political Instability in Latin America," *Journal of Peace Research,* No. 3, 1967, 209–227.

Miller, John C. *Origins of the American Revolution.* Stanford: Stanford University Press, 1943, 1959.

Miller, Linda. *World Order and Local Disorder: The United Nations and Internal Conflicts.* Princeton: Princeton University Press, 1967.

Mintz, Alexander. "A Re-Examination of Correlations Between Lynchings and Economic Indices," *Journal of Abnormal and Social Psychology,* XLI (April 1946), 154–160.

Morgan, Edmund S. (ed.). *The American Revolution: Two Centuries of Interpretation.* Englewood Cliffs: Prentice-Hall, 1967.

Moore, Barrington Jr. *Social Origins of Dictatorship and Democracy: Lord and Peasant in the Making of the Modern World.* Boston: Beacon Press, 1966.

Morrison, Denton E. "Relative Deprivation and Rural Discontent in Developing Countries: A Theoretical Proposal," Paper read at the Annual Meeting of the American Association for the Advancement of Science, 1966.

Myers, R. C. "Anti-Communist Mob Action: A Case Study," *Public Opinion Quarterly,* XII (Spring 1948), 57–67.

Nadel, George. "The Logic of the *Anatomy of Revolution,* with Reference to the Netherlands Revolt," *Comparative Studies in Society and History,* II (July 1960), 473–484.

Narayan, Jayaprakash. "The Nature of the Revolutionary Situation around the World," Paper read to the Conference on "The United States in a Revolutionary World," Princeton University, April 2, 1968.

Nash, Phileo. "The Place of Religious Revivalism in the Formation of the Intercultural Community on Klamath Reservation," In Fred Eggan (ed.). *Social Anthropology of North American Tribes.* Chicago: University of Chicago Press, 1937, 377–442.

National Advisory Commission on Civil Disorders. *Supplemental Studies.* Washington, D.C.: U.S. Government Printing Office, 1968.

Nawawi, Mohammed Ansori. "Regionalism and Regional Conflicts in Indonesia," Ph.D. Dissertation, Department of Politics, Princeton University, June 1968.

Needler, Martin C. *Anatomy of a Coup D'état: Ecuador 1963.* Washington, D.C.: Institute for the Comparative Study of Political Systems, 1964.

Neumann, Sigmund. "The International Civil War," *World Politics,* I (April 1949), 333–350.

Neumann, Sigmund. "The Structure and Strategy of Revolution: 1848 and 1948," *Journal of Politics,* XI (August 1949), 532–544.

Nieburg, H. L. "The Threat of Violence and Social Change," *American Political Science Review,* LVI (December 1962), 865–873.

Nomad, Max. *Aspects of Revolt.* New York: Bookman Associates, 1959.

Nomad, Max. *Political Heretics from Plato to Mao Tse-Tung.* Ann Arbor: University of Michigan Press, 1963.

Norbeck, Edward. "African Rituals of Conflict," *American Anthropologist,* LXV (December 1963), 1254–1279.

Oberschall, Anthony, "Rising Expectations, National Unity and Political Turmoil," Paper Read at the Annual Meeting of the African Studies Association, November 1967.

O'Connell, J. "The Inevitability of Instability." *Journal of Modern African Studies,* V (No. 2, 1967), 181–191.

Oduho, Joseph and William Deng. *The Problem of the Southern Sudan.* London: Oxford University Press, 1963.

Olson, Mancur Jr. "Economic Development and Guerrilla Warfare: The War of the Country Against the City," Unpublished Paper. Princeton: Center of International Studies, Princeton University, 1966 (Mimeographed).

Olson, Mancur Jr. "Rapid Growth as a Destabilizing Force," *Journal of Economic History,* XXIII (December 1963), 529–552.

Osanka, Franklin M. (ed.). *Modern Guerrilla Warfare: Fighting Communist Guerrilla Movements, 1941–1961.* New York: The Free Press, 1962.

Packard, George R. III. *Protest in Tokyo: The Security Treaty Crisis of 1960.* Princeton: Princeton University Press, 1966.

Palmer, Robert R. *The Age of the Democratic Revolutions: A Political History of Europe and America 1760–1800.* Princeton: Princeton University Press, 1959.

Paret, Peter. *French Revolutionary Warfare From Indochina to Algeria: The Analysis of a Political and Military Doctrine.* New York: Praeger, 1964.

Paret, Peter and John W. Shy. *Guerrillas in the 1960's.* rev. ed. New York: Praeger, 1964.

Parsons, Talcott. "Certain Primary Sources and Patterns of Aggression in the Social Structure of the Western World," In Lyman Bryson, Louis Finkelstein, and Robert M. MacIver (eds.). *Conflicts of Power in Modern Culture.* New York: Conference on Science, Philosophy, and Religion, Seventh Symposium, 1947.

Parsons, Talcott. "Some Reflections on the Place of Force in Social Process," In Harry Eckstein (ed.). *Internal War: Problems and Approaches.* New York: The Free Press, 1963.

Passos, Alaor S. "Developmental Tension and Political Instability: Testing Some Hypotheses Concerning Latin America," *Journal of Peace Research,* No. 1, 1968, 70–86.

Patch, Richard W. "Peasantry and National Revolution," In Kalman H. Silvert (ed.). *Expectant Peoples: Nationalism and Development.* New York: Random House, 1963.

Payne, James. "Peru: The Politics of Structured Violence," *Journal of Politics,* XXVII (May 1965), 362–374.

Petras, James and Maurice Zeitlin. "Miners and Agrarian Radicalism," *American Sociological Review,* XXXII (August 1967), 578–586.

Pettee, George. *The Process of Revolution.* New York: Harper, 1938.

Pike, Douglas. *Viet Cong: The Organization and Techniques of the National Liberation Front of South Vietnam.* Cambridge: M.I.T. Press, 1967.

Pinkney, David H. "The Crowd in the French Revolution of 1830." *American Historical Review,* LXX (October 1964), 1–17.

Pool, Ithiel de Sola. "Village Violence and International Violence." *Peace Research Society (International) Papers,* IX (1968), 87–94.

Powell, Elwin H. "Reform, Revolution, and Reaction as Adaptations to Anomie," *Review of Mexican Sociology,* XXV (1963), 331–355.

Pulzer, Peter G. J. *The Rise of Political Anti-Semitism in Germany and Austria.* New York: Wiley, 1964.

Putnam, Robert D. "Toward Explaining Military Intervention in Latin American Politics," *World Politics,* XX (October 1967), 83–110.

Pye, Lucian. *Guerrilla Communism in Malaya: Its Social and Political Meaning.* Princeton: Princeton University Press, 1956.

Pye, Lucian. "The Roots of Insurgency." In Harry Eckstein (ed.). *Internal War: Problems and Approaches.* New York: The Free Press, 1963.

Rapoport, David C. "Coup D'État: The View of the Men Firing Pistols," In Carl J. Friedrich (ed.). *Revolution.* New York: Atherton Press, 1966.

Rapoport, David C. "The Political Dimensions of Military Usurpation." *Political Science Quarterly,* LXXXIII (December 1968), 551–572.

Rapoport, Anatol. *Fights, Games, and Debates.* Ann Arbor: University of Michigan Press, 1960.

Reed, Nelson. *The Caste War of Yucatan.* Stanford: Stanford University Press, 1964.

Reeve, Sidney A. *The Natural Laws of Social Convulsions.* New York: E. P. Dutton, 1933.

Reeves, Ambrose. *Shooting at Sharpeville: The Agony of South Africa.* Boston: Houghton Mifflin, 1961.

Report of the National Advisory Commission on Civil Disorder. Otto Kerner (Chairman). New York: Bantam Books, 1968.

Richardson, Lewis F. *Statistics of Deadly Quarrels.* Pittsburgh: Boxwood Press, 1960.

Ridker, Ronald G. "Discontent and Economic Growth," *Economic Development and Cultural Change,* XI (October 1962), 1–15.

Roberts, Ben C. "On the Origins and Resolution of English Working-Class Protest." In Hugh Davis Graham and Ted Robert Gurr (eds.). *Violence in America: Historical and Comparative Perspectives.* Washington, D.C.: National Commission on the Causes and Prevention of Violence, 1969.

Robertson, Priscilla. *Revolutions of 1848: A Social History.* Princeton: Princeton University Press, 1952.

Rosberg, Carl G. Jr. "The Mau Mau as a Political Mobilization Institution," Paper Read at the Seventh Annual Meeting of the African Studies Association, Chicago, October 1964.

Rosberg, Carl G. Jr. and John Nottingham. *The Myth of "Mau Mau": Nationalism in Kenya.* New York: Praeger, 1966.

Rose, R. B. "Eighteenth-Century Price Riots and Public Policy in England," *International Review of Social History,* VI (No. 2, 1961), 277–292.

Rosenau, James N. "Internal War as an International Event," In James N. Rosenau (ed.). *International Aspects of Civil Strife.* Princeton: Princeton University Press, 1964.

Rosenstiel, Annette. "An Anthropological Approach to the Mau Mau Problem." *Political Science Quarterly,* LXVIII (September 1953), 419–432.

Rosenthal, Joel T. "The King's 'Wicked Advisers' and Medieval Baronial Rebellions," *Political Science Quarterly,* LXXXII (December 1967), 595–618.

Rotberg, Robert. "The Lenshina Movement of Northern Rhodesia," *Rhodes-Livingstone Institute Journal,* XXIX (June 1961), 63–78.

Rowe, James W. "Argentina's Restless Military," In Robert D.

Tomasek (ed.). *Latin American Politics: Studies of the Contemporary Scene.* Garden City: Doubleday, 1966.

Rudé, George. *The Crowd in the French Revolution.* London: Oxford University Press, 1959, 1967.

Rudé, George. *The Crowd in History: A Study of Popular Disturbances in France and England, 1730–1848.* New York: Wiley, 1964.

Rudé, George. "Prices, Wages, and Popular Movements in Paris During the French Revolution," *Economic History Review,* VI (April 1954), 246–267.

Rudé, George. *Revolutionary Europe, 1783–1815.* Cleveland: World, 1964.

Rudé, George. "The Study of Popular Disturbances in the 'Pre-Industrial' Age," *Historical Studies: Australia and New Zealand,* X (May 1963), 457–469.

Ruiz, Ramon Eduardo. *Cuba: The Making of a Revolution.* Amherst: University of Massachusetts Press, 1968.

Rummel, Rudolph J. "A Field Theory of Social Action with Application to Conflict within Nations," *Yearbook of the Society for General Systems Research,* X (1965), 183–204.

Rummel, Rudolph J. "Dimensionality of Nations Project: Orthogonally Rotated Factor Tables for 236 Variables," New Haven: Department of Political Science, Yale University, 1964 (Mimeographed).

Rummel, Rudolph J. "Dimensions of Conflict Behavior Within and Between Nations," *General Systems Yearbook,* VIII (1963), 1–50.

Rummel, Rudolph J. "Testing Some Possible Predictors of Conflict Behavior Within and Between Nations," *Peace Research Society, Papers,* I (1963), 79–112.

Russett, Bruce M. "Inequality and Instability: The Relation of Land Tenure to Politics," *World Politics,* XVI (April 1964), 442–454.

Sanger, Richard H. *Insurgent Era: New Patterns of Political, Economic, and Social Revolution.* Washington, D.C.: Potomac Books, 1967.

Scaff, Alvin H. *The Philippine Answer to Communism.* Stanford: Stanford University Press, 1955.

Scalapino, Robert A. "Communism in Asia: Towards Comparative Analysis," In Robert A. Scalapino (ed.). *The Communist Revolution in Asia: Tactics, Goals, and Achievements.* Englewood Cliffs: Prentice-Hall, 1965.

Schapiro, Jacob S. *Movements of Social Dissent in Modern Europe.* Princeton: Van Nostrand, 1962.

Schattschneider, E. E. "Intensity, Visibility, Direction and Scope," *American Political Science Review*, LI (December 1957), 933–942.

Scheffler, H. W. "The Genesis and Repression of Conflict: Choiseul Island," *American Anthropologist*, LXVI (August 1964), 789–804.

Schelling, Thomas C. *The Strategy of Conflict*. Cambridge: Harvard University Press, 1960, 1963.

Schuman, Frederick L. *The Nazi Dictatorship: A Study in Social Pathology and the Politics of Fascism*. New York: Knopf, 1935.

Schwartz, David C. "A Theory of Revolutionary Behavior." In James C. Davies (ed.). *When Men Rebel and Why*. New York: The Free Press, 1970.

Schwartz, David C. "On the Ecology of Political Violence: 'The Long Hot Summer' as a Hypothesis," *American Behavioral Scientist*, XI (July-August 1968), 24–28.

Schwartz, David C. "Political Alienation: A Preliminary Experiment on the Psychology of Revolution's First Stage," Paper Delivered at the Annual Meeting of the American Political Science Association, New York, 1967.

Schwarz, Solomon M. *The Russian Revolution of 1905: The Workers' Movement and the Formation of Bolshevism and Menshevism*. Gertrude Vakar (tr.). Chicago: University of Chicago Press, 1967.

Seton-Watson, Hugh. *Nationalism and Communism*. New York: Praeger, 1964.

Seton-Watson, Hugh. "Twentieth Century Revolutions," *Political Quarterly*, XXII (July 1951), 251–265.

Shepperson, George and Thomas T. Price. *Independent African: John Chilembwe and the Origins, Setting, and Significance of the Nyasaland Native Uprising of 1915*. Edinburgh: Edinburgh University Press, 1958.

Shogan, Robert and Tom Craig. *The Detroit Race Riot: A Study in Violence*. Philadelphia: Chilton Books, 1964.

Shubs, Peter. "Revolutionary Symbology: Comparative Case Studies of the American and Indian Independence Movements." Paper read at the Annual Meeting of the American Political Science Association, New York, 1969.

Siegel, Bernard. "Defensive Cultural Adaptation." In Hugh Davis Graham and Ted Robert Gurr (eds.). *Violence in America: Historical and Comparative Perspectives*. Washington, D.C.: National Commission of the Causes and Prevention of Violence, 1969.

Silvert, Kalman H. *The Conflict Society: Reaction and Revolution in Latin America*. New Orleans: Hauser Press, 1961.

Silvert, Kalman H. "The Costs of Anti-Nationalism: Argentina," In Kalman H. Silvert (ed.). *Expectant Peoples: Nationalism and Development*. New York: Random House, 1963.

Simon, W. B. "Motivation of a Totalitarian Mass Vote," *British Journal of Sociology*, x (December 1959), 338–345.

Smelser, Neil J. *Social Change in the Industrial Revolution*. Chicago: University of Chicago Press, 1950.

Smelser, Neil J. *Theory of Collective Behavior*. New York: The Free Press, 1963.

Solomon, F. et al. "Civil Rights Activity and Reduction in Crime Among Negroes," *Archives of General Psychiatry*, xii (March 1965), 227–236.

Sorel, Georges. *Reflections on Violence*. T. E. Hulme (tr.). New York: Peter Smith, 1915, 1941.

Sorokin, Pitirim. *Social and Cultural Dynamics, Volume III: Fluctuations of Social Relationships, War and Revolutions*. New York: American Book Company, 1937.

Sorokin, Pitirim A. *The Sociology of Revolution*. Philadelphia: J. B. Lippincott, 1925.

Soule, George. *The Coming American Revolution*. New York: Macmillan, 1935.

Springer, Philip B. "Disunity and Disorder: Factional Politics in the Argentine Military," In Henry Bienen (ed.). *The Military Intervenes: Case Studies in Political Development*. New York: Russell Sage, 1968.

Starner, Frances Lucille. *Magsaysay and the Philippine Peasantry: The Agrarian Impact on Philippine Politics, 1953–1956*. Berkeley: University of California Press, 1961.

Stokes, W. S. "Violence as a Power Factor in Latin American Politics," *Western Political Quarterly*, v (December 1952), 445–468.

Stone, Lawrence. "Theories of Revolution." *World Politics*, xvii (January 1966), 159–176.

Strausz-Hupé, Robert, et al. *Protracted Conflict*. New York: Harper and Row, 1959, 1963.

Taft, Philip and Philip Ross. "American Labor Violence: Its Causes, Character, and Outcome." In Hugh Davis Graham and Ted Robert Gurr (eds.). *Violence in America: Historical and Comparative Perspectives*. Washington, D.C.: National Commission on the Causes and Prevention of Violence, 1969.

Tannenbaum, Frank. "On Political Stability," *Political Science Quarterly*, lxxv (June 1960), 161–180.

Tanter, Raymond. "Dimensions of Conflict Behavior Within and Between Nations, 1958–1960." *Journal of Conflict Resolution*, x (March 1966), 41–64.

Tanter, Raymond. "Dimensions of Conflict Behavior within Nations, 1955–60; Turmoil and Internal War," *Peace Research Society Papers,* III (1965), 159–184.

Tanter, Raymond and Manus Midlarsky. "A Theory of Revolution," *Journal of Conflict Resolution,* XI (September 1967), 264–280.

Thomas, Dorothy S. and Richard S. Nishimoto. *The Spoilage.* Berkeley: University of California Press, 1946.

Thompson, Sir Robert. *Defeating Communist Insurgency.* New York: Praeger, 1966.

Thornton, Thomas Perry. "Terror as a Weapon of Political Agitation," In Harry Eckstein (ed.). *Internal War: Problems and Approaches.* New York: The Free Press, 1964.

Tilly, Charles. "A Travers le Chaos des Vivantes Cités," Paper Read at the Sixth World Congress of Sociology, Evian-les-Bains, September 1966.

Tilly, Charles. "Collective Violence in European Perspective." In Hugh Davis Graham and Ted Robert Gurr (eds.). *Violence in America: Historical and Comparative Perspectives.* Washington, D.C.: National Commission on the Causes and Prevention of Violence, 1969.

Tilly, Charles. "Reflections on the Revolutions of Paris: An Essay on Recent Historical Writing," *Social Problems,* XII (Summer 1964), 99–121.

Tilly, Charles. *The Vendée.* Cambridge: Harvard University Press, 1964.

Tilly, Charles and Louise. "Popular Participation in the French Revolution," Unpublished Paper, Joint Center for Urban Studies of M.I.T. and Harvard University, December 1965 (Mimeographed).

Tilly, Charles and James Rule. *Measuring Political Upheaval.* Princeton: Center of International Studies, Princeton University, Research Monograph No. 19, 1965.

Timasheff, Nicholas S. *War and Revolution.* New York: Sheed and Ward, 1965.

Tolles, F. B. "Non-Violent Contact: The Quakers and the Indians," *Proceedings of the American Philosophical Society,* CVII (April 15, 1963), 93–101.

Trotsky, Leon. *The History of the Russian Revolution.* Ann Arbor: University of Michigan Press, 1957.

Tse-tung, Mao. *Mao Tse-tung on Guerrilla Warfare.* S. B. Griffith (tr.). New York: Praeger, 1961.

Tse-tung, Mao. *On the Protracted War.* Peking: Foreign Language Press, 1954.

Ulam, Adam B. *The Unfinished Revolution.* New York: Random House, 1960.

U.S. Department of Labor, Manpower Administration. *The Detroit Riot: A Profile of 500 Prisoners.* Washington, D.C.: Author, March 1968.

Vatikiotis, P. J. (ed.). *Egypt Since the Revolution.* New York: Praeger, 1968.

Venturi, Franco. *Roots of Revolution: A History of the Populist and Socialist Movements in Nineteenth Century Russia.* Isaiah Berlin (tr.). New York: Knopf, 1960.

Viles, Perry. "Participants and Elites in French Revolutionary Politics, 1789–1795," Philadelphia: Foreign Policy Research Institute, University of Pennsylvania, n.d. (1968). (Dittoed).

Vittachi, Tarzie. *Emergency '58: The Story of the Ceylon Race Riots.* London: Andre Deutsch, 1959.

Vittachi, Tarzie. *The Fall of Sukarno.* New York: Praeger, 1967.

Von der Mehden, Fred R. "Political Violence in Burma and Thailand: A Preliminary Comparison," Paper Read at the Annual Meeting of the Asian Studies Association, Philadelphia, March 1968.

Wada, George and James C. Davies. "Riots and Rioters," *Western Political Quarterly,* X (December 1957), 864–874.

Wainhouse, Edward R. "Guerrilla War in Greece, 1946–49: A Case Study," In Franklin M. Osanka (ed.). *Modern Guerrilla Warfare: Fighting Communist Guerrilla Movements, 1941–1961.* New York: The Free Press, 1962.

Wallace, Anthony F. C. "Revitalization Movements," *American Anthropologist,* LVIII (April 1956), 264–281.

Walter, E. V. "Power and Violence," *American Political Science Review,* LVIII (June 1964), 350–360.

Walter, E. V. "Violence and the Process of Terror," *American Sociological Review,* XXIX (April 1964), 248–257.

Walton, Jennifer G. "Correlates of Coerciveness and Permissiveness of National Political Systems: A Cross-National Study," M. A. Thesis, San Diego State College, June 1965.

Wanderer, Jules J. "1967 Riots: A Test of the Congruity of Events." *Social Problems,* XVI (Fall 1968), 193–198.

Walzer, Michael. "Revolutionary Ideology: The Case of the Marian Exiles," *American Political Science Review,* LVII (September 1963), 643–654.

Wedge, Bryant. "The Case Study of Student Political Violence: Brazil, 1964, and Dominican Republic, 1965," *World Politics,* XXI (January 1969), 183–206.

Weiker, Walter F. *The Turkish Revolution 1960–1961: Aspects of Military Politics.* Washington: The Brookings Institution, 1963.

Welsh, William A. "A Game-Theoretic Conceptualization of the Hungarian Revolt: Toward an Inductive Theory of Games," Athens: Department of Political Science, University of Georgia, 1968 (Mimeographed).

Wheatley, Charles. "Military Coups and their Effects in Terms of Political Development," Princeton: Center of International Studies, Princeton University, 1968 (Mimeographed).

Wilkenfeld, Jonathan. "Domestic and Foreign Conflict Behavior of Nations," *Journal of Peace Research,* No. 1, 1968, 56–69.

Willer, David and George K. Zollschan. "Prolegomenon to a Theory of Revolutions," In George K. Zollschan and Walter Hirsch (eds.). *Explorations in Social Change.* Boston: Houghton-Mifflin, 1964.

Williamson, Robert C. "Toward a Theory of Political Violence: The Case of Rural Colombia," *Western Political Quarterly,* XVIII (March 1965), 35–44.

Willner, Ann Ruth. "Some Forms and Functions of Public Protest in Indonesia," Paper Read at the Annual Meeting of the Asian Studies Association, Philadelphia, 1968.

Wilson, B. R. "An Analysis of Sect Development," *American Sociological Review,* XXIV (February 1959), 3–15.

Wilson, David A. "Nation-Building and Revolutionary War," In Karl Deutsch and William J. Foltz (eds.). *Nation-Building.* New York: Atherton Press, 1963.

Wilson, Frank L. "French-Canadian Separatism," *Western Political Quarterly,* XX (March 1967), 116–31.

Wintringham, Thomas Henry. *Mutiny: Being A Survey of Mutinies from Spartacus to Invergordon.* London: Mott, 1936.

Wolfe, Bertram David. *Three Who Made A Revolution: A Biographical History.* New York: Dial Press, 1948.

Wolf, Charles Jr. *Insurgency and Counterinsurgency: New Myths and Old Realities,* Santa Monica: RAND Corporation, Paper P-3132-1, July 1965.

Wolfe, Leon. *Lockout: The Story of the Homestead Strike of 1892.* New York: Harper and Row, 1965.

Wolfgang, Marvin E. and Franco Ferracuti. *The Subculture of Violence: Towards an Integrated Theory in Criminology.* London: Tavistock, 1967.

Wolin, Sheldon. "Violence and the Western Political Tradition," *American Journal of Orthopsychiatry,* XXXIII (January 1963), 15–28.

Woolman, David S. *Rebels in the Rif: Abd El Krim and the Rif Rebellion.* Stanford: Stanford University Press, 1968.

Worsley, Peter M. "The Analysis of Rebellion and Revolution in Modern British Social Anthropology," *Science and Society,* XXV (Winter 1961), 26–37.

Worsley, Peter M. *The Trumpet Shall Sound: A Study of "Cargo" Cults in Melanesia.* London: MacGibbon and Kee, 1957.

Wright, Quincy. *A Study of War.* Chicago: University of Chicago Press, 1942.

Yalman, Nur. "Intervention and Extrication: The Officer Corps in the Turkish Crisis," In Henry Bienen (ed.). *The Military Intervenes: Case Studies in Political Development.* New York: Russell Sage, 1968.

Yoder, Dale. "Current Definitions of Revolution," *American Journal of Sociology,* XXXII (November 1926), 433–441.

Young, Crawford. *Politics in the Congo: Decolonization and Independence.* Princeton: Princeton University Press, 1965.

Young, Roland and Henry A. Fosbrooke. *Smoke in the Hills: Political Tension in the Morogoro District of Tanganyika.* Evanston: Northwestern University Press, 1960.

Zawodny, J. K. "Unexplored Realms of Underground Strife," *American Behavioral Scientist,* IV (September 1960), 3–5.

Zeitlin, Maurice. *Revolutionary Politics and the Cuban Working Class.* Princeton: Princeton University Press, 1967.

Zinner, Paul E. *Revolution in Hungary.* New York: Columbia University Press, 1962.

Zolberg, Aristide R. "The Structure of Political Conflict in the New States of Tropical Africa," *American Political Science Review,* LXII (March 1968), 70–87.

"Political Conflict: Perspectives on Revolution." *Journal of International Affairs,* XXIII (No. 1, 1969), 1–118.

"Six Views of the Nigerian War," *Africa Report,* XIII (February 1968), 8–49.

"Students and Politics." *Daedalus,* XCVII (Winter 1968), 1–317.

Supplementary Bibliography on Group Conflict and Political Violence

Canetti, Elias. *Crowds and Power.* New York: The Viking Press, 1960, 1963.

Diaz del Moral, Juan. *Historia de las Agitaciones Campesinos Andaluzas.* Madrid: Alianza Editorial, 1929, 1967.

Drachkovitch, Milorad M. (ed.). *The Revolutionary Internationals, 1864–1943.* Stanford: Stanford University Press, for the Hoover Institution on War, Revolution, and Peace, 1966.

Feuer, Lewis S. *The Conflict of Generations: The Character and Significance of Student Movements.* New York: Basic Books, 1969.

Garson, David. "The Politics of Collective Violence in America: 1863–1963." Ph.D. dissertation, Department of Government, Harvard University, 1969.

Gude, Edward W. "Batista and Betancourt: Alternative Responses to Violence." In Hugh Davis Graham and Ted Robert Gurr, (eds.). *Violence in America: Historical and Comparative Perspectives.* Washington, D.C.: National Commission on the Causes and Prevention of Violence, 1969.

Horowitz, Irving Louis. "The Struggle is the Message." Paper prepared for the Task Force on Group Protest and Violence, National Commission on the Causes and Prevention of Violence, September 1968 (Mimeographed).

Hudson, Michael. "Political Violence and the Transfer of Power: Some Longitudinal Comparisons." Paper read at the Annual Meeting of the American Political Science Association, New York, 1969.

Huizinga, Johan. *The Waning of the Middle Ages.* London: E. Arnold, 1924.

Hundley, James R., Jr. "The Dynamics of Recent Ghetto Riots," *University of Detroit Journal of Urban Law,* XLV (Spring-Summer 1968), 627–639.

Leites, Nathan and Charles Wolf, Jr. *Rebellion and Authority: An Analytic Essay on Insurgent Conflicts.* Santa Monica: RAND Corporation, 1969.

Lipset, Seymour M. *Political Man: The Social Bases of Politics.* Garden City: Doubleday, 1960.

Loomis, Charles P. "In Praise of Conflict and its Resolution." *American Sociological Review,* XXXII (December 1967), 875–890.

Mitchell, Edward J. "Inequality and Insurgency: A Statistical Study of South Vietnam," *World Politics,* XX (April 1968), 421–438.

Moreno, Francisco Jose. *Legitimacy and Stability in Latin America: A Case Study of Chilean Political Culture.* New York: New York University Press, 1970.

Nesvold, Betty A. et al. "Regime Coerciveness and Political Instability." Paper read at the Annual Meeting of the American Political Science Association, New York, 1969.

Nieburg, H. L. *Political Violence: The Behavioral Process.* New York: St. Martin's Press, 1969.

Nun, José. "A Latin American Phenomenon: The Middle-Class

Coup." In James Petras and Maurice Zeitlin (eds.). *Latin America: Reform or Revolution?* Greenwich: Fawcett, 1968, 145–185.

Petras, James. "Revolution and Guerrilla Movements in Latin America: Venezuela, Guatemala, Colombia, and Peru." In James Petras and Maurice Zeitlin (eds.). *Latin America: Reform or Revolution?* Greenwich: Fawcett, 1968, 329–369.

Rubenstein, Richard. *Rebels in Eden.* Boston: Little, Brown, 1970.

Skolnick, Jerome H. *The Politics of Protest.* Washington, D.C.: National Commission on the Causes and Prevention of Violence, 1969.

Taylor, Philip A. M. (ed.). *The Origins of the English Civil War: Conspiracy, Crusade, or Class Conflict?* Boston: D. C. Heath, 1960.

Walter, E. V. *Terror and Resistance: A Study of Political Violence.* New York: Oxford University Press, 1969.

INDEX

Index

Note: Specific occurrences of violence, and sets of related events, are indexed under the country in which they occurred. Organizations and movements are similarly indexed except when they are cross-national in nature.

Books Written Under the Auspices of the

CENTER OF INTERNATIONAL STUDIES

Princeton University

Gabriel A. Almond, *The Appeals of Communism* (Princeton University Press 1954)

William W. Kaufmann, ed., *Military Policy and National Security* (Princeton University Press 1956)

Klaus Knorr, *The War Potential of Nations* (Princeton University Press 1956)

Lucian W. Pye, *Guerrilla Communism in Malaya* (Princeton University Press 1956)

Charles De Visscher, *Theory and Reality in Public International Law*, trans. by P. E. Corbett (Princeton University Press 1957; rev. ed. 1968)

Bernard C. Cohen, *The Political Process and Foreign Policy: The Making of the Japanese Peace Settlement* (Princeton University Press 1959)

Myron Weiner, *Party Politics in India: The Development of a Multi-Party System* (Princeton University Press 1957)

Percy E. Corbett, *Law in Diplomacy* (Princeton University Press 1959)

Rolf Sannwald and Jacques Stohler, *Economic Integration: Theoretical Assumptions and Consequences of European Unification*, trans. by Herman Karreman (Princeton University Press 1959)

Klaus Knorr, ed., *NATO and American Security* (Princeton University Press 1959)

Gabriel A. Almond and James S. Coleman, eds., *The Politics of the Developing Areas* (Princeton University Press 1960)

Herman Kahn, *On Thermonuclear War* (Princeton University Press 1960)

Sidney Verba, *Small Groups and Political Behavior: A Study of Leadership* (Princeton University Press 1961)

Robert J. C. Butow, *Tojo and the Coming of the War* (Princeton University Press 1961)

Glenn H. Snyder, *Deterrence and Defense: Toward a Theory of National Security* (Princeton University Press 1961)

Klaus Knorr and Sidney Verba, eds., *The International System: Theoretical Essays* (Princeton University Press 1961)

Peter Paret and John W. Shy, *Guerrillas in the 1960's* (Praeger 1962)

George Modelski, *A Theory of Foreign Policy* (Praeger 1962)

CENTER PUBLICATIONS

Klaus Knorr and Thornton Read, eds., *Limited Strategic War* (Praeger 1963)

Frederick S. Dunn, *Peace-Making and the Settlement with Japan* (Princeton University Press 1963)

Arthur L. Burns and Nina Heathcote, *Peace-Keeping by United Nations Forces* (Praeger 1963)

Richard A. Falk, *Law, Morality, and War in the Contemporary World* (Praeger 1963)

James N. Rosenau, *National Leadership and Foreign Policy: A Case Study in the Mobilization of Public Support* (Princeton University Press 1963)

Gabriel A. Almond and Sidney Verba, *The Civic Culture: Political Attitudes and Democracy in Five Nations* (Princeton University Press 1963)

Bernard C. Cohen, *The Press and Foreign Policy* (Princeton University Press 1963)

Richard L. Sklar, *Nigerian Political Parties: Power in an Emergent African Nation* (Princeton University Press 1963).

Peter Paret, *French Revolutionary Warfare from Indochina to Algeria: The Analysis of a Political and Military Doctrine* (Praeger 1964)

Harry Eckstein, ed., *Internal War: Problems and Approaches* (Free Press 1964)

Cyril E. Black and Thomas P. Thornton, eds., *Communism and Revolution: The Strategic Uses of Political Violence* (Princeton University Press 1964)

Miriam Camps, *Britain and the European Community 1955–1963* (Princeton University Press 1964)

Thomas P. Thornton, ed., *The Third World in Soviet Perspective: Studies by Soviet Writers on the Developing Areas* (Princeton University Press 1964)

James N. Rosenau, ed., *International Aspects of Civil Strife* (Princeton University Press 1964)

Sidney I. Ploss, *Conflict and Decision-Making in Soviet Russia: A Case Study of Agricultural Policy, 1953–1963* (Princeton University Press 1965)

Richard A. Falk and Richard J. Barnet, eds., *Security in Disarmament* (Princeton University Press 1965)

Karl von Vorys, *Political Development in Pakistan* (Princeton University Press 1965)

Harold and Margaret Sprout, *The Ecological Perspective on Human Affairs, With Special Reference to International Politics* (Princeton University Press 1965)

Klaus Knorr, *On the Uses of Military Power in the Nuclear Age* (Princeton University Press 1966)

Harry Eckstein, *Division and Cohesion in Democracy: A Study of Norway* (Princeton University Press 1966)

Cyril E. Black, *The Dynamics of Modernization: A Study in Comparative History* (Harper and Row 1966)

Peter Kunstadter, ed., *Southeast Asian Tribes, Minorities, and Nations* (Princeton University Press 1967)

E. Victor Wolfenstein, *The Revolutionary Personality: Lenin, Trotsky, Gandhi* (Princeton University Press 1967)

Leon Gordenker, *The UN Secretary-General and the Maintenance of Peace* (Columbia University Press 1967)

Oran R. Young, *The Intermediaries: Third Parties in International Crises* (Princeton University Press 1967)

James N. Rosenau, ed., *Domestic Sources of Foreign Policy* (Free Press 1967)

Richard F. Hamilton, *Affluence and the French Worker in the Fourth Republic* (Princeton University Press 1967)

Linda B. Miller, *World Order and Local Disorder: The United Nations and Internal Conflicts* (Princeton University Press 1967)

Henry Bienen, *Tanzania: Party Transformation and Economic Development* (Princeton University Press 1967)

Wolfram F. Hanrieder, *West German Foreign Policy, 1949–1963: International Pressures and Domestic Response* (Stanford University Press 1967)

Richard H. Ullman, *Britain and the Russian Civil War: November 1918–February 1920* (Princeton University Press 1968)

Robert Gilpin, *France in the Age of the Scientific State* (Princeton University Press 1968)

William B. Bader, *The United States and the Spread of Nuclear Weapons* (Pegasus 1968)

Richard A. Falk, *Legal Order in a Violent World* (Princeton University Press 1968)

Cyril E. Black, Richard A. Falk, Klaus Knorr, and Oran R. Young, *Neutralization and World Politics* (Princeton University Press 1968)

Oran R. Young, *The Politics of Force: Bargaining During International Crises* (Princeton University Press 1969)

Klaus Knorr and James N. Rosenau, eds., *Contending Approaches to International Politics* (Princeton University Press 1969)

James N. Rosenau, ed., *Linkage Politics: Essays on the Convergence of National and International Systems* (Free Press 1969)

CENTER PUBLICATIONS

John T. McAlister, Jr., *Viet Nam: The Origins of Revolution* (Knopf 1969)

Jean Edward Smith, *Germany Beyond the Wall: People, Politics and Prosperity* (Little Brown 1969)

James Barros, *Betrayal from Within: Joseph Avenol, Secretary-General of the League of Nations, 1933–40* (Yale University Press 1969)

Charles Hermann, *Crises in Foreign Policy: A Simulation Analysis* (Bobbs-Merrill 1969)

Robert C. Tucker, *The Marxian Revolution Idea: Essays on Marxist Thought and Its Impact on Radical Movements* (W. W. Norton 1969)

Harvey Waterman, *Political Change in Contemporary France: The Politics of an Industrial Democracy* (Charles E. Merrill 1969)

Cyril E. Black and Richard A. Falk, eds., *The Future of the International Legal Order, Volume I: Trends and Patterns* (Princeton University Press 1969)

Richard A. Falk, *The Status of Law in International Society* (Princeton University Press 1970)

Ted Robert Gurr, *Why Men Rebel* (Princeton University Press 1970)

C. S. Whitaker, Jr., *The Politics of Tradition: Continuity and Change in Northern Nigeria, 1946–1966* (Princeton University Press 1970)

Henry Bienen, *Tanzania: Party Transformation and Economic Development* (Princeton University Press 1967, rev. ed. 1970)

Klaus Knorr, *Military Power and Potential* (D. C. Heath 1970)

Richard A. Falk and Cyril E. Black, eds., *The Future of the International Legal Order*, Vol. II, *Wealth and Resources* (Princeton University Press 1970)

Leon Gordenker, ed., *The United Nations in International Politics* (Princeton University Press 1971)

Cyril E. Black and Richard A. Falk, eds., *The Future of the International Legal Order*, Vol. III, *Conflict Management* (Princeton University Press 1971)

Harold and Margaret Sprout, *Toward a Politics of the Planet Earth* (Van Nostrand Reinhold Co. 1971)

Francine R. Frankel, *India's Green Revolution: Economic Gains and Political Costs* (Princeton University Press 1971)

Cyril E. Black and Richard A. Falk, eds., *The Future of the International Legal Order*, Vol. IV, *The Structure of the International Environment* (Princeton University Press 1972)

Gerald Garvey, *Energy, Ecology, Economy* (W. W. Norton 1972)

Richard H. Ullman, *The Anglo-Soviet Accord* (Princeton University Press 1973)

Klaus Knorr, *Power and Wealth: The Political Economy of International Power* (Basic Books 1973)

Henry Bienen, *Kenya: The Politics of Participation and Control* (Princeton University Press 1974)

Gregory L. Massell, *The Surrogate Proletariat: Moslem Women and Revolutionary Strategies in Soviet Central Asia, 1919–1929* (Princeton University Press 1974)

R. J. Vincent, *Nonintervention and International Order* (Princeton University Press 1974)